ArtScroll Judaica Classics®

הגות בפרשיות התורה

STUDIES

Published by

Mesorah Publications, ltd

ArtScroll/ירושלים בע"מ אַרטסקרול/
Jerusalem, ltd.

IN THE WEEKLY PARASHAH

The classical interpretations of major topics and themes in the Torah

by
Yehuda Nachshoni

translated from the Hebrew by
Shmuel Himelstein

FIRST EDITION
First Impression . . . March, 1989

Published and Distributed by
MESORAH PUBLICATIONS, Ltd.
Brooklyn, New York 11232

Distributed in Israel by
MESORAH MAFITZIM / J. GROSSMAN
Rechov Harav Uziel 117
Jerusalem, Israel

Distributed in Europe by
J. LEHMANN HEBREW BOOKSELLERS
20 Cambridge Terrace
Gateshead, Tyne and Wear
England NE8 1RP

THE ARTSCROLL JUDAICA CLASSICS ®
STUDIES IN THE WEEKLY PARASHAH
Vol III: Vayikra
© *Copyright 1988, by* MESORAH PUBLICATIONS, Ltd.
4401 Second Avenue / Brooklyn, N.Y. 11232 / (718) 921-9000

ISBN:
0-89906-937-1 (hard cover)
0-89906-938-X (paperback)

Typography by CompuScribe at ArtScroll Studios, Ltd.
4401 Second Avenue / Brooklyn, N.Y. 11232 / (718) 921-9000

Printed in the United States of America by Noble Book Press Corp.
Bound by Sefercraft, Quality Bookbinders, Ltd. Brooklyn, N.Y.

❧ Table of Contents

Kedoshim

Emor

Behar

Bechukosai

ספר ויקרא

Vayikra

Vayikra – ויקרא

I.

The Function of the Sacrifices

Sacrifices are the subject of our *parashah*. In Hebrew the word קָרְבָּן — sacrifice — explains their purpose, which is לְקָרֵב, to draw Israel closer to their Father in Heaven. Upon the destruction of the Temple and the cessation of the sacrifices, prayer replaced the sacrifices, although the latter is the preferred method, since it draws one closer to the Creator through actions rather than through intentions alone.

According to the Torah, the commandments are not to be fulfilled only on the mental level, but must be acted out. This is in keeping with the nature of man who, born with five senses, expresses his innermost feelings through deed and action. The major aspects of the sacrifice ritual for the one bringing them are *s'michah* — the laying of the hands on the head of the animal — and *vidui* — the confession of sins — both of which lead man to regret his past evil deeds and to repent. The influence of the Temple sacrifices was enormous, which is why our prayers express a longing and yearning for the restoration of the Temple Service: "Return the *Kohanim* to their Service and the *Levi'im* to their psalm and song." All the same it is clear that the ultimate goal of the sacrifices is to serve as a means by which to arouse our hearts; this being best achieved by action, as man is limited by his corporeal senses.

Those who would distort the content of Judaism support their contentions by resorting to the prophets, who they claim were opposed to the sacrifices. The truth is that the prophets were only against the sacrifices when they were an end unto themselves. The prophets criticized the masses and the uneducated for whom the sacrifices were an end, rather than the means by which to return to God with all their hearts.

We already find Shmuel, the first prophet [recorded in the Prophetic Books], rebuking Shaul (*I Shmuel* 15:22): "Has Hashem as great delight in burnt offerings and sacrifices, as in obeying the voice of Hashem? Behold, to obey is better than sacrifice, and to hearken [more desirable] than the fat of rams." In reprimanding Shaul, Shmuel was certainly not rejecting the idea of sacrifice as a means to bringing one to proper intentions, for the prophet himself expressed his dissatisfaction with Shaul for not waiting for him before offering sacrifices when he was under attack by the Philistines (ibid. ch. 13).

The same is true for the Prophet Yeshayahu, who admonished the people (*Yeshayahu* 1:11,16), " 'To what purpose is the multitude of your sacrifices unto Me?' says Hashem: 'I am full of the burnt offerings of rams, and the fat of fed beasts; and I do not desire the blood of bulls, or of lambs, or of he-goats ... Wash yourself, make yourself clean; put away the evil of your doings from before My eyes; cease to do evil.' " Yet it is the same Yeshayahu who says later (56:7), "I will bring them to My holy mountain, and make them joyful in My house of prayer: their burnt offerings and their sacrifices shall be accepted upon My Altar."

The Prophet Yirmiyahu too expressed himself in harsh terms concerning the sacrifices, when he stated (*Yirmiyahu* 6:20), "Your burnt offerings are not acceptable, nor your sacrifices sweet unto Me." Yet he prophesied of the ideal future, when (17:26): "They shall come from the cities of Yehudah and from the places about Jerusalem ... bringing burnt offerings, and sacrifices, and meal offerings, and incense," and (33:18): "Neither shall the *Kohanim* and the *Levi'im* lack a man before Me to offer burnt offerings, and to burn meal offerings, and to do sacrifice continually."

All this shows explicitly that the prophets were rebuking the people for failing to draw the proper conclusions from their sacrifices. These should have served as a means for drawing closer to God and His commandments rather than as an end to themselves. The moral leaders of our time, as well, rebuke those who believe that by prayer alone they fulfill their obligations to Heaven, and warn them not to imagine that through prayer alone they are doing a favor for Hashem, Blessed is He. Rather, their duty is to observe all the *mitzvos* and to behave in a pure and sanctified manner. Thus, King David, in the fiftieth psalm (verse 13), relates Hashem's admonition: "Do I eat the flesh of fat beasts, or drink the blood of goats?"

The prophet who causes the greatest turmoil in regard to the sacrifices is Amos, who says (5:25), "Did you offer unto Me sacrifices and meal offerings in the wilderness forty years, O House of Israel?" It is this verse that the negators of the Torah and prophecy quote in their opposition to the concept of the *korbanos*. But it is clear that the meaning of the verse is that Hashem does not want sacrifices without the observance of His commandments or without having Him alone in mind, as is seen from the conclusion (v. 26): "You have borne Sikus your king and Kiun your images, Kochav your god, which you made to yourselves." Thus the intention of all the prophets is clear. After all, how can anyone negate the entire sacrificial system commanded by the Torah? Rather, as we mentioned, the sacrifices have a single purpose: to draw Israel close to their Father in Heaven by the kind of physical act that stimulates contemplation. Thus the prophets railed against confusion of the superficial with the essential; whereby the means becomes the end, as King David said (*Tehillim* 51:18,19), "For You do not desire sacrifice; else would I give it: You do not delight in burnt offering. The sacrifices of God is a broken spirit: a broken and a contrite heart, O God, You will not despise." In order to achieve this purpose, God commanded us to offer sacrifices when the Temple existed, just as we have been commanded about prayer, which fulfills this same purpose when there is no Temple.

The whole doctrine of the sacrifices occupies a major and fundamental role in drawing Israel closer to their Father in Heaven. This was manifested during the Second Temple era, too, when the sacrificial service of the *Kohen Gadol* inspired the observers to repent, in accord with the teaching of the *Tannaim* in those days. That is why our desire is so strong for the return of those days and to see again the *Kohanim* engaged in the Temple Service.

◄§ Rambam and the Doctrine of the Korbanos

Rambam (Maimonides) wrote two major works, one for the general Jewish public, entitled *Yad HaChazakah* or *Mishneh Torah*, and the other, known as *Moreh Nevuchim* — *the Guide for the Perplexed*. By the latter's title, we can see that this work was meant for *Rambam's* contemporaries who were weak in their faith, and who, influenced by the prevalent Greek philosophy, wanted to understand the reasons for the various commandments in the Torah, as he writes in his introduction to the book. In the other vast compendium, *Mishneh Torah*, which is the practical guide for all the actions of the general Jewish public, *Rambam* devotes a full volume to all the laws pertaining to the sacrifices, something that the later *halachic* codifiers do not.

In the laws governing *me'ilah* — the wrongful use of objects that have been sanctified to Hashem and the Temple — *Rambam* discusses at length that one should not search for logical explanations or reasons for the *mitzvos*, even though that is exactly what he does in the *Moreh Nevuchim*. To those who seek such reasons, he quotes the verse in *Sh'mos* (19:24): "They should not break the ranks to ascend to God, lest He burst forth upon them." *Rambam* in *Mishneh Torah* classifies the *korbanos* as being in the realm of *chukim* — statutes — whose reasons are unfathomable by man (as opposed to *mishpatim* — laws — which are logical to man). He cites our Sages, who taught that the entire world continues to exist only because of the merits of sacrifices. He concludes the chapter by warning all to heed the *chukim*, which he notes precede all the other commandments in the Torah: "As it states, 'You shall observe My *chukim* and My commandments.'" Again, in his introduction to the Order of *Kodashim*, he stresses the importance of learning the sacrificial service even now when the laws are not applicable:

> Due to our great sins, the matter of the *korbanos* has been lost in our days, and there are very few people who study it, and it is not remembered by even those who do, for there is no concrete act to establish the habits. And there is none who asks, expounds, or who is interested.

Elsewhere, *Rambam* writes of the value of the sacrifices, in keeping with the teachings of the Torah and *Chazal*.

In *Moreh Nevuchim* (section 3), however, *Rambam* provides a reason for the sacrifices, which does not seem to be in accord with *Chazal's* understanding. He suggests that the sole reason for the sacrifices was to wean Israel away from idolatry:

> They were used to a form of worship which included fire, and were raised (in an atmosphere which included) sacrificing animals on which they placed idols ... It was for this reason that God preserved these kinds of worship, but transferred them from (the worship of) creatures and imaginary matters, and commanded us (to sacrifice) to Him, may He be praised.

In Chapter 46, *Rambam* offers a rational explanation for the various kinds of sacrifices, and he states that the animals which Israel were commanded to sacrifice were thought to be gods by different nations in ancient times. The sheep was the god of Egypt. The goat was the god of Chaldea, and cattle were the gods of India. The Torah therefore commanded that these abominations of the various nations be slaughtered, so as to uproot idolatry from the hearts of Israel and to bring Israel closer to God; and it is for this purpose that the *korbanos* were instituted.

Ramban (Nachmanides), on this *parashah*, finds no justification for *Rambam's* explanations in *Moreh Nevuchim*, even though fully aware of the different approach in *Mishneh Torah*. He refers to the former as "nonsense," and asks: "How can *Rambam* say that the purpose of the sacrifices is to uproot idolatrous thoughts from the hearts, when the Torah states clearly in numerous places that the *korban* is "a sweet savor unto Hashem"? *Ramban* also cites both Hevel and Noach, who brought sacrifices, as proof that there is no connection between the *korbanos* and the beliefs of the Chaldeans and Egyptians, who did not yet exist in those days. Similarly, Bilaam set up seven altars and brought sacrifices to Hashem. Did *he* too wish to uproot vain beliefs? asks *Ramban*.

As a result of these questions, *Ramban* provides other explanations for the sacrifices, based both on *kabbalah* and the literal meaning of the texts. According to him, the literal significance of the sacrifice is that it causes man to be subservient to God, as the animal's ordeal is seen as a substitute for (the life) of the one bringing the *korban*. *Ramban*, though, prefers the *kabbalistic* explanation, which is that the sacrifices have their effect in the Heavenly strata.

Abarbanel, who offers his own interpretation of the sacrifices, defends the honor of *Rambam* by responding to *Ramban's* attacks. According to him, *Rambam* is on firm ground when he suggests that the offering of sacrifices is not the highest stage in the service of God, and that there are higher levels, these being prayer and moral behavior. Many prophets did, in fact, criticize ritual that does not lead to spiritual heights. Adam and his sons offered sacrifices with the purest of motives, whereas those who followed, even before the time of Noach, fell into error and were idolatrous. Hashem knew that man could not be severed from his customary practices at once, and He therefore allowed him the practices of the sacrificial system, provided that their purpose is for the sake of Heaven. Thus *Rambam* is right in·contending that prayer and the study of Torah are higher levels of the worship of Hashem. *Abarbanel* quotes *Midrash Rabbah* on *Vayikra* 22 as proof that one may regard the sacrificial system as a means to wean man away from idolatry:

> It was taught by R' Yishmael, since Israel was forbidden to eat non-sacrificial meat in the desert, the Torah obliged them to bring their *korbanos*, which the *Kohen* would slaughter and receive [the blood to sprinkle on the Altar]. R' Pinchas said in the name of R' Levi: "This is analogous to a king's son who was brutish, and who habitually ate all types of carrion. The king said: 'Let him always eat it at my table, and on his own he will stop eating these.' Thus,

as Israel chased after the Egyptian idolatry ... and brought their sacrifices in a forbidden manner, the Holy One, Blessed is He, said: 'Let them sacrifice their offerings to Me in the Tent of Assembly, and they will forsake idolatry.' "

This midrash is clearly in keeping with *Rambam's* statement that the purpose of the sacrifices was to separate the people from idolatry. (A number of later authorities bring proof to *Rambam's* view from this midrash, but they overlook the fact that Abarbanel preceded them.)

R' David Zvi Hoffman, in his introduction to the book of *Vayikra*, explains convincingly why it is an error to bring proof from the above midrash. In his opinion, it is impossible that *Chazal* would compare the sacrifices to "carrion." Neither did *Rambam* himself go so far, since he did not disqualify the sacrifices themselves, if only for their educational value. R' Hoffmann has a different version of the text of the midrash, which states, "This will always be at my table," rather than the version that Abarbanel quoted, "Let him always eat it at my table." There is a vast difference between the two versions. The phrase "this will always be on my table" refers to what precedes it, namely non-sacrificial meat. Thus, what R' Pinchas is saying in the name of R' Levi is that the Jews were forbidden to eat non-sacrificial meat during their sojourn in the desert so as to accustom them to always eat in Hashem's House — the place where the sacrifices were brought, and by this means they would be weaned from idolatry.

Accordingly, it is not the sacrifices themselves that serve to separate one from idolatry, but the requirement to eat the meat of the sacrifices in Hashem's House, together with the ban on other meat, which accomplishes this. Thus, as in the analogy, the king's son will sit at his father's table and will forsake his bad ways and customs. But Heaven forbid that we interpret the midrash to mean that sacrifices in themselves have no value, and are only meant to separate man from idolatry. R' David Hoffman has his reservations regarding *Rambam's* explanation; instead he too holds that the sacrifices have symbolic significance.

The Gaon of Dvinsk, in his *Meshech Chochmah*, seeks to reconcile *Rambam's* view with those of his opponents. He says that *Rambam's* statement that the sacrifices were intended to separate the Jews from idolatry refers to those sacrifices that were brought on *bamos* — local altars — which were an interim step in Israel's service in the period before the Temple. Although these local altars had no sanctity, they nevertheless served as an educational tool to root out idolatry from the people's hearts. All agree, however, that the service in the Temple was a lofty action, binding our world with the upper worlds. Thus the Gaon of Dvinsk also explains the words of King David (*Tehillim* 51:16), "For You do not desire sacrifice; else would I give it: You delight not in burnt offering." This refers to the *bamos*, but (ibid. 18-19), "Do good in Your favor unto Zion: Build the walls of Jerusalem. Then shall You be pleased with the sacrifices of righteousness" — this refers to the Temple, where the *korbanos* are sacrifices of righteousness.

◄§ The Principle of the Akeidah (the Binding of Yitzchak) in the Korban

Innumerable reasons, explanations and studies appear in our literature regarding the sacrifices. The author of *Akeidas Yitzchak* sees the sacrifice as a way for man to express his thanks to God. The Torah fathomed the real mentality of man, and discerned that sacrifices are a proper means of expressing one's thanks. *Maharal* of Prague sees the sacrifices as constituting the annulment of man's own being before the glory of God. *Ma'asei Hashem* views the sacrifice as man's renewal of himself. Man frees himself from the yoke of his sins, and can turn over a new leaf, free of guilt-feelings. The kabbalists see *korbanos* as God's gift to mankind to offset the attributes of *midas hadin* — strict justice, while the literal interpreters of the Torah regard the *korbanos* as having the effect of offering "a life for a life." *Kuzari* dwells on *korbanos* at length in Section II, Chapter 26, and explains that the purpose of the sacrifice is to bind the upper world to the lower world, but he concludes:

> I am not, Heaven forbid, determining that the purpose of this service is for the reasons that I gave, but what is more wondrous and exalted, for this is the Torah of God, Blessed is He. Whoever accepts it completely without attempting to be overwise with his own intelligence is better than one who attempts to be wise in it and to delve into it. But one who has fallen from that highest level and has chosen to delve (into the Torah), it is better that he achieve wise findings, rather than be inclined towards faulty reasoning and doubts that lead to destruction.

It would seem that what is still missing is the basic understanding of the role of "man-sacrifice" in the concept of the *korbanos*. The Jewish view of this is expressed in the *Akeidah* — when Avraham was willing to sacrifice Yitzchak his son to Heaven, but God arranged for a ram to appear and to be sacrificed instead, and promised to remember Avraham's holy readiness to the merit of his descendants. The place where this occurred is, by our tradition, on the Temple Mount. The fact that sacrifices were later offered on this same spot arouses memories of the *Akeidah*, so that we realize that sacrifices are by God's command a substitute for man.

The commentators' explanation that the sacrifice is "a life for a life" is deeper than is generally understood. The *korbanos* are tangible evidence of the *Akeidah* and the willingness of Avraham, the founder of our nation, to offer such a sacrifice, from which his descendants derive their willingness for self-sacrifice for Judaism throughout the generations. Indeed, this is hinted at by *Chazal* in *Midrash Rabbah* on *Vayikra*: "When Israel would offer the daily sacrifice — the *amid* — on the Altar and recite the phrase: 'Northward before the Lord,' the Holy One, Blessed is He, would remember the *Akeidah* of Yitzchak." I think that this point is the central one in the sacrifices, and am surprised that the Torah commentators do not note this. The only commentator who emphasizes the *Akeidah* in relationship to the *korbanos* is R' David Hoffman, but he deals primarily with the action of safeguarding man's life by the substitution of a ram, rather than the act of remembrance of the sanctity of the Jewish people as personified by the *Akeidah*. Perhaps this is the meaning of the verse: "If a person of you will bring a sacrifice," being a veiled allusion to the link between self-sacrifice and the act of the *korban*, as already indicated by Rabbeinu Bachya in his commentary. This allusion relates to Avraham's original sacrifice, which was substituted by an animal, and which has, for all generations, become the symbol of the sanctity of the Jewish people.

II.

Why Is no Honey Mixed in?

Much has been said in *halachah*, *aggadah*, and even Jewish philosophy about the prohibitions against honey — *d'vash* — and leaven, and the requirement of salt, with any sacrifice (see *Vayikra* 2:11). The investigations even branch out to include an examination of the nature of honey. The term itself generally includes not only honey from bees, but also the syrup that exudes from fruit, whereas in regard to the *bikkurim* — the bringing of first fruits to Jerusalem — it is limited solely to the syrup emanating from dates.

Rashi explains the word d'vash as follows: "*Any* sweet substance derived of fruit is d'vash." His generalized statement does not indicate how he expanded it to include more than the date syrup to which it applies in regard to bikkurim. Rashi's commentators, such as R' Eliyahu Mizrachi and Taz in his Divrei David and others, find a source for Rashi's explanation in the verse which follows the prohibition against using d'vash, where it is said (Vayikra 2:12), "You shall offer them as first fruits unto the Lord." According to Chazal in Menachos 58, this refers to the offerings of the two loaves of showbread and the bikkurim, where d'vash and leaven are permitted. From that fact, Rashi concludes that d'vash is any fruit sweetener since bee honey was not permitted to be brought as bikkurim.

Mishneh LaMelech, on Chapter 5 of Rambam's Hil. Issurei HaMizbe'ach, wonders why bee honey is forbidden with sacrifices, if the d'vash of the bikkurim is obviously only date syrup. Chasam Sofer in his responsa, Orach Chaim 198, asks the exact opposite: Why do we take it for granted that the d'vash, mentioned in connection with bikkurim, refers only to date syrup and not bee honey? He searches to find a convincing reason, and concludes that the word d'vash, in general, refers to any sweet exudation. However with regard to bikkurim, the Torah commands that they shall be the "first". And the "first" of the sweet exudations is date syrup alone.

It appears to me that the deduction that d'vash, in connection with bikkurim, refers to date syrup is a simple one, based on smichus — on the juxtaposition of the words "oil-yielding olive and d'vash" (Devarim 8:8). Referring to the Seven Species for which Eretz Yisrael is renowned, the Torah lists five of the species and two others which exude their products. Thus, just as olive oil is a product which is exuded from the olive, d'vash is a product which is exuded from the date.

Even so, it is apparent that the word d'vash in general, except for bikkurim, means bee honey. This is why Rashi stresses that here it refers to "a sweet substance from fruit." Based on the inference explained by Rashi's commentators, Chazal deduced that d'vash includes sweet substances from fruit, but did not need to deduce that it includes bee honey, for that is the common use of the term. In fact, Philo of Alexandria mistakenly explained the word d'vash in our verse to mean bee honey, for this reason. But Philo erred because d'vash in our context here includes more, as deduced from the verse, "You shall offer them as first fruits unto the Lord," as we quoted above.

Rambam in his *Moreh Nevuchim* 3:46, following his method, explains these commandments as being aimed at uprooting Israel from the Emorite ways. He states that the idolaters sacrificed leaven rather than bread, and that they sacrificed sweet things. At the same time, they did not put any salt on their sacrifices, so as to ensure that the blood would remain in the animal's body, as part of their worship of the god Mars. On the other hand, I have seen commentators who hold that the emphasis in the Torah (*Vayikra* 2:13), "And every sacrifice of your meal offering shall you season with salt," shows clearly the opposite of *Rambam's* interpretations, for the meal offering — *minchah* — has no blood, and thus one cannot associate it with any idolatrous ritual.

Chasam Sofer too, in his commentary on the Torah, offers his own proof against *Rambam's* explanation. R' Aaron Halevi, in his *Bedek HaBayis*, explains the verse, "upon all your sacrifices shall you offer salt," as indicating that the remnants of the sacrifice that are eaten by the *Kohanim* must also be salted. On the other hand, the *Kohanim* were permitted to eat the showbread and the *bikkurim* together with leaven and *d'vash*. The question thus confronts us: If the *Kohanim* too are required to eradicate the traces of the pagan sacrifices (as we see from the fact that they must salt those portions of the sacrifices that they themselves eat), why are they permitted leaven and *d'vash*?

This would seem to indicate that there is no rational explanation for these laws, but that they are Divine decrees. Thus, when the Torah states (*Vayikra* 2:13), "neither shall you suffer the salt of the covenant of your God to be lacking," it is not because the Torah wishes to eradicate the Emorite ways, but rather it is "a covenant of God" for "upon all your sacrifices shall you offer salt and even the remnants of the sacrifices must be salted when eaten by the *Kohanim*, even though the *Kohanim* are not commanded to take special measures to distance themselves from idolatry." *Rashba*, however, disagrees with R' Aaron Halevi, and holds that there is no need for the *Kohanim* to add salt to the remnants of the sacrifice which they themselves eat. If so, the whole line of reasoning just cited is of course invalid. But *Rambam's* reason is difficult in itself. After all, what difference does it make how the idolaters offered their sacrifices, when the entire purpose of the *korbanos* is to wean the Jews away from the Emorite practices? The latter offered sacrifices to their gods, and Israel was commanded to offer *korbanos* to Hashem. Why then in regard to salt, leaven and *d'vash* were we ordered to remove ourselves from them totally, as opposed to the very institution of sacrifices which we were commanded to observe?

Tur gives a simple reason why leaven and *d'vash* should be forbidden. Leaven causes gaps in the *minchah* — meal offering — as does *d'vash*, whereas the *kometz* — the handful that had to be taken by the *Kohen* — had to be complete. According to him, there is also a simple reason for requiring salt, so as to ensure that the sacrifice is not tasteless, for food which is inedible may not be sacrificed in accord with the rule that anything unfit to present to a human king cannot be offered on the Altar.

Abarbanel also offers a logical reason for the prohibition against leaven, for if one added leaven he would have to wait for the flour to rise, and that might result in the sacrifice being offered beyond its fixed time. *D'vash*, on the other hand, works in the opposite way, for it breaks down its host product, and people might rush to bring the sacrifice before it is consumed. Thus the Torah forbade the addition of either one of these ingredients, since they interfere, in opposite ways, with the sacrifice being brought at its proper time.

Abarbanel notes also two other interesting opposites. Leaven by itself is not fit for human consumption and is therefore not suitable to be offered to God, while *d'vash* stimulates one's appetite, thus there is a chance that the *Kohanim* will lick it before the sacrifice takes place. A number of other reasons, of a symbolic nature, are offered elsewhere by Abarbanel and may be found in other sources. There are also numerous *halachic* and rational reasons in the different commentaries. *Ba'alei HaTosafos* see the three ingredients — leaven, *d'vash*, and salt — as a single unit. Since we must place salt on all our sacrifices, we are therefore forbidden to add leaven or *d'vash*, neither of which absorbs salt, and which are not fit to be eaten with salt. The *acharonim* — later rabbinic authorities — also seek a natural or halachic explanation why leaven and *d'vash* should be forbidden.

Torah Temimah holds that the Torah forbade the use of honey because it is exuded by a non-kosher insect, the bee. Man, on the other hand, may personally partake of honey, as it is kosher since the bee merely exudes the fruit juices it collected, but honey cannot be sacrificed to God because of its repellent origins. This is also the reason that the garments used by the *Kohanim* contained no silk, which is derived from a non-kosher insect.

Chinuch states, in regard to leaven and *d'vash*: "As to the source of this commandment, it is very difficult to find even a hint." Nevertheless, he seeks symbolic explanations, although he prefaces this by stating:

I have already announced, at the beginning of my work, that my intention in giving these reasons is to give the young men reasons when they first begin to study, so as to accustom them to the fact that the words of the Torah have reasons and functions, so that they will accept these on the level of their habitual way of thinking, each according to his intellectual level.

⊷§ Symbolic Reasons

The Chassidic and *d'rush* commentators see leaven as the symbol of the evil inclination, which *Chazal* referred to as "the leaven in the dough." Honey symbolizes the desires and lusts of the world, all of which one should shun, for they make it harder for man to draw closer to Hashem. This symbolism is already found in the *rishonim* — the earlier rabbinic authorities — Abarbanel, *Chinuch*, and is especially developed by Rabbeinu Bachya. According to the latter, leaven symbolizes the evil inclination of idolatry. Regarding the *Pesach* sacrifice, too, it is written (*Devarim* 16:3), "You shall not eat *chametz* with it"; for the *Pesach* sacrifice also comes for the purpose of distancing us from idol worship.

D'vash in *gematria* is numerically equivalent to *ishah* — woman. The first woman, Eve, was the one who enticed Adam into eating of the forbidden fruit.

Yet the degree to which one must keep from leaven and from *d'vash* is not identical. For example, the *Kohanim* eat *d'vash* with the remainder of the *minchah* — the meal offering — but remain forbidden to partake of any leaven. The Gaon of Lutzk, author of *Oznayim LaTorah*, explains this: Our Sages tell us that the *Anshei Knesses Hagedolah* — the Men of the Great Assembly — succeeded totally in destroying the evil inclination to indulge in idolatry, but they refrained from totally abolishing the evil inclination for adultery, for the world cannot exist without the urge for procreation. The difference between the two inclinations is symbolically seen in comparing the difference between leaven and *d'vash*. The first is never permitted, while the second is permitted with the remainder of the *minchah*.

Chasam Sofer sees the three substances of leaven, *d'vash* and salt as symbolic of "envy, lust and urge for honor." Leaven symbolizes the urge for honor which results from haughtiness. *D'vash* symbolizes the lusts of this world. Salt symbolizes envy, for as *Chazal* tell us, at the time of Creation the lower waters envied the upper waters. The Torah therefore commanded that salt be added to each sacrifice, so as to raise the lower waters, represented by salt, to the highest level. Lust and conceit do not have any positive dimension, therefore they should be abolished totally and are forbidden, even in the most minute amount. Envy, though, does have a positive aspect, as it is said, "the envy of Sages increases wisdom." As Shlomo stated (*Koheles* 4:4), "the prerequisite for accomplishment is that one man envies another." The Torah therefore enabled the offering of salt — symbol of envy — on the Altar, but totally excluded leaven and *d'vash* — symbols of conceit and lust.

R' Yosef Zvi Dushinski varies this theme in his *Toras Maharitz*. The lower waters, he writes, wished to unite and to ascend upward, and they were therefore worthy of being offered on the Altar. This is the object lesson for each person to learn: that he must strive to link up with what is above. Thus the meaning of "neither shall you suffer the salt of the covenant of your God to be lacking" is that salt should be a constant reminder to seek to draw closer to God.

The Rebbe of Kotzk gives a symbolic message to this *parashah*. In his curt style, he writes: "No leaven and no honey — not too sour and not too sweet." In other words, in serving God, one should not be too sour nor too sweet, not too simple and not too abstract. The later Tzaddikim of Kotzk and their disciples extended this concept. One of the great Torah Sages of our generation, who was not associated with the Chassidic world, the Gaon, R' Yosef Shaul Nathansohn, in his *Divrei Shaul*, although he does not mention the Tzaddik of Kotzk, similarly rejects extremes in the service of God when he states that the Torah wishes man to choose the middle road, and not to stray into side alleys or fanaticism, in keeping with the well-known golden path dictum of *Rambam*.

✑§ When is Salt a Covenant?

Salt as a covenant appears in a number of places in *Tanach*. Ibn Ezra's explanation that the covenant is an oath not to sacrifice something tasteless is surprising: Why should there be such an oath? *Rivash's* interpretation, as well as that of a number of other early commentators, is that salt symbolizes eternity, for salt does not change or decay. This is also the spirit in which R' Samson Raphael Hirsch explains it. The covenant of salt directs Israel not to change or modify the laws of Sinai, just as salt never changes.

"*Chadash* — new — is forbidden by Torah law," (a reference to the new crop of wheat that may not be used until the *omer* is brought on the second day of *Pesach*, but which is also taken to mean that "new innovations and practices" are forbidden) says the *Chasam Sofer*, and this explains the symbolism of salt on our tables.

Chazal in *Menachos* 21 learn from the verse (*Vayikra* 2:13), "neither shall you suffer the salt of the covenant of your God to be lacking," that one should make sure to use salt which is never "lacking". This means the salt of *Yam Hamelech* (the Dead Sea), in the region of Sodom, namely natural salt rather than that manufactured by man. *Sifsei Kohen* offers an interesting explanation, linking the latter requirement to the fact that Sodom was destroyed by brimstone and salt. Hashem commanded us to remember that event when we eat so that we be certain to engage in charitable acts and be hospitable to strangers, as a safeguard against the punishment visited upon the wicked people of Sodom who did not practice these good deeds.

Ramban sees salt as a unified combination of diametric opposites. On the one hand, it is derived from water, whose purpose is to rain upon the earth and make it bloom, yet, when the sun causes water to evaporate, the result is salt and brimstone. Salt, which combines in itself both fire (of the sun) and (life-sustaining) water, is therefore the symbol of the royalty of Israel, for King David was noted for his mercy to Israel and his ruthlessness to his enemies. It therefore states (*II Divrei HaYamim* 13:5), "to him and to his sons a covenant of salt."

Kli Yakar sees salt as a symbol of variety. It symbolizes the total sovereignty of God in all conditions and circumstances, whether over fire or water, justice or mercy. *HaKesav VeHaKabalah* also follows that path. As evidence that one of the elements of salt is fire, he quotes *Chazal* in the fourth chapter of *Shabbos*, where it is stated that salt is one of those materials which contribute heat and steam to its host. Accordingly, the use of salt is intended to counteract the idolatrous worship of either fire or water that predominated in the pagan world. It is salt in the sacrifice that proclaims the dominion of God over both elements.

Chasam Sofer points out that the Torah only speaks of a "covenant of salt" in reference to the *minchah* — the meal offering, whereas in regard to other sacrifices it simply states: "upon all your sacrifices shall you offer salt." In all the other types of sacrifices, salt could possibly be understood as a seasoning for the meat. Regarding the *minchah*, though, one cannot interpret it that way, because salt would not normally be used there as a seasoning. This thus clearly indicates the Torah's purpose to proclaim "the covenant of your God."

ᴥᔥ Why is D'vash not Added?

"If a *kurtov* (a certain measure) of *d'vash* was added, no person could withstand its smell," says Bar Kappara in a comment on the formula of the *k'tores* — incense — described in the Talmud (*Kereisos* 6:1). If so, continues Bar Kappara, "Why not add *d'vash*?" His answer, "because the Torah said so," arouses astonishment among the commentators. What did he mean? But after having delved into the current subject and having seen that the *chukim* of the Torah are not understandable by man regardless of all the attempts to explain them, we can appreciate the words of the Rebbe of Kotzk who said that Bar Kappara meant to teach us that we ought not be overly sophisticated on Torah study nor attempt to ascertain that which is above our understanding. Instead, we should accept all simply "because the Torah said so." "If a *kurtov* of *d'vash* was added, no person could withstand its smell." But if we refrain from adding honey because the Torah instructed us so, then the *mitzvah* acquires its proper flavor, and is "a sweet savor unto Hashem."

III.

Sinning through Negligence

The Torah begins with a general principle (*Vayikra* 4:2): "If a soul shall sin through negligence, in any of the commandments which Hashem has commanded not to be done." It concludes by mentioning the individuals involved in the various types of negligence, these being: a) The anointed *Kohen*; b) the Sanhedrin (referred to by the verse "the entire congregation"); c) the king (or *nasi*); d) any individual. The sin offering that is to be brought by an anointed *Kohen* or the Sanhedrin is a bull, that of the *nasi* is a he-goat, and the sin offering of an individual is a she-goat. The sacrifices of the first two are burned completely, while those of the last two are not burned completely.

Throughout the ages, our commentators have offered explanations for the differences in the laws involved, and for the differing phraseology in the Torah regarding the manner of sinning. Thus, for the anointed *Kohen* and the Sanhedrin, the Torah phrases it "אִם — if —

the person sins," implying a doubt. In regard to an individual, on the other hand, it is phrased "כִּי — if — a soul shall sin," which too implies a doubt, but with an increased probability of the sin being committed. With the *nasi*, on the other hand, the Torah states it as a certainty: "When (אֲשֶׁר) a *nasi* sins." Grammarians suggest that the word *asher* before a noun has the same meaning as if it had been written after a noun, thus yielding, in essence, "a *nasi* who (*asher*) sins." *Zohar* and certain *d'rush seforim* prefer to explain the verse literally, for they feel a king simply is unable to remain free of sin; his pride *must* lead him to transgress. The text appears to invite homiletic interpretation of each letter and word, but the commentators do not devote much time to this type of commentary. They prefer, instead, to discuss the astounding fact that negligence — *shogeg* — too, is considered to be a sin, for which one must bring a sin offering. We will devote our interpretation to this aspect.

The Gaon of Lutzk ties the phrase, "If a soul shall sin," to the characteristic nature of sins committed through negligence. The difference between the deliberate and the negligent act is only apparent in the soul of the individual, and not in his body. The body commits the same sin, whether deliberately or negligently, but the soul differentiates between the two, indicating whether it was committed intentionally or unintentionally. When one sins intentionally, the saintly *Or HaChaim* states, his soul is removed, and it is for this reason that *Chazal* say that the wicked are considered to be dead even as they live, since their soul is completely gone. On the other hand, when one sins through negligence, his soul is not removed, but is instead blemished. It must be repaired by means of a sacrifice, and thereby drawn closer to holiness. In the case of an intentional sin, one cannot repair the damage caused by the sin through the act of sacrifice, for there is no blemish in the soul. Instead, the soul has simply been removed.

Akeidah explains this somewhat differently. If one sinned through negligence, only his body committed the sin, and therefore the sacrifice of the body of an animal can be effective to remedy the sin. On the other hand, one who sins intentionally has sullied his soul, and how then can the sacrifice of the body of an animal serve to purify the person's soul?

◆§ Sin Creates a Blemish

Ramban too explains the reason for the *chatas* — the sacrifice brought for a sin committed through negligence — as relating to the blemish caused to the person's soul. He says:

As the power of thought is within the soul, and it is this which committed the sin through negligence, (the Torah) therefore mentions the soul here. And the reason for the sacrifices that are brought for the soul that sins through negligence is because all sins lead to the disgrace of the soul and are a blemish upon it, thereby making it unworthy of being received by its Creator ... Were this not so, then all the fools of the world would be worthy of coming before Him. Therefore, the soul which sins through negligence must bring a sacrifice, to enable it to draw closer to God who gave it, and for this reason (the Torah) also uses the word, "soul".

Chinuch, though, views sacrifice as an educational act, which is only effective for sins through negligence, and not for those that are intentional. This is because one's heart is drawn after one's actions. Thus, if a person sins, it is not enough for him simply to say that he has repented and will not sin again, but he must take many actions: He must take a sacrifice from his flock; bring it to the Temple, and carry out all the rules pertaining to the sacrifice. By doing so, he will realize the greatness of his sin, and will not sin again. In addition, the fact that animals resemble man in composition, except for man's use of the process of thought, leads the sinner to realize that his sin came about because he did not use his ability to think. Instead, he acted like the animal which is being sacrificed in his stead. This should lead him to think in the future, so that he will not sin again. The Torah reasons that by bringing a sacrifice, man will regret his actions and his sin will be atoned. But this comparison of one's actions to the thoughtless animal sacrificed in his stead cannot apply to a deliberate sin, where the person was deliberately sinning against God.

Abarbanel has a different view. The sacrifice brought by the person who sinned is his punishment and a monetary loss, and that will prevent him from doing evil. In his introduction to *Vayikra*, Abarbanel states that Hashem wished to caution Israel against sinning before Him and against violating His commandments. As people can sometimes err and do something which they had not planned to do, Hashem decided to punish them through their money, so that it would make an impact on their spirit and soul, and they would be careful not to sin again. It is for this reason that the sinner must bring a *chatas*, which is a monetary punishment, so that he will straighten his ways and be most careful not to sin through negligence.

Other commentators note that the sacrifice brought for a sin of negligence was instituted by the Torah because of one's temptation to feel that he has not really done anything wrong. *Chazal* have already said that if a scholar who should know better negligently hands down a wrongful ruling, it is considered as if he sinned deliberately, whether he ruled for himself or for others. R' Menachem the Babylonian said that the punishment for a sin through negligence is a great one, because the person "remains calm and says that a soul that sins through negligence should not be punished." He must therefore bring a sacrifice, so as to make him aware that he has indeed sinned.

The word *cheit* is used uniquely for sins through negligence, whereas those carried out deliberately are referred to as *avon* and *pesha*. According to R' David Zvi Hoffman, the essence of the *cheit* is that the person was not careful and therefore sinned. The Jewish people were commanded (*Vayikra* 18:30), "And you shall guard My commandment" and (*Bereishis* 18:19), "they shall guard the way of God", meaning that we must institute all the necessary safeguards and precautions to prevent coming near to the violation of Torah commandments. It is for this reason that even a sin through negligence requires atonement. This does not apply to a person who committed a sin through absolutely no fault of his own (*oneis*), which does not require a sacrifice, for the Torah exempts an *oneis*.

R' Samson Raphael Hirsch also explains the nature of *cheit* as stemming from unthinking carelessness. When committing such a sin, the person is not taking care to ensure that what he is doing is in accordance with the Torah law. He is not "fearful of My word," as Yeshayahu puts it in Chapter 66. This lack of fear of what he is doing is the major dimension of the sin through negligence. Thus an element of *pesha* accompanies the *cheit*.

◆§ A Hidden Tie Between Man and Sin

The Lubavitcher Rebbi, in his unique fashion, explains the concept of sin caused through negligence in a simple psychological way. According to him, a sin caused through negligence requires atonement, because even though it was committed unintentionally and without the person's desiring to do so, the fact that the person was even able to commit the sin proves that he is not at the proper level of behavior. Had he been at that level, he would not have sinned through negligence, as it states (*Mishlei* 12:21), "No evil will happen to the righteous." What the person who commits a sin caused through negligence is guilty of, is allowing his animalistic qualities to govern his past behavior, and it is this which brought him to the condition where he is capable of committing a sin through negligence.

Those actions which a person commits unwittingly, without thought or intention, indicate his nature, where his involvement lies, and what his pleasures are. The actions of the righteous person, whose delight is in God, are good and sanctified, while the one who commits a sin through negligence indicates that his pleasures are derived from an impure source.

When a person commits a sin caused through negligence, in a certain respect his deficiency is greater than that of a person who sinned deliberately, for when a person deliberately commits a sin of his own free will, it does not necessarily reflect a deep spiritual tie between him and the sin which he committed. Rather it is likely that his entire link with the action is limited to the time of its performance, and is confined merely to the level of his intention and consciousness at the time. On the other hand, an action performed negligently is proof of the person's essence, and is a greater link between the sin and his essence than that between a person and a sin committed deliberately. The person who sins negligently does so because he is drawn instinctively to perform such actions, until he actually sins.

This explains the saying of *Arizal* that whoever is careful about even the smallest particle of *chametz* on *Pesach* is guaranteed not to sin the whole year. Yet, if we say that man has the power of free will, he should certainly always be at liberty to choose the path that he will follow. How then can one state so categorically that one who is scrupulous about even the slightest quantity of *chametz* for eight days loses this free will?

The explanation of this is that *Arizal* is referring to sins committed through negligence. It is possible for a person to commit a sin deliberately, God forbid, because he always has free will and he may do as he desires. But a sin through negligence, which is committed unintentionally, will not happen to the one who is careful about *chametz*, because such observance affects his entire being to the extent that he is more saintly and therefore will not be drawn to commit such sin.

The Lubavitcher Rebbi continues along these lines to explain why one who transgresses a doubtful prohibition — *safek issur* — (e.g., by eating a piece of fat that might or might not have been kosher) is more stringently penalized than a person who transgresses a *vadai issur* — a definite prohibition. The former brings an *asham talui* — a "doubt" offering — while the latter only brings a *chatas*, which costs considerably less. If a person knows definitely that he committed a sin through negligence, this shows that his ties to evil existed even before he performed the action, and it was these that caused him to commit the sin, although he was unaware of doing so. But at least, afterwards, he realizes that he has sinned, and he knows now that he has indeed faltered. Where, however, he is not even sure that he has committed a sin, he is in danger of congratulating himself that he did nothing wrong. But this just shows that the person has an even deeper tie to evil, since he does not even know that he is in need of improvement.

One who commits a sin through negligence is still in essence a good person. His sin is a contradiction of this essence and is foreign to him. He, therefore, realizes ultimately that he has transgressed against Hashem's will. He feels bad about this uncharacteristic behavior, which disturbs his essence. (The animal-like element in him has merely surrounded him and drawn him to evil, but does not become his essence; on the contrary, it exists in opposition to his essence.) On the other hand, where a person may have transgressed a sin but congratulates himself that he has done nothing wrong, this becomes part of his essence, inasmuch as he feels no contradiction or disturbance to his equanimity, since he does not feel he has sinned.

The sources of the Lubavitcher Rebbe are kabbalistic and Chassidic works, drawn from the wells of Divine wisdom, but I found a clear and explicit source in *Midrash Tanchuma* on *Vayikra*, where we read: "Our Sages learned: A *mitzvah* draws another in its wake, and an *aveirah* — a sin — draws another in its wake. A person should be distressed by a sin committed through negligence, because it creates an opening for future sin, both unintentional and deliberate. A person should rejoice over a *mitzvah* which he performed, because of the many *mitzvos* which will come his way in the future. Therefore if one sinned through negligence, it is not a good sign, as it states (*Mishlei* 19:2), 'even without knowledge the soul is not good.' " According to this midrash, sins of negligence are a bad sign for the future and the same is implied regarding the past, since one sin draws another in its wake, and the present sin is an indication that the person sinned in the past, this having led to the present sin.

If the person was without a defect in his roots, he would not be able to transgress without being aware of it. A beautiful explanation of this was given by my rebbi, the Gaon, R' Yosef Zvi Dushinski, in explaining the verse (*Vayikra* 4:2), "If a soul should sin through negligence any of all the commandments of Hashem which are not to be done." With the righteous person, all the organs of his body assist him to perform the *mitzvos*. Avraham performed the *mitzvos* as the organs of his body showed him, as we read with regard to the *Akeidah*: "and he sent forth his hand." His hand was not acting of its own volition, for it was

Hashem's will that Avraham should not sacrifice his son. Avraham needed to compel his own hand, against its will, to do what he thought had to be done. A person who has not previously committed a sin and is unscathed would necessarily find his organs reacting against something forbidden. The person who acts out one of the things "which ought not to be done" does so because his body was not sanctified as it should be.

Tiferes Shmuel also adds a sharp Chassidic insight. One who sins through negligence reveals not only his sin, but also his separation from the community. Had he been attached to the community he would never have sinned, just as anything attached to the ground cannot become *tamei* — ritually unclean. The community is the soil in which the person grew, and it is because he is so uprooted from it that he sins: "If a single soul shall sin through negligence." He sins because he is a "single soul," and not part of the entire community.

◈§ The Guilt of the People

The relationship between the sin of the individual and that of the entire community is stated in the Torah with regard only to the anointed Kohen — the *Kohen Gadol*, as it is written, "If the anointed Kohen sins so as to bring guilt — *ashmas ha'am* — upon the people. . ." *Chazal* in *Midrash Rabbah* provide an analogy: "Woeful is the place whose doctor is ill, and the watchman blind in one eye, and the defending attorney in a capital case becomes the prosecuting attorney." The guilt of the people — *ashmas ha'am* — means that the people must suffer when their leader sins, and must be punished through his actions. The *d'rush* and Chassidic works add to this a wealth of ideas. "Each generation and its leaders," the Chassidic works tell us, means that the leaders draw their essence from the people. If the people are wise, the leaders, too, are exalted, while if the people are lacking in various qualities, the leaders sink with the people. The guilt of the people leads to the decline of its leaders; had the people not been sinners, their leaders would not have sunk that low. Various *d'rush* works explain the midrash as meaning that even the smallest sins of the leaders have a negative influence on the entire community, and as a result the latter commit deliberate sins.

R' David Zvi Hoffman's interpretation is different, in that he explains the verse according to its literal meaning. When the *Kohen Gadol* sins, it is the sin of the people, who are dependent on him to atone for them and to pray for them. The *Kohen Gadol* leaves the people in a state of non-atonement. The meaning of the word *asham* (translated until now as "guilt") is a debt, which, by God's law, must be paid. The *Kohen Gadol* is the representative of the nation, and his condition reveals theirs. As long as the *Kohen Gadol* is free of sin, the Jewish people are said to be fulfilling their duties, but when the *Kohen Gadol* has sinned, his debt applies to the entire people, because they did not choose the proper person who could atone for them.

R' David Zvi Hoffman rejects the interpretations of the secular Bible critics, who claim that the Torah only applies this law where the *Kohen Gadol* had been acting in his capacity as a representative of the people before Hashem, rather than as an individual. This view is simply unfounded. The Torah does not recognize any difference between sins committed as a functionary and those committed privately. We are told regarding the *Kohanim*, "they shall teach Your laws," and they must therefore be examples in their private as well as their public lives.

Rashbam explains that since the *Kohen* is required to teach the nation, his sinning causes the people to sin as well. If that is what the Torah wishes to convey, though, would it not have been more appropriate to refer to *chatas ha'am* (sin), rather than *ashmas ha'am* (guilt)? *Rashi's* interpretation therefore seems more understandable, when he writes that the meaning is, "When the *Kohen Gadol* sins, it is the *ashmah* of the people, for they are dependent on him to atone for them and to pray for them, and he has become sullied."

R' David Zvi Hoffman offers evidence in support of *Chazal* who interpret "the whole congregation of Israel" as a reference to when the Sanhedrin erred in its ruling. He brings numerous proofs for this interpretation.

(a) The word used for congregation, *eidah*, derives from a root referring to "assembling," thus referring to the assembly of the Sanhedrin.

(b) In *Bamidbar* 10:3, we read: "And when they shall blow [the trumpets], all the assembly (*eidah*) shall assemble themselves to the entrance to the Tent of Assembly." This, of course, refers to the representatives of the people, since the entire community could not assemble there.

(c) In *Bamidbar* 35:24-25, it states, "Then the congregation (*eidah*) shall judge" and "And the congregation shall rescue." These verses refer to a normal *beis din* — court of Torah law — whereas the reference to "*all* the assembly (or congregation)" must be referring to the *Great Beis Din*, the Sanhedrin.

(d) In *Bamidbar* 27:21 we are told concerning Joshua: "At his word shall they go out, and at his word they shall come in, both he, and all the congregation (*eidah*) of the Children of Israel with him, and all the congregation" (*eidah*). We see that there is a difference between "the congregation of the Children of Israel" and "all the congregation."

(e) In *Bamidbar* 25:6 the Torah states, "And, behold, one of the Children of Israel came and brought unto his brethren a Midianite woman in the sight of Moses, and in the sight of all the congregation (*eidah*) of the Children of Israel." One cannot interpret *eidah* to mean the entire congregation, because it would be physically impossible for all to see.

(f) In *I Melachim* 12:20, it states: "And it came to pass, when all Israel heard that Yerovam had come again, that they sent and called him unto the congregation (*eidah*) and made him king over all Israel." Again, we see a distinction between all "Israel" and "the congregation."

(g) In our *parashah*, there are two terms used for the community: "the whole assembly (*eidah*) of Israel," and "the community" (*kahal*). The first refers to the *Great Beis Din* and the second to the community as such.

R' David Zvi Hoffman also shows how correct *Chazal* were when they explained that the word *nasi* (commonly translated as leader or prince) refers to the king, and not to the heads of the tribes as thought by Ibn Ezra and other commentators. In *Yechezkel* 34:24 we read: "And my servant David a *nasi* among them." This means that he was the king among them. The word *nasi* implies someone greater than the rest of the people. When the Torah uses the word *nasi* without qualifying whether it is referring to a person who is the head of a family, a tribe, or the people as a whole, it must be referring to the person who is greater than all others. The proof of this is from the phrase in our *parashah*, "If a soul should sin through negligence of all the commandments of Hashem, *his God*, which are not to be done." This must be referring to the greatest person in the nation, above whom is only Hashem, as it is written in *Devarim* 17:19, in regard to the king, "that he may learn to fear Hashem his God."

These interpretations of *Chazal* are in keeping with the spirit of the verses, and in accordance with the literal meaning of the text.

IV.

Between Man and Hashem
and Between Man and His Fellow-Man

he beginning of Chapter 5 of *Vayikra* constitutes a declaration that sins between man and his fellow-man are also sins between man and Hashem, and that Jewish morality is based on Divine morality. R' Akiva analyzes this assumption in a clear fashion:

> Why does the verse state (*Vayikra* 5:21), "and commit a trespass against Hashem"? This is because every lender and borrower, or he who negotiates a transaction, does so with witnesses and a deed. Therefore, whoever denies (any detail), denies the witnesses and the deed. But if someone leaves a deposit with his fellow, and does so without wanting anyone to know, except for the Third between them, then, when the deposit is denied, he denies it to the Third between them.

What R' Akiva says is clear: When one trusts a person, he is trusting the Divine part of that person's soul. One who denies a deposit is denying Hashem, Who sees and is not seen, and Who knows all, for it is upon Him that the one who left the deposit relied, rather than upon witnesses. In this spirit, and in line with the other commentators, *Shaloh* explains: "See and perceive how far reaching is the sin of one who denies a debt. Even though it is only a monetary question, nevertheless he is denying Him, may He be Blessed."

R' David Zvi Hoffman and many other commentators explain the literal meaning of the text: "And commit a trespass (*me'ilah*) against Hashem." Moral sin in matters between man and his fellow-man is referred to as *me'ilah* against God, not because the person took a false oath, since neither the oaths of witnesses, in v. 1 of this chapter, nor using God's name in vain, in v. 4, is referred to as "a *me'ilah* against Hashem." Rather, a *me'ilah* against God is the injury caused to the other man's right and his ownership.

Noteworthy is the fact that the type of false oath (*shvu'as sheker*) in our instance is not considered by the Torah to be as serious as when one deliberately swears falsely (*shvu'as zadon*) for which, we are told, Hashem will not absolve the person who swore. Thus we see that a sacrifice helps to atone for the present type of false oath. The reason, according to *Meshech Chochmah*, is that a false oath in this case is somewhat of an involuntary act that results from the denial of a debt. "To confirm his words and to release himself from his fellow-litigant he swears falsely, without the intention of desecrating His name, may It be Blessed. He is acting, as it were, involuntarily, forced by the wickedness of his heart. But He who knows man's intentions and nature knows that it is man's tendency to swear in these instances." The basic sin in this *parashah* is the abuse of the ownership of a person and his rights, and that constitutes a trespass against Hashem. On the other hand, giving a false oath, which is an act against God, is considered as only a sin through negligence — a *shogeg* — and an involuntary act for which there is atonement.

Rabbeinu Bachya explains that the repetition of the wording, "And if he sins and is guilty (*ashem*)," is meant to stress this principle, namely that a sin against one's fellow-man also means guilt (*ashem*) against God. The social morality is also Divine morality.

Ohel Yaakov, by the Dubno Magid, explains at great length, using *d'rush*, the tie between sins against God and sins against one's fellow-man. Shlomo said in *Mishlei* (6:1-2), concerning one who has become involved in debt to his fellow, "My son, if you are surety for your friend, if you have stricken your hand with a stranger, you are snared with the words of your mouth, you are trapped with the words of your mouth." This appears, at first, to be repetitious: Why "you are snared" and "you are trapped"? But *Chazal* in *Midrash Rabbah Vayikra* 6 say: " 'My son, if you are surety for your friend. . .' The word 'friend' (רֵעַ) refers to the Holy One, Blessed is He, as it is said (*Mishlei* 27:10), 'Do not abandon your Friend and the Friend of your father.' " A sin committed against God is called a "snare," because it is comparable to one who stumbles against a stone and injures himself. For this there is a remedy: He may apply the proper medicine and be healed. But a sin committed against one's fellow man is called a "trap," because it is comparable to one who has been captured by others and thrown into the guardhouse. The remedy is no longer in his own hands. He can only be saved by others — that is, by the forgiveness of those he has injured.

Now we can understand the flow of these verses written by the wise King Shlomo: "My son, if you are a surety to your Friend" — that is, the Holy One, Blessed is He — and in addition "you have stricken your hand with a stranger"; that is, your fellow-man, then the result is that "you are snared with the words of your mouth," and moreover, "you are trapped with the words of your mouth," meaning you have committed the type of sin which is an offense both against God and man. In that case, you must follow the advice offered in the next verse: "Do this ... since you have fallen into the hand of your friend; go, humble yourself, and encourage your friend." In other words, first appease your friend and rectify the sin against him, and only then can you repent before Hashem. This is also what we see in our present *parashah*. First the Torah writes (*Vayikra* 5:15-16): "If a soul commits a trespass (*me'ilah*), and sins through negligence, in the holy things of Hashem; then he shall bring for his *me'ilah* unto Hashem a ram without blemish ... and the *Kohen* shall make atonement for him with the ram of the *asham* — trespass offering — and it shall be forgiven him."

Afterwards, the Torah states (*Vayikra* 5:21-25), "If a soul sins, and commits a trespass against Hashem, and lies unto his neighbor in that which was delivered him to keep ... and lies concerning it, and swears falsely ... Then it shall be, because he has sinned, and is guilty," that the first thing he must do is to "restore that which he took violently away," and only thereafter "shall he bring his *asham* unto Hashem." That is, as *Chazal* tell us (*Bava Kama* 110),

> If a person returned what he stole, and afterwards brought the required guilt offering, he has fulfilled his obligation [the guilt offering is valid]. If he brought the guilt offering and afterwards returned what he stole, he has not fulfilled his obligation [the guilt offering is invalid].

In *Bava Basra* (88b), *Chazal* deduce from this *parashah* that stealing from a person is worse than stealing from Hashem, and that the Torah is more stringent about *mitzvos* between man and his fellow-man than it is about *mitzvos* between man and God.

R' Yosef Zvi Dushinski uses *d'rush* to explain this *Gemara* through the verses in our *parashah*. It states here: "If a soul sins, and commits a *me'ilah* against Hashem, and lies unto his neighbor ... in any of all these that a man does, sinning therein." Repentance requires that a person who has committed numerous sins should offset them by the performance of many *mitzvos*. This remedy, however, refers to *mitzvos* between man and Hashem. When it comes to sins between man and his fellow-man, such as theft or cheating, the *mitzvos* that follow will be of no avail, for they too are being performed in sin with money obtained illegally, and whatever good the sinner does is a *mitzvah* which comes through an *aveirah*. This is the meaning of "If a soul sins, and commits a *me'ilah* against Hashem, and lies unto his neighbor," in which case, "in any of all these that a man does, sinning therein" — whatever he does afterwards is considered a sin, and all the *mitzvos* he performs are mixed with sin. It is for this reason that there is no way to be forgiven unless the person appeases all those he wronged and returns all that he stole.

The basic underlying theme of our *parashah* is that there is no social morality without Divine morality. A defect in one's human morality is a defect in one's Divine morality, and a *me'ilah* against Hashem.

◄§ And Lies to His Neighbor

In all the sins against one's fellow-man described in this chapter, we are told that the person has (v. 21)''lied to his neighbor." Only in regard to withholding wages is it written, "or has abused (*ashak*) his neighbor." There are commentators who state that the three previous sins — namely a) denying having received a pledge, b) *tesumes yad* — which *Rashi* interprets as denying facts about a loan or partnership, and c) theft — involve the illegal transfer of items from one domain to another. Withholding wages, though, does not involve such transfer. The Torah did not add the phrase of "and lied to his neighbor" in the case of withholding wages, because the whole act consists of deceiving his neighbor. This unique feature of the sin called *oshek* — i.e., that the Torah does not mention "lying" in connection with it — is the basis for Yonasan ben Uziel and the Targum Yerushalmi who state that *oshek* refers to deliberately bad advice given to one's neighbor. The latter commentary leaves us wondering what sort of oath there should be for having given bad advice. No doubt that the two *Targum* translations had a source for their interpretation, whereby even bad advice is an offense against Divine morality and a trespass against Hashem.

The interpretation of *tesumes yad* by the two *Targumim* suits that of Ibn Ezra who states that it refers to one who denies an obligation arising from a partnership. *Rashi*, though, interprets it differently, as applying also to one who denies a loan. But *Rashi's* interpretation in our *parashah* is different from the explanation of R' Chisda in *Bava Metzia* 48a, that *tesumes yad* refers to one who "sets aside a utensil as security for his loan." According to the latter interpretation, the person being sued does not deny the loan itself, but denies that a particular utensil was set aside. *Rashi* in *Bava Metzia* explains that where a particular utensil is set aside, "this is like a deposit for if he simply denied a loan by itself he would not be required to bring a sacrifice of a (false) oath, as (the money involved) was lent in order to be spent."

R' Chisda interpreted the oath for *oshek*, too, as referring to where "he set aside a utensil for his *oshek*." According to R' Chisda, the sacrifice required for a false oath applies only where there was a denial of the special utensil that was set aside. In his commentary on the Torah, though, *Rashi* explains the denial as referring to the loan itself, or to the wages due the worker.

The *acharonim* are amazed by the ruling of *Rambam* in *Mishneh Torah* that the sacrifice for a false oath applies to the person who denies the facts and swears falsely in regard to a loan and the wages of a worker. They ask: Why did *Rambam* obviously ignore the ruling of R' Chisda that the denial must be relative to a utensil specially set aside for the purpose? This question is not necessarily so severe, since *Rambam* may hold like *Ramban*, *Rashba*, *Ran*, and *Ritva*, who state that R' Chisda's purpose was not to inform us that without a special utensil being set aside there is no sacrifice for a false oath. Rather, what R' Chisda was conveying is that even though the person is suing for the utensil that he did not have possession of and the person being sued denies that there even was such a utensil but does not deny the debt or the wage itself, this denial too requires a sacrifice for a false oath.

Ramban also explains why R' Chisda mentions that "he set aside a utensil." The Torah states (*Vayikra* 5:23): "He shall restore that which he took violently away, or the thing which he has deceitfully gotten." This implies a reference to a specific object, where the same item that was illegally taken is returned intact, unlike where one does not return exactly the same item that was taken, such as money which is lent out to be spent and replaced. Thus, R' Chisda gave an explanation that fits the language of the Torah passage. But he would admit that, in actuality, loans too can require a sacrifice for a false oath, where the person denied the loan and then swore to that fact. This is probably the opinion of *Rambam*, which is why we need not wonder why he does not mention R' Chisda's ruling.

The commentators expound at length in their interpretations of R' Chisda, and what compelled him to explain as he does. *Maskil LeEisan* provides a beautiful interpretation in his *Mitzpeh LeEisan* on *Bava Kama* 48. According to him, R' Chisda is consistent with his view in *Bava Metzia* 111 as to what is considered *oshek* and what is considered to be theft: " 'Go and come back, go and come back,' that is *oshek*. 'I owe it to you, but I will not give it to you,' that is *gezel* — theft." On this, R' Sheishes asks: "For what *oshek* does the Torah hold one culpable? (For that) similar to a deposit, where the person denied the money." (According to R' Sheishes, then, the two cases described by R' Chisda would not be *oshek*, for there is no denial of the debt itself.) But according to the way R' Chisda interprets it, namely that he put aside a special utensil, there is no problem. Here we are referring to where the person denied that a utensil was put aside, thus resembling the case of a deposit.

P'nei Yehoshua, on *Kesubos* 42, notes that according to the Sages, R' Chisda's reason is only valid in accordance with *Reish Lakish*, who holds that "money does not make an acquisition," or, in this case, that the person to whom the loan or the worker's wages are due, is not considered to be in the possession of anything belonging to the other person. Thus, the reason that the Torah did not require one to bring a sacrifice in the case of *tesumes yad* (unlike the other three cases listed above), is that, as the person suing for the money does not have anything belonging to the other, the latter obviously was never guilty of denying something belonging to another. R' Chisda thus specifies that only where a special utensil was set aside will there be need for a sacrifice, for a denial in such a case is indeed a denial of something belonging to another. It follows that, according to us, where we rule in accordance with R' Yochanan that by Torah law a person to whom money is owed for a loan or for work done is considered in possession of the other person's property, the latter is required to bring a sacrifice for a false oath when he denies the loan or the wages. According to R' Yochanan's view, in opposition to that of Reish Lakish, we are not forced into interpreting the verse as applying to where the person set aside a utensil. Thus *Rambam's* opinion is upheld.

But in terms of the literal meaning of the Torah text, why did the Torah not repeat *tesumes yad* in regard to bringing a sacrifice, and instead limited itself to stating (*Vayikra* 5:23), "he shall restore that which he took violently away, or the thing which he has deceitfully gotten, or that which was delivered him to keep, or the lost thing which he found"?

R' David Zvi Hoffman answers that for the other prohibitions or *me'ilos*, one must return whatever was owed before he brings his sacrifice, and must first rectify the damage before offering the *asham*. In *tesumes yad*, though, which, according to the *rishonim* refers to a loan, the person who receives the loan is not required to return the loan before the sacrifice, for the whole purpose of a loan is to permit the borrower to use the item borrowed. This may also be the source for *Rashi's* explanation of the words of R' Chisda as to why *tesumes yad* refers to a loan, for *Chazal* state in *Bava Metzia* 48: " 'Or all that about which he has sworn falsely' (*Vayikra* 5:24) — this (additional phrase) includes *tesumes yad* to be returned." And if *tesumes yad* referred to a loan, should it not be for spending? But *Ramban* deduces the exact opposite from *Chazal*. There is only need for a verse to tell us that the amount must be returned and not one to teach us that the person must offer a sacrifice in such a case, for it is obvious that the person must bring a sacrifice for swearing falsely even where he denies a monetary debt.

This explanation, which *Ramban* brings in the name of Rabbeinu Chananel, appears difficult, for if so, to be returned means that the person is obligated to return the object, and not that the obligation comes before the sacrifice. Indeed, Rabbeinu Chananel explains that this refers to a utensil, and as the person did not perform an act of acquisition, he is not required to return it. But in this case, too, we can then ask what "to be returned" comes to include. It is possible that it comes to include such cases where the person did acquire the object, and he later went back and left the object with the other person, as *Chazal* explain about *oshek*. But incidentally the Torah teaches us another point, that if the person did not acquire it he is not required to return it. That, though, is only in regard to a utensil, but the lender himself certainly must return the loan after bringing his sacrifice, and he is also obligated to bring a sacrifice for a false oath, according to *Ramban*.

⇜§ He Shall Make Restitution of the Principal

Chizkuni explains that the literal meaning of the above verse (*Vayikra* 5:24) is that one must pay back his theft, or what he denied or lied about, before he brings his sacrifice (deduced from the word בְּרֹאשׁו — which is taken to mean "before"), as stated in *Bava Kama* 110: "If he brought his *asham* sacrifice before he brought (i.e., paid back) his theft, he has not fulfilled the obligation [of the sacrifice]." Thus, according to *Chizkuni*, this statement of the *Gemara* is found explicitly in the verse.

Kli Yakar explains this in a similar fashion, when he states that Hashem is willing to forgo His turn, commanding the person to first return the theft and only thereafter to bring his *korban asham*. *Rashi* and the other commentators, though, hold that when the verse states בְּרֹאשׁו, it is a reference to the principal that must be returned. R' David Zvi Hoffman supports this interpretation with the verse "When you count the heads" (ראש), which proves that ראש refers to an amount.

Ibn Ezra explains this in a similar fashion, namely that one must pay the principal or the value of the principal. The Torah's requirement that 'a fifth part' is to be added to the return payment of the theft is described by *Chinuch* as teaching us that simply returning what was stolen does not effect an atonement. The thief must also be punished so that he does not take lightly the sin of appropriating someone's money by reasoning that he will return it at his leisure. The fact that he must add a fifth of the value when he repays the theft will act to dissuade a person from taking that which does not belong to him. *Kli Yakar* holds that the fifth is compensation paid to the person from whom the object was stolen, in that his object was not in his possession and he was thus unable to use its value for investment purposes. Apparently, the profit a person would reap on an investment is one fifth. *Chasam Sofer*, though, holds that the added fifth is due to the fact that the thief has committed a sacrilege (*me'ilah*) against Hashem as well. Theft, after all, is not only a sin against man but also against Hashem for which one must pay the penalty of one fifth for *me'ilah*.

Ibn Ezra offers an interesting explanation on the verse "he shall add his fifth to it." According to him, the verse means that one must add two fifths of the value. (This interpretation is based on the fact that the Torah writes *v'chamishisav* — the plural form — rather than *v'chamishiso*.) Although the Torah also writes (*Bamidbar* 5:7) *v'chamishiso*, that refers to a person who came forward of his own free will and confessed his theft. Such a thief adds only one fifth of the value. Here, though, where witnesses came and testified the person had stolen the object, he must pay two fifths. This interpretation, however, is contrary to *Chazal*, who explain the plural form of *v'chamishisav* as indicating that there are occasions when one must pay many fifths on a single principal, such as where a person was obligated to pay a fifth extra, denied this, took an oath, admitted his wrongdoing, thus becoming obligated to add one fifth to the original fifth, and then denied this fifth, took an oath, admitted, etc. However, Ibn Ezra himself states in *Bamidbar* 5:7 that "the transmitters of the Law said [that the plural form means] fifths of fifths; and their knowledge is broader than ours." All the commentators oppose Ibn Ezra's interpretation that the plural form *v'chamishisav* relates to where witnesses testified against the thief, and state that here too no witnesses appeared and the person confessed voluntarily; as *Rashi* and the others comment: "It shall come to pass if he sins and is guilty — when he realizes by himself that he must repent and must confess."

Indeed, the verses in the Torah seem to refer to one who steps forward voluntarily to atone for and to rectify his sin, without being forced to do so. As such, it appears that our *parashah* teaches us the severity of sins against one's fellow-man. We see that the person who wishes to repent must first return what he stole, and only thereafter does he bring a sacrifice to atone for his sin against Hashem.

So too does *S'forno* explain the verses (*Vayikra* 5:23,25), "He shall restore that which he took violently away ... And he shall bring his *asham* unto Hashem" — that the sacrifice does not atone for a person until he has appeased his fellow. Rabbeinu Bachya also explains the phrase, "in the day of his guilt," to mean that on the day that the person realizes his sin he must return the theft, and he cannot postpone its return. As *HaTorah V'HaMitzvah* on *Toras Kohanim* explains: " 'Then it shall be, because he has sinned, and is guilty,' what shall he do? 'He shall immediately restore.' " *Chizkuni* explains that one who steals must immediately repay the theft to the one from whom he stole on the day he brings his guilt offering, or, in other words, that the sacrifice does not serve to atone for the sin until after the person has repaid the theft.

Chazal in *Toras Kohanim* and elsewhere note that the meaning of "in the day of his guilt" is open to various interpretations, but all commentators concur that the *parashah* conveys the serious nature of sins between man and his fellow-man, which cannot be atoned for unless one first appeases his fellow; that these sins are also *me'ilah* against Hashem, and that one must compensate the offended person by payment of an added fifth.

V.

The Offering for a Theft Trespass — Asham Gezeilos — and Its Nature

Ramban in our *parashah* seeks to find the difference between the *chatas* and *asham* offerings. One cannot say that the *chatas* must be a female animal, for there are certain *chatas* sacrifices that are of bulls and he-goats. Similarly, one cannot say that the *chatas* is brought for more severe sins, for a *metzora* (one suffering from a form of leprosy caused by sin) brings two he-goats, one as a *chatas* and one as an *asham*, for the identical sin. What, then, is the difference between the two, and why are they two separate categories?

Ramban offers his own novel interpretation, that an *asham* is brought for a more severe sin, the kind for which one deserves to be wiped off the face of the earth, and quotes various verses with a similar Hebraic root in support of this. *Chatas*, however, refers to a person who diverged from the proper path, similar to the same Hebrew root used for one whose aim in shooting is off the mark. Thus, the sacrifice for deliberate sins — *meizid* — such as theft or for having relations with a *shifchah charufah* — a half-freed female slave — requires an *asham*.

An exception is the *asham me'ilos* sacrifice which is brought where one negligently (i.e., not deliberately) used sanctified objects, this being a sin stemming from negligence and therefore less severe. Even so, it requires an *asham*, because the sin is a severe one for it involved an act against Hashem. Thus this sacrifice is called an *asham*, since it indicates the guilt — *asham* — of the person who committed a severe sin.

By the same token, an *asham talui*, brought where a person is unsure if he did or did not commit a sin, indicates the severity of the situation, for the person might delude himself into believing that he has not committed any sin. As a result, the Torah is even more severe in a case of a doubtful sin than in one where a definite sin was committed, and requires one to bring a ram costing silver *shekels*, whereas if one knows he sinned, all he must bring is a *chatas* whose cost is only a *danka*, a small coin. The Torah therefore refers to the sacrifice in the former case as an *asham* so as to indicate to the person involved that if he regards the matter lightly and does not bring a sacrifice, he will be destroyed (*shameim*) by his sin. That is why the Torah stresses "he was guilty (*asham*) to Hashem, it is an *asham*," or, in other words, that the person is regarded as a sinner by Hashem, who knows all of man's deeds. If he did indeed sin to Hashem, he will be punished.

Similarly, when an *asham* is brought (*Vayikra* 5:1): "If a soul sins, and hears the voice of swearing," it is because the man sinned deliberately in swearing falsely, and the type of *korban* required indicates the severity of the sin.

Unlike *Ramban's* view that the *asham* indicates the severity of the sin, R' David Zvi Hoffman explains that a *chatas* is brought when a blemish has been made in the soul aside from the sin against Hashem, while an *asham* indicates that the sin is primarily against Hashem. A person whose sin requires a *chatas* has sinned first against his own soul, for he has moved it away from drawing closer to Hashem, and he causes his soul to be separated and cut off from holiness. It is for such sins that one must bring a *chatas* sacrifice, to atone for the soul. Thus the *chatas* is brought by those who became *tamei* — ritually impure — such as the woman who gave birth, the *metzora* (a form of leprosy), the *zav* and the *zavah* (a person with a pathological genital discharge). The *parah adumah* — "red heifer" — is also called a *chatas*. The birds used in the ritual of purifying a home (*Vayikra* 14:49) are also referred to as being used *l'chatei es habayis* — "to atone for sin as regard to the house."

According to R' David Zvi Hoffman, the above-mentioned instances of purification are not only to purify the soul, but to purify the Altar or the Temple. Each sin makes the Temple ritually impure, as stated by *Chazal*: "It causes the *Shechinah* to depart from Israel." In the *chatas* of

Yom Kippur, the Torah states in *Vayikra* 16:16, "And he shall make an atonement for the holy place from the impurity of the Children of Israel." So too in (*Vayikra* 16:19), "And he shall sprinkle the blood upon it with his finger seven times, and purify it, and hallow it from the uncleanness of the Children of Israel." The sprinkling of the blood of the *chatas* on the Altar is referred to in the verse as purifying the Altar.

Similarly, when the bulls were brought when the Altar was first dedicated, it states (*Vayikra* 8:15), "and he put it upon the horns of the Altar round about with his finger, and purified the Altar." The blood of the sacrifices of the *Kohen Gadol* and the entire congregation had to be brought inside the Sanctuary, because through their sins the inner Sanctuary was defiled, whereas when an individual committed a sin through negligence there was only a need to purify the outer Altar. We see, therefore, that the purpose of sprinkling the blood is to draw the sinner closer to Hashem by purifying his soul, and by purifying the Altar which he has defiled by his actions. However, besides the fact that a person who sinned is removed from Hashem's Altar, he is also subject to a punishment as well, in that he now carries a sin. This obligation is fulfilled by the *chatas* that he brings when the *emurim* — portions of the sacrifice — are burned on the Altar and other parts are eaten by the *Kohanim*, as it states (*Vayikra* 10:17), "And He has given it to you to bear the sin of the congregation, to atone for them before Hashem." As *Chazal* tell us: "The *Kohanim* eat and the owners receive atonement." If the sin penetrated into the Sanctuary though, "Every *chatas* which is brought to the Tent of Assembly . . . shall not be eaten; it shall be burned by fire." One then needs another symbolic action with the meat which represents the sin, which is to take it out of the camp and burn it.

All this applies if a person definitely knows that he committed a sin whose atonement requires a *chatas*. In such cases, the Torah commanded that one must use purification — *chitui*. However in those cases where a *chatas* is inappropriate, one brings an *asham* instead, so as to remove the sin against Hashem. It is thus clear that regarding a *chatas*, although the sin involves an infringement against the Divine, the sin in one's soul is nevertheless greater. The obligation, therefore, is classified as a *chatas*, and only incidentally is also an *asham*.

But there are instances where the sin — the *asham* — against Hashem is greater than against oneself. In such cases, the sacrifice must be an *asham*, and only incidentally could also be called a *chatas* — an atonement for one's soul. It is for this reason that where there is an infringement of the Divine, either directly or indirectly, such as by a sin between man and his fellow man, one must always bring an *asham*. This can be seen in the case of the *asham* brought for theft, where the

Torah states, "He shall make restitution of the principal," that is, he must pay his debt by returning the principal. So too does it state (*Vayikra* 5:24), "He shall give it unto him to whom it pertains," namely to the person to whom he owes it. "But if the man has no kinsman to whom to recompense the *asham*, let the *asham* be returned unto Hashem, to the *Kohen*" (*Bamidbar* 5:8). From this we see that the *asham* is a repayment for rights which had been infringed on. This applies to the *asham* of *me'ilah*, the *asham* of armed robbery, and the *asham* of a half-free female slave. Because of the obvious infringement, one must bring a sacrifice that is worth at least two *shekalim*. As for the *nazir* who has transgressed on his oath to Hashem, he must also repay his debt by recounting the days of his *nezirus* and by bringing an *asham* (*Bamidbar* 6). A *metzora*, too, is one afflicted by his sin against his fellow through *lashon hara* — slander — as explained by *Chazal*, and, therefore, he too brings an *asham*. But in these latter cases, where the infringements are not obvious, the value of the *asham* need not be two *shekalim*.

As to an *asham talui*, which is brought in place of a *chatas*, since one does not know if he committed a sin, the more stringent rules of the *asham* apply. Those sins for which one must bring a *korban oleh v'yored* (a sacrifice which varies based on the person's financial ability) are, firstly, for a false oath, an oath of testimony, and a personal oath (*sh'vu'as bitui* — such as swearing that one will not eat bread), and are similar to the oath taken on a deposit. Their primary element is infringement of rights, and thus the sacrifice to be brought is an *asham*.

⋙ If a Soul Sins and Commits a Trespass Against Hashem

In brief, R' David Zvi Hoffman's interpretation is that the *chatas* is brought where the sin primarily affects the soul, whereas the *asham* is brought where the sin is primarily against Hashem rather than the person's soul. As to sins between man and his fellow, they are in the latter category, as is indicated by the words in the Torah, *u'ma'alah ma'al ba'Shem* — "he commits a trespass against Hashem," which R' Samson Raphael Hirsch interprets to mean that a sin against one's fellow-man is a rebellion against Hashem. Hashem sees and hears all. The sinner used the name of Hashem to deny the truth, therefore his sin is a trespass against Hashem. In the same vein, R' Akiva says in *Sifra*:

> Why does it state *u'ma'alah ma'al ba'Shem*? It is because the lender and the borrower or those who negotiate a transaction do so

only with a written contract and witnesses. Therefore, when the person denies it, he has denied the witnesses and the written contract. But a person who deposits something with another wants no one else to know about it, except for the third party (i.e., Hashem) who is involved. Then, when he denies the pledge, he is making a denial against the third party.

While the *Sifra* is only referring to the denial of a deposit, the significance of R' Akiva's point is that when one makes such a denial, he is making the denial against Hashem, and it is, by extension, as if he denied the very existence of Hashem.

Oznayim LaTorah, as well as Chassidic works, explains *u'ma'alah ma'al ba'Shem* as a lesson to us that there is no such thing as human morals without fear of Hashem. When a person sins against his fellow, it is proof that he has no faith, as when Avraham said to Avimelech, "For I said there is no fear of Hashem in this place, and they will kill me." The lack of faith in Hashem is the causative factor which leads to the infringement on social morals. The Torah therefore insisted on the return of a theft before one brings his *asham* sacrifice to Hashem. Thus the Torah states (*Vayikra* 5:23), "he shall restore that which he took violently away, or the thing which he has deceitfully gotten, or that which was delivered him to keep, or the lost thing which he found," and only thereafter does it state, "And he shall bring his *asham* unto Hashem." *S'forno* notes here:

"The sacrifice does not atone unless the person first appeased the one he harmed before he brings his sacrifice, as our Sages tell us in Tractate *Yoma*: 'If he brought his *asham* before he brought (i.e., returned) his theft, he has not fulfilled his obligation' " (*Yoma* ch. Yom HaKippurim).

Rashi and the other commentators explain the verse, "He shall make restitution *b'rosho*" to mean that one must first pay the amount of the "principal"(רֹאשׁ) and thereafter the one-fifth penalty, but *Chizkuni* and *Kli Yakar* explain that he must "first" (בְּרֹאשׁ) pay back the theft, and only afterwards brings his sacrifice.

R' David Zvi Hoffman notes that the Torah in each case stipulates that financial restitution must be made before the sacrifice is offered, except for *tesumes yad*, which is the case of a loan. A loan is given to be spent, and one is therefore not required to return it immediately. It is enough for the person to admit that he owes the loan and to obligate himself to pay for it, and then to bring his *asham*. *Chazal*, though, in *Bava Metzia* 48a, state: " 'Or all that about which he has sworn falsely'

(*Vayikra* 5:24). This comes to includes *tesumes yad* (in those items) that must be returned, (even though) the Torah did not explicitly write that it must be returned." As to what the ruling is, one must look to the *halachic* authorities.

In any event, the *me'ilah* against Hashem is not removed until the person has repaired the *me'ilah* against his fellow-man. As *Chazal* say in *Yoma* 85b: "Sins between man and Hashem, *Yom Kippur* atones for. Sins between man and his fellow-man, *Yom Kippur* does not atone for until he appeases his fellow-man." The same is taught in *Bava Kama* 9: "One who steals the value of a *p'rutah* from his fellow and swears (falsely) to him, he must go after him, even until Medea." *Tiferes Yisrael* explains — and some attribute it to the Gaon of Vilna — that the *mishnah* mentions "Medea" because money was considered worthless there, as it states (*Yeshayahu* 13:17), "Behold, I will stir up the Medes against them, which do not regard silver; and as for gold, they do not desire it." What the *mishnah* tells us is that even though a *p'rutah* has no value in Medea, one is still obligated by all means to return the theft.

◦§ Me'ilah Constitutes a Change

Earlier in this *parashah*, *Rashi* comments on the verse (5:15), "If a soul commits a trespass (*ki sim'ol ma'al*)," through the misappropriation of property belonging to the Temple. He explains that *me'ilah* always implies that a change has transpired. *Turei Zahav* in his *Divrei David* finds this surprising, since there is no change from one domain to another when one commits *me'ilah* with a deposit or *tesumes yad*. Mizrachi suggests that change is only implied in reference to the *me'ilah* in the above verse, but *Divrei David* does not accept this distinction, since *Rashi* himself emphasized the word "always." He explains that *me'ilah* with a pledge or *tesumes yad* also includes a change of domain, by virtue of the person having sworn falsely. The change, however, is in the sinner whose false oath causes him to leave the domain of his Creator and enter another domain, so that his behavior is similar to idolatry.

This interpretation is somewhat difficult, for the change in domain relates in this case not to the object but to the sinner. *Ha'amek Davar* explains, however, that when the person swears falsely, he removes the object from the owner's domain and into his own, in accordance with what Rav states in *Bava Kama* 106, that an oath gives one possession. And even according to the Talmud's conclusion that one does not acquire possession through an oath, the oath still is effective in making him responsible for any subsequent accidental damages. Thus, the acquired responsibility causes the item pledged to change its status.

Kli Yakar explains the change of possession differently. The Torah uses the word חֲטָא before *me'ilah*, where the offended party is a fellow Jew, as stated: "if a soul sins — תֶחֱטָא — and is *mo'el*." In regard to *me'ilah* of *hekdesh* — the misappropriation of sanctified objects — on the other hand, the Torah reverses the order: "If a soul is *mo'el* and sins — וְחָטְאָה — through negligence." The difference is in the character of the sins. Where one denies money and swears falsely, he sins once against his fellow and twice against Hashem. The Torah calls the sin against Hashem *me'ilah*, for *me'ilah* implies a change. This person has changed from the ways of his Creator. Hashem is good to all, yet the person did not repay Him as he should have. The sinner thus changes from the way a person should act, and instead of showing his gratitude to Hashem, he demonstrates ingratitude. In fact, the word *me'ilah* does not suit the sin against one's fellow, for he did him no favor with either the deposited or stolen object. When a person steals from *hekdesh*, though, the word *me'ilah* in the Torah precedes that of *cheit*, for as soon as he has benefited from the *hekdesh* he has stolen from Hashem. The use of *me'ilah* twice — וּמָעֲלָה מַעַל — by the Torah is to tell us that one commits *me'ilah* even if he did not eat of the *hekdesh*. Afterwards the Torah uses the word חֲטָא to show that there is a sin here against man as well, for one who commits *me'ilah* has also stolen the portion of the sacrifice to which the *Kohanim* are entitled.

Chazal, though, in *Bava Basra* (ch. 8) provide a different reason why the Torah, in our *parashah*, placed *cheit* before *me'ilah*: "It is worse to steal from a human than to steal from 'on High,' for in the former (the Torah) mentions *cheit* before *me'ilah*, and (in the latter) it mentions *me'ilah* before *cheit*."

Rashbam explains the different wording in the Torah in that when one steals from another human he is considered a sinner the instant he steals the object, while in stealing from *hekdesh* he only transgresses after he has any enjoyment from the object. It is for this reason that the Torah in the latter case uses the concept of *me'ilah* before *cheit*, for if the person does not derive any enjoyment he has not committed *me'ilah*.

The commentators also examine why it is that the Torah states that (*Vayikra* 5:21) "if he lies against his neighbor" (*ba'amiso*) rather than "if he lies to his neighbor" (*la'amiso*). *Ha'amek Davar* explains the expression according to *Rambam*, *Hil. Edus* 17, that "You shall not give false witness against your neighbor" means through your neighbor, "and whoever testifies based on hearsay, simply repeating what his neighbor told him, is a false witness." Here too, the word *b'amiso* means through his neighbor, indicating that the latter sued him and he denied the charge. If, however, his "neighbor" did not sue him, he is not liable.

Torah Temimah, though, quotes *Chazal* in *Shavu'os* 32, who interpret this in the exact opposite fashion. It states there: "An oath on a pledge applies whether one swears on his own initiative or that of others. What is the reason? 'If he lies against his neighbor' (applies) in any event." In other words, had the Torah written *la'amiso*, I would have said that only where there is someone suing can there be a denial, but since it states *ba'amiso*, it implies in any event. *Or HaChaim* explains the verse according to the literal meaning of the text. "If he lies against his neighbor" implies that by his false oath, the man makes his neighbor out to be a liar or one who denies matters. With a lost object, on the other hand, the Torah states, "And he will deny it," for by his denial the man does not imply that the other person is a liar.

⋓ When He Has Sinned, and is Guilty — Ashem

Rashi explains the above verse as referring to a person who recognizes he has sinned and wishes to repent and confess. He must then return the stolen item and bring an *asham*. *Rashbam* and *Targum Yehonasan* introduce that same meaning into the sentence: "On the day of his guilt" — namely, on the day that he recognizes his guilt.

According to *Kli Yakar*, as soon as a person feels he is guilty, he must immediately return the stolen object, for when a person sins he normally does not feel guilty about what he has done; he rationalizes in all sorts of ways that he need not return the object, for the other person owes it to him, and that is why he stole what he did. But when he blames himself for his action, that is already a level of repentance. Therefore, says *Oznayim LaTorah*, he should hasten to return the object that day, for if he delays until the following day he will again find a way to rationalize his actions to himself.

Ha'amek Davar explains that the return of a stolen object must be "on the day that he is guilty," but the sacrifice may be delayed until the person comes to Jerusalem for one of the three pilgrimage festivals (*shalosh regalim*). Others explain that the Torah is telling us that even if a person returns an object on the day he stole it, he must still pay the added one-fifth of its value.

Toras Kohanim explains that "On the day that he is guilty" means "at the time that he stole it." (In *Bava Metzia* 43, there is a dispute among *Tannaim* whether the person has to repay what the object was worth at the time the verdict was rendered or what it was worth at the time that he illicitly used it.)

Rabbeinu Bachya says even though these sins can be repaid, theft is still a severe sin, for sometimes a person is unable to find the person whom he stole from, as, for example, if the person died or moved far away. Also, it is possible the thief may lose all his money and not have the money to pay restitution. Sometimes there may not even be an identifiable person to repay, such as where the person steals public funds and doesn't know whose money he took. *Chida* mentions an interesting point. A negative commandment which is "linked to a positive commandment" (נִתָּק לַעֲשֵׂה) does not carry a punishment of lashing (*malkos*).

For example, the prohibition against taking a mother bird along with her eggs is not punishable by lashes, since it is linked to a positive commandment — that of sending away the mother bird. If so, asks *Chida*, why shouldn't *all* negative commandments be exempt from lashing? After all, they are linked to the positive commandment of repentance (*teshuvah*). He answers as follows. When there is a generalized prohibition — לָאו שֶׁבִּכְלָלוּת — one does not receive *malkos* — 39 lashes — because when the לָאו includes a number of categories it is not as severe as a specific לָאו. By the same token, the עֲשֵׂה — positive commandment — to repent is a generalized one, and therefore is not as major as a specified one. For that reason, the לָאו is not considered as "linked" to a positive commandment — עֲשֵׂה.

Tzav – צַו

I.
Urgency Where Monetary Loss Is Involved

At the beginning of this *parashah*, *Rashi* quotes *Toras Kohanim*: "The word *tzav* — command — implies urgency — *zeiruz* — immediately, and in future generations. R' Shimon said: 'Where there is monetary loss, the Torah was necessarily mindful of the need for urgency.'"

Malbim's Torah U'Mitzvah explains at length the three meanings of the word *tzav*, these being: (a) urgency, (b) immediately and (c) in future generations; and the fourth meaning of R' Shimon, namely a reference to cases where a monetary loss is involved. Whenever the Torah uses the word *vayedaber* it means either that it is relating an episode or that it is giving a command. *Tzav*, though, always implies an order, and comes to stress one of the three possible conditions: (a) *zeiruz* — urging one to complete the action speedily, as in (*Bereishis* 44:1), "And he (Yosef) commanded (*vayetzav*) the steward of his house, saying, 'Fill the men's sacks with food.'" So too do we see in the verse (*Sh'mos* 1:15,22), "And the King of Egypt spoke to the Hebrew midwives ... And Pharaoh charged (*vayetzav*) all his people." While Pharaoh only spoke to the midwives, he charged his people to carry out his orders. (b) speedy completion of the task within a very limited time, as R' Avraham Sofer writes in *Mikneh Avraham* regarding the categories of verbs: "Then comes the imperative — *tzav* — which indicates immediate implementation; and after that comes the future tense." The imperative tense thus indicates an action to be taken within a limited period of time, while the future tense indicates an unlimited period of time; (c) continuity in generations to come, such as the legacies (*tzava'os*) that fathers leave their children, or the *mitzvos* of Hashem that were given for all generations.

In the Torah, we find that the verb *tzav* always expresses at least one of these meanings, as, for example, (*Bereishis*) "And he commanded (*vayetzav*) the first saying ... Thus shall you say to my master, Esav." In this case, the command is not for future generations. On the other hand, when the word *tzav* is preceded by such commands as: "Speak — *daber* — to the Children of Israel," or "Say — *emor* — to the Children of Israel," *tzav* implies all three meanings, as in the verse, "Command (*tzav*) Aaron," in our *parashah*; *tzav* in regard to lighting the *menorah* (*Vayikra* 24); *tzav* in sending forth those that are *tamei* (*Bamidbar* 5); *tzav* in the daily *tamid* sacrifice (*Bamidbar* 28), and *tzav* relating to inheritances (*Bamidbar* 34). Thus the rule that *tzav* has three meanings only applies where it is directed at all of Israel. In fact where the Torah stated, "And Avraham circumcised ... as Hashem commanded (*tzivah*) him," there was a need for a *gezeirah shavah* — a comparison of similar wording — of the verb *tzivah* (see *Kiddushin* 29) to teach us that the commandment applies to all generations. Similarly, in the *beraisa* of *yud-gimmel middos* (the Thirteen Hermeneutic Principles by which laws are derived from verses), we employ a principle known as *binyan av* to indicate that certain *mitzvos* were meant by the Torah to be observed both at the time they were given and afterwards. The *binyan av* in question compares the concept of *tzav* when sending forth those who are *tamei* (*Bamidbar* 5) to the lighting of the *menorah* (*Bamidbar* 28), the first of which could have been mistakenly interpreted to apply only immediately, and the second to only apply for the future. With the *binyan av*, we deduce that what they have in common is that both apply immediately and for future generations. And from these we deduce that whenever the Torah states *tzav*, it refers to the immediate time and to future generations. R' Shimon, though, adds another condition in regard to *tzivui*, and that is that it applies where there is a monetary loss. *Sifre* on *Naso* adds: "*Tzivui* always represents monetary loss, except in one instance (*Bamidbar* 34:2): 'Command (*tzav*) the Children of Israel: When you enter the land.' " There the Torah merely urges the Jews to divide up the land, which does not entail any monetary loss, and is not both "immediately" and "for future generations."

Chizkuni states that *zeiruz* is mentioned here because people might be lazy in regard to keeping the fire burning on the Altar and cleaning out the ashes of the Altar. There is also a potential for monetary loss if the *olah* sacrifice is not done properly, for then the person will have to bring another in its place. This reason for *zeiruz* is mentioned by *Torah Temimah*.

Chazal stated that the verse teaches us that the burning on the Altar of the *cheilev* fat and the other organs of the sacrificial animal is permitted the entire night. They nevertheless limited the time of burning until midnight, so as to ensure that people do not go beyond the allotted time, which would be a Torah prohibition. That is why the Torah itself urged one to be quick, by using the word "tzav." The verse (Vayikra 6:2), "It is the olah, the olah shall remain upon the Altar all night unto the morning," could lead one to feel that he had the whole night ahead of him, and hence to tarry beyond the allotted time. Zeiruz is indicated so that one will be certain to burn the parts before the deadline set by the Torah.

Chasam Sofer says that the Torah stipulated zeiruz as this is a commandment which is "immediately and for future generations." With such a commandment, one must be concerned that it will not become mere routine. The Torah thus comes with its message of zeiruz — telling us to regard the performance of the commandment each day as something new. Akeidah has an original interpretation. The tzav of "for future generations" refers to the institution, in future generations, of prayer in place of sacrifices, in accordance with the verse (Hoshea 14:3), "We will render the bulls with our lips." He also explains a verse in Tehillim (51:15-16), "O Hashem, open my lips; and my mouth will tell Your praise. For You do not desire sacrifice; else would I give it." He reads the word כִּי in the second sentence, which is generally translated "for," as meaning "if" in this context, and brings other examples of this usage. Thus, according to him, "if" a time should come when Hashem does not desire the sacrifices, such as after the destruction of the Temple, then "O Hashem, open my lips; and my mouth will tell Your praise."

◆§ Does R' Shimon Differ or Does He Merely Add to the Other Explanations?

As we noted in the previous section, R' Shimon adds a fourth interpretation of the word tzav. R' Shimon's words are ambiguous, and it is unclear whether he is disagreeing with the previous Tanna, or whether he is merely adding to his thoughts. Ramban, at the end of his comments, concludes that Sifre on Parashas Naso proves that R' Shimon comes to argue with the previous Tanna. Sifre states: "R' Shimon omeir" — "R' Shimon says," and this style of wording is generally accepted to imply that the person disagrees with the previous statement. Sifra, though, phrases it as "amar R' Shimon" — "said R' Shimon" — and this language is inconclusive.

At the beginning of his comments, though, Ramban states that R' Shimon's interpretation does not apply to the olah sacrifice in our parashah, for here the Kohanim suffer no monetary loss, even though the *olah* is entirely burned. On the contrary, they gain on the sacrifice, for the hide belongs to them. In this instance, R' Shimon undoubtedly agrees with the first *Tanna* that *tzav* indicates an act that is immediate, and for future generations. What R' Shimon is adding is that on occasion, the word *tzav* need not imply something immediate or for future generations, but where there is a question of monetary loss, such as where the Torah uses *tzav* in regard to the oil for the *menorah* or to command the Jews to set aside cities for the *Levi'im*. However, even in our *parashah*, it could possibly be said that the word *tzav* refers to a monetary loss, for the *minchah* brought daily by the *Kohen Gadol* and that brought by a regular *Kohen* the first day he begins his Temple service are given by the *Kohen* from his own grain, this then being monetary loss, in which case there is need for the use of the word *tzav*.

The commentators on *Rashi* are also divided as to the meaning of R' Shimon's dictum. R' Eliyahu Mizrachi holds that R' Shimon's words are "an added condition," and are meant to expand the concept of *tzav*, so that in addition to the three conditions of the first *Tanna* one must also resort to a fourth one — that of monetary loss. However, where there is no monetary loss, although the three other conditions of urgency, immediacy and for future generations exist, *tzav* would be inappropriate. But that does not mean that R' Shimon intended that the fourth condition of monetary loss would be sufficient by itself without the other three. In *Toras Kohanim* we deduced from *a binyan av* from two verses that wherever the Torah uses *tzav*, it means "urgency, immediately, and for future generations." *Chazal*, too, in *Kiddushin* 29 quote this in the name of *Tanna d'bei R' Yishmael*. It thus follows that R' Shimon's comment is only an addition, and even then not in all instances. Thus *Sifre* explains that in regard to the division of *Eretz Yisrael* the Torah states: "Command the Children of Israel," and that only means *zeiruz*.

According to *Mizrachi*, monetary loss in the case of the *olah* is the result of anxiety and effort involved in keeping the fire burning the entire night long, and in donning the special garments. This effort is more demanding on a person than is monetary loss, and therefore the Torah urges *zeiruz* through the use of *tzav*.

Levush HaOrah explains this in a different fashion. Earlier in *Vayikra* the Torah spoke of a *nedavah* — a freewill offering — brought as an *olah*, where the word *tzav* is appropriately absent, since there is no need to urge a person to give a *korban* voluntarily. Here, however, the subject is the sacrificial process, in which the *olah* is burned in its entirety, and where the owner gains nothing; so the Torah urges the *Kohanim* to sacrifice the offering with *zeiruz*, and not to bother the owner of the animal unnecessarily, lest the owner regret bringing the sacrifice for all the trouble involved. If a person entertains such thoughts when bringing a sacrifice, it is almost as if *chulin* — an unsanctified animal — had been brought into the Temple courtyard, for the animal's sanctity can be terminated by such thoughts. The Torah therefore made a point of stressing to the *Kohanim* the need for *zeiruz*. That is why R' Shimon adds his comment that "*zeiruz* is especially necessary where there is a monetary loss."

In the sacrifices mentioned in the previous *parashah*, such as the various *chatas* and *asham* sacrifices, the owners at least have the benefit of atonement for their sins. By the *shelamim* sacrifice, the owner actually derives a tangible benefit, for he receives a part of the meat to be eaten. In the latter three types of sacrifices, then, there is no need to fear that the person might regret bringing the animal. In the case of a freewill *olah*, though, the owner has no benefit out of the sacrifice; and all he has is monetary loss. There is, therefore, reason for concern that if the *Kohanim* are lazy and delay the bringing of the sacrifice, the owner might begin to regret his action. As a result, the Torah insists on the need for *zeiruz* here.

Maharal in *Gur Aryeh* holds that the "monetary loss" involved is that the *Kohen* must forsake his other work, for in the proof-text quoted by R' Shimon (*Bamidbar* 5:2), "Command the Children of Israel and have them send forth [those who are ritually impure] from the camp," *tzav* is also used in the context of monetary loss that results from having to forsake one's work. The Torah urges the *Kohanim* to deal with Heavenly concerns, even if this entails neglecting their own work.

On the other hand, *Turei Zahav* in *Divrei David* holds that the fact that the *Kohanim* receive no benefit from the *olah* is the monetary loss involved, just as where one who prevents another from making a profit is said to have caused the other a monetary loss. In general, the sacrifices involve a benefit to the *Kohanim* [since they eat the parts allotted to them] and the *Kohanim* will surely work with alacrity and will not be lazy, so as to ensure that no other *Kohen* might precede them and deprive them of the opportunity to serve. In the case of the *olah*, though, which is burnt up in its entirety, the *Kohanim* might become lazy, and therefore the *Kohanim* are urged — *tzav* — to act industriously — with *zeiruz*.

Chanukas HaTorah, by R' Heschel of Cracow, asks: How can one say that there is no benefit to the *Kohanim* in the case of an *olah*, when, as *Ramban* pointed out, they receive the hide? He answers that this refers to the *olah* sacrifices that were offered in the desert, which, according to *Chazal*, did not need to be flayed before being burned. Thus in that case the *Kohanim* enjoyed no benefit whatsoever. This is what *Rashi* means when he states that """zav* applies immediately and for future generations." "Immediately" refers to the time that the Jews were in the desert. Thus, when R' Shimon states there is a monetary loss, he is correct, for in the case of the *olah* in the desert the *Kohanim* indeed got nothing, and there was cause for concern that they might be lazy or that they might have the wrong thoughts at the time, thus rendering the sacrifice *pigul* or unfit.

K'sav Sofer has a similar comment on *Ramban's* words. According to him, R' Shimon is referring to the *minchas chavitin*, which the *Kohanim* sacrificed of their own grain, thereby entailing a monetary loss. This appears, though, to be difficult, for why is there a need for *zeiruz* in the tenth part of an *ephah* of flour that was brought daily by the *Kohen Gadol*, and by a regular *Kohen* on the day that he began to serve, if the *Kohanim* had grain that was given to them as either *terumah* or *ma'aser*, without having to exert themselves for it? The answer is that at that time the Jews were still in the desert, where the *Kohanim* received no *terumah* or *ma'aser*. They had to buy their own fine flour from merchants who brought it from far away, and it was therefore very expensive. (See *Rambam Hil. Korbanos*, ch. 2. This requires further study.)

Torah Temimah has another explanation of the dispute between the first *Tanna* and R' Shimon. According to him, this dispute is the same as one between R' Elazar and R' Akiva in *Chagigah* 6b, as to whether the *olas tamid* — the *olah* that was brought twice daily — was already sacrificed when the Jews were still in the desert, or whether the Jews only began sacrificing it once they reached *Eretz Yisrael*. R' Elazar holds that the *olas tamid* was not offered in the desert, because the Jews had been reprimanded by Hashem for the sin of the Golden Calf. Only after the Jews entered *Eretz Yisrael* did they begin to bring the *tamid*. R' Akiva, though, holds that the *tamid* was offered in the desert as well. According to this, one can say that the first *Tanna* of the *Sifra* agrees with R' Akiva, and therefore *tzav* refers to immediately and future generations, whereas R' Shimon holds that the *tamid* was not offered in the desert, and therefore he interprets *tzav* to refer to a monetary loss.

◈§ Where There Is a Monetary Loss

We have already explained *Ramban's* view and those of the commentators on *Rashi* as to what "monetary loss" means in this *parashah*. But there are many commentaries on this topic, and it is worth quoting them here, for they carry a wealth of ideas, both in terms of *halachah* and *hashkafah*.

Or HaChaim rejects all the explanations brought by us above, and he sees them all as constrained answers. According to him, it is possible that monetary loss refers back to the need to have logs on the Altar constantly. According to *Chazal*, there were three fires going. The third had no purpose whatsoever except to fulfill the verse, "A permanent fire shall burn on it." The reason the Torah warned of the need for *zeiruz* here is because of the superficially "wasteful" practice involved. While it is true that no individual suffered a monetary loss thereby, there was a monetary loss for the public. Thus, the Torah urges us not to be stingy in this regard, but to fulfill our duty to have a fire burn continuously.

Pa'aneach Raza holds that the monetary loss involved is that the *Kohanim* must be awake the entire night, which leaves them incapable of working at their occupations during the day, and, furthermore, they may be forced to hire people out of their own pocket so as to ensure that they do not doze off.

Kli Yakar too holds that *zeiruz* is meant to prevent the *Kohanim* from falling asleep, for *zeiruz* is needed where one might be lazy. *Kli Yakar* also brings verses to show that laziness is related to sleep. Thus there is reason for concern that laziness might bring the *Kohanim* to fall asleep, and then they will ruin the sacrifice. From this, the Torah deduced that the *Kohanim* are indeed *zerizim* — eager and alert — because they are urged by the Torah not to doze off, but to be involved with the sacrifices the entire night long.

Kli Yakar, however, explains the idea of monetary loss in a different fashion. The *olah* is brought to atone for evil thoughts. We find in the *Yerushalmi*:

> Once R' Yochanan lost his wallet, and they asked him Torah and he did not know. They said to him: 'Is it because you lost your wallet that you lost your mind?' He told them: 'One's mind depends on one's heart, and the heart is dependent on the wallet.'

This is proof that a monetary loss confuses, and leads one to think evil thoughts. Now, *Chizkuni* states that the monetary loss occurs where a *Kohen* does not offer the sacrifice properly, for then he must offer a second, and the first represents a loss. In such a case, where there is a monetary loss, he will become confused both in heart and mind, leading him to think evil thoughts, whereby his second sacrifice is a *mitzvah haba'ah b'aveirah* — a *mitzvah* which occurs through a forbidden act. In such circumstances, *Chizkuni* asks, how can the second sacrifice fulfill its purpose of atoning for an evil thought, when it itself, because of the monetary loss, is a *mitzvah haba'ah b'aveirah* brought on by evil thoughts? Thus the *Kohen* needs a special *zeiruz* when he brings an *olah*.

Chanukas HaTorah, though, explains the concept of *zeiruz* in the word *tzav* in a simple fashion. *Chazal* tell us that "Greater is one who is commanded to do something and does it, than one who is not commanded and does it." *Tosafos* in *Kiddushin* 31 explain that the reason for this is that a person who has been commanded to perform a *mitzvah* is afraid that something might occur which would prevent him from fulfilling the *mitzvah* properly. That is not true for one who was not commanded to do it, who has no such concerns. Therefore, in a place where there is a *tzav*, one needs a special *zeiruz* to perform what was commanded, because the person must overcome his evil impulse — which is stronger within him because he was commanded to perform the action.

Nachlas Yaakov Yehoshua explains that the reason for the *zeiruz* is based on what *Chazal* tell us at the end of *Menachos*: "Whoever studies the laws of the *olah* is as if he sacrificed an *olah*." Therefore everyone can rationalize to himself and decide to study the topic rather than actually sacrifice an *olah*. The Torah therefore urges specifically to bring a sacrifice, even though this will involve a monetary loss.

Chasam Sofer gives a *hashkafah* insight that is diametrically opposite from the previous view. The *Kohanim* receive a benefit from the sacrifices, including even the *olah*, whose hide they are given. There is, therefore, reason to fear that because of their self-interest they may not tell the people the rule that "Whoever studies the laws of the *olah* is as if he sacrificed an *olah*." The Torah, therefore, warns the *Kohanim* and tells them, "This is the law of the *olah*" — that they must teach the people this law even though they might suffer a monetary loss as a result.

The Rabbi of Lida gives an almost identical interpretation. The *Kohanim* gain when the Jewish people sin [because they eat a portion of the sin-offering], and one must therefore be concerned that because of their monetary loss they will not teach the people Hashem's ways and will not warn them not to sin. This is the *zeiruz* to the *Kohanim*: that they should not forget that their primary task is to teach people the Torah, so that they do not sin. The Torah recognizes man's weakness, even if he is a *Kohen*, and it warns him not to allow his own egotism to impinge on his work by placing secondary matters above the main goal.

II.

The Tamid Sacrifice of the Kohen Gadol

In our *parashah*, Chapter 6 verse 12 and further, the *Kohen Gadol* is commanded to sacrifice a *minchas tamid* (literally, "perpetual *minchah*" — or meal offering) each morning and evening, to parallel the *olas tamid*, the morning and evening *olah* brought each day on behalf of the whole Jewish people. In reality, this twice-daily *minchah* of the *Kohen Gadol* is not totally identical with the community *olah*, since the *Kohen* would bring only a single *olah*, half of which was sacrificed in the morning and half in the evening. Even so, *Chinuch* in Positive *Mitzvah* 136 maintains that the purpose of this *mitzvah* is to make the agent of the community resemble the community itself,

> and it is appropriate for such a man to bring a personal sacrifice perpetually, just as the *tamid* brought by the community; and just as two are brought perpetually daily, he too is obligated to sacrifice his *minchah* twice daily... One cannot compare the inspiration received when a person offers his own special sacrifice to that received when he brings a sacrifice to which he is only a partner, for this is something which is known and experienced by everyone: that which is his alone inspires him more.

We will discuss later the manner in which this *minchah* was made, but based on the fact that it is a special *minchah* for a special task, Abarbanel sees in it elements of all the other *menachos* (the plural form of *minchah*). There are four types of *menachos*: *minchas soles* — "of fine flour"; *minchas machavas* — "of a shallow pan"; *minchas ma'afei tanur* — "baked in the oven"; and *minchas marcheshes* — "of a deep pan." The *minchah* of the *Kohen Gadol* is known by *Chazal* as *minchas chavitin* — the "shallow-pan *minchah*" — and is referred to this way in *I Divrei HaYamim*, 40:31. Nevertheless, it contains elements of all the *menachos*. It is made of fine flour, like the *minchas soles*; it is made in a shallow pan, like the *minchas machavas*; it is also deep fried, like the *minchas marcheshes*, and while still soft, it is baked, as the *minchas ma'afei tanur*. Thus we see that it represents all four of the other *menachos*, and its importance is prominently emphasized. We will yet discuss the reason for this importance according to Abarbanel.

Chazal in *Menachos* learn from here that the first time a *Kohen* enters into the Temple service, he must bring an additional *minchah*, which is known as the *minchas chinuch* (see *Menachos* 51). The *Gemara* concludes (*Menachos* 78) that a plain *Kohen* who had not yet served in the Temple and who was anointed as the *Kohen Gadol* must bring three *menachos*: (a) *minchas chinuch* for entering the Temple service, (b) *minchas chinuch* of the *Kohen Gadol*, (c) *minchas chavitin*. *Rambam* rules that way as well. It is surprising that *Kesef Mishneh* gives as *Rambam's* source the *Yerushalmi Shekalim*, for there only two *menachos* are mentioned: the *minchas chinuch* and the *minchas chavitin*. It would seem that *Rambam's* source is the *Bavli Menachos* 78. This, though, requires further deliberation. *Rambam's* words themselves are also surprising, for he writes that "all three are prepared identically," and yet he himself states in *Hil. Ma'aseh HaKorbanos* that in the case of *minchas chavitin* each loaf is divided into two parts, for the morning and evening, while the *minchas chinuch* is not divided up but is brought as a whole.

Mishneh LaMelech wishes to answer that what is identical is the way all are made, but the way they are brought is different. However, according to *Toras Kohanim* on our *parashah*, there are also differences in the way the *menachos* are brought. The *minchas chavitin* requires three *logim* of oil and must be mixed with hot water, but not the *minchas chinuch*. *Mishneh LaMelech* leaves the question open.

R' S.D. Mendelson, in the *Mossad Harav Kook* edition of *Rambam*, notes the source as *Menachos* 71, but there the *Gemara* discusses the *minchas chinuch* of *milu'im*, brought at the time that the *Mishkan* in the desert was sanctified. That *minchas chinuch* was eaten by the *Kohanim*, unlike the *minchas chinuch* for future generations, which was totally burned. (See the note by *Shitah Mekubetzes* there.)

It is also surprising that all those who compiled lists of the 613 *mitzvos* list only a single *mitzvah* here, and that is *minchas chavitin*, while in reality there are three *menachos* here which are independent of one another. I have not found any commentators who have commented on this. It might be that this supports the contention of R' David Zvi Hoffman, that the only *mitzvah* specified in the Torah here is the *minchas chavitin*, whereas the *minchas chinuch* is only *halachah l'Moshe mi'Sinai*, a law handed down to Moshe orally at Sinai, even though *Chazal* deduced it from a verse, as explained below. The verse in this case is but an *asmachta* — a verse used by *Chazal* to support a point — and that is the reason why the other two *menachos* are apparently not included in the 613 *mitzvos*.

Rambam in *Hil. Klei HaMikdash* 5:7 rules that the *Kohen Gadol* must live in Jerusalem. The commentators on *Rambam* do not note a source for this. R' S. D. Mendelson, in the *Mossad Harav Kook* edition of *Rambam*, notes the source as a *mishnah* in *Sanhedrin* 18, which states that "he goes out with them to the gateway of the city." It appears, though, that the source is in *Tosafos Sukkah* 47, לִינָה, that even one who brings a sacrifice of wood must afterwards lodge overnight in Jerusalem. So too did *Rambam* rule in *Hil. Bikkurim* 3:14. Thus, as the *Kohen Gadol* brings a *minchas chavitin* each day, he must live permanently in Jerusalem.

৵ Chazal's Deductions and the Meaning of the Verses

Verse 13 is somewhat difficult in terms of the *p'shat*, the literal meaning of the text, and requires an explanation. It begins: "This is the sacrifice of Aharon and his sons that they shall sacrifice to Hashem on the day he is anointed." We thus see that the verse refers to the sacrifice to be brought on the day of being anointed. Yet the verse continues: "a perpetual *minchah*, half of it in the morning and half of it in the evening." The verse also starts with a plural verb, "they shall sacrifice," and then continues, "he is anointed," which is the singular form. It is not clear whether the Torah is referring to the *Kohen Gadol* or to a plain *Kohen*. But in verse 15 it adds that the son of Aharon, who succeeds him, shall bring a sacrifice, "as a perpetual statute," and there it is clear that the Torah is referring to the *Kohen Gadol*. When does the *Kohen Gadol* bring his sacrifice? On the day he is anointed. Why, then, is it called a continual sacrifice? And if this refers to the *Kohen Gadol*, why does the Torah state "Aharon and his sons"?

Chazal in *Menachos* 51 discuss the meaning of these verses, and conclude that two sacrifices are involved here: (a) the *minchas chinuch* which all the *Kohanim* bring, both the *Kohen Gadol* and plain *Kohanim* (as suggested by the use of the plural form, "they shall sacrifice" — Aharon by himself and his sons by themselves); (b) *minchas chavitin*, which only the *Kohen Gadol* brings. The verse is then divided into two parts: The first part refers to the sacrifice of Aharon and his sons, each succeeding *Kohen Gadol* brings on the day he is anointed; a tenth of an *ephah* of fine flour mixed with oil; and the second part refers to the *minchas tamid*, which is brought every day, half in the morning and the other half in the evening.

Again the *Gemara* asks:

> Does the term "his sons" mean plain *Kohanim*, or *Kohanim Gedolim*? When (the Torah) states: "And the *Kohen* who is

anointed in his place from among his sons shall make it," this refers to the *Kohen Gadol*. How then do I (interpret) "his sons"? These are plain *Kohanim*.

But this is difficult in light of another interpretation by *Chazal* on the verse: "And the *Kohen* who is anointed in his place from among his sons shall make it," whereby we deduce that the *kehunah gedolah* passes down by inheritance. If so, what proof is there for the previous contention that "Aharon and his sons" refers to plain *Kohanim* as well? Ibn Ezra's and *Rashbam's* explanations, which are in accordance with the literal meaning of the text, are also difficult, for they explain verse 13 "Aharon and his sons" to refer to the sons of Aharon, the *Kohanim*, who become *Kohen Gadol* in his stead. This interpretation is unnecessary, as verse 15 says exactly that.

It is also difficult to see in the literal meaning of the text the words of *Chazal* that this refers to two *menachos*: (a) *minchas chinuch*, and (b) *minchas chavitin*, for the verse includes everything together, and states: "On the day he is anointed, a tenth of an *ephah* of fine flour as a perpetual *minchah*, half of it in the morning and half of it in the evening." Judging by the plain meaning of the text, it would seem that Ibn Ezra interpreted the words "on the day he is anointed" to read as if written, "from the day he is anointed," which means that from that day on, the *Kohanim* must bring a *minchas tamid* each morning and evening.

HaKesav VeHaKabalah explains that the word "This" at the beginning of the verse refers to both sacrifices, i.e., both the *korban chinuch* and the *korban tamid* require a tenth of an *ephah*. But according to this interpretation, there is no reference here to the fact that the *korban tamid* is only to be brought by the *Kohen Gadol*, and the *korban chinuch* is brought by plain *Kohanim*. While verse 15 does mention "the anointed *Kohen*," there it speaks of inheriting the post, and not about the law of the *menachos* itself.

R' Samson Raphael Hirsch explains the exact opposite, that "this is the sacrifice of Aharon and his sons that they shall sacrifice on the day he is anointed" refers to the sacrifice that Aharon and his sons are to bring as a *minchas chinuch*. The verse then goes on to describe this like the *minchah*: "a tenth of an *ephah* of fine flour, like the perpetual *minchah*," which is a reference to the tenth of an *ephah* of fine flour that the *Kohen Gadol* would always bring as *minchas chavitin*.

But R' David Zvi Hoffman sees this interpretation as forced, for the *minchas milu'im* — offered by Aharon and his sons when the Tabernacle was first consecrated — which is a *minchas chinuch*, came before the *minchas tamid*, so why would the Torah describe the *minchas chinuch* in terms of the *minchas tamid*? R' David Zvi Hoffman therefore holds that the Torah here refers only to the *minchas tamid*, and no other *minchah*. He explains the words "on the day he is anointed" as Ibn Ezra explained it, namely "from the day of anointing," i.e., that the *minchas tamid* was to be brought from the day that Aharon was anointed. The Torah relates this sacrifice to "Aharon and his sons," even though only the *Kohen Gadol* brought it, just as in Chapter 16, verses 6 and 11, which refer to the sacrifice that Aharon brought, the Torah states twice, "He shall atone for himself and for his household," which, *Chazal* say, refers the first time to his actual household, namely his wife and children, and the second to all the *Kohanim*, who are known as "Aharon's house." Thus, this sacrifice that Aharon brings is described as "the sacrifice of Aharon and his sons," because it is brought daily by the *Kohen Gadol* not only for his sake, but for all the *Kohanim* as well. The words "as a perpetual statute to Hashem" come to teach us that this sacrifice which the *Kohen Gadol* brings each morning and evening comes in return for the *menachos* given to the *Kohanim*, of which we are told in verse 11, "a perpetual statute (*chok olam*)." The word *chok* can mean "food" (compare *Bereishis* 47:22 and *Mishle* 30:8), so the phrase implies *lechem tamid* — "perpetual food." For the *lechem tamid* that the *Kohanim* receive perpetually, they show their appreciation by returning *chok olam laShem* — a "perpetual statute" (or "food") to Hashem and by this they announce that they are ready to serve Hashem, in return for the numerous sacrifices that Hashem awarded them.

According to this, the Torah does not specifically mention the *minchas chinuch*, and it appears to be *halachah l'Moshe mi'Sinai* (I mentioned above that this view is supported by the fact that the *minchas chinuch* is not listed in the 613 *mitzvos*). But the Torah does provide a *remez* — hint — regarding this *mitzvah*, when during the days of *milu'im* Aharon brought a *minchas chinuch* on his behalf and on behalf of his sons (see *Sh'mos* 29). Since the *Kohanim* of future generations did not participate in that particular *minchas chinuch* which came as a *minchas milu'im*, it meant that in future generations each and every *Kohen* would have to bring his own *minchas chinuch*.

However, the Torah itself states specifically that the *Kohen Gadol* must bring a *minchas chavitin* on the day he is anointed. Afterwards, *Chazal* deduce that the *kehunah gedolah* passes down by inheritance, and that is learned from the verse, "And the *Kohen* who is anointed in his place from among his sons shall make it."

✌︎ The Law of Inheritance of the Kehunah Gedolah

Chazal in *Horiyos* 11 learn from the above verse that the *Kohen Gadol* bequeaths the *kehunah gedolah* to his sons, but that the son also must be anointed. Thus *Rambam* deduces it in *Hil. Klei HaMikdash* (1:7) from this same verse.

Tosefes Brachah explains that this verse is really elliptical, and it is as if it had stated: "And the *Kohen* who is anointed, when he dies, in his place one from among his sons shall make it." We find a similar elliptical form in *II Melachim* 8:16, "And in the fifth year of Yoram the son of Ahab King of Israel, Yehoshafat King of Yehudah, Yehoram the son of Yehoshafat King of Yehudah began to reign." On this, *Radak* comments that the verse is elliptical, and is to be understood to mean "and Yehoshafat King of Yehudah died." So too in *II Shmuel* 17:3, the verse states: "The man whom you seek; so all the people shall be in peace," instead of: "the man whom you seek will die, and all the people will be in peace."

Abarbanel too explains that our verse refers to the inheriting of the *kehunah gedolah*, and states that "the leaders of the Israelite nation are the king and the *Kohen Gadol*. Both leadership roles are compared in the verse (*Eichah* 2:6): 'Hashem ... has despised in the indignation of His anger the king and the *Kohen*.' This verse is a reference to the leaders of the nation, the former the civil and the latter the spiritual leader, whose positions are exalted. Therefore, just as when a king dies his sons succeed him ... the same applies to the *Kohen Gadol*."

But *Avnei Shoham* by R' Moshe Leib Shachor wonders why the Torah had to tell us in three different places that the *Kohen Gadol* is succeeded by his sons: once in our *parashah*; a second time in *Acharei Mos* regarding the *Yom Kippur* sacrificial service: "And the *Kohen* who is anointed and who shall fill his hand to serve in place of his father shall atone," from which *Toras Kohanim* deduces that "the son takes priority over any other person" (and this is also stated in *Yoma* 72b); And finally, the third time, in regard to wearing the clothes of the *kehunah gedolah* in *Tetzaveh* (*Sh'mos* 29:30), "And the son that is the *Kohen* in his stead shall put them on seven days, when he comes into the Tent of Assembly to minister in the holy place." In *Yoma* 72 and 73, the *Gemara* deduces from this that the position of the *Kohen Gadol* is transferred to his sons after him. Why then do we need three separate verses to teach us this? What is even more surprising is that *Rambam* in *Hil. Klei HaMikdash* (4:20) deduces that the *kehunah gedolah* is inherited from the fact that the kingship is inherited, and writes, "It states regarding the king, 'He and his sons among Israel.' This teaches that the kingship is hereditary

. . ." from which *Rambam* learns that the same applies to the *Kohen Gadol* and the other high offices. But what about the three verses from which we learn the same law regarding the *Kohen Gadol*? This requires further investigation.

Chasam Sofer in *Sh'eilos U'Teshuvos Orach Chaim* 12 asks the opposite: Why does the *Gemara* in *Yoma* 72 use a verse to show that inheritance applies to the *Kohen Gadol*, when we already know that the law applies to kings? He answers that the *Kohen Gadol* is a matter dealing with *kedushah* — sanctity — and therefore we need a special verse to learn this. That is why *Rashdam* wrote in *Teshuvah* 85 that all appointments of Torah scholars, *poskim* and the rabbinate are not handed over by inheritance, and he brings a statement from *Yoma* that there are three crowns: That of royalty and of *kehunah gedolah* are bequeathed to one's sons, but not the crown of Torah. But then does it not say: "For him and his sons after him"? The answer is that matters dealing with *kedushah* are different in that they are not hereditary, except for the *kehunah gedolah*, for which we have a separate verse in the Torah. By this *teshuvah*, *Chasam Sofer* supports the ruling that a rabbinic position is not hereditary. But in the following *teshuvah*, 13, he states that that was only at the times of *Chazal*, where the rabbinate was an appointment solely of *kedushah* and not of service. In our days, though, where the rabbi is subject to his community and must serve its needs, this appointment is no worse than any other, and is conveyed by inheritance just as the other leadership roles pass to children.

◄§ Abarbanel's Reasons for the Minchas Chavitin

Abarbanel gives a number of reasons for the *minchas chavitin* of the *Kohen Gadol*. (a) This *korban* parallels the morning and evening *tamid* sacrifices brought on behalf of the public. The *Kohen Gadol* in this matter is acting as agent of the entire nation (this reason was brought by us in the name of *Chinuch*). (b) *Chazal* said: "Adorn yourself first, and then adorn others." It is therefore appropriate for the one on whom Israel depends as its agent to atone for it, to always be in a state of atonement, by means of his own *korban tamid*. (c) Each day the *Kohanim* eat of the *menachos* that the Jewish people have brought. Now the *Kohanim* come to prove, with the sacrifice that they themselves offer, that their intention is not to fill their bellies, for here they offer of their own grain; but that they are fulfilling a duty to Hashem. (d) The *minchas tamid* is a way of thanking Hashem for the gifts which He granted to the *Kohanim*. (e) The *Kohen* takes a full fistful of each *minchah* to put on the Altar, but as he might have erred and not taken the full amount, the *Kohen Gadol* brings a *minchah* each morning and evening as one who repays what he stole. (f) This *minchah* is meant to have sinners consider their sins and repent, when they see that even the *Kohen Gadol* brings a sacrifice each day to atone for his sins. Thus they will think that if *he* must atone for his sins, all the more must they. (g) This modest sacrifice of a tenth of an *ephah* leads the *Kohen* to be modest and to submit to Hashem. (h) The poor that can afford no more than a tenth of an *ephah* will not be ashamed with the sacrifices that they bring when they seė that the *Kohen Gadol* brings no more. (i) The *Kohen Gadol* brings a sacrifice each day for the sin of the Golden Calf.

It is worth noting here the words of *Rambam* in *Moreh Nevuchim* 3:41, that the reason this sacrifice is burned up completely is that if the *Kohen* would eat it, it would appear as if he had not sacrificed at all. *Rivash*, *Chizkuni*, *Pa'aneach Raza* and others all elaborate on this. When a Jew brings his *minchah*, he burns a *kometz* — a handful — of it, and the rest is eaten by the *Kohanim*, who are the servants of Hashem. But if a *Kohen* would only burn the *kometz* that he picks up using his three fingers, what would his gift to Hashem consist of, but a small, almost insignificant amount? Neither does it resemble the *chatas* and *asham* of *Kohanim*, for there the *cheilev* fat and the *emurim* are burned. The Torah therefore obligated the *Kohanim* to burn their *minchah* in its entirety, and then they will feel that they too brought a sacrifice to Hashem.

III.

You Shall Eat No Blood

The *rishonim* and *acharonim* give many reasons why *cheilev* (a certain fat of the animal) and blood are forbidden to us, while it is a *mitzvah* to sacrifice them on the Altar. Abarbanel states that blood and *cheilev* symbolize, in the words of *Yeshayahu* (1:18), "Though your sins be as scarlet, they shall be as white as snow." Blood is *red*, while *cheilev* is *white*. To explain why we are forbidden to eat the two, Abarbanel stresses *Rambam's* and *Ramban's* reasons.

According to *Rambam* in *Moreh Nevuchim*, the prohibition against *cheilev* is for health reasons, but the prohibition against blood is meant to wean Israel from idolatry, which in those days was linked to blood. "And know," writes *Rambam*, "that blood was very unclean in the eyes of the Zaba (a type of idolatry of those days). Yet they nevertheless ate it, thinking that it is the food of the spirits. When one ate it he was joining with the spirits, and would be able to tell the future. And there were people who found it difficult to swallow blood — for it is something which man's nature rejects — so (instead) they would slaughter an animal and collect the blood in utensils or in a ditch, and would then eat the slaughtered meat next to its blood, thinking that by their actions the spirits would drink the blood which is their food, while they ate the meat, thus bringing about love, comradeship and friendship with (the spirits), for they all ate together at the same table and at one sitting, and then they assumed that those spirits would come to them in a dream, and would tell them the future and help them."

These were all ideas, continues *Rambam*, which people believed in those days and were universally accepted, with none demurring as to their validity. The Torah thus came to remove this evil doctrine, and forbade the consuming of blood. In order to stress the importance of this law, the Torah stated (*Vayikra* 17:10): "I will set My face against that soul that consumes blood," just as the Torah states in regard to those that worship Moloch, "I will set My face against that man." This language is found nowhere else except in regard to the consuming of blood and the practice of idolatry. Yet the Torah made blood into something pure, and commanded that it be sprinkled on Aharon and his sons, and on the Altar, for their purification. And it made it into an entire Divine service, to pour it there [on the Altar] and not to gather it, as it is said (*Vayikra* 17:11) "And I gave it [the blood] to you on the Altar, to atone for your souls." And it commanded us to pour out the blood of any animal, even if it is not a sacrifice, for we are commanded: "You shall spill it on the ground as water." Then, when the Jews continued in their rebellion and followed the prevailing doctrines which believed that by eating meat containing blood one could commune with the spirits, Hashem commanded that the Jews were not to eat any plain meat at all in the desert, and restricted them to eating the meat of sacrifices brought to Him.

Ramban in *Parashas Acharei Mos* brings *Rambam's* explanation. He says that "these are logical words, but the verses do not teach this," for the Torah states specifically that the reason for the prohibition is (*Vayikra* 17:11), "For the life-force of the flesh is in the blood," and this is repeated in *Devarim*: "But be strong not to consume the blood, for the blood is the life-force, and you shall not consume the life-force with the meat."

To explain the prohibition against consuming blood, *Ramban* gives us the historical background. When Hashem created the world, the lower creatures were made for man's needs, for only man recognizes his Creator. Even then, Hashem only permitted the eating of vegetation and not animals, as it states in *Bereishis* (1:29), "And Hashem said, Behold, I have given you every herb bearing seed, which is upon the face of all the earth, and every tree, including the fruit of a tree yielding seed; to you it shall be for food."

When the flood occurred and mankind was saved because of Noach, Noach offered animals as sacrifices, which Hashem accepted. It was then that Hashem permitted the eating of meat, as it states (*Bereishis* 9:3), "Every moving thing that lives shall be meat for you; even as the green herb have I given you all things," for they were meant for man. Thus Hashem permitted the use of the flesh of animals, for these creatures were created for man's enjoyment and his needs. But the life-force (i.e., the blood) in these creatures was to serve to atone for man but not for it to be eaten, for a living creature may not consume the life-force of another. All lives belong to Hashem, both those of man and animal. After all, every living creature [to some extent resembles man, in that it knows enough to flee from danger and to seek that which is pleasurable to it. Living creatures are devoted to those to whom they are accustomed and love them, as dogs love their masters. It is for this reason [i.e., the similarity between the life-force of man and animal] that it is forbidden to eat the life-force of a living creature.

Ramban also brings two other reasons for this prohibition in his commentary on *Vayikra* 17:13, and these are brought down in detail by Rabbeinu Bachya. (a) The Torah states (ibid. v.11) , "And I have given it to you on the Altar to atone for your lives." We are forbidden to consume blood because it is meant for the Altar, to atone for man. We may then ask: Why are we forbidden to consume the blood of those kosher species which are not offered on the Altar, such as deer and chickens? We can answer that Hashem wanted to separate us from all blood, so that we should not err. (b) The blood is the life-force of the animal, in which are found its natural instincts. We are therefore forbidden to mix animal blood with our blood, for we received the Torah and it is proper for us to have our lives untainted so that we will be able better to understand higher concepts. We were commanded to be merciful, but if we would eat blood it would form cruelty and coarseness in us, and our souls would become close to that of the animals, for — unlike foods — blood is not simply digested by the body, but remains as is, and affects the person's very being. It is this that the Torah writes, "for the life-force of the flesh is in the blood." It is not proper to mix a temporal life-force [that of an animal] with an external one [that of man].

Yet with regard to *Devarim* 12:23, " Only be sure that you do not consume the blood," *Ramban* writes, using the same reasoning as does *Rambam* in *Moreh Nevuchim*, that the blood was used to conjure up the spirits, where the people would drink it and then foretell the future. It is for this reason that the Torah warned us to be strong and not consume the blood, even if as a result we would be able to tell the future.

The other commentators explain this stress in a different fashion. Blood, says *Rashbam*, is concealed deep in the organs, and one must be sufficiently strong willed to remove it from there.

Rabbeinu Bachya explains that blood strengthens the body of the person consuming it, and therefore the Torah promised physical strength to those who refrain from consuming it.

But R' David Zvi Hoffman proves that the commandment is one of compassion and mercy from what follows afterwards in the verse, "in order that it shall be good for you," as is stated in regard to honoring one's parents and sending away the mother bird before one takes its young. Before the Flood, humans were forbidden to kill and eat any living thing. Only after the Flood was meat permitted. At the same time, we were commanded: "But the flesh in its life-force, its blood, you shall not eat" (*Bereishis* 9:4). It is true that according to *Chazal* this commandment refers to the prohibition of eating flesh or a limb from an animal which is still alive, but at the same time the quality of compassion is stressed, as part of the entire foundation of this commandment. At Sinai, Israel was warned not to spill the blood of cattle, unless the animal was offered as a sacrifice to Hashem. In *Vayikra* 17:4, this is considered as if one committed murder. Even when the Torah did permit the slaughtering of animals as sacrifices, it forbade eating the blood, which contains the life-force. This prohibition continued in force later on, when the Torah permitted the slaughter of animals purely for food. Eating blood together with the meat is deemed a cruel act. Although Hashem granted man limited dominion over the animals, man must take care not to consume the life-force of the animal. It is precisely because of the fact that *shechitah* was permitted in general that there is a need to be especially strong not to eat the meat together with the life-force of the animal. This reason is also that given by *Chinuch*. He states that besides creating a bad nature within a person, the very consumption of blood is an act of cruelty, for the one who consumes blood swallows the life-force of the animal, the force that kept it alive. Animals, too, have a life-force, even if it is not marked by human intelligence, and it is not fitting for the way of compassion to eat that life-force.

Abarbanel combines two views, those of *Rambam* and *Ramban*. On the one hand, *Rambam's* explanation that the reason is because of the worship of spirits is questionable according to *Ramban*, on the basis of the various verses which indicate that the prohibition derives from the fact that blood is the life-force. On the other hand, *Ramban's* view is also questionable, since in *Acharei Mos*, regarding the prohibition against spilling blood outside, the Torah states (*Vayikra* 17:7), "They shall no longer sacrifice their offerings to spirits," thus showing that the prohibition is directed against the worship of spirits. Abarbanel therefore concludes that the Torah provides two reasons that indicate two separate prohibitions. The Torah forbids one to slaughter sacrifices outside the place designated by Hashem or to spill the blood outside the designated place. Abarbanel mentions the reason given by *Rambam* for this, as it states here, "They shall no longer sacrifice their offerings to spirits." In addition to the prohibition of spilling the blood outside the designated place, though, there is another prohibition against consuming any blood, even if it is not from a sacrifice, and the reason for this prohibition is that of *Ramban*, for the blood is the life-force. One needs both reasons: (a) so as to forbid slaughtering outside the designated place, and (b) so as to forbid the eating of any blood.

As noted, these reasons originate with Abarbanel's predecessors, except that he added to them somewhat; but he also adds other reasons:

(a) Blood is the life-force of the body, by which this force penetrates all of one's organs and veins. Hashem ordered that we sacrifice the blood of animals instead of man. Man sinned with his life-force, and he must therefore rectify matters through a life-force. "For the life-force of the flesh is in the blood" refers to man's own life-force and soul. The purpose of the blood of the sacrifice is to atone for man and to take his place, and not to be man's food.

(b) When blood of an animal is consumed, it joins with the blood of the person eating it, and makes his nature coarse. The other things one eats change in the digestive process but blood remains intact and is not digested, so that man's life-force merges with the life-force of the animal he has consumed. "Therefore did I say to the Children of Israel, no soul among you shall consume blood." This latter reason was also given by Abarbanel's predecessors, but it is he who stresses the Torah's reference to "the Children of Israel," whereby the prohibition is particularly meaningful for those whose name (*ki sarisa im Elohim* — *Bereishis* 32:29) indicates their standing with Hashem and whose soul is removed from animalistic impulses. Hashem tells us: "You should be perfect in your beliefs and your qualities and you are therefore not to eat blood, for the blood is the life-force, and I do not want the animalistic life-force to merge with your spiritual life-force."

(c) The blood of animals is in place of the soul of man. It carries with it the animal's equivalent of the human life-force. We cannot see the life-force but we can see the blood. If one consumes the blood, it is as if he had eaten the body and life-force of the animal together, and already the sons of Noach were forbidden to eat a live animal. Abarbanel adds that the reasons given in the Torah include all three of the above.

Akeidah also explains the reason for the prohibition in accordance with *Ramban* and Abarbanel, and states that by consuming blood there is a fusion of man's life-force with that of the animals, and man acquires animalistic lusts. He expands the explanation of the reason for sprinkling the blood on the Altar, for the life-force of all flesh is in the blood. The sprinkling of the blood symbolizes man's sacrifice of his own soul on the Altar. Man must be willing to sacrifice his life for the sanctification of Hashem's name.

Chazal in *Berachos* 54 said: " 'With all your soul' — even if He takes your soul." Yonasan testified about David (*I Shmuel* 19:5), "For he put his life in his hand, and slew the Philistine." And Yotam said (*Shoftim* 9:17), "For my father fought for you, and placed his soul in the balance." Yiftach also said (*Shoftim* 12:3), "I put my life in my hands, and passed over against the children of Ammon." All of these men were willing to sacrifice their lives for their nation, their city, and the glory of Hashem. If, however, a person endangers his life for his own enjoyment, for glory or a monetary award, he deserves to lose his life, as David said when three of his mighty men risked their lives to bring him water to drink (*II Shmuel* 23:17): "Far be it from me, O Lord, that I should do this: Is not this the blood of the men that went in jeopardy of their lives?" He then refused to drink the water they had brought, and "poured it out to Hashem."

Other commentators also deal with the reason for the prohibition. The Torah explains the prohibition regarding *cheilev* and blood as a result of their being sanctified on the Altar. In regard to *cheilev*, it states (*Vayikra* 7:25), "Whosoever eats *cheilev* of an animal of the species that is sacrificed as an offering to Hashem." Also in regard to blood, the Torah states (ibid. 17:11), "For the life-force of the flesh is in the blood, and I gave it to you on the Altar to atone." Yet, one cannot conclude that this is the only reason for the prohibition. After all, while the Torah forbade the eating of *cheilev*, it did not forbid us to eat "the kidneys, the lobe of the liver, and the fat tail," which are also placed on the Altar. And as for the blood, that of other kosher animals (e.g., deer) is also forbidden, even though their blood is not sprinkled on the Altar and is not used for atonement.

Oznayim LaTorah cites *Chazal* in order to show that it is not the fact that they are offered on the Altar that makes *cheilev* and blood forbidden. *Chazal* tell us in *Menachos* 5:

> It is a *kal vachomer* (*a fortiori*): If a blemished animal, which is permitted to man, is forbidden (to be sacrificed) to the Most High, a *treifah*, which is forbidden to man, is certainly forbidden (to be sacrificed) to the Most High. *Cheilev* and blood will (be used to) prove (against this reasoning), for they are forbidden to man and are permitted to the Most High.

But if we say that the reason for the prohibition of *cheilev* and blood is because they are sacrificed on the Altar, then what analogy can be made regarding other prohibitions from the fact that these are prohibited? For *cheilev* and blood, which are meant for the Altar, are different from the other prohibitions. We are therefore forced to say that this was not the reason for their prohibition, even though the Torah stresses the fact that they are sacrificed on the Altar in regard to the prohibition.

R' David Zvi Hoffman, however, holds that since this prohibition appears among the laws regarding sacrifices, its reason is linked to the sacrifices. The Torah does not say (*Vayikra* 11:43), "do not make your souls loathsome and you will become unclean through them," or (*Sh'mos* 22:30) "you shall be holy people to Me," in regard to *cheilev* and blood as it does with other forbidden foods. This is a sign that this prohibition is not due to health considerations, but is rather only symbolic in content. This is shown in the verses (*Vayikra* 3:16), "all *cheilev* is to Hashem," and (ibid. 17:11) "the blood shall atone for the soul." That which a person sacrifices as an offering to Hashem he dare not eat himself, out of awe. Blood is meant to atone for man's soul, and symbolically represents the spiritual, namely the Divine in man, and therefore man should not ingest blood into his body. With this, R' David Zvi Hoffman rejects the explanation of R' Samson Raphael Hirsch that the reason for the prohibition against *cheilev* and blood is the same as for all other prohibited foods, namely that these introduce into the body matter which disturbs his spiritual renewal.

Later, in *Parashas Acharei Mos*, R' David Zvi Hoffman states that the prohibition against consuming blood is linked to that of slaughtering animals outside the Temple. No animal should be slaughtered unless it is brought as a sacrifice to Hashem. The blood of animals is meant to serve on the Altar as an atonement for men who have sinned. The life-force of the animal symbolizes man's soul, thus that which atones for him and which is offered on the *Mizbe'ach* (Altar) in place of his soul ought not be permitted to enter into his body. Just as man's soul and his body are separate, in that the former comes from Hashem and the latter from the earth, so too is the blood of animals, which is intended by Divine statute to symbolize man's soul, not to be ingested as food into man's body.

⊷§ Against Materialism

A new explanation of the prohibition against *cheilev* and blood is given by R' Isaac Breuer in his *Nachaliel*. Blood is the active portion of the animal's body. Its actions are what keep the animal alive. The *cheilev* is the reserve of the animal, upon which it sustains itself in an emergency. Both symbolize animalistic life.

The philosophy pursued by materialism is correct in maintaining that there is no difference between the life of man and that of animals. That is the true part of the falsehood. But materialism is a lie, because according to it, all of man's life is but animalistic, and he has no opportunity to overcome this and to sanctify it.

Man sacrifices his own *cheilev* and blood when he sacrifices the *cheilev* and blood of various animals. Materialism is correct in claiming that there is no difference between one *cheilev* and another and between one blood and another. But it is precisely because of the identity between man's blood and *cheilev* and those involved in the act of sacrifice that there is a prohibition of eating *cheilev* and blood, so as to keep them apart from man's *cheilev* and blood, thereby stressing that materialism is false. Man's *cheilev* and blood are meant to be holy to Hashem. The very fact that there is so serious a prohibition associated with the offering of the sacrifices indicates to us that it is not the *cheilev* or blood of the animal, but man's own *cheilev* and blood that he is offering on the Altar so as to atone for his soul.

Hashem has not yet rebuilt His destroyed Altar for close to two thousand years, and no *Kohanim* are serving in the Temple. Our blood and *cheilev* no longer ascend before Hashem to atone for our souls, but this severe prohibition — which indicates the identity and the differences between the animalistic life of man and the animal life of animals — this prohibition — whose source is in the *Bais HaMikdash* and the *korbanos* — is a perpetual statute for all generations, regardless of where one lives, for it separates the Jew from materialism, and whoever transgresses this is cut off from his people.

The preceding refers to the prohibition of *cheilev*. As to blood, it is the life-force and the active component of animal life, which supports and maintains all parts of the body. The very fact of animalistic life is a secret which we cannot fathom, just as we are unable to understand the strong bond between the blood and the animalistic desire. This bond surely exists, since blood is the energy of animalistic life as long as it is controlled by the animalistic desire, as indicated by the Torah's acknowledgement that "the life-force is in the blood."

Materialism implies that all blood is identical. According to it, man has no different a life than any other creature, for all have the same animalistic life. The severe prohibition that the Torah imposed a number of times on the consuming of blood divided for all generations man's animalistic urges and those of animals. Do not eat the meat of animals in which the traces of "its life-force" still exist. After all, the very act of eating is animalistic. Is not the very act of eating support of the materialistic view which has woven a web of falsehood around the truth? The Torah says: "Strengthen yourself!" When you eat meat, do not eat the "life-force" with the meat. "Strengthen yourself!" is the Torah's warning against the lure of materialism. One must be very strong so as to always be able to differentiate between blood and blood, between life-force and life-force, between human desire and animalistic desire. It is on this differentiation that Judaism is founded.

Shemini – שְׁמִינִי

I.

A Foreign Fire
that Hashem Had not Commanded

he reason that Nadav and Avihu died is mentioned in the Torah: "And the sons of Aharon took each his censer, and they put in them incense. And they offered before Hashem foreign fire which He had not commanded them." Yet *Chazal* and the midrashim give numerous reasons and explanations as to what their sin was and why they died. There are some commentators who praise Aharon's sons and consider them as exceptional people. The sons meant what they did for the best and did more than they were commanded. But they were punished because no man has the right to do more or less in the *avodah* — the Divine service — than he is commanded.

Different commentators find serious fault in the actions of Aharon's sons. Some claim that they showed disrespect for the *Mishkan*, the *korbanos*, and the Divine service: (a) They entered the *Mishkan* wearing the robes of a regular *Kohen* rather than those of a *Kohen Gadol*. (b) They had previously imbibed wine. (c) They brought in a foreign fire, which they took from a stove and not from the outer Altar. (d) They offered a sacrifice which they had not been commanded to bring.

Other commentators accuse the sons of improper behavior which discredited the *kehunah*: (e) that they did not take wives because of their conceit, for they felt that no other family was as distinguished as theirs, and (f) they did not have children.

There are also commentators who find other *halachic* or moral blemishes in the performance of Aharon's sons: (g) they determined the *halachah* in the presence of their rebbi (Moshe). (h) They were among those of whom it was said (*Sh'mos* 24:11), "And they ate and drank, and they saw Hashem." (i) They awaited the death of Moshe and Aharon, so that they could take over the leadership of the nation. (j) They were not friendly to one another.

But there are those among *Chazal* who place the cause of their deaths on their exaggerated enthusiasm. This explanation states that they saw a flame coming down from Heaven and wished to add love to love (*Sifra* 26). Yet, other explanations have been given of their sin and punishment.

This great number of interpretations demands an explanation. After all, the Torah specifies what the sin was, so why is there need to add so many further sins to that given there? While it is true that *Chazal* deduce their different interpretations from the verses themselves, it is still difficult to understand why they did not limit themselves to what the Torah states specifically. Most of the commentators state that *Chazal* found the severity of the punishment difficult to comprehend if the entire sin consisted of doing that which they were not commanded.

Baal HaTurim, Ba'alei HaTosafos and Rabbeinu Yosef Bechor Shor explain the verse, אֲשֶׁר לֹא צִוָּה אֹתָם — "which He did not command them" — in a way whereby the words are rearranged: אֲשֶׁר צִוָּה אֹתָם לֹא — "that He commanded them not to." In other words, there was a specific commandment to them not to do what they did, and yet they did so.

Taz in *Divrei David* says that the redundancy in the words bothered *Chazal*: "And it consumed them, and they died before Hashem." From this *Chazal* concluded that they were already deserving of death, even before this last act of theirs.

But it appears to me that *Chazal* were bothered by the fact that it is a *mitzvah* to bring fire from outside. *Da'as Zekeinim Mi'Ba'alei HaTosafos* senses this, and states: "For indeed it is a *mitzvah* to bring a fire from outside, after fire had already come down from the Heavens. But prior to that it was forbidden to bring fire from the outside, for by doing so it diminished the Glory of Heaven, as if the sacrifice had been consumed by fire from man. And even though earlier the Torah states, 'And a fire went out from Hashem,' that was a fire meant for the sacrifices and not for the incense."

Rashbam also explains it along these lines, and adds that they brought a foreign fire even before the fire came down from Heaven, for the incense of the morning comes before the burning of the limbs of the daily *tamid*. Thus, before the fire came down from Heaven, they had taken their censers to offer incense on the golden Altar, and had placed fire in their censers, and there is a specific commandment not to do so. Thus we find that Eliyahu said (during his confrontation with the prophets of Ba'al on Mt. Carmel, *I Melachim* 18:25): "Do not place fire there," since he wished to have the Divine Name sanctified when fire came down from heaven. According to this interpretation, the fire that burned

Aharon's sons was the same fire that came from on High so that there were not two instances of fire coming down, as appears from the verses.

It appears that this uncertainty as to the meaning of the verses brought *Chazal* to search for another sin, one which is not mentioned in the Torah. *Sh'eilos U'Teshuvos HaRosh*, at the end of Section 13, asks how, according to *Chazal*, Nadav and Avihu were punished for transgressing prohibitions of which they had not yet been commanded, such as not to imbibe wine or strong drink.

Similarly, he asks how they could have been punished for wearing the four garments of the regular *Kohanim* rather than the eight required of the *Kohen Gadol*, when they were not *Kohanim Gedolim*. His answer is that in any case they had to be punished; for if indeed they were regular *Kohanim* and were thus only required to wear four garments, they were forbidden to enter the inner chamber, where only the *Kohen Gadol* is permitted. This answer, however, still presents difficulties. For in any case they should not have been doubly punished, both as regular *Kohanim* and as *Kohanim Gedolim*. If it is true that they were punished for entering the inner chamber, then they must have been regular *Kohanim*; and should not have been punished for wearing only the four garments.

It is interesting that *Targum Yehonasan* translates the phrase "after the death of the two sons of Aharon," as follows: "After the two sons of Aharon, the *Kohanim Gedolim*, died." What is his source that they were *Kohanim Gedolim*? Some change the language in *Yehonasan* from the plural form to the singular, so that the Aramaic verse reads: "the two sons of Aharon, the *Kohen Gadol*," namely that Aharon was the *Kohen Gadol*. But that too is difficult. What is the *Targum* then adding? This requires further study.

ᥧ The Nature of the Sin According to Our Early Rabbis

Our early rabbis were divided on the sin of Nadav and Avihu. There are those who say that the sin consisted of what the Torah states, namely introducing foreign fire, and there are others who maintain that the sin was that they introduced foreign incense. The source for this dispute is that there is no specific commandment not to bring in foreign fire. On the contrary: *Chazal* in *Yoma* learned from a verse (*Vayikra* 1:7), "And the sons of Aharon shall put fire on the Altar," that even though fire came down from Heaven, it was nevertheless a *mitzvah* to bring fire from the outside (see previous section). We will see later how those commentators who see the sin as the introduction of foreign fire interpret this section.

Rashbam, as mentioned earlier, explains simply that they brought a foreign fire to offer incense on the inner, golden Altar, in accordance with the law that the offering of incense takes place before the burning of the limbs of the *tamid*. Their sin consisted of not waiting for fire to descend from Heaven, but in first bringing in fire from the outside. It is true that on the other days they were commanded to bring fire from outside, but on that day they were not commanded to do so, for Hashem wished to have His name sanctified by the appearance of fire from Heaven. This interpretation is similar to the one we brought above in the name of the *Ba'alei Tosafos*, but as mentioned this is difficult, for they had not been commanded about the prohibition involved, and why were they punished when they had not been warned?

R' Koppel Reinitz, in his commentary on *Ba'al HaTurim*, quotes a certain commentator that a warning against such action is contained in the verse (*Sh'mos* 30:9), "You shall not offer up on it foreign incense," upon which *Rashi* comments that any freewill offering of incense is considered foreign. Thus the fire which they brought for the purpose of the incense was also considered foreign fire.

Ibn Ezra too says that their sin was that the fire they took for the incense was not fire that came from Heaven but from outside, and they did this on their own, for they had not been commanded to bring the incense with foreign fire. The Torah refers to it as "foreign" because they had not been commanded to do so.

R' Benzion Firer brings proof that this is the way in which the Torah indicates its intent. It states in *Bamidbar* 18: "And a foreigner (זָר) shall not draw near to you," by which the Torah warns us against doing that which we were not commanded. The prohibition against a foreign element refers to either (a) a person who is not a *Kohen* bringing the sacrifice, or (b) a *Kohen* who carries the action out without being commanded to do so.

Rabbeinu Bachya brings almost the same idea in the name of *Ra'avad*, but he adds that Nadav and Avihu, rather than taking fire from the Altar for the incense as commanded in the verse (*Vayikra* 16:12), "And he shall take a full censer of coals of fire from upon the Altar," were afraid that that fire would be sufficient only to burn up the sacrifice, but not the incense. Their sin consisted of a lack of faith in the ability of the fire from on High — a fire which is limitless — to perform the necessary task.

R' Sa'adiah Gaon, too, in notes in a volume published by *Mossad Harav Kook*, explains that their sin was that they brought foreign fire from outside. He states that the sons of Aharon misinterpreted the verse (ibid. 1:7), "And the sons of Aharon the *Kohen* shall place fire on the Altar," to mean that Hashem commanded them to bring fire from outside into the *Mishkan*, for the *olah* (burnt offering), whereas all that the Torah had commanded was that they should burn the wood. This is in accordance with the view of *Chazal* that their sin consisted in ruling the *halachah* in front of their rebbi, for they should have asked Moshe what Hashem had meant and not done by themselves what they thought Hashem had meant.

R' Baruch Epstein, in *Torah Temimah*, holds that even though they were indeed required to bring fire (and in this they did not misconstrue Hashem's command), they still sinned in ruling *halachah* in front of their rebbi. Thus we find in *Berachos* 31b that when Shmuel ruled *halachah* in front of his rebbi, Eli the *Kohen*, that *shechitah* may be done by a non-*Kohen*, it was considered as ruling before his rebbi, even though Eli told him, "What you said is correct." In the final analysis, though, *Torah Temimah* finds it difficult to explain it this way. After all, the Torah states, "which He did not command," and yet they were indeed commanded to bring fire from the outside, as *Chazal* tell us in *Yoma* 21. He therefore explains that the *mitzvah* to bring fire from the outside means to bring fire from elsewhere to the outer Altar, where the animals were sacrificed, whereas the *mitzvah* for the inner Altar is to bring fire only from the outer one, as explained in *Yoma* 53. Their error consisted of bringing fire from elsewhere to the inner Altar, which they ruled to be the same as the outer Altar. (*Tosafos* in *Yoma* 21 explains this differently.)

Chizkuni, by contrast, adopts the interpretation mentioned earlier, namely that even though the Torah states that they brought in foreign fire, their sin consisted of bringing in their own incense. The incense had to be brought from the public, and as incense cannot be brought without fire, the Torah refers to it as "foreign fire" although the intent is foreign incense. The phrase, "which Hashem did not command them," really means "which He commanded them *not* to," as found in the verse (*Sh'mos* 30:9), "And you shall not offer foreign incense." An example of this is found in the verse (*Yirmiyahu* 7:31), "Their sons and their daughters which I did not command them," where too the meaning is, "Which I commanded them not."

S'forno, too, explains that they sinned in offering foreign incense on the inner Altar. They thought that just as one brings the incense after the *tamid* sacrifice, in honor of the presence of the *Shechinah*, so too was it appropriate to offer new incense to welcome the revelation of Hashem. Indeed they might have been correct had they been commanded to do so, but their sin was that they did what they did without being commanded.

Most commentators hold that the incense that Nadav and Avihu brought was offered on the inner Altar as required, but *Tosafos* in *Eruvin* 63 (מאי דרוש) wish to prove that they offered it on the outer Altar, and this was a special Divine ruling for that particular instance.

Ramban, however, in *Parashas Acharei Mos*, explains that the offering was in the *Ohel Moed* on the inner Altar, for Aharon too only brought his incense into the *Ohel Moed*, and they had no reason to depart from the procedure of their father. *Ramban* writes this in order to refute the opinion of Ibn Ezra, whom he quotes to the effect that they went in further than their father, and brought the incense into the Holy of Holies.

Abarbanel deduces from the verses a number of sins that Nadav and Avihu were guilty of when they brought the incense. (a) It is true that the *Kohen* who offers the incense is chosen by lot. On *Yom Kippur*, though, only the *Kohen Gadol* offers the incense. The eighth day of the days of *milu'im* was a holy one, just as *Yom Kippur*. Nadav and Avihu, who were regular *Kohanim*, were therefore forbidden from bringing the incense. (b) On the eighth day of the *milu'im*, Moshe was acting as the *Kohen Gadol*. He was the only one permitted to perform the Divine service on that day, and it was forbidden for others to do any part of it. (c) The incense must be brought by a single *Kohen*, and here it was brought by both.

He also adds, quoting *Ramban*, that there is another sin here, that in the case of incense the fire must be put down first and the incense put upon it, but they put the incense down first. I have not found where *Ramban* writes this, but there is a comment of *Ramban* that might be interpreted this way. If one studies Rabbeinu Bachya, Ricanti and *Ramban* on *Parashas Vayikra*, on the verse "An offering of sweet savor," one will find that *Ramban* is referring here to the interpretation of the kabbalists, that in his offering Aharon turned to "the attribute of strict justice," and therefore a fire blazed forth from the attribute of strict justice and consumed his sons.

Akeidas Yitzchak offers a unique interpretation of the sin of the sons of Aharon. They brought the incense because they lacked faith. They did not believe that the fire came from Heaven but thought that it was caused spontaneously by the specific list of ingredients used in preparing the incense, which made the mixture explode. They therefore brought incense to see if they too could have the mixture burst into flames. This interpretation is interesting, but it is difficult to fit it into the Torah verses, for the Torah states clearly that they brought "strange fire." Was the fire then caused by the distinct list of ingredients brought by Nadav and Avihu?

◆§ Adding Love to Love

Earlier, we brought the view of *Sifra* that Nadav and Avihu added love to love and went beyond the proper limits by exceeding what they had been commanded to do. This explanation is found quite frequently in the Chassidic literature. It is interesting that *HaKesav VeHaKabalah* explains the words "and it consumed them" in the sense of a sacrifice, as if to say that their zeal was accepted by Hashem and as a result "they died." This interpretation is in keeping with that of the kabbalists such as R' Chaim Vital in his *Eitz HaDa'as HaTov* and in other works which compare the death of Nadav and Avihu to the *misas neshikah* ("death by a kiss") mentioned in *Idra Rabbah*. He brings proof that such a lofty action as that of Nadav and Avihu draws the soul from the body to its Creator. *Chazal* too say that when the Torah was given, the souls of all of Israel departed from their bodies because of their great love of Hashem and that Hashem later revived them all with the dew of resurrection.

The Lubavitcher Rebbi has a remarkable discourse on this in his discourses on *Parashas Acharei-Kedoshim* 5724. In summary, he says that even though the righteous man in his worship of Hashem may leave his physical reality, he must still return after his worship to the lower regions. Nadav and Avihu only knew how to leave their material reality, but did not know how to return. They left their earthly framework and drew so close to Hashem that "they died." This is the meaning of *Chazal*'s statement that they served Hashem "with incomplete clothes," meaning that they did not know that one also needs a physical garb and must remain in this garb and not shed it. This too is what *Chazal* meant when they said that Nadav and Avihu did not marry wives or have children. By this, *Chazal* pointed out that Nadav and Avihu reached the lofty rung of Ben Azzai (who also never married), but did not reach the rung of R' Akiva, "who came in whole and went out whole." R' Akiva knew the secret of how to depart from his physical reality, but also how to return to it.

The Torah warned the *Kohen Gadol* (*Vayikra* 16:2-3,6): "And Hashem said unto Moses, Speak unto Aharon your brother, that he should not come at all times into the holy place . . . Thus shall Aharon come into the holy place . . . and make an atonement for himself, and for his house." *Chazal* tell us that his house refers to his wife. Even when the *Kohen Gadol* ascends to the loftiest spiritual realms, he may not forget his human existence and "his house," which is a part of his existence.

According to *Sifsei Tzaddik* (brought in *Torah Kvall* by R' Alexander Zusya Friedman), Nadav and Avihu deserved to die, for doing what they were not commanded. Had they done only what Hashem commanded them, they would have seen the fulfillment of "and they shall live by them." The Torah grants man life so that he should not cease to exist.

Sefas Emes quotes his grandfather, *Chiddushei HaRim*, that their main downfall lay in that they did what they were not commanded. He says:

> The main aspect of the performing of a *mitzvah* is the power of the command, and this exceeds all special intentions. Now Nadav and Avihu were the greatest Sages of the generation and they had holy intentions, unifications, and hidden meanings in their deeds, but they were nevertheless punished for not doing what they had been commanded. How much more is this true on the positive side: where one who performs a *mitzvah* the way it was commanded, even though he knows nothing, is considered as if he had concentrated on all the profound interpretations.

It appears to me that that is what the Torah means when it writes later: "This is the thing which Hashem commanded, and the glory of Hashem will appear to you." All the commentators wonder: What is this thing? After all, nothing is mentioned here. However the Torah tells us a major and basic principle and says: "This is the thing" — this is what Hashem wants: "that which Hashem commanded, you are to do." Only that which He commanded. No more and no less. Aharon obeyed this command, and therefore a fire came from Hashem and consumed his sacrifice. But Nadav and Avihu did not obey, and therefore the fire came forth and consumed them.

In *Parashas Ki Sisa*, many commentators say that in the sin of the Golden Calf the Jews confused one form of Divine service with another, concerning which they had not been commanded. It is for this reason that in regard to the construction of the *Mishkan*, it is specified that each detail was constructed as Hashem commanded them. In our case, Nadav and Avihu repeated the sin of doing what they were not commanded to do. In this, they were repeating the sin of the Golden Calf of which the Torah tells us (*Sh'mos* 32:8), "They departed quickly from the way which I commanded them, and made themselves a graven calf." We can therefore understand the words of *Chazal* on the Torah's phrase (*Devarim* 9:20), " 'And against Aharon did Hashem become very angry' — this means the destruction of his children." The sin of Aharon's sons recalled the sin of the Golden Calf. The severe punishment in this case, too, was meant to warn people not to do anything but that which Hashem commanded. No more and no less.

II.

The Sacrifices on the Eighth Day of Milu'im

At the beginning of our *parashah*, Aharon and the Children of Israel were commanded about the special sacrifices on the eighth day of the *milu'im* — of the sanctification of the *Mishkan* and the *Kohanim* in the desert. The commentators question the purpose of these special sacrifices, as well as the differences between the sacrifices of Aharon and of the Children of Israel. Israel was ordered to sacrifice a "male goat" as a *chatas*, while Aharon himself was ordered to bring "a calf, the son of a bull" for a *chatas*. As opposed to this, Israel was to bring a calf and a lamb for an *olah* and Aharon was to bring a ram for an *olah*. On the other days of the *milu'im*, Aharon was commanded to bring a bull, while on the eighth day he was to bring a calf.

Later, in verse 7 of chapter 9, Moshe says to Aharon: "offer your sin offering and your burnt offering, and make an atonement for yourself and for the people." In other words, the people were to gain atonement through Aharon's sacrifice, while immediately afterwards we are told: "and offer the offering of the people, and make an atonement for them." Thus we see that the sacrifice for the people was meant as atonement for the people.

The commentators also discuss how the sacrifices were offered. In regard to Aharon's *chatas*, we are told, "And the flesh and the hide he burned with fire outside the camp." What was the purpose of this burning? After all, a *chatas* whose blood was put on the outer Altar did not require burning. *Rashi* says: "We do not find an outside *chatas* that is burned, except for this [on the eighth day] and that of the [first seven days of the] *milu'im*, and all [these exceptions] were in accordance with a specific command."

But not all commentators accept this explanation. In regard to the *chatas* of the nation we are also told, "And he offered it for sin, as the first." On this *Rashi* comments that it was offered in accordance with the rules of a *chatas*, just as Aharon's calf. The question is then asked: Was this *chatas* too burned? And what is the difference between the various *chatas* sacrifices?

At first, *Ramban* wishes to say that these sacrifices were meant for the dedication of the *Kohanim* for their sacred work — the *avodah* — just like the *minchas chavitin* brought by the *Kohen Gadol* on the day he was anointed. Afterwards, though, he follows in the footsteps of *Chazal*, that the calf was brought to atone for the sin of the Golden Calf, but that Israel as a whole also had to bring a goat to atone for the sin of the selling of Yosef, of which we are told (*Bereishis* 37), "and they killed a goat, and dipped the coat in the blood." *Ramban* quotes the words of *Toras Kohanim*: "You sinned at the beginning and sinned at the end. You sinned in the beginning, as it states, 'and they killed a goat, and dipped the coat in the blood'; and you sinned at the end, as it states, 'They made a graven calf which I did not command them.' Let him bring a goat to atone for the event of the goat, and let him bring a calf to atone for the event of the calf."

The various *drush* works discuss at length the link between the sale of Yosef and the sin of the Golden Calf, as shown in *Toras Kohanim*, which sees the issue in the context of having a "beginning and an end." We will bring a number of explanations on this. *Ramban* notes that the *chatas* of Aharon was identical to his sacrifice on *Yom Kippur*, and the *chatas* of the entire nation was identical to its *chatas* on *Yom Kippur*. R' Chaim Dov Chavel notes that the *chatas* of Aharon was not entirely identical to the one he brought on *Yom Kippur*, for there the sacrifice was a bull — a פַּר — while here it was a "calf, the son of a bull"— עֵגֶל בֶּן בָּקָר.

Ibn Ezra, though, according to *Ezrah Lehavin*, explains that there is no difference between the two terms. R' David Zvi Hoffman nevertheless points out that according to *Chazal* an עֵגֶל is in the first year, an עֵגֶל בֶּן בָּקָר is in the second year, and a פַּר בֶּן בָּקָר is in the third year. Based on the above, *Ramban* deduces that this *chatas* was burned, although Moshe had not said this explicitly for the פַּר of *Yom Kippur*, on which this sacrifice is molded, was burned. Thus, the *chatas* of the people also had to be burned, just as on *Yom Kippur*. The question then arises: What was the difference between the method of sacrificing the *chatas* of Aharon and the *chatas* of the people? This requires further study.

◆§ To Atone for the Sin of the Golden Calf

The commentators follow in the footsteps of *Chazal*, that the *chatas* brought by Aharon was meant to atone for the sin of the Golden Calf. *Midrash Tanchuma*, *Targum Yehonasan*, *Rashi* and almost all commentators on the Torah state that the two calves — of Aharon and of the people — both come to atone for the sin of the Golden Calf. None of the commentators has any other explanation for the *chatas*, or for the *olah* brought for the people.

R' Eliyahu Mizrachi questions this explanation, for the *Kohen Gadol* was not permitted to enter the *Kodesh Kodashim* in his golden garments, because an accuser (i.e., gold) cannot become a defender (of those who sinned with the Golden Calf). If so, how can a calf serve as a *chatas*? He answers that only inside the *Kodesh Kodashim* is the accuser not allowed to serve as the defender. This is what the *Gemara* states precisely in *Rosh Hashanah*, after having asked: But are not the golden garments worn by the *Kohen Gadol* outside (the *Kodesh Kodashim*)? To which the *Gemara* answers that the prohibition applies only inside the *Kodesh Kodashim*. The *Gemara* then asks: Why cannot the *shofar* which is used outside the *Kodesh Kodashim* be taken from a calf? To this, the *Gemara* replies that as the *shofar's* specific task is to serve as a reminder to Hashem, it is, as if it were, used inside the *Kodesh Kodashim*. What we clearly see from this is that concern for the "accuser becoming the defender" generally applies only inside the *Kodesh Kodashim*. Mizrachi says, though, that there are different פָּרִים (adult bulls) — such as those of the *Kohen Gadol*; of *ha'alem davar* — where due to an error in a rabbinic ruling, the people sinned — and of the *Kohen Gadol* on *Yom Kippur* which are all brought in the *Kodesh Kodashim*. Why then do we not say on these that "an accuser cannot become a defender"? He answers this by saying that in all these cases the animals are not slaughtered inside the *Kodesh Kodashim* but only their blood is sprinkled there, and therefore this rule does not apply.

R' Baruch Epstein, in *Tosefes Brachah*, comments that the rule only applies to an enduring reminder of the sin, such as the gold garments which remind us of the Golden Calf. Where, however, the calf is slaughtered, that act annuls the memory of the sin, and one cannot say that an accuser has become a defender. This interpretation, that *Tosefes Brachah* provides, appears earlier in *Yefei To'ar*. Another question that *Tosefes Brachah* asks is also dealt with earlier by the Rebbe, R' Heschel, in his *Chanukas HaTorah*. *Tosefes Brachah* asks how the calf for a *chatas* was slaughtered in public to atone for the sin of the Golden Calf. After all, the Torah states: "the place where the *olah* is slaughtered, the *chatas* shall be slaughtered." The similar location is required, we are taught by *Chazal*, to avoid embarrassing the repenter, since those present will say that he is sacrificing an *olah* rather than a *chatas*. *Tosefes Brachah* answers that *Chazal* in *Sotah* 32 state that the above verse applies to a *chatas* being brought for other sins, whereas the sin of idolatry must be made public. Hashem therefore ordered Aharon to sacrifice the calf of the *chatas* publicly. This interpretation was already brought in *Chanukas HaTorah* to explain *Rashi*, who states that the purpose of the publicly offered *chatas* is: "To tell you that this was the atonement for the Golden Calf." In other words, this *chatas* was slaughtered in public "to tell" us that their sin was that of idolatry.

R' Shlomo Ganzfried in *Aperion* answers the question simply. He says that we avoid any reminder of a sin when the reminder is not meant to atone for that sin; but when the entire purpose is to atone for that sin, we are even obligated to remedy the sin by means of the very thing that caused it. He brings numerous proofs of this from *Chazal*. Therefore, since the Jews sinned with the Golden Calf, they brought a bull to atone for that sin.

Rabbeinu Bachya (who also says that the reason Aharon brought a *chatas* of a calf was to atone for the act of the Golden Calf) explains why Israel's calf is an *olah*, and Aharon's is a *chatas*. With the Golden Calf Aharon did not sin in thought, for he meant what he did for the sake of Heaven. This is evident from the verse, which states (*Sh'mos* 32:35), "Which Aharon made" after the Torah has already stated (ibid. v. 4): "And he took it from their hands, and he formed it with a graving tool, and made it into a graven calf." The Torah wishes to stress that Aharon's only sin consisted of the action of shaping the calf. It was for this reason that he brought a *chatas* as is prescribed for an action. An *olah* sacrifice, on the other hand, is brought because of one's thoughts, and since Israel sinned in thought as well, its *olah* had to be a calf.

Akeidah also follows this line, and states that Aharon sacrificed a *chatas* because he only sinned in deed. Israel, however, brought the required goat for the sin of idolatry, as specified in *Bamidbar* 15, but since their idolatry involved a calf, they also brought a calf.

Ralbag also holds that the sacrifices brought by Israel were those prescribed by the Torah for worshiping idolatry through negligence: a goat for a *chatas* and a bull for an *olah*. According to him, a calf (עֵגֶל) and a bull (פַּר) are the same thing. Aharon was also required to bring a sacrifice, because he was at least the cause. In accordance with this, Ibn Ezra explains the verse (*Vayikra* 9:7), "and make an atonement for yourself, and for the people." There is indeed a special atonement for the people, but in order for that atonement to be effective, you must first bring your own sacrifice for atonement, and after you have atoned and are free of sin, you can atone for the people.

⋞§ And He Offered It for Sin, as the First

According to *Rashi*, the meaning of וַיְחַטְּאֵהוּ — "and he offered it for sin" — is that he offered the *chatas* of the people according to the *halachos* of an ordinary *chatas*. *Sifra* as well as *Chazal* in the *Gemara* state: "Just as the first followed the procedure of a *chatas*, so too does this one follow the procedure of a *chatas*; just as the first needs sprinkling (of the blood) on the four corners (of the Altar), so too does this one need sprinkling on the four corners."

Malbim in *HaTorah VeHaMitzvah* finds a number of differences between the two, in regard to the transporting of the blood and in the burning of the sacrifice. Likewise, according to the different *Targumim* the similarity between the two is only in the sprinkling of the blood. *S'forno* is the only commentator who concludes that the sacrifice of the people was also burned, even though it was a *chatas*, just as the *chatas* of Aharon was burned. This interpretation is unlike that of *Chazal*; but according to Ramban's interpretation that we brought above, that Aharon's *chatas* was burned just as his *chatas* on *Yom Kippur*, there is no reason why the *s'ir* (goat) *chatas* of the people should not also be burned just as their *chatas* of *Yom Kippur*.

But I have also seen *Kli Chemdah*, who writes that indeed, before the sin of the Golden Calf, all of Israel was at the highest level, that of a kingdom of *Kohanim* and a holy nation, and was under the direct intervention of Hashem. After the sin, though, the tribe of Levi was chosen to serve before Hashem, and Israel only obtained atonement through the *Kohanim*. It was for this reason that their *sa'ir*, whose blood was put on the outside Altar, was not burned, as was that of the *Kohanim*, to teach thereby that there was a difference between them and the *Kohanim*. But that only applied to the *s'ir chatas*, whose blood was not brought inside the Sanctuary; in this case, the sacrifice of Israel was not burned, but the *Kohanim* ate the meat and the owners received atonement. But on *Yom Kippur*, when all of Israel repented and returned to their previous status before the sin of the Golden Calf, the blood of their *sa'ir* was sprinkled inside, so as to stress that internally all are one, and therefore their *sa'ir* needed to be burned.

This explanation is of course more *d'rush* than *p'shat*, and these matters still need further study, in terms of *p'shat*, as to what the difference is between the *chatas* of Aharon and that of the nation. It is also worth examining what *Rashi* means when he states that the term "as the first" refers to the calf. What does he wish to convey by this? Does he wish to tell us that whatever was done to the calf was also done to the goat of the nation, including burning? According to Mizrachi and *Gur Aryeh*, *Rashi's* purpose is to explain that the term "the first" refers, not to Aharon's *olah* of a ram, but to his *chatas* of a calf. This, *Rashi* deduced from the word וַיְחַטְּאֵהוּ, "he treated it as a *chatas*." This, however, still requires further study, and the commentators have left room here for someone to distinguish himself by clarifying the matter.

◆§ The Selling of Yosef and the Sin of the Golden Calf

It would appear that the linking in the midrash between the selling of Yosef and the sin of the Golden Calf is purely a chance one, in that these were both sins committed by Israel, one dealing with a goat and the other with a calf. Since these are the two sacrifices that are brought, the midrash linked the two sins to the two sacrifices that were brought when the *Mishkan* was dedicated. But the words "in the beginning" and "at the end" in the midrash indicate more than a casual link. Various *d'rush* works give their own explanations for the linkage. In concluding our comments on this *parashah*, we will cite a number of these interpretations. Although they are *d'rush*, in interpreting the Torah, one should not discriminate against any of the four basic approaches known as *pardes* (פַּרְדֵּס): *p'shat* (פְּשָׁט), the plain meaning; *remez* (רֶמֶז), hints and allusions; *d'rush* (דְּרָשׁ), homiletical interpretation; and *sod* (סוֹד), the hidden kabbalistic meaning. All four have their source in the earlier and later Sages. *Kesav Sofer* sees a direct link between these two events. *Rashi*, following in the footsteps of *Chazal*, mentions earlier on *Sh'mos* 32:4,

> There are those who say that Michah [an idolater mentioned in *Shoftim*] was there (when Aharon was throwing the gold into the fire), having been rescued from among the babies crushed in brick-molds in Egypt, and he had in his possession either a Divine Name or a medallion upon which Moshe had written "Rise up, ox! Rise up, ox!" so as to raise Yosef's coffin from the Nile (Yosef is compared to an ox), and [Michah] threw [the medallion] into the furnace and the (Golden) Calf emerged (*Sanhedrin* 101).

Thus there is a clear link between Yosef and the Golden Calf. Yosef was sold by his brothers into Egypt, and was eventually buried there. The Jews were obligated to raise his coffin from the Nile, for which Moshe used an engraved medallion, and this medallion was instrumental in making the Golden Calf.

Meshech Chochmah also explains matters according to *d'rush*. Yosef, rather than rightfully rebuking his brothers in an attempt to influence their behavior, went instead to his father and spoke *lashon hara* about them. In order to remedy his sin, his brothers threw him into a pit filled with snakes, and as a result he was eventually sold to Egypt and this later led to the Jews' exile in Egypt. Now, with the making of the Golden Calf, it became clear that Yosef had been right in not rebuking them, for Chur, who rebuked the Jews about the Golden Calf, was killed as a result. Thus the sin of the Golden Calf again brought to the fore the sin of the selling of Yosef.

R' Yechezkel Lifshitz in *HaMidrash VeHaMa'as* sees the following link between the two: *Midrash Bereishis Rabbah* (4:13) states that the brothers were angry at Yosef for what they foresaw in the future, namely that Yeravam ben Nevat, one of Yosef's descendants, would renew the worship of the calf. Until the sin of the Golden Calf, the complaint of the brothers had its merits. But when the Jews who emerged from Egypt made the Golden Calf, the brothers were deprived of their righteous anger for their own children were now among those who had been involved in making the Golden Calf. In that case, how could they now complain about Yosef whose more remote descendants would do the same in the future? Therefore, the Jews were charged with sinning "at the beginning and the end."

◆§ This is the Matter Which Hashem Commanded You to Do

The commentators are puzzled at what matter Israel was commanded to do, for after all, the service in the *Mishkan* was done only by Aharon. (See Ibn Ezra and the question in the commentary of *Even Ezer*.) S'forno explains that the Torah refers here to the *semichah* — the laying of hands — on the *olah* and *chatas*, but this is not mentioned specifically in the Torah.

Or HaChaim holds that the reference is to what the Torah states later: "And all the people drew near and they stood before Hashem." The Torah stressed *before Hashem* rather than before the Tent of Assembly, for the purpose was to set their hearts and minds to be worthy of the privilege of standing before Hashem, and it was to this end that they were commanded, "This is the matter which Hashem commanded you to do," namely to remove the *orlas levavchem*, "uncircumcision of their heart," which separates Israel from Hashem.

Thus, we see in *Toras Kohanim*: "Moshe said to Israel, 'Remove the *yetzer hara* from your hearts, so that you will all be united in fear and in a common purpose, to serve the All-Present. Just as He is Alone in the world, so shall your service be to Him alone, as it states, 'And you shall remove the uncircumcision of your hearts.' Why? Because (*Devarim* 10:16-17), 'Hashem, God is the God of Gods and the Lord of Lords.' Therefore the Torah states here that if you do the matter which Hashem commanded you to do, "The glory of Hashem will appear to you." (See *Malbim* who also explains this *Sifra* using *d'rush*.)

Avnei Shoham by R' Moshe Leib Shachor also explains *Toras Kohanim* in accordance to what we said above, that the atonement here was for the sin of idolatry. *Toras Kohanim* interprets the verse, "This is the matter which Hashem commanded you to do," to refer to the commandment (*Sh'mos* 20:3) "You shall have no strange gods before Me," just as *Chazal* (*Sanhedrin* 99) explained the verse (*Bamidbar* 15:31), "For he has despised the word of Hashem and has violated His commandments," as referring to idolatry, since the latter is the act by which the commandments of "I am Hashem" and "You shall have no strange gods" are despised. As *Rashi* explains, these two commandments are "the word of Hashem," for they are the only two commandments that Hashem Himself spoke to all of Israel. With this we understand the *Toras Kohanim*: "This is the matter which Hashem commanded you to do," namely that these are the words that you heard from Hashem himself. *Toras Kohanim* continues by telling us that:

> Moshe said to Israel, "Remove the *yetzer hara* from your hearts, so that you will all be united in fear and in a common purpose, to serve the All-Present; just as He is Alone in the world, so shall your service be to Him alone, as it states, 'And you shall remove the uncircumcision of your hearts.' Why? Because 'Hashem, God, is the God of Gods and the Lord of Lords.' If you do this, then 'The glory of Hashem will appear to you.'"

Toras Kohanim wishes to explain here the word *ta'asu* — "to do." There is doing in removing the evil inclination from your hearts; this is how one fulfills the commandment: "And you shall remove the uncircumcision of your hearts." The sacrifices come to atone for the sin of the Golden Calf; you must now continue the process, by doing the *mitzvah* of nullifying the *yetzer hara* of idolatry.

III.

The Voice of the Father, the King — and God

According to *Chazal*, eating forbidden foods contaminates the soul. Even repentance does not erase the contamination, but only brings forgiveness and pardon. There are literally thousands of references in the *Gemara* to the destructive effect that eating non-kosher food has upon the soul and the spirit. The *Gemara* tells us (*Yoma* 39b): "Do not read it (*Vayikra* 11:43) וְנִטְמֵתֶם (*venitmeisem* — in the Torah the word is written without the א) 'you shall become *tamei*'; but as וּנְטַמְתֶּם, *unetamtem*" (as the word appears in the Torah), implying "you shall become dull hearted."

On the verse (*Vayikra* 11:2), "this is the beast that you shall eat," *Chazal* tell us in the midrash that this is as in the verse (*Tehillim* 40:9), "I delight to do Your will, O Hashem: Your Torah is within my innards." What this means is that one cannot observe the wishes of the Torah and that of Hashem unless the innards are pure, by means of eating pure foods. Eating the various forbidden foods, according to *Chazal*, infects the person who eats them. In *Shabbos* 145 we are told: "Why are non-Jews tainted? Because they eat swarming and creeping things."

Zohar says: "Whoever eats forbidden foods is infected with the 'Other Force,' and an unclean spirit rests upon him, and it appears as if he has no part in Hashem the Most Holy. And whoever becomes unclean, by eating such foods, worships idolatry, for idolatry is an 'abomination' (*Devarim* 7:26), and regarding forbidden foods it is written: 'You shall not eat any abomination' (ibid. 14:3)... and such a person is unclean in this world and in the World to Come."

Our Sages are so stringent about this that it is a specific law in *Shulchan Aruch Yoreh De'ah* 81, that a woman who nurses a Jewish child should not eat forbidden foods [i.e., even if a sick woman is permitted to eat non-kosher foods prescribed to remedy her condition, she should not nurse a child] and it is all the more true that one should not allow an infant to eat non-kosher foods. Although *halachah* does not absolutely require one to stop a child from eating things which are only forbidden by rabbinic law, one should nevertheless stop him from doing so because it makes him dull hearted in the future.

On the verse (*Vayikra* 11:45), "For I am Hashem who took you out of the Land of Egypt," *Chazal* tell us that,

> It was learned in the Beis Midrash of R' Yishmael, "Had I not brought Israel up (הֶעֱלֵיתִי) out of Egypt but as the other nations, that would have been enough for them, and that in itself would be a benefit (מַעֲלְיָיתָא) for them."

Kli Yakar explains the reason for this: Egypt is lower than *Eretz Yisrael*, and therefore its earth is more base. In regard to swarming creatures, the Torah says אַל תְּשַׁקְּצוּ — "do not make yourselves abominable" — while in regard to creeping creatures, it states לֹא תִטַּמְּאוּ — "do not make yourselves *tamei*." *Tumah* is worse than abomination, because creeping things swallow more of the earth. Man was created to walk upright, with his head pointed to the Heavens. The closer his head is to the earth, the closer he is to the dust, and that makes him more *tamei*. "For I am Hashem Who took you out," Who took you out of a lower and more *tamei* place to one which is higher and holy, and it is therefore your duty to suppress the earth element within yourselves, and to separate yourself as much as possible from *tumah*.

Kesav Sofer has a beautiful interpretation of *Chazal*. After *Chazal* state that the entire reason why Hashem brought Israel up from Egypt was because they did not contaminate themselves with swarming creatures, they ask: "Is then their reward (for doing so) greater than (wearing) *tzitzis* or (maintaining accurate) weights?" To this, the answer given is that, "Indeed the reward may not be greater, but these are detestable to eat." This seems strange, for why should there be a greater reward for not eating something which is detestable? But, says *Kesav Sofer*, *Chazal* mean that there is a greater reward for not eating such things if the person's motivation is not because they are detestable, but because that is what the Torah commanded. This is as *Chazal* tell us: "A person should not say, 'I do not like pork,' but (rather) 'I certainly like it, but the Torah forbids it.'" This is the greatness of Israel, because of which Hashem brought them up out of Egypt. They overcome their nature and detest creeping and swarming creatures, not because they are detestable, but because that was Hashem's command.

The Rav of Kutno also has an interpretation that fits into the *p'shat*, based on a specific verse. It is impossible to have the *Shechinah* rest on a body which contaminates itself with forbidden foods, "For I am Hashem who took you out of the Land of Egypt," and you cannot have the *Shechinah* rest upon you there, in an abominable and *tamei* place.

According to S'forno, the laws of *tumah* and *taharah* — of ritual uncleanliness and cleanliness — and of kosher and *treif* — of food that may and may not be eaten — were given after the sin of the Golden Calf. Israel needed a means to purify and sanctify themselves. Until the sin of the Golden Calf they were worthy of having the *Shechinah* rest upon them without any intermediate means, as it states (*Sh'mos* 20:21), "Wherever I will have My name mentioned, I will come to you and bless you," and as promised us for the World to Come (*Vayikra* 26:11), "and I will place My dwelling within them and My soul will not detest you." But after the sin of the Golden Calf, Hashem refused to let His *Shechinah* dwell among them, as it states (*Sh'mos* 33:3), "I will not come up in your midst." Afterwards, with his prayers, Moshe was able to have the *Shechinah* rest in their midst through the *Mishkan*, its vessels, its servants, and its sacrifices, until they merited (*Vayikra* 9:23) "And the glory of Hashem appeared to all the nation" and the descent of fire from the Heavens. At that time, Hashem saw fit to rectify the people's nature by giving them laws regarding their food and procreation, and He told them which things defile the soul. He also prohibited (intercourse with) the *niddah* (a woman with a menstrual emission), *zavah* (one with a bloody genital emission not at the time of the regular menstrual cycle) or *yoledes* (a woman who has just given birth), so as to sanctify their descendants and to purify them of all *tumah*. Had the Jews not sinned, they would not, according to S'forno, have needed any such means for sanctifying themselves with the holiness of Hashem.

◄§ Is there a Reason for the Prohibition?

In addition to the specific reason given by the Torah, namely the *tumah* and detestation of forbidden foods, the commentators deal with logical and natural explanations of the prohibition against eating certain foods. *Rambam* in *Moreh Nevuchim* (3:48) proves that the forbidden foods are harmful to the body. According to him, it is not the signs of a kosher animal that make it kosher, nor do the signs of a non-kosher animal make it non-kosher. These signs only serve to indicate which animals are permitted and forbidden — of themselves, because Hashem knew of the injury that forbidden foods cause to man.

Ramban on *Vayikra* 11 also says that there are forbidden creatures whose damage to health is apparent to people.

But Abarbanel comments on these statements and says:

> Far be it from me to believe this, for then the Torah given by Hashem is no more than a minor medical treatise, and this is not in keeping with its greatness and eternity. In addition, we ourselves see that the other nations do eat these forbidden foods, and this does not in any way affect their health. In addition, if the reason is medical, then there are also various plants which are harmful, yet the Torah does not forbid them.

As a result of this, Abarbanel holds that it is clear that the Torah did not forbid these for medical reasons but because of the invisible effects they have on man's soul. The Torah never refers to such foods as "harmful." *Tumah* refers to the soul. The Torah wishes to prevent the defilement of the soul caused by eating non-kosher foods. Foods which are *tahor* create blood which is *tahor*, while food which is *tamei* creates blood which is *tamei*. In addition, foods which are *tamei* are linked to various forms of idolatry. In different countries even today all types of detestable creatures are eaten as part of idolatrous services. The Torah therefore referred to these as *to'evah* — abominations — a word which, as is known, relates to idolatry.

R' David Zvi Hoffman also uses Abarbanel's reasons to question *Rambam's* and *Ramban's* views that the reasons for the prohibitions are medical. He adds other questions to those posed by Abarbanel, as, for example, if the reasons are medical, why did the Torah conceal this fact? After all, people would be more scrupulous in the observance of these laws if they knew that eating such items would be harmful to their health.

He brings various reasons for the prohibition. For example, there are those who see this as a means by which to separate us from idolatry. The Egyptians deified various animals. The Torah therefore decreed that certain of these animals are to be used for sacrifices to Hashem, and through this these particular species were then permitted as food, while the others are *tamei*. Others tend to see these laws as a means by which to separate Israel from the other nations. The Jewish people were given special dietary laws

> so that they would keep apart from the other nations, and so that they might be marked as a singular nation, or so that they might feel themselves exalted above the others as a holy nation, and they would remain separate from the other nations.

R' David Zvi Hoffman rejects this view. There is no basis in our *parashah* for claiming that the reason for the *kashrus* laws is to separate us from others. On the contrary, the Torah writes the opposite: It is because Israel was separated by Hashem to be holy that they were forbidden to eat meat which is abominable or *tamei*.

R' David Zvi Hoffman also rejects the view that the seemingly negative comments about the non-kosher animals stem from an approach of good and bad in the Creation. One who delves into the Torah does not find a negative approach in itself to non-kosher animals, and one is forbidden to pain such animals just as one is forbidden to pain kosher animals. Thus we read (*Sh'mos* 23:5), "If you see the donkey of your enemy falling under its load, you shall surely help with him." From this we learn that the Torah does not have an absolutely negative approach to certain types of animals which Jews are forbidden to eat.

R' David Zvi Hoffman therefore explains the *parashah* in the spirit of R' Samson Raphael Hirsch. With this *mitzvah*, Hashem paved a way for Israel to play a spiritual function in the world. Indeed we find a certain amount of separation among various animals among other nations as well, and Noach already differentiated between the kosher and non-kosher species and brought sacrifices only from the former.

Just as recognizing the existence of Hashem brought man to seek ways to draw close to his Creator and to use sacrifices for this purpose, so too did this recognition lead him to use those species of animals which are closer to man's nature.

Later, when Israel was chosen at Sinai to become a nation of *Kohanim*, the Torah decreed that they might only eat animals of those species which may be offered as sacrifices, and to slaughter them the same way that sacrifices are slaughtered. Before that, man was permitted to eat only vegetation. The conditions later on caused Hashem to grant permission for man to eat meat, but only within the limitations of observing Hashem's *mitzvos*. At first, only the meat of sacrifices was permitted to be eaten. Later, other meat was also permitted, but this permission too was subject to stringent limitations, all following the pattern of the sacrifices and the way these are rendered permissible for the Altar.

R' Samson Raphael Hirsch in his *Chorev* discusses the hidden effect on one's soul of eating non-kosher food, to the extent of changing the person's nature and character. He says: "Just as the sanctity of the Temple can be defiled, so too your own bodily temple can become defiled by *tumah*." Thus one must preserve his body so as to keep it holy. By eating forbidden foods, man's animalistic force will gain strength and will tip the scales to the side of evil. Hashem knows and recognizes the characteristics of every thing. He recognizes our individuality and the composition of the forces within us.

Do you recognize the nature of the world which surrounds you? The nature of your individuality? The way you are maintained? The relationship between the powers of the body and their relationship to the powers of the soul? When you recognize all these, you will understand; and if you do not understand, follow the Lord your God who took you out of the Land of Egypt.

◆§ The Influence on Man Internally

Akeidah explains in depth the injurious nature of forbidden foods on man's soul. His words serve as a source for some of the commentators brought above. Hashem did not leave out anything in His world. He created all creatures and knows the general good in each case. One cannot ask why He created this particular creature or that one, just as one cannot ask why, in man's body, each organ is separate and the entire body does not consist only of a heart or of a head. Each organ has its own unique purpose, and the same is true for each creature. Just as man's body has a variety of organs, so too does Hashem's world have a variety of creatures. One can only understand the glory of this plan if he can recognize its total extent and orderliness, and that is not given to man.

In this incredible plan, which is absolutely beyond man's comprehension, Hashem gives expression to His love for Israel, the nation which is more remarkable than any other, in that it is subject to Hashem's *hashgachah p'ratis* — His personal attention. The Torah was given to Israel to improve their character, and thereby they will be qualitatively better than the others. Not only did Hashem order us to restrict our appetites so as to purify us, but He also commanded us not to eat those foods which develop coarseness. People's digestion suits the variable nature of human beings. A farmer eats coarse foods, while the refined foods of kings are strange to him. People's natures vary in accordance with the climate, the type of work in which they are engaged, and their diets. Those who live near the North or South Pole are small in stature, and are different in intelligence and ability, to the extent that some act like wild men of the jungle, even eating their own children. By the same token, the food of the Holy Nation, the Jewish people, is different from that of the other nations.

Akeidah refutes those who claim that the reason for these food restrictions is medical, for the prohibition applies even when a small quantity of forbidden food is mixed with a large quantity of permitted food, although the danger to one's health is then almost non-existent. The reason for the prohibition is only because forbidden foods form bad characteristics. Proper belief is to be found only in the hearts of those who serve Hashem and who observe His commandments, as it states (*Tehillim* 51:10), "Create in me a clean heart, O Hashem; and renew a right spirit within me." Forbidden foods stultify those who eat them, as *Chazal* tell us: " 'This you shall not eat' (*Vayikra* 11:4) — This is what is seen in (*Tehillim* 18:31), 'the word of Hashem is refined.' The commandments were only given to refine mankind."

Chazal in *Midrash Tanchuma* gave an analogy of a doctor who went to visit two patients. He saw that one had a terminal illness, so he told the members of the person's household to give him whatever he asked for. Then he saw another who would live, and prescribed specific foods the patient should eat and warned him not to eat certain other foods. Those who were there asked the doctor why he permitted one patient to eat everything, while he restricted the other's diet. The doctor answered them, "The second patient will live, so I told him what to eat and what not to eat, whereas the first is terminally ill, so I told him he can eat whatever he wants." Thus Hashem permitted the non-Jews to eat all creeping and swarming creatures, but for the Jews who are to remain alive, He told them (*Vayikra* 20:26), "Be holy for Me, because I am holy," and (ibid. 11:43) "Do not make your souls abominable." The message contained in this midrash is the need for us to rectify and exalt ourselves through the laws of *kedushah* and *taharah* — sanctity and ritual cleanliness — for the good of our souls.

This does away with the view of those who see the laws of *kashrus* as being on medical grounds, says *Kli Yakar*. Using medical grounds to explain these laws can only serve to lead non-Jews astray and make them think that by keeping the laws they will be more healthy. The midrash therefore says that this is not the reason, and that the purpose for the *mitzvah* is to keep our souls pure. The non-Jews are not commanded to do so, for in any event they do not have a superior soul.

According to *Kli Yakar*, this concept is also to be found at the beginning of the *parashah*. "And Hashem spoke to Moshe and Aharon and said to them." The commentators have given various explanations for the Hebrew word אֲלֵהֶם — "to them." But according to *Kli Yakar*, this hints at the fact that such foods form coarseness and cruelty among those who eat them. The effect of forbidden foods is on the soul. They form coarseness and cruelty, for whatever is derived from the *tamei* becomes like it. The proof of this is that if a cow is born from a donkey, the *halachah* is that the cow is forbidden to be eaten. This teaches us that the creature which gives birth leaves its imprint on the one to which it gave birth. The Torah says (*Vayikra* 11:4): "This is what you shall not eat (מִמַּעֲלֵי הַגֵּרָה וּמִמַּפְרִסֵי הַפַּרְסָה) from among those which chew the cud and from among those which have split hooves." The extra letter *mem*, meaning "from among," which modifies the phrase, "*from among* those which chew the cud and *from among* those which have split hooves," comes to teach us that even if there are animals which have both signs of *kashrus* but were born of non-kosher animals, such as a cow born from a camel, etc., they are not kosher. On this we are told (*Iyov* 14:4), "Can something *tahor* come from something *tamei*?" After all, each child is part of its mother, and where impurity leaves its mark upon the progeny, there is no possible way to alter it.

Tazria – תַזְרִיעַ

I.

Why Do the Actions of Bris Milah Take Precedence over the Observance of Shabbos?

hazal deduced various *halachos* of *milah* from the verse "and on the eighth day the skin of his *orlah* shall be circumcised." The Hebrew word וּבַיּוֹם — "and on the (eighth) day" — teaches us that a *bris milah* is performed only during the day, i.e., after sunrise (*Megillah* 20a); that the *bris milah* takes precedence over the observance of the *Shabbos* day (*Shabbos* 132 — The concept of "precedence" here — דּוֹחֶה in Hebrew — refers to the fact that even though a *bris milah* involves certain violations of the *Shabbos* laws, it is nevertheless permitted on *Shabbos* if that is the eighth day since the child is born (the day of birth is counted as well); and other *halachos* are deduced from every word in the verse. The verse in question is mentioned almost parenthetically, in the context of the laws of *tumah* — ritual impurity — that apply to a woman who gives birth, as will be clarified later. The law that the *bris milah* must be performed on the eighth day appears earlier in the Torah (*Bereishis* 17:12), "And he that is eight days old shall be circumcised among you, every male child in your generations." It is because of the repetition of the verse here that it is used to derive so many *halachos*.

Tosefes Brachah explains why *bris milah* takes precedence over *Shabbos*. On the surface, since both are a sign — *os* — of the covenant between Israel and Hashem, there should be no reason for the *mitzvah* of *bris milah* to take precedence over *Shabbos*. But *Chazal* in *Sanhedrin* 58 say that a non-Jew who observes *Shabbos* deserves capital punishment, as it is written (*Bereishis* 8:2), "Day and night they shall not rest." Now, the one difference between the Jew and the non-Jew is the *bris milah*. Without the *mitzvah* of *bris milah*, Jews, too, would have been forbidden to observe *Shabbos* because of the Divine edict to all of creation, that "Day and night they shall not rest." It follows, therefore, that the *mitzvah* of *bris milah* is what obligates the Jew to keep *Shabbos*. As such, the *bris milah* is a first *kedushah* — state of holiness — which leads to a second. If there is no *bris milah*, there is no keeping of *Shabbos*. It is thus proper that *bris milah* should take precedence over *Shabbos*, because it makes one obligated to keep *Shabbos*. (The same idea expressed by *Tosefes Brachah* is to be found in *Chiddushei HaRitva* on *Sukkah* 43.)

Tosefes Brachah also answers the commentators who ask why *bris milah* takes precedence over *Shabbos*, when *shofar* and *lulav* do not. As regards the latter, *Chazal* fear that a person may carry the *shofar* or *lulav* four *amos* — cubits — in a *reshus harabim* — a public domain — to ask a Torah Sage about the relevant *halachos*, and therefore we do not use either when the *Yom Tov* coincides with *Shabbos*. Why then are we not concerned that the *mohel* will carry the knife four *amos* in the *reshus harabim*? R' Baruch Epstein answers this as follows: In regard to *Rosh Hashanah* and *Sukkos*, which fall on the 1st and 15th of *Tishrei* respectively, our generations are no longer expert in determining the New Moon; thus it is theoretically possible that the *Yom Tov* that coincides with *Shabbos* should, in fact, have fallen on Sunday. *Chazal* therefore forbade the use of the *shofar* or *lulav* on *Yom Tov* which falls on *Shabbos*. In regard to *bris milah*, though, it is perfectly clear which is the correct day, for the Torah specifies "the eighth day," even if this is *Shabbos*, and *Chazal* therefore did not forbid the *bris milah* from being held on that day.

There are also various explanations why the *bris milah* may not be performed at night. A beautiful interpretation is given by R' Benzion Firer in his *Hegionah Shel Torah*. When blood is spilled for the purpose of a *mitzvah*, it is done in broad daylight. Only the criminal spilling of blood takes place in the shadow of night. People do not hide their honest deeds in the dark. The Torah says (*Bereishis* 17:26), "On this very day Avraham and his son Yishmael were circumcised." Here, the *Tosafos* in *Da'as Zekeinim* comment: "What is meant by 'on this very day'? It means at the height of the day." As *Kli Yakar* explains, Avraham was not content merely to ensure that his *bris milah* would take place during the day and not the night, but made sure to perform it in broad daylight, at the height of the day, when all would be present, since he was not afraid of those who might see.

In a similar vein, cases which may entail the death penalty are also judged only during the day. *Chazal* tell us in *Sanhedrin* 34: From where do we deduce this? R' Shimi bar Chiye said, "a verse states (*Bamidbar* 25:4), 'Hang them up before Hashem against the sun.' " Furthermore, not only is one not judged at night but a person who is sentenced to death cannot be executed at night, for, as the *Gemara* states, "Should he be executed at night? (This cannot be done, because) one needs 'against the sun.' "

This applies not only to humans, but to animals as well. Sacrifices are brought only during the day, for Israel was commanded to bring its sacrifices only during the day and not at night. Just as sacrifices are slaughtered only during the day, so too must the sprinkling of their blood take place on the day that the animals are slaughtered, as the Torah states (*Vayikra* 7:16), "on the day when he offers his sacrifice," implying that the offering of the blood is on the day of the sacrifice. Indeed, if the sun sets, the blood may no longer be sprinkled (*Rambam Hil. Ma'asei HaKorbanos* 4:1, based on *Zevachim* 56).

On the other hand, when it comes to spilling of blood of animals which is not within the framework of a *mitzvah*, there is no reason to boast about our deed, as *Chinuch* explains in *Mitzvah* 157:

> Why is one to cover it (the blood of a slaughtered beast or fowl) with earth? Among the foundations for this *mitzvah* is that the life-force depends on the blood, as (the Torah) says in regard to the prohibition against blood. It is therefore fitting for us to cover the life-force and to conceal it from the eyes of the beholders before we eat the meat, for by eating the meat while the blood is before us we impart a measure of cruelty to our souls.

This does not apply to the blood of sacrifices, where there is no imperfection in our actions. In that case we do not acquire any measure of cruelty, for this is the commandment of the Torah. It is for this reason that sacrifices are brought specifically during the day, in broad daylight.

Oznayim LaTorah explains the connection between the *mitzvah* of *bris milah* and the previous topic in the Torah — the *tumah* of a woman who has just given birth. When a non-Jewish male wishes to enter the ranks of Judaism, he must have the two signs of *taharah* — ritual purity: *tevilah* in a *mikveh*, and a *bris milah*. But when a male is born a Jew, his parents have already preceded his birth by an act of *taharah*, that being the *tevilah* that a woman undergoes when she observes the laws of *niddah* and *tevilah*, as the Torah states (*Vayikra* 12:2), "According to the days of the separation for her infirmity shall she be unclean." Thus, when a son is born in *taharah*, "on the eighth day the skin of his *orlah* shall be circumcised," so that he now has both signs of *taharah*. So too did Shlomo say (*Koheles* 11:2), "Give a portion to seven, and also to eight." On this, *Chazal* expounded,

"Give a portion to seven" — this refers to the seven days of *niddah*; "and also to eight" — this refers to the eight days of *bris milah*. Hashem said: "If you observe the (seven) days of *niddah*, I will give you a son and you will circumcise him on the eighth day." This is (the promise contained in) "and on the eighth day the skin of his *orlah* shall be circumcised" (*Niddah* 31).

Thus we see the two are linked together, both symbolizing signs of *taharah*. We can also understand why the *parashah* of the woman giving birth follows that of the animals which may be eaten. After the Torah has told us which creatures are *tahor* and which are not, it concludes, "This is the Torah of the beasts, and of the fowl, and of every living creature," and then it continues to tell us the laws concerning man and his signs of *taharah*.

⋑§ The Fate of Man and the Fate of the Beast

Midrash Rabbah on *Emor*, chapter 27, draws a parallel between man and beast. There we are told:

"Man and beast, You will save them, O Hashem (*Tehillim* 36:7)." R' Yitzchak said, "The judgment of man and of beasts is equal. With regard to man it is stated: 'And on the eighth day his foreskin shall be circumcised.' And with regard to animals it is stated (*Vayikra* 22:27): 'From the eighth day on, he will be acceptable as a sacrifice.' "

It is thus that Rabbeinu Bachya deduces in *Parashas Lech Lecha* that the *mitzvah* of the *bris milah* is like a sacrifice, and just as the blood of a sacrifice atones on the Altar, the blood of the *bris milah* also atones. That is also the reason why the *mitzvah* is on the eighth day, for a sacrifice only atones when the animal is at least eight days or older. Moreover, the festival meal at a *bris milah* is seen by Rabbeinu Bachya as part of the sacrifice. Just as we are told by a sacrifice (*Sh'mos* 29:33), "And they shall eat those things with which the atonement was made," so too is there a festive meal on the day of the *bris milah*.

Tosefes Brachah, though, learns the purpose of the meal at the *bris milah* from what *Chazal* tell us (*Niddah* 31),"Why did the Torah ordain *milah* on the eighth day?" There, we are told that it is a *mitzvah* of the Torah to have *simchah* — rejoicing — and all agree, as *Rashi* explains, that all rejoice at a festive meal. Thus it is not just a custom, for, as *Chazal* tell us, "Why did the Torah ordain" that there must be *simchah*? which implies a festive meal. R' Baruch Epstein is therefore surprised at those commentators on the *Shulchan Aruch* and the *Gra* who search for a source for the required festive meal. The *Torah Temimah* is difficult to understand. The *Gra* does not seek a source, but explains the source found in *Pirkei d'Rebbi Eliezer*, 29, which derives from the verse (*Bereishis* 21:8), "And Avraham made a large feast on the day that his son Yitzchak was weaned," that one makes a festive meal on the eighth day when a child has his *bris milah*. *Pirkei d'Rebbi Eliezer* learns the word "weaned" — in Hebrew הַגָּמֵל — as if it was composed of two separate elements — ה, which is five, and גָּמֵל, as the letter *gimmel*, which is three, thus adding up to eight, the eighth day on which Yitzchak entered the *bris milah*. *Avnei Shoham*, who quotes *Pirkei d'Rebbi Eliezer*, adds a note of his own, that not only is this a *se'udas mitzvah*, but it is also a *se'udas hoda'ah* — a thanksgiving meal — by the woman who has given birth, for emerging from danger.

Regarding the equation between man and beast we made earlier, we can add that *Rambam* in *Moreh Nevuchim* 3, chapter 49, explains that the reason why *bris milah* is on the eighth day is due to the fact that each animal is weak when first born, and for the first seven days after its birth is still as if in its mother's womb; during that time it might well die, as if it had been stillborn or aborted. Only by the eighth day is the animal considered to have survived its birth. And it is on this day that the Jewish male has his *bris milah*. This period of seven days, says *Rambam*, is a fixed measure, not subject to individual conjecture. The source of this is in *Midrash Rabbah*, at the beginning of *Parashas Ki Seitzei* and in *Yalkut Shimoni Parashas Lech Lecha*, *remez* 84. R' Baruch Epstein then asks: Why is it that for the *bris milah* the child is considered to have survived his birth if he reaches his eighth day, while the *pidyon haben* — the redemption of the firstborn male — requires waiting thirty days? He answers as follows. In most cases, if a child lives for seven days after birth, he will survive. For a minority of children, though, one cannot establish this until the child is thirty days old. In regard to *bris milah*, we follow the majority, for most children are healthy after seven days. With *pidyon haben*, though, there is a monetary obligation involved, for the father must give five *sela'im* to a *Kohen* to redeem his son, and the rule is that one does not follow the majority in questions of financial obligations. Thus one must wait for thirty days, at which time there is no longer a doubt that the child will survive.

⋅ఈ Seven Denotes Perfection

Chazal in *Niddah* 31 ask: "Why did the Torah say that *bris milah* is on the eighth day? So that it should not be that all rejoice, while his father and mother are sad." *Rashi* explains that the question of the *Gemara* is why the *bris milah* takes place on the eighth day rather than on the seventh. *Maharsha* comments וְהוּא דָחוּק — "that is strained." He says that had it not been for *Rashi's* comments, he would have explained *Chazal's* question to mean why it was that the Torah states that the *bris milah* should be on the eighth day after the woman gives birth, as if to connect the law of *bris milah* to the law that pertains to women who give birth. On this, the *Gemara* answers that the connection between the two is "that it should not be that all rejoice, while his father and mother are sad" because the mother is still ritually impure (*t'me'ah*). The Torah therefore waited until the woman is no longer *tamei* — on the eighth day — and then commanded that the child be circumcised.

Torah Temimah says that had it not been for what *Rashi* wrote, he would have explained the question of the *Gemara* as to why the Torah made the *bris milah* on the eighth day rather than on the day the child is born, as for example in the case of a non-Jewish infant slave, who is circumcised on the day he is born. This interpretation is already brought in *Or HaChaim*. It nevertheless would seem that the question of the *Gemara* is indeed as *Rashi* explained it, as to why the *bris milah* should not be on the seventh day, as indicated by *Chazal* in *Shabbos* 132: "(The word) שְׁמִינִי — 'eighth' — is meant to exclude the seventh day." According to *Or HaChaim*, though, the *Gemara* should have said that the word שְׁמִינִי is meant to exclude the day of the child's birth.

We must nevertheless explain why the *Gemara* assumes that the seventh day should be more appropriate for *bris milah* than the eighth day. The commentary of *Tosefes Brachah* is very logical, for he points out that the number seven is often used to indicate perfection. For example, we find that after the *molad* — the point at which the new moon begins to appear — for a period of seven days the moon grows a little each day and becomes more complete. It is for this reason that according to one opinion in *Shulchan Aruch, Orach Chaim* 426, *kiddush levanah*, the blessings recited over the New Moon, should not take place until the eighth day after the *molad*, for by then its light is complete.

We also find seven as a completion of matters in *II Melachim* (4:35), "And the boy sneezed seven times and revived." Again we find there (5:14), "He immersed himself seven times in the Jordan and his skin became like the skin of a small boy." Similarly, when a person is a *zav* or *zavah*, the disease ends after seven days. We also have seven days of festivities after a wedding and seven days of mourning, for during the course of seven days both joy and mourning are exhausted. Seven also represents the number of days of the week, the number of years in a *shemittah* cycle, the number of *shemittah* cycles in a *yovel*, the number of branches of the *Menorah* in the *Beis HaMikdash*, the number of sprinklings on *Yom Kippur*, and innumerable other matters. *Rashi's* question, then, is why the *bris milah* should not be on the seventh day, for seven always implies a completion.

Torah Temimah explains that the reason the eighth day was chosen for the *bris milah* is so that the child will have lived through a *Shabbos* before the event, since *Shabbos* strengthens and heals a person. We find this in the Midrash: "Before *Shabbos* came, the world was weak and trembling, and when *Shabbos* came, its powers were strengthened." This reason, and the support from the words of *Chazal*, are brought by *Or HaChaim*. But the source for this is *Mechilta* on *Sh'mos* 31, which states, "Great is *Shabbos*, for the infant is not circumcised until he has lived through a *Shabbos*, as it states, 'And at the age of eight days every male shall be circumcised among you.' " Thus we see clearly that the reason the *bris milah* is on the eighth day is so that the infant will have lived through a *Shabbos*. This idea is not, as *Torah Temimah* thought, merely *d'rush*.

◈§ So that All Will Rejoice

There is a direct link in our *parashah* between birth and *bris milah*, in that while the Torah discusses the *tumah* and *taharah* of the woman who has given birth, it mentions — incidentally, as it were — that on the eighth day the child has his *bris milah*. It is as if the Torah had written, "and on the eighth day the skin of his *orlah* shall be circumcised," so as to give the mother time to recover, become ritually pure (*t'horah*), and participate in the joy of entering her child in the *bris* of Avraham Avinu. This is in keeping with *Chazal*, who state that the reason for the *bris milah* on the eighth day is so that there should not be a situation where all are rejoicing, while the father and mother are sad.

The Torah speaks of the *bris milah* as something which is obvious, and links it to the end of the mother's *tumah*. It is in this spirit that *Netziv* explains it in both *Ha'amek Davar* and *Harchev Davar*. According to his interpretation, already in the days of Avraham, husband and wife kept apart for a number of days after the woman gave birth. It was for this reason that the *bris milah* was set for the eighth day. *Avnei Shoham* quotes, in this regard, the words of R' Assi in *Shabbos* 135: "One whose mother is *t'me'ah* due to giving birth is circumcised on the eighth day, and one whose mother is not *tame'ah* due to giving birth (e.g., if the birth took place when the mother was non-Jewish, and she converted the next day) is not circumcised on the eighth day, as it states, 'If a woman conceives a seed and bears a male... she shall be *t'me'ah* seven days.... and on the eighth day the skin of his *orlah* shall be circumcised.' " R' Shimon bar Yohai, too, who gives the reason for the *bris milah* on the eighth day so as not to have all rejoicing while the father and mother are sad, connects the *mitzvah* of the *bris milah* with the woman who conceives and bears.

II.
The Transition from Tumah to Taharah

The differences between the *tumah* following giving birth to a son and that following giving birth to a daughter; the nature of the *tumah*; the obligation to bring a *korban* as atonement; the link between the *tumah* and the requirement to have the *bris milah* on the eighth day — all of these have been topics that the commentators on our *parashah* have discussed.

R' Samson Raphael Hirsch holds that the *tumah* and *taharah* here serve as an educational tool for man, so as to have him rise above his physical characteristics, and to impose moral and ethical standards on his body and his actions. The Torah refers to the action which precedes giving birth as *tazria* — conceiving seed. This is a physical term which applies equally to all life, such as (*Bereishis* 1:12), "grass yielding seed" — *mazri'a zera*. Because of the spiritual effect which this action involves, the Torah requires man to ascend by the power of his will and thoughts above his physical dimension, and to impose a moral and spiritual dimension upon his actions, a dimension stemming from the *Shechinah* itself. This is the reason for the *halachos* involved in the act of giving birth, whose source is the recognition of the superiority of the spirit in the world. It offers proof that man is different from other creatures.

In his introduction to the *parashah* of *tumah*, R' David Zvi Hoffman also develops this idea, using his own method. He classifies *tumah* into three categories, analogous to the three categories of spiritual sanctification. These are: (a) *tumah* through the dead; (b) *tumah* related to sexual relations, including *ba'al keri* — one who has a seminal emission — *zav* and *zavah* (a man or woman with a pathological genital discharge), *niddah*, and a *yoledes*, a woman who gave birth; (c) *tumah* of *negaim*, various plagues in one's body or other objects.

In the first category, the person is only excluded from the *Machaneh HaShechinah* — the Camp of the *Shechinah*. The second category excludes one even from the *Machaneh HaLevi'im* — the Camp of the Levites. And the third category goes even further, excluding one even from the *Machaneh Yisrael* — the Camp of Israel. Paralleling these are three levels of acts which drive a person from *kedushah* — sanctification. These are: (a) sins between man and God; (b) sins between man and himself and his soul; (c) sins between man and his fellow-man. The first, revolt against the Kingdom of Heaven, causes the punishment of death, the opposite of eternal life in the presence of the *Shechinah*. By the same token, sacrifices to false gods are the sacrifices of the dead. This category is thus clearly analogous to the *tumah* of the dead.

The second category, man's *tumah* related to sexual relations, stems from an exaggerated amount of frivolity and sensuality. One who is afflicted with these faults must distance himself not only from the camp of the *Shechinah*, but even from the camp of those who are close to Hashem. Finally, the *tumah* of *negaim* is a result of sins between man and his fellow-man, as we see where Miriam became a *metzora'as* for speaking *lashon hara*, and the Torah placed the command of (*Devarim* 24:8) "guard against the *nega* of the *tzara'as*" next to that of "remember what Hashem your God did to Miriam." This *tumah* requires social ostracism — being driven from contact with any other person — so as to prevent the damage caused by one who poisons society.

Rabbeinu Bachya and other early authorities hold that the *tumah* of childbearing goes back to the sin of Eve, as a result of which the world was changed. Had it not been for that, then (*Yechezkel* 16:7), "I would have caused you to multiply as the sprout of the field" — humans would bear children without lust or passion. *Kli Yakar* even finds a hint at this interpretation. According to him, this is what the Torah means when it writes, "she shall become pure from the source of her blood," namely from the earliest source of her blood, as *Chazal* tell us in *Eiruvin* 100: " 'I will greatly multiply your suffering' (*Bereishis* 3:16) refers to the blood of *niddah*."

Paane'ach Raza also has a new interpretation along these lines, when he writes that the Torah decreed seven days of *tumah* for childbirth, just as the seven days of mourning for someone who died. Both of these matters — natural childbirth and death — were decreed because of the sin of Adam, and their *tumah* is similar.

I do not normally engage in kabbalah, but in my heart I think that it is possible that the three types of *tumah* which R' David Zvi Hoffman categorizes stem from the original contamination of the serpent, and especially in the light of the fact that *Chazal* say that the serpent was suffering from a *nega*; hence, this is the worst category of *tumah*. It is possible that the greater degree of *tumah* when a woman gives birth to a girl is also due to the fact that Chavah sinned more than Adam.

The Tzaddik of Kotzk has a beautiful interpretation of this topic. The key to giving birth lies in the hands of Hashem, as the Torah says (*Bereishis* 29:31), "And Hashem opened her womb." There is thus a spiritual influence of the *Shechinah*, the Divine Presence, in childbirth. If this influence departs, *tumah* comes in its place, just as when the soul departs the body, *tumah* takes over.

◆§ The Tumah for a Male and that for a Female

Many of the commentators of the Torah explain that the reason why the *tumah* after giving birth to a daughter is twice the length of that after giving birth to a son is due to physical and natural processes. A female exudes more substances into its mother's womb than does a male, and the process of eliminating these after childbirth is thus more lengthy and complex than after the birth of a boy.

Ramban and Ibn Ezra even explain that this has been verified biologically. Abarbanel also follows this path, but he expands the explanation to the days of purification after the days of *tumah*. In the case of giving birth to a male, the *tumah* lasts for seven days, followed by thirty-three days of purification, and in these last thirty-three days there is also a certain degree of *tumah* in that the woman is still forbidden to eat *kodashim* — sanctified foods. The total of both periods together is forty days. In the case of giving birth to a female, though, the *tumah* is fourteen days, while the period of purification thereafter amounts to sixty-six days, giving a total of eighty days. These two periods correspond to the time until the shape of the fetus is formed in the womb, for according to *Chazal* this is forty days, while according to R' Yishmael a male is discernible from the forty-first day and a female from the eighty-first day. Nature proves, says Abarbanel, that R' Yishmael is correct. During the period that the fetus is being shaped, blood and other fluids are secreted into the mother's womb so as to shape the child, therefore Hashem's wisdom saw need to cleanse the body for a corresponding number of days after childbirth.

S'forno also sees the reason of the woman's *tumah* as due to the fact that during this time the child is nourished by decayed matter and the *tumah* of *niddah*, because of the wastes which are still being discharged from the woman. When a girl is born, this process takes longer than when a boy is born. The reason that the Torah ordered that the *bris milah* take place on the eighth day is by that time the *tamei* blood with which the child was nourished has been consumed, and he has become fit to take on *kedushah* and to enter the holy covenant of the *bris milah*.

R' David Zvi Hoffman also links the *bris milah* on the eighth day to the *tumah* of seven days, and says that the Torah might have reduced the number of days a woman is *tamei* after the birth of a son to seven days so that she can be *t'horah* at her son's *bris milah*, or, possibly, that the *bris milah* itself may have the effect of speeding up the *taharah*. This interpretation is in keeping with that of the great kabbalist, R' Avraham Azulai, in his *Ba'al Bris Avraham*, where he writes that the purpose of the *bris milah* on the eighth day is to eliminate the *tumah* which the *niddah* imparts to the woman who gives birth. This, he explains, is alluded to in the verse (*Koheles* 11:2), "Give a portion to seven, and also to eight," which may be understood as linking the seven days of *tumah* to the sanctity of the *bris milah* on the eighth day.

There is a clear hint at the substantive link between *bris milah* and what preceded it in *Targum Yehonasan*. He says: "And on the eighth day she is permitted (to her husband), and the *orlah* is cut from the child." Here the link between the two is stressed, with the emphasis being that both the woman and the child enter a stage of *taharah* on the eighth day.

In his *Oznayim LaTorah*, the Gaon of Lutzk explains beautifully that the entering of a son into the covenant of Avraham is done by *tevilah* in a *mikveh* and by the *bris milah*, as is the case where a non-Jew converts to Judaism. With a convert it is he who undergoes both rituals himself. In the case of the birth of a son of a Jewish mother, it is the woman who goes to the *mikveh*, while the son undergoes the *bris milah*.

Chazal in *Niddah* 31 say:

> His students asked R' Shimon bar Yochai: "Why did the Torah say that for a male the mother is *t'me'ah* for seven days, and for a female she is *t'me'ah* for fourteen days?" He told them: "When a woman is in the throes of labor pains, she impulsively swears that she will have no further (sexual) relations with her husband. When

she gives birth to a male and all rejoice, she takes (her vow) back after seven (days), and when she gives birth to a female where all are sad, she takes [the vow] back after fourteen days."

What *Chazal* do not specify is why all are happy when a son is born. *Rashi* explains that the people are happy because of the festive meal at the *bris milah*. *Maharsha*, though, says that they are happy that a male was born because he will not have to suffer the pains of childbirth in the future.

Maharsha's explanation is difficult, for if that is so, why are all happy? Only the parents' joy should be justified. But it is possible that the joy is linked to the removal of the *orlah* and the rectification of the sin of Adam, as we mentioned. The *bris milah* brings the child and his mother into the world of *taharah* and removes the impurities through the power of the *mitzvah*. But when a female is born, she reminds us of Chavah and the contamination brought to the world because of her.

◄§ The Reason for the Korban

According to Abarbanel, the *korban* brought by the woman who has given birth is a sacrifice of thanks to Hashem, for having made remarkable miracles and for having saved her from the pain and danger of childbirth. This is the reason for the *olah* — burnt offering — that is brought. But she must also bring a *chatas* — a sin offering — for by this she accepts Hashem's judgment and announces that she did not suffer and feel pain without reason, but rather because of her sins, as in the saying by our Sages, "There is no pain without sin."

Chinuch and *Ramban* also explain the nature of the *korban* as gratitude for the woman's recovery. *Ramban* sees this as an act of prayer and supplication to Hashem, where the woman asks that her bleeding should cease and that she should become pure, "for Hashem, Blessed is He, heals all flesh and performs wonders." *S'forno*, though, sees the *korban* as a means of directing the woman's thoughts to matters of *kedushah*, after a period during which her attention had been directed to her concealed organs and to her physical and material needs. This is identical to the interpretation of R' Samson Raphael Hirsch which we brought at the beginning of the *parashah*, and was evidently the latter's source.

The Gaon of Dvinsk introduces a new idea on this in his *Meshech Chochmah*. This sacrifice is a *korban r'iyah* — a *korban* brought when one appears at the *Beis HaMikdash*. A woman who has given birth is forbidden to come to the *Beis HaMikdash* during the entire period of her "purification." Now she is again able to come to it, and she brings a *korban* as her thanks for having regained her strength, in accordance with the verse, (*Sh'mos* 23:15), "and none shall appear before Me (i.e., in the *Beis HaMikdash*) empty."

According to *Chazal* in *Niddah*, the *chatas* comes to atone for the woman's return to her family, for when she endured her labor pains she swore that she would have no sexual relations with her husband. The Rav of Lutzk has a beautiful comment on this. According to the Torah, a rich woman who gave birth brings a turtledove or a young pigeon. He notes that when a woman must bring a *korban oleh v'yoreid* (a *korban* which varies based on whether the person is rich or poor), a poor woman must bring two turtledoves or young pigeons, so that the *korban* brought by a rich woman after childbirth is only half that, and we find nothing similar to this law elsewhere. He explains this beautifully. In *Niddah*, *Chazal* ask: "Should not the woman then bring a *korban* for (having taken) an oath?" and *Rashi* explains the question to be that the woman should have had to bring either a sheep or goat rather than a fowl. The *Gemara* does not answer this question, but as this *chatas* comes because the woman took an oath not to have any sexual relations with her husband, it is fitting that she should bring a single bird and not a pair of turtledoves or young pigeons. This way, she will see the anguish of the remaining bird which pines for its mate and does not seek another, and she will learn to be devoted to her husband under all circumstances, even when she is suffering the pains of labor. With this, he also explains why the Torah mentions the dove before the pigeon. While many commentators have already discussed this, the Rav of Lutzk writes that the Torah wished to show the woman the devotion of the dove to its missing mate, for if it can no longer find happiness with its dead spouse, the bird will remain alone for the rest of its life because of its longing for its mate.

The commentators on the Torah note with surprise that in the *parashah* dealing with the woman who gives birth, the Torah mentions the *olah* that she must bring before the *chatas*, even though the law — including in this case — is that the *chatas* is brought before the *olah*. In *Zevachim*, Chapter *Kol Tadir*, *Chazal* tell us that "the Torah only mentioned *olah* first for *mikra'ah* (lit., "its reading"), but as for sacrificing, the *chatas* comes first." If so, we should ask why the Torah mentioned the *olah* first for *mikra'ah*. And what, indeed, is *mikra'ah*? There are innumerable explanations of this.

A very penetrating answer is given by *Avnei Azel*. *Chazal* state that whoever studies the laws of the *olah* is considered as if he himself had brought an *olah*. All the same, there is a difference between the order in which the sacrifices are brought and in which they are recited. In *Shulchan Aruch, Orach Chaim* 1, we are told that each morning one should say the *korbanos* according to the following order: *olah, shelamim, chatas,* and *asham.* We know that in the actual *korban,* the *chatas* was brought before the *olah,* and indeed *Magen Avraham* asks why we recite the *korbanos* in the order we do, and answers this question in his own way. This, says *Avnei Azel,* is the meaning of the *Gemara* that "the Torah only mentioned it first for *mikra'ah,*" namely for the order in which the *korbanos* are recited, and not to indicate that the *olah* comes before the *chatas.*

◄§ Childbirth as a Sign of the Attribute of Mercy

Chazal give a reason why the period of *tumah* after the birth of a boy is only seven days rather than fourteen as for a girl. This is an example of Hashem's mercy, "so that all should not be rejoicing while his father and mother are sad." The *bris milah* on the eighth day is also explained by *Chazal* as Hashem's mercy:

> Why is an infant circumcised on the eighth day? That the Holy One, Blessed is He, was merciful to him, to wait until he is strong enough, and just as He is merciful to man, He is merciful to animals, as it states (*Vayikra* 22:27), "and from the eighth day and on it shall be accepted for an *olah* unto Hashem."

Zohar also compares man to the animals in this regard, but the comparison refers to the nature of the *korban. Bris milah,* too, is considered as a *korban* that man offers to Hashem. The fact that the verse, "and on the eighth day the skin of his *orlah* shall be circumcised," appears in the midst of the verses dealing with the *tumah* and *taharah* of the woman who has given birth, allows for various kabbalistic interpretations side by side with the different *halachos* that *Chazal* deduced from it. *Shabbos* is also included here within this framework of sanctification of one's life. We find a blend here of the sanctity of time (*Shabbos*), the sanctity of man (the *bris milah*), and the sanctity of place (the *korban*).

Sefas Emes explained the words of *Chazal* on the verse (*I Shmuel* 2:2), "There is no rock (צוּר) like our God" — that there is no artist (צַיָּר) like our God. Hashem created man as a hidden form within an outer form. Man, by his actions, removes one form and puts on another, thus exposing his inner form. By removing the *orlah* during the *bris milah,* the true inner form of the Jew emerges. The Lubavitcher Rebbi expands this idea to the *halachic* dimension as well, in regard to a *bris* milah which is held after the appointed time. He says that if the delay was due to אֹנֶס — unavoidable circumstances — then when the *bris milah* is finally held it is considered to have been held at the appointed time, for the light which will shine forth after the *bris milah* was there in potential, but its revelation was delayed. Once the *bris milah* is held, it is as if the light had been shining retroactively from the appointed time.

R' Isaac Breuer in *Nachliel* gives a striking definition of *kedushah* and *tumah*. Whatever aids in fostering the false belief that man is no more than an advanced animal and that there is nothing after death, is *tumah*. As opposed to this, whatever is distant from death and helps to raise man above the animals is *taharah*. But *taharah* is not the final step; instead it is a station on the way to *kedushah*, "for I am *kadosh*" (*Vayikra* 19:2). Hashem is by His nature *kadosh*. Man was given the nature of constantly striving to attain *kedushah*. The Torah teaches us how to free ourselves of our slavery to our passions and to climb the rungs of *kedushah*. But do not ever think that you reached *kedushah* in your life, "for I am *kadosh*," and My *kedushah* is infinite (*Melo HaOmer*).

Abarbanel says that in *Parashas Kedoshim* the Torah repeats all the *mitzvos* mentioned before, so as to stress that they are to be performed in an atmosphere of *kedushah*, and not as a matter of rote performance. It is true that the Ten Commandments and the other *mitzvos* dealing with morals and modesty would be rules that man would impose on himself naturally, even if not commanded to do so by Hashem. For the Jew, though, the only reason for performing them lies in his need to attain *kedushah*, and for no other reason. It is for this reason that *Parashas Kedoshim* was given in a public gathering of the entire nation — so as to obligate all of Israel, together, to observe all the moral and ethical commands, out of a desire to attain *kedushah*, and thereby to ensure that the nation will be stable and enduring.

According to *Rambam* in *Moreh Nevuchim* 3:47, the meaning of קְדשִׁים תִּהְיוּ is to sanctify yourselves by observing the *mitzvos*. It is from this observance that Israel's *kedushah* is derived. R' Zadok Hakohen of Lublin also develops this concept in his own way. When we perform a *mitzvah*, we declare אֲשֶׁר קִדְּשָׁנוּ בְּמִצְוֹתָיו — "Who has sanctified us with His *mitzvos*" — so that we can proclaim that the *mitzvos* are the basis for *kedushah*. If then a person says that it is hard for him to observe the *mitzvos* properly, Hashem tells him, "I am holy," and I will help you in this. *I am the source of kedushah*, and this *kedushah* spreads from Me to all those who try to emulate My ways, as in the statement of *Chazal*: "Whoever sanctifies himself below is sanctified from above." "You shall be holy, because I am holy "(ibid.). You do not need to create the *kedushah* because it is already there, and if you observe the *mitzvos*, that *kedushah* will cling to you, whether you are aware of it or not.

III.
Tzara'as — Disease or Divine Retribution?

I n *Arachin*, *Chazal* list seven causes of *tzara'as* — the leprosy-like ailment of the *metzora* described by the Torah. However, innumerable instances in *Shas* and the Midrash stress that *tzara'as* is a punishment for *lashon hara*. *Chazal* took the word צָרַעַת to be a combination of מוֹצִיא רָע meaning "utters (lit., 'takes out') evil." The Torah placed the sin of Miriam, who was guilty of *lashon hara*, next to the verse of הִשָּׁמֶר בְּנֶגַע הַצָּרַעַת — "take heed of the plague of *tzara'as*" (see *Devarim* 24:8);for immediately after this verse it states: "Remember what Hashem your God did to Miriam." Based on this, the commentators see the first verse as a warning and the second as the resulting punishment.

Some *rishonim*, such as *Ramban* and others, learn from this that when a person is guilty of *lashon hara* he has also violated an עֲשֵׂה — a positive commandment — contained in the words of the Torah: "Remember what Hashem your God did to Miriam," in addition to the לָאו — the negative commandment. This is the way *Ramban* puts it: "According to my opinion, this is a real *mitzvas asei* such as "Remember the *Shabbos* day to sanctify it" (*Shemos* 20:8). *Ramban* also criticizes those who do not include it among the *mitzvos asei* in their listing of the 613 *mitzvos*.

Rambam, who does not list the remembrance of Miriam among the 613 *mitzvos*, nevertheless mentions it in the laws regarding the *tum'ah* of the *tzara'as*, chapter 16: "On this matter, the Torah warns us and says: 'Take heed of the plague of *tzara'as* ... Remember what Hashem your God did unto Miriam.' " In various places in the *Yad HaChazakah*, *Rambam* notes that *tzara'as* is a supernatural punishment for the sin of *lashon hara*. *Rambam* also explains in *Hil. Metzora* chapter 16 the fact that the *metzora* must be isolated in order to keep him from repeating the same sin, "that he should not indulge in the speech of the wicked, which is frivolity and *lashon hara*."

R' Isaac Breuer in *Nachliel* says that *Rambam* in his *Mishneh Torah* deliberately mentions the *tzara'as* that attacks one's home or garments before the kind which is visited upon one's own body, so as to include them all in one overall category and to stress that just as *nega'im* — "plagues" — of one's home and garments are not natural events, neither is *tzara'as* of the body a natural event.

Penetrating are the interpretations of *Chafetz Chaim*, the Magid of Dubno and others on the fact that the *metzora's* purification is dependent on the word of the *Kohen*. According to them, the Torah meant to teach the *metzora* an object lesson in the power of man's speech, for "Life and death are within the power of the tongue." This way, the *metzora* will appreciate the enormity of the sin of *lashon hara*.

According to this interpretation, each Jew is affected by both natural and supernatural phenomena. Blemishes on the soul affect the body as well, causing bodily illness which proclaims to all that the person has sinned.

◆§ A Contagious Disease

In *Moreh Nevuchim* 3:47, *Rambam* attributes to *tzara'as* the natural characteristics of a contagious disease, which requires the person to be isolated. At the same time, he writes:

> The main interpretation is the universally accepted one, i.e., that it comes for the sin of *lashon hara*, and this change begins with the walls (of one's house). If the person did *teshuvah* the goal is achieved. And if he continues with his rebelliousness, the change spreads to the utensils of his servants and those of his own home. If he continues to be rebellious, it spreads to his clothes, and afterwards to his body. This was an accepted phenomenon as the (curse of death visited upon the) *sotah* — the wife suspected of infidelity (*Bamidbar* 5:11-31).

After all of *Rambam's* attempts to explain *tzara'as* by natural means, he concludes: "It was a sign and miracle in Israel so as to warn them against *lashon hara*." The source of *Rambam's* statement that one's servants' utensils and those of his own home are also afflicted by *tzara'as* is unclear.

As opposed to *Rambam*, there are other *rishonim* who wish to explain the phenomenon in natural terms. *Ralbag* even wishes to explain *nega'im* of one's garments and home in terms of the scientific terminology of his time. According to him, natural heat decreases progressively as a result of increased humidity, and this eventually destroys various substances.

Abarbanel mocks this explanation and refers to it as being "imaginative and absurd." He too, though, gives a medical explanation for *tzara'as*, even though it occurs because of one's sins. According to him, wool and flax absorb the decay in the body of the *metzora*. The Torah feared that after a *metzora* had been pronounced *tahor* he might go back to using the same clothes and shoes he had used before, and this way he might become reinfected. It was for this reason that the Torah required the clothes to be burned. The Torah did not require this of silk or metal, because "their material is so strong that they will not be ruined by being exposed to man."

Rabbeinu Bachya also comments that "*tzara'as* is a contagious disease; [the bird used in the purification process] is therefore to be sent 'into the field' (*Vayikra* 14:7), to a place where there are no people, so that the *tzara'as* will not infect others."

But R' Samson Raphael Hirsch brings numerous proofs that *tzara'as* is not a natural disease, as certain rationalistic commentators explain on the basis of the fact that the *metzora* must be isolated.

R' David Zvi Hoffmann cites the proofs of R' Hirsch and adds to them: a) שְׁחִין — boils — of Egypt (see *Devarim* 28:27), which are incurable, nevertheless do not make one *tamei*. b) *tzara'as* that spreads to the entire body is not *tamei*. c) When one's home is afflicted with *nega'im*, the Torah orders that all the utensils be removed from it before the *Kohen* comes and pronounces the house *tamei*. If the *tum'ah* is infectious, all utensils which came in contact with the *tzara'as* should also be *tamei*. d) According to *halachah*, a bridegroom in the festivities of the first week of his marriage is not required to have *nega'im* on his body examined. Similarly, during the *regel* — the pilgrimage festivals — the *metzora* is released from the requirement to be isolated, and it is just during such times of festivities and rejoicing that he has the greatest chance of coming in contact with others. e) The signs of *tzara'as*, as described in the Torah, do not correspond to any infectious disease known to medicine. f) Even the most infectious plagues known to medicine are not found to vary in contagiousness in accordance with the color and appearance of the sores.

One can add numerous proofs to these. The *halachah* is that *gerim* — converts — and *toshavim* — those who have accepted the seven *mitzvos b'nei Noach* — do not become *tamei* from *nega'im* (*Mishnah*

Nega'im 3). Similarly, if a person removed the signs of *nega'im* before the *Kohen* arrived, the person is *tahor* (ibid. 7:4). Also, in case of doubt about a *nega*, the person is *tahor* (ibid. 5:1). These and other proofs show that the Torah and *Chazal* did not link *tum'ah* and *taharah* to a contagious disease, but ruled in accordance with the principles set down by Moshe from Sinai. It is surprising that those commentators who interpreted *tzara'as* as a natural phenomenon ignored all the above-mentioned proofs.

It is worthwhile bringing here what *Midrash Tanchuma* writes about a *Kohen* who thought that *tzara'as* was a natural phenomenon. When he became impoverished and wanted to leave *Eretz Yisrael*, he called his wife and said to her: "As people come to me to check their *nega'im*, let me teach you how to view the *nega'im*. If you see the hair of a man where the roots are dry, you can tell that he is afflicted. Hashem created for each hair a root (lit. מעין, "wellspring") of its own, from which it is nourished. If the root dries up, the hair dries up." His wife said to him: "If the Holy One Blessed be He created a root for each single hair to support that hair, is it not only logical that the Holy One Blessed be He should supply you, who are a person and who has so many hairs, and who must support your children, with an income?" And she did not permit him to leave the country.

We can see from this story that certain *Kohanim* also saw the *tzara'as* as a natural disease and thought that they were able to teach others who were not *Kohanim* how to diagnose it.

⋖§ The Crime and Its Punishment

As mentioned, *Chazal* and the various commentators accept that *tzara'as* comes as a punishment for *lashon hara*, but there is no explanation as to why *nega'im* are the suitable punishment for *lashon hara*. *Chazal* in *Arachin* state that the *metzora* is isolated because he "separated between man and wife and between man and his fellow." *Maharal* of Prague explains this as follows: A person who speaks *lashon hara* undermines the peace of society and of the people living in that society. This type of behavior is: "...an alien thing, not worthy of having anything in common with human society; as a result whoever departs [from acceptable behavior] deserves — and it is only fitting that it is so — to be afflicted with *nega'im*, which separates him totally from everyone, so that he is entirely alone."

This explanation clarifies the measure for measure involved in this punishment, for as *lashon hara* crumbles society and moves people apart one from the other, the punishment of one who has arisen against society is that he be exiled from that society and be forced to remain apart from it. Thus we at least understand what the *nega'im* accomplish, for they move the person apart from society. But this does not explain what connection a *nega* should have to *lashon hara*. And what is the connection between *lashon hara* and *tzara'as*? It appears to me that this punishment recalls the behavior of the primeval serpent in Eden who is mentioned on numerous occasions with regard to *lashon hara*. *Chazal* explain the verse (*Koheles* 10:11), "Will the serpent bite without a whisper? And a gossip achieves nothing" as follows:

> In the future, the animals will gather and come to the serpent and tell it: "A lion mauls and eats, a wolf tears apart and devours, but what enjoyment do you have?" It will answer them: "And what did the gossip achieve?"

In these words of *Chazal*, we can understand the severity of the sin of *lashon hara*. One who speaks *lashon hara* cannot justify his actions in the way done by other sinners who are overcome by their lusts. This sinner is like a serpent, which bites without receiving any physical benefit while doing so. He is similar to the serpent in other ways as well. "He separated between man and wife and between man and his fellow" — as the primeval serpent did in Eden. He is also similar in the sort of calamity he brings upon his victims. "Life and death are within the power of the tongue" and "*lashon hara* kills three people" (the person who tells it, the one who listens, and the person about whom it is told), just as the serpent brought about death on all of humanity. There are many other comparisons between the serpent and the teller of *lashon hara*. What is most interesting is that *Chazal* consider the snake to be a *metzora*, and even said: "the primeval snake, because it spoke *lashon hara* about its Creator, was made a *metzora*" (*Midrash Tanchuma*, *Metzora* 2). *Chazal* also said that "the scales of the snake are *nega'im*" (*Shemos Rabbah* 3). It would seem that this is the source of the words of *Chazal* regarding the link between the sin of *lashon hara* and *tzara'as*. One who speaks *lashon hara* is a snake in the guise of a man, for the primeval serpent also walked upright, according to *Chazal* in *Sotah* 9, and ate the same foods as Adam. It was the serpent's sin which brought about: *nega'im* of clothing (that man had to wear clothing), *nega'im* of housing (Adam was chased out of the Garden of Eden), and *nega'im* of the body (death came to the world). Indeed the "whisperer," the one who speaks *lashon hara*, has an uncanny resemblance to the primeval serpent, and it is logical that his punishment should be a similar one, for the punishment of *nega'im* is what the one who speaks *lashon hara* and the snake have in common.

✒ Removal From the Human Experience

The disciples of the *Besht* said in the name of their rebbi that what *Chazal* meant when they equated מְצֹרָע with מוֹצִיא רָע "drawing out" or "speaking" evil, was that one who speaks *lashon hara* "draws out the evil — the רָע — from its roots." Many try to understand this comment. It would seem that the *Besht* is in accordance with his view, that all the characteristics and attributes that exist in the world were created for a positive end so that they can be used for essential goals, and — as the *Besht* puts it — evil too is a footstool to good. The view of the great Chassidic leaders is well known: that Hashem must also be worshipped with one's *yetzer hara*, or, as *Chazal* put it: בְּכָל-לְבָבְךָ — "with all your heart" (*Devarim* 6:6) means that we must serve Hashem with our *yetzer hara* as well as with our *yetzer tov*. In this way the *tzaddikim* "sweeten" evil and integrate it with good. Thus, R' Simchah Bunim of Pshischa said that *apikorsus* — heresy — also has a function. For example, if a poor person comes to you and asks for charity, don't rely on trust that Hashem will take care of him, but assume that if you don't help him he may, God forbid, die of hunger.

Lashon hara is different. It bites without any other goal. It utilizes man's animalistic instinct only for evil purposes, simply to destroy and tear apart, just as a wild animal. Indeed it is even worse than a wild animal, for animals enjoy eating their prey after tearing it apart, but *lashon hara* is like the snake who derives no pleasure from the damage he inflicts. The isolation of the person who engages in *lashon hara* is meant to announce to all that this man has abandoned his human roots and has left human culture. This is evidently the reason *nega'im* affect a person's home and garments, for such a person does not deserve to drape himself with the outward symbols of society and civilization.

This idea is related in unusual clarity by one of the Chassidic giants, who was able, in a short passage, to give expression to the Chassidic outlook on this matter. The following are the words of *Sefas Emes* on *Parashas Metzora*:

> In every thing there is a mixture of evil and good. And so with man. In general the good overcomes the evil, for there is more good. But one must be careful not to exclude evil from the community. So too does it state, "Guard your tongue from evil and your lips from speaking deceit...seek peace and pursue it,' which means that (the evil) is to be engulfed by the common good, as indicated in the act of *taharah* of the *metzora*, which includes "spring water" and "two living birds." The emphasis is to return to

the source and to cleave to the root, and when one is within the common good he can be rectified.

In another place in the same *parashah*, *Sefas Emes* writes:

"The *yetzer hara* that Hashem gave man, too, is in no way a contradiction to the service of Hashem, as long as one remains within the community, as it states, "with both your *yetzarim*" Only he who cuts himself off from the community is misusing his *yetzer hara*. This is perhaps what is denoted by the 'two living birds': that both *yetzarim* as originally given by Hashem are *tahor*, as it is stated, 'The soul which You placed in me is *tahor*'(from the *Shacharis* prayers), and man has sufficient purity (*taharah*) within himself, as long as he does not cut himself off from his roots."

The idea expressed here is that mentioned in the entire Chassidic literature, namely that our bad characteristics, just as the *yetzer hara*, were also created to serve Hashem, and they too can be "alive" and add to our *kedushah*, holiness. We must only be sure not to use any characteristic of ours for total evil, for by doing so we uproot these characteristics from their Divine tie. It is understandable that the *metzora*, who separated between man and his wife and between man and his fellow-man, has by that removed himself from the community and cut himself off from the source of life. To rectify this, he has to include himself in the community so that his *yetzer hara* will return to the source of life and will serve Hashem in its assigned role. This is the idea we brought above in the name of the *Besht*, that one who speaks *lashon hara* has excluded himself from the community and has cut himself off from the source, and that is the reason for his *tumah*.

R' Eliezer Lipmann Lavie, in his *Otzar Ma'amarim*, quotes *Pri Tzaddik* on *Tikunei Zohar*: "One who does not observe the three meals of *Shabbos* is afflicted by the *nega* of *tzara'as*." He explains that the three meals represent our *avos* Avraham, Yitzchak and Yaakov. The *avos* also represent the three concentric "camps" in which the Jewish people were arranged as they camped in the wilderness. Avraham represents the inner camp, *Shechinah*, the *Mishkan*, because he brought the *Shechinah* to the world. Yitzchak is linked through his quality of *gevurah* (strength) to the intermediary camp of the Levites (*Zohar*, *Shimini* 39). Finally, Yaakov represents the Camp of *Yisrael*, because he was the founder of the twelve tribes of Israel, and infused all Israel with sanctity. A *metzora* is sent outside all the camps and has no place in the Camp of *Yisrael*. It is for this reason that *Chazal* said that Gechazi, who became a *metzora*, has no place in the World to Come. Similarly, *Shabbos* is a "daughter crowned by the three *avos*," and one who doesn't have the three *Shabbos* meals has excluded himself from all the camps, and is described by the *Zohar* as becoming, God forbid, a *metzora*. This is similar to the idea presented earlier.

Metzora – מְצֹרָע

I.

The Law of the מוֹצִיא רָע

he Torah regards *tzara'as* as a spiritual disease, which is cured by removing those causes which brought about the affliction. *Chazal* list many sins which are punished by *nega'im*, but the substantive sin where the Torah implies the cause of this affliction is *lashon hara*.

Miriam was afflicted with *tzara'as* because she spoke *lashon hara* against Moshe. The Torah also places the reminder of Miriam's behavior side-by-side with the command to beware of *tzara'as* (*Devarim* 24:8-9). Further, the fact that the Torah describes the one afflicted with *tzara'as* as a מְצֹרָע hints to the composite of the words מוֹצִיא רָע — issuing evil," as noted by *Chazal*. This helps us understand the Torah's command, וְהוּבָא אֶל־הַכֹּהֵן — "he shall be brought to the *Kohen*" (*Vayikra* 14:2) — which otherwise would seem unintelligible. After all, the *halachah* is that the *Kohen* is the one who must go out of the three camps to the *metzora*, and not that the *metzora* comes in to the *Kohen*. But it appears that this phrase too indicates the true nature of the disease, for the Torah does not state that the person is to see a doctor, but rather that he requires a *Kohen*. Only a spiritual healer can help, as in the verse (*Malachi* 2:7), "For the *Kohen's* lips should keep knowledge, and they should seek the Torah at his mouth." Thereafter, the Torah prescribes in great detail how this spiritual healer can cure the person and make him *tahor* from his *tumah*.

Or HaChaim explains the verse (*Vayikra* 14:2), "This shall be the law of the *metzora* in the day of his *taharah*: he shall be brought unto the *Kohen*" — it is on the day of his *taharah*, purification, that we have the clearest proof that his disease was a spiritual one, and that the law of the person afflicted with *tzara'as* is that of the מוֹצִיא רָע. Natural skin disease stems from infection and decay, and makes the person extremely depressed. The natural treatment for one afflicted with a skin disease should be cheering him up and improving his living conditions and his clothing. In the case of *metzora*, though, the Torah tells us to act in exactly the opposite way. The person is to be completely isolated, and "his clothes shall be torn and the hair on his head shall be unshorn..." (ibid. 13:45). When we see that the person who has accepted the Yoke of Heaven has become cured, in spite of treatment that was contrary to our medical expectations, it is a clear sign that his sins caused the disease rather than some physical infection. When the Torah states, "This shall be the law of the *metzora* in the day of his *taharah*," it is on that day that it will become clear to all that the disease came about because he was guilty of מוֹצִיא רָע, and not for any other reason. Had the disease been a physical one, it would not have been cured by the measures he took.

Chasam Sofer explains the verse which follows the one quoted above in a similar fashion. This verse states (*Vayikra* 14:3), "Behold, if the plague of *tzara'as* is healed in the afflicted one (*tzarua*)." When the *Kohen* looks at the *metzora* in the spiritual capacity of his priestly office and observes that the soul's ailment which the Torah calls *nega tzara'as* has gone, he then orders the person to become *tahor* and to bring a *korban*.

Many commentators, both *rishonim* and *acharonim*, explain this *parashah* along similar lines. Had there not been a link between the spiritual and the material aspects of this disease, there would be no logic in the way it is treated. *Alshech* says that an external manifestation of a spiritual illness, such as *tzara'as*, was only to occur in an enlightened generation, where sinners were an exception. In our times though, one cannot have such a manifestation, or else we would all be afflicted with *tzara'as*. It is because of Hashem's mercy for us that He removed this disease from our midst, so that we can survive in spite of our spiritual weakness.

Chazal in *Arachin* state that the need for two live birds to purify the *metzora* is because birds twitter, just as the *metzora* twittered away with his *lashon hara*. The commentators explain that the *gemara* was not surprised at the fact that birds are used for *taharah*, but only that one must bring two birds. As, however, the sin was *lashon hara*, which required two participants — the one who told it and the one who listened — the person must atone for it by bringing two birds, so as to remember his sin and to be careful for the future. There are those who note, though, that bringing two birds is common, as in the sacrifices brought by the *zav* and *zavah*, so why did the *gemara* not question the use of two birds elsewhere? The answer is that in the other places one does not have to bring two species. The sacrifice is either cattle or sheep or birds. In the case of the *metzora*, however, the Torah obligated him to bring sheep as well as birds. Thus the question of *Chazal* is why two species are brought by the *metzora*, and they answer that the birds come to remind the *metzora* that his idle chatter caused his sin.

Ramban, however, is unsure of how to understand *Chazal* there. *Chazal* in *Chullin* 140, and in *Toras Kohanim*, state that the *metzora* must use: "Birds which are *tahor*, and not *tamei*." This would imply that the term צִפּוֹר ("bird") refers to all species of birds which are *tahor*. How then can we assume that all of these twitter? After all, there are birds that are *tahor* but do not emit any sounds at all. After a lengthy discussion, *Ramban* concludes that *Chazal* were referring to birds of the field, צִפֳּרֵי דְרוֹר, all of which twitter. One of these species, the *snunit* (swallow), is *tamei*; hence *Chazal* needed to specify that only a *tahor* species may be used.

◆§ The Difference between Kedushah and Tum'ah

R' David Zvi Hoffmann, in his introduction to the laws of *tumah* and *taharah*, takes a clear position that the *nega'im* which appear are a symbol of the sins against society. It is the role of the *Kohen* to announce that a person who has a detrimental effect on the society is to be isolated from it. Social evils generally occur when there is a clash between the individual and society. If, while isolated, the person who is *tamei* regains his equilibrium, he is healed and afterwards becomes *tahor*. R' Hoffman quotes one opinion that the laws of the *metzora* are sanitary measures but rejects this, quoting convincing proofs of R' Samson Raphael Hirsch, which show that according to modern medicine many of the regulations governing the *metzora* would serve to spread the disease even further, whereas, according to the Torah, these are ritually pure. One who looks into the laws of the *metzora* is forced to say that they are based on *nistar* — a "hidden," kabbalistic interpretation, as are many similar topics.

To a certain extent, the *taharah* here is like the goat that was sent away by the *Kohen Gadol* on *Yom Kippur*, and to a certain extent like the dipping of the hyssop sprigs in blood just before the Jews left Egypt, the purpose being to keep away any destructive forces. The *rishonim* all comment on this, each illuminating a different point.

Ibn Ezra, in his explanation of the use of the *erez* (cedar tree) and *eizov* (hyssop bush; see *Vayikra* 14:4), notes: "The *metzora*, a house which has *nega'im*, and the *tumah* of the dead are all similar, and they are all like the *Pesach* of Egypt." (In the *Pesach* of Egypt, Hashem commanded the Jews to take a hyssop branch, to dip it into blood, and to sprinkle the blood on the doorposts and lintels of their houses, so as to keep away the destructive angel.)

Ramban also mentions here the goat of Yom Kippur. He provides a rational reason why the bird was dipped in blood and then sent away into the field, i.e., that this is to prevent the tzara'as from infecting other people. But after quoting Toras Kohanim, which states that one is forbidden to send the bird to either the desert or the sea, he concludes that the purpose of sending away the bird cannot be simply to prevent the spread of infection. After all, the bird would be further from people if it was in the desert rather than somewhere in the countryside. Hence, he compares this bird to the scapegoat of Yom Kippur. There, he explains, the purpose is to appease an evil spirit of the desert, while here the appeasement is directed towards forces which "fly in the field." Rabbeinu Bachya explains that these are destructive forces on a lower level than the "prince of the desert who receives bribery on Yom Kippur." The Kabbalah deals with this topic at length.

Studying the parashah of metzora leads man to a clear recognition that the entire parashah is based on Kabbalah. The commentators strive to find symbolic and ethical interpretations, but they do so only in regard to specific details and not regarding the nature of the disease or the taharah process, which remain sealed to us, even though we do know from Chazal what the cause is.

Chasam Sofer in his derashos sees the tumah of tzara'as as much greater than that of the tumah in Egypt and that of the dead. In the Pesach of Egypt they brought only a hyssop, and with the goat of Yom Kippur all that was used was a crimson "tongue" of wool; whereas with a metzora one uses a crimson "tongue" of wool, hyssop and cedar wood. He explains the symbolism of this according to d'rush. On Yom Kippur, we free ourselves from the yetzer hara. This is symbolized by the crimson "tongue," as in the verse (Yeshayahu 1:18), "Though your sins be as crimson, they shall become as white as snow." On the first Pesach, the Jews were freed from the bondage of other nations, and as a result, Hashem told them to use the hyssop, which is the smallest of bushes. This is meant to symbolize that Hashem chose us (Devarim 7:7), "not because you were more in number than any people, for you were the fewest of all people." In the case of metzora, however, there is an addition of the cedar, which symbolizes that only if the metzora is like a cedar, which does not bear fruit (i.e., he does not cause others to sin), can he become tahor. Of course this interpretation is not in keeping with the p'shat, the plain meaning of the verses, but it does alert us to the special significance of the taharah of the metzora, which, due to the lack of any simple explanation, gives us the opportunity for various kinds of symbolic interpretations.

It is also worth delving into why it is that on *Yom Kippur* the decision as to which goat will be slaughtered and which will be sent away alive is determined by lot, whereas in the case of the *metzora* the bird that is chosen to be sent away is decided by the *Kohen*.

◆§ And He Will be Brought to the Kohen

Various *rishonim* and *acharonim* labor to explain the meaning of the words, "And he will be brought to the *Kohen*" (*Vayikra* 14:2), which contradicts what the Torah says later: "And the *Kohen* shall go out of the camp" (ibid. v. 3) implying that the *Kohen* goes to the *metzora*, and not vice-versa. *Chazal* in the Midrash explain the first verse as being equivalent in meaning to "and he will come to the *Kohen*," where the first word וְהוּבָא ("he will be brought") is to be understood as if it had been written as two words: וְהוּא בָא ("he will come"). But this does not change much, because according to *halachah* the *Kohen* goes out to the *metzora*.

Ramban explains that what the Torah meant to tell us is that the *metzora* cannot become *tahor* without the pronouncement of the Kohen, even if he has been healed from his *tzara'as*. This interpretation follows *Toras Kohanim*, which states that the verse comes to teach us that all matters relating to the *metzora*, such as the *shechitah* of the bird, the sprinkling of the blood of the bird, shaving the *metzora*, and so on are to be carried out under the supervision of the *Kohen* (see *Malbim's HaTorah VeHaMitzvah*). *Ramban* explains further that the day that the *metzora* is healed from his *nega* he immediately begins with *taharah*, as directed by the *Kohen*. This interpretation also follows *Chazal*, who say that "he shall not delay." According to this, the meaning of "on the day that he becomes *tahor*" refers to the day that he is healed from his *nega*, on which day he is to be brought to the *Kohen* even against his will if he does not begin the *taharah* process on his own. Ibn Ezra also follows this path, and states that he is to be brought to the *Kohen* "whether he wishes to or not."

S'forno gives an interesting interpretation which is the basis for a new *halachic* insight. Not only did the Torah require the *Kohen* to go out to the *metzora*, it also required the *metzora* go out to the *Kohen*. Thus the Torah requires the *metzora* to come to the nearest possible place so that the *Kohen* should not have to travel any great distance. The *metzora* is to be brought to the closest point outside the camp, so that the *Kohen* can see him without excessive effort.

R' Yosef Bechor Shor also explains it along these lines. The *Kohen* and the *metzora* meet at an intermediate station, and both therefore go out from their own places. The Gaon of Lutzk in his *Oznayim LeTorah* explains the reason for this commandment. One cause of *nega'im* is pride. If the *Kohen* would go to the *metzora*, the latter would be conceited by that fact. Therefore he has to come to the *Kohen*.

Sifsei Kohen takes the exact opposite approach. The *Kohen* must go out to the *metzora* to show him respect. This is because the *metzora* who was sent out of the camp was publicly humiliated; now that he has been healed, he is entitled to be shown respect in compensation. It is for that reason that the *Kohen* goes out to him.

Ohel Yaakov explains that the stress on "He will be brought to the *Kohen*" is so that the *metzora* will learn an ethical lesson in realizing that life and death are in the power of the tongue. The *Kohen* takes him out of his *tumah* through the word of his mouth. He does not become *tahor* until the *Kohen* says the word "*tahor*." This is measure for measure, for he became *tamei* because of his words.

My rebbi, author of *Chakal Yitzchak*, of Spinka, sees this as an ethical lesson for the *Kohen* as well. "And the *Kohen* shall go out of the camp." The leader must go out to the people if he wishes to save them from sin. The task of the *tzaddik* is not to go up to the heavens as Chanoch did, but instead to be like Avraham, of whom we are told, "That he will command his sons" (*Bereishis* 18:19). *Chakal Yitzchak* quotes *Chasam Sofer* who explains this at length. This Chassidic interpretation fits in well with the view that both the *Kohen* and the *metzora* must leave their own place and must meet along the way of *taharah* for sake of the nation.

◄§ Four Tools of Taharah

There are four items that are used in the purification of the *metzora* before he brings his sacrifices: a) cedar wood; b) crimson "tongue" of wool; c) hyssop; d) two live birds. One of the birds is slaughtered, while the second is dipped in the blood of the first and is set free outside the city. *Chazal* and the different commentators alike explain the purposes of these actions, using symbolic and conceptual ideas.

Rashi, following *Chazal*, explains that the birds and the cedar wood are symbols of the factors causing *tzara'as* (birds twitter, thus symbolizing *lashon hara*; the cedar wood symbolizes pride). The scarlet wool and the hyssop, on the other hand, are symbols of rectifying the sin (the person is to make himself as humble as the worm found in the berries from which the crimson dye is made or as a hyssop).

Abarbanel sees these four items as symbolic of bringing the person back to his previous state materially and spiritually, and improving his characteristic nature. The disease of *tzara'as* has four negative symptoms: a) the flesh is dead and has no feeling; b) it is moist and decayed; c) the person is pale and his liver does not function; d) he has a bad body odor. In addition, he is excluded from both the *Machaneh Shechinah* and from the *Machaneh Yisrael*. The Torah commanded the *taharah* and the sacrifice against these two exclusions. The *taharah* indicates the person's physical well-being, and the sacrifice, his spiritual well-being. The two birds symbolize that he has been revived, while the cedar wood symbolizes that he is now fresh and no longer decaying; the scarlet thread indicates that his blood is flowing; and the hyssop that his body odor is now sweet.

R' David Zvi Hoffmann also sees in this a symbolic action as a sign. This person has finally realized his place in human society. He understands that without law and morality man cannot exist on this earth. The bird which is slaughtered over water symbolizes the person's willingness to give up his arbitrary nature for the sake of the success of humanity and of the law. The live bird which is dipped in the blood of the dead bird is to be set free in the fields as a symbol of the desire to have wanton actions far removed from the city, to the place where wild animals roam. After all, the existence of every society is dependent on each person being willing to make compromises for the benefit of that society.

Chizkuni sees the bird which is sent away as a symbol of human freedom which has been regained by the person who, having had *nega'im*, had sat alone and in isolation from society. Now he can return to that society, just as the bird which was once in a cage is now set free. *Chizkuni* goes on to say that the purpose of dipping the live bird in the blood of the dead bird is so that birds of the same species will look upon it as a foreigner in their midst and will kill it, and it will not be used for another *metzora*. This is the meaning of the verse (*Yirmiyahu* 12:9), "Is My heritage unto Me as a painted bird? The birds round about are against her." What is a painted bird? This refers to a bird which is stained with the blood of its fellow. When *Chazal* said that the bird may be eaten, that refers to a case where it is caught before its fellows killed it.

The need that the commentators found to seek symbolic interpretations such as these proves that the basis of this *parashah* is not to be found in the plain meaning, but is in *nistar*, as revealed by the masters of the Kabbalah.

II.
The Opinion of Akeidas Yitzchak on the Metzora

hazal in this *parashah* state that *tzara'as* appears on account of the sin of *lashon hara* (*Arachin* 15), and there is therefore a need to search for a direct link between the sin and the means which the spiritually and physically ill *metzora* must use to purify himself from the sins of his disease. Below we will give the explanation of one of our great Torah thinkers of previous generations, R' Yitzchak Aram'ah, in his well-known *Akeidas Yitzchak*.

R' Yitzchak ben Aram'ah devotes his words to explaining a midrash on our *parashah* which seems surprising:

> There was a certain peddler who would wander among the towns near Tzippori, and would announce: "Who wishes to buy the elixir of life?" All the people would assemble before him. R' Yannai was sitting and studying. He said to him: "Come here and sell it to me." He said to him: "You and those like you do not need it." (R' Yannai) beseeched him, so the peddler came over and brought him the book of *Tehillim* and showed him (*Tehillim* 34:13), "What man is he that desires life, and loves many days, that he may see good?" And what does it say after that? "Keep your tongue from evil, and your lips from speaking guile." R' Yannai said: "So too did Shlomo say (*Mishle* 21:23), 'Whoever guards his mouth and his tongue, guards his soul from troubles.' " R' Yannai said: "All my life I would read this verse and did not know where it was explained until that peddler came and informed me 'What man is he that desires life?' Moshe therefore warned Israel: זֹאת תּוֹרַת הַמְצֹרָע — This is the law of the *metzora* — מוֹצִיא רָע.' "

The various *darshanim* are puzzled at how R' Yannai was so astounded by the words of the peddler. What did he hear that he had not known previously? In which way did he find that *Parashas Metzora* was clearer to him now?

R' Yitzchak Aram'ah explains the words of R' Yannai in a philosophical type of introduction on the nature of man and life. One of the characteristics of man, which singles him out among all living creatures, is his power of speech. On the verse, וַיִּפַּח בְּאַפָּיו נִשְׁמַת חַיִּים — "And He breathed into his nostrils the breath of life" (*Bereishis* 2:7) — *Onkelos* explains that Hashem gave man the ability to speak. We are not referring here to the ability to utter sounds in the technical sense but to man's ability to think, which is expressed in his speech. It is written, "Man has the processes of thought, but the speech of the tongue is from Hashem" (*Mishlei* 16:1). Man's thought and his speech are linked together, and represent his superiority over all other living creatures. We know that a person who does not have the ability to speak — to express his thoughts to others by speech — is not halachically within the category of "man" (see *Terumos* ch. 1), because a man who is deprived of the power of speech is missing the unique characteristic which distinguishes man from the other creatures.

Since speech determines the essence of man, it must have special qualities. If one's speech does not have such qualities, it is no different than the chirping of a bird. It is as if a person took a royal robe and used it to clean out a garbage can. It is for this reason that *Chazal* were praised for never having uttered an idle word in their lives (*Sukkah* 28).

Rambam, in his commentary on *Avos*, at the end of the first chapter mentions that a certain wise man was asked why he was always quiet when he sat with company. He answered that a) *lashon hara*, *rechilus* (tale-bearing) and foul language are totally evil; b) to praise people has good and bad points; c) to discuss events which have occurred is neither good nor bad; d) wisdom and philosophy are good. "As to the first three," the wise man said, "I don't talk about these at all. As to the fourth, I would talk about it, but I would be considered strange in a society which doesn't understand such matters, and that is why I remain silent."

Rambam divided the different forms of talk into four categories, but R' Shimon b. Gamliel said: "All my life I grew up among *chachamim* and I found nothing better for the body than silence," namely that even the wisdom in a person's heart deserves to be limited and restricted, as in the words of *Chazal* that one should always teach his *talmidim* בְּדֶרֶךְ קְצָרָה — using brevity. As opposed to this, *Chazal* regard a person who is boastful and who does not know how to control his speech a fool. They compare the latter's speech to the hollow-sounding noise produced by a single coin that rattles about in an otherwise empty container.

Even in discussing matters of wisdom it is good for a person to speak little, and this is all the more so when it comes to frivolity, vulgar language or *lashon hara*. A person who uses his speech to harm others cannot be considered as "a speaking creature," but rather, as Shlomo referred to him in *Mishlei* 26:18, "A mad man who casts firebrands, arrows, and death." The man's lips send forth stones thrown by a sling to kill others. David said about Shim'i (*I Melachim* 2:8), "who cursed me with a grievous curse in the day when I went to Machanayim." But when the *navi* described the event (*II Shmuel* 16:13), he stated, "And he cursed as he went, and threw stones at him, and cast dust." This is in keeping with the idea that a person who talks *lashon hara* about another is as if stoning him with stones.

This is certainly not the activity that elevates man above the other creatures. This negative behavior can be divided into three categories: a) One who uses his power of speech simply for evil purposes, condemning the just and justifying the wicked; b) One who damages another through speech but acts as if he is doing it for the sake of Heaven, where, for example, he may act as if jealous for the honor of a *rav*, judge, etc.; c) One who responds in kind to a person who insulted him. The last category is of course the least of the three, but that too is considered as if the person had stoned his fellow, even though the other threw the first stone. It was in regard to these three categories that *Chazal* composed the prayer (*Berachos* 17), which we add after our *Shemoneh Esrei*: אֱלֹהַי נְצֹר לְשׁוֹנִי מֵרָע — "My God, guard my tongue from evil" — this refers to plain *lashon hara*; וּשְׂפָתַי מִדַּבֵּר מִרְמָה — "and my lips from speaking deceitfully" — referring here to a person who acts as if what he is doing is for the sake of Heaven; וְלִמְקַלְלַי נַפְשִׁי תִדֹּם — "And may my soul be silent to those who curse me" — here we refer to the third category, the person who responds to another's insults. All three instances remove a person from the framework of humanity, because he has exploited his power of speech for other purposes than that of "the speaking creature." Both David and Shlomo, on numerous occasions in *Tanach*, spoke at length about how evil *lashon hara* really is.

⊰§ The Evil of Lashon Hara

Moshe Rabbeinu spoke out more than anyone else against evil speech, which removes its speaker from life. He warned Israel that זֹאת .... תּוֹרַת הַמְּצֹרָע — This is the law of the *metzora* — מוֹצִיא רָע. It is well known that *Chazal* (in *Nedarim* 64) consider the *metzora* as if he were dead, the reason being that by his behavior he made an animalistic use of his power of speech and took himself out of the ranks of the "speaking creatures." As a result, he is considered as dead. In *Midrash Rabbah* (*Vayikra* 16), *Chazal* tell us: "R' Yehoshua ben Levi said: 'The word תּוֹרַת is used five times in regard to the מְצֹרָע ... to teach you that one who speaks *lashon hara* is as if transgressing all five *chumashim* of

the Torah. That is why Moshe warned Israel, "תּוֹרַת הַמְצֹרָע ... זֹאת —
This is the law of the *metzora* — מוֹצִיא רָע."

And indeed one who examines the five *chumashim* finds that in each there is a warning against *lashon hara*. In *Bereishis* we find the very first sin of the serpent who tempted Eve by speaking *lashon hara* against Hashem, when he said (*Bereishis* 3:5), "For God knows that in the day you eat thereof, then your eyes shall be opened, and you shall be as gods, knowing good and evil." This *lashon hara* brought death to the world, and a curse to both the one who spoke it and the one who listened.

Again we are told in *Bereishis* of how, through Yosef's talking *lashon hara* against his brothers, the Jews were eventually forced into exile in Egypt. At the end of *Bereishis*, we find the rectification of that sin when we are told (50:16), "And they sent a messenger unto Yosef saying, 'Your father commanded before he died, saying, So shall you say unto Yosef: Forgive, I pray you, the trespass of your brethren.' " All of this indicates that "death and life are in the power of the tongue" (*Mishlei* 18:21).

At the beginning of *Shemos* (2:14), we find that the *rasha* — wicked man — tells Moshe, "Do you intend to kill me as you killed the Egyptian?" This was a case of *lashon hara* where the speaker shoots forth arrows, and as actually happened (*Shemos* 2:15): "Pharaoh heard this thing, and he sought to slay Moshe." *Chazal* add that the latter is what Moshe meant when he said (ibid. v. 14), "Surely this thing is known." It was this experience with *lashon hara* that led Moshe to finally realize the reason for Israel's being in *galus*. And similarly in *Nedarim* 64 on the verse (*Shemos* 4:19), "For all the men who sought your life are dead," *Chazal* explain that they were considered dead because they had either become *metzora'im* or lost all their possessions because of the sin of *lashon hara*.

Vayikra is full of denunciations of the sin of *lashon hara*. In it we find the entire *parashah* of *metzora*, which is a warning against speaking *lashon hara*. In *Parashas Kedoshim* we also find specific commandments (*Vayikra* 19:16): "You shall not go as a talebearer among your people: Neither shall you stand beside the blood of your neighbor." This teaches us that one who is a talebearer is as if he shed his neighbor's blood. Actually, *Akeidah* provides numerous other instances throughout *Tanach* where *lashon hara* is linked to shedding blood.

In *Bamidbar*, we have the story of Miriam, who suffered from *tzara'as* because of *lashon hara*. There were also the spies who were guilty of speaking evil of *Eretz Yisrael*, a sin which kept the Jews in the wilderness for forty years. That sin, which occurred on *Tishah B'Av*, was the forerunner of so many other calamities which would take place that day, where, as Hashem told the people (*Ta'anis* 29), "Today you cried without cause. I will give you cause for crying on this day for all generations." There was also Korach and his followers whose controversy led to their being swallowed up by the earth and by fire. We find also in *Bamidbar* the sin of those men who spoke against Moshe and Aharon who were punished by the fiery serpents.

The book of *Devarim* begins with a stern warning by Moshe against the sin of *lashon hara*, where, on the phrase "between Paran and between Tofel," *Onkelos* explains that they complained about the manna. So too did Moshe say to them (1:27), "And you murmured in your tents, and said, 'Because Hashem hated us, He brought us forth out of the land of Egypt.' " And again, when all the people were assembled at Mount Gerizim, one of the curses was directed against "he who smites his fellow secretly" (*Devarim* 27:24), this referring to *lashon hara*, as with Doeg the Edomite. In the light of the above, we understand that a person who speaks *lashon hara* is transgressing all five *chumashim* of the Torah as well as all of *Nach*, and his punishment is a clear one: He becomes a *metzora* — מוֹצִיא שֵׁם רָע, for it only proper that such a person should be ostracized and separated from other people.

◆§ What Was New in the Peddler's Words?

The peddler of Tzippori, in the midrash cited earlier by R' Yitzchak Aram'ah, did not teach R' Yannai anything new that he had not known before. What the peddler did was to clarify the severity of the sin of *lashon hara* in a very succinct form. First, the peddler did not content himself with his personal knowledge of the seriousness of this sin. Instead, he made a point of proclaiming it in the city streets, and publicizing it within the community that had come to engage in *lashon hara* as a matter of routine. In this, the peddler followed the footsteps of the *avos*, whose service of Hashem went beyond that of Chanoch, of whom we are told, "And Chanoch walked with God" (*Bereishis* 5:22), or Noach, of whom it is said, "With God Noach walked" (ibid. 6:9). Instead, Avraham *Avinu* showed us the course we are to follow: "For I know him, that he commands his sons and his house" (ibid. 18:19). Avraham called in the name of Hashem, and was followed in this by his holy sons and disciples. This was the method the peddler also adopted. And that was why R' Yannai found the peddler's behavior so remarkable, particularly the man's courage to preach the unpopular, and to proclaim the Torah's attitude toward *lashon hara*.

In addition, R' Yannai was impressed with the peddler's perception in that he understood that one's power of speech is the essence of true life, of man's life on earth. The peddler made it clear when he announced, "What man is he that desires life?" This way, he stressed that man's life is inextricably linked to his power of speech and to the contents of that speech. This was a remarkable perception which astounded R' Yannai, who now viewed the peddler as an educator teaching people the way to behave and the essence of life, by stating clearly that the secret to man's life and his superiority over other creatures lies solely in limiting, guarding and sanctifying one's speech. Second, in most cases, people see their lives in a different light, based on their own subjective wants and desires. Here came this peddler and told everyone what the essence of life is in objective terms, without regard for what people feel or desire. Third, R' Yannai was impressed with the clarity of the man's words, in stating that "Keep your tongue from evil, and your lips from speaking guile" is the very basis and essence of life.

In all of this, as we mentioned, the peddler did not show any great originality but exposed the simple truth, which, because of its simplicity, is so often ignored. This is like the story of a certain wise doctor who wrote down all the secrets that he had learned about medicine during his life in a book which he sealed. When the book was opened after his death, it stated there that the plants in Greece are useful as remedies for disease. People immediately began to flock to Greece to pick these plants, but when they tried them, they found that the plants were of no use. All were utterly astounded, because the doctor had been one of the greatest, and how could he have left such advice which seemed so clearly wrong? Finally, along came a wise man and explained it: the doctor had not been referring to the actual plants that grow in Greece, but to the ideas and philosophy of the country, which have the ability to heal the soul of man.

That was what the peddler·was doing when he announced that he had found an elixir for life. When the people then approached him and asked him for this cure for their physical ailments, he explained to them that what he was "selling" was not meant as a physical cure, but as one for man's spiritual diseases. And what is that cure? "Keep your tongue from evil, and your lips from speaking guile."

ఆ§ The Peddler in the Guise of the Kohen

The *Kohen* who comes to pronounce the *metzora tahor* is the peddler in the above story. It is when the *Kohen* sees that the *metzora* has truly repented that he orders him to take two birds, for, as R' Yehudah ben R'

Shimon said (*Midrash Rabbah* 16): "Birds are noisy. Let the sound (of the birds) atone for the sound (of the *lashon hara*)." One of the birds must then be slaughtered over water in an earthenware container, as a symbol that the source of all life — being the power of speech — was changed by the *metzora* to an earthenware vessel, as stated by the prophet (*Eichah* 4:2), "The precious sons of Zion, comparable to fine gold, how are they esteemed as earthen pitchers, the work of the hands of the potter!" In addition, the *Kohen* orders the *metzora* to take cedar wood and crimson wool as a symbol of the latter's evil talk, whereby he made great people small and small people big. Then the *Kohen* orders him to wash his clothes; he must remedy his "clothing," and only then is the *metzora* permitted back into the camp. But he still cannot go to his own tent until a further seven days have passed, during which he rectifies his thoughts. Finally, on the eighth day, he must wash his clothes again, and is then permitted to go back to his own tent. Even then, he cannot appear before Hashem until he has brought his sacrifices. Then the *Kohen* must sprinkle blood on the former *metzora's* cartilage and the thumb of his right hand and large toe of his right foot, for he was guilty to Hashem with his ear for listening to *lashon hara*, and with his hand, which represents action, and with his foot, which symbolizes the last words of the peddler: "Seek peace, and pursue it." Then his sin is finally atoned and it will be well with him and his tent.

III.

What is the Purpose of the Isolation?

The fact that the *metzora* is isolated outside the three camps provides a basis for the discussion of whether *tzara'as* is a natural disease or is something supernatural, and whether the isolation is meant as a punishment to the *metzora* or merely as a way to keep him away from others and thereby to prevent the infection from spreading.

Da'as Zekeinim MiBa'alei HaTosafos says that the person is isolated for the benefit of others, because this disease is contagious and can spread to other people. The *metzora* must be separated so that other people are not harmed. He adds that "he shall dwell alone" (*Vayikra* 13:46), as the Torah requires, means that he must also be separated from his wife, and not only because he infects her, but because due to his sickness marital relations are difficult for him.

Chizkuni also explains this verse as a commandment for the man to refrain from marital intercourse, but he interprets the words מְחוּץ לַמַּחֲנֶה מוֹשָׁבוֹ (ibid.) — that he must reside outside the camp — as a preventive measure so as not to infect others. *Tur* adds that "the nature of this disease is such that whoever deals with [the *metzora*] or even talks to him is infected with the disease." In keeping with this, he explains that the verse (ibid. v. 45), וְעַל שָׂפָם יַעְטֶה — that he must cover his face to his lips — means that the *metzora* must cover his mouth so that he does not infect others by his breath.

Rivash also follows this path, and says that the purpose of the isolation is to protect others from the disease and not because of the *tumah*.

Oznayim LeTorah sees the disease as the reason that the Torah also says וְעַל שָׂפָם יַעְטֶה, which *Chazal* interpret as meaning that he must act as an אָבֵל — a mourner. The *metzora* is, as it were, mourning for himself while still alive, for not only is a *metzora* considered as if he were dead, but the *tzara'as* destroys entire parts of his body, to the extent that his limbs fall off him even during his life. Aaron said about his sister Miriam, who was suffering from *tzara'as*: "Let her not be like a dead person," and even added, "half of whose flesh is eaten away" (*Bamidbar* 12:12). The *metzora* sees his limbs dying while he is still alive and he mourns for them. At the same, though, *Oznayim LeTorah* says that the isolation of the *metzora* is because of *tumah* and not because of his disease. The Torah therefore stresses: "He is *tamei*, he will sit alone, his habitation will be outside the camp" (*Vayikra* 13:46). This is to teach us that the isolation is due to the *tumah* and not for any other reason, for if the reason had been due to disease, the person could have been isolated within the camp and there would be no reason to remove him from all the camps. Thus, the final words of the verse, "his habitation will be outside the camp," are meant to explain the beginning of the verse, "he is *tamei*."

Rambam in his commentary on the Mishnah (*Nega'im* 12) says that *tzara'as* is supernatural, and is under no circumstances a natural disease. The *metzora's* isolation is intended to seclude him from other people so that they may be relieved of the damage caused by his tongue. This isolation is, according to him, in keeping with what *Chazal* wrote: "As he separated with his *lashon hara* between man and his wife and between man and his fellow, he too is to be separated."

Chinuch does not see the isolation as a punishment but as a means to have the person begin thinking about his actions and to do *teshuvah*, and to have him realize the sin which he committed against society. Incidentally, he explains the saying of *Chazal*: בְּמִדָּה שֶׁאָדָם מוֹדֵד, מוֹדְדִים לוֹ — "The same way a man measures, it is measured for him." *Tzara'as* is not an act of retribution that is visited upon the sinner, but a natural outcome, just as a person who walks among thorns is bound to be pricked by them. When a person does evil to others, he brings evil upon himself. Here too, as the person caused evil to society, he is cast out by it, and by that means he realizes the evil which he did to it.

Sifsei Kohen sees the person's total isolation from others as a means to achieve a spiritual cure. If he were allowed the company of other people who were *tamei*, they could all console each other. Living alone, on the other hand, he necessarily begins to reflect upon his ways.

According to *Rivash*, the only reason for this isolation is that the *metzora* has been banished by society. Thus he is obligated by the Torah to announce his presence with the words: "*Tamei! tamei!*" (ibid. v. 45) since he must maintain his seclusion and suffer his banishment. *Akeidah* holds that the isolation is meant to ensure that the person does not infect anyone else with his moral corruption. He too regards this disease as contagious, but not physically; the contagion is spiritual.

Oznayim LeTorah, however, sees the purpose of isolation as an educational tool, to teach the *metzora* the value of society and the importance of it. According to *Chazal*, this person engaged in *lashon hara* and thereby crumbled society. If he must live in isolation, he will realize how essential society is for the preservation of the world. *Chazal* therefore say in *Nedarim* 64 that "a *metzora* is considered as dead." His isolation outside society makes his life unbearable, because there is no life except within human society.

It is quite possible that all three interpretations can be merged into one. The person is isolated from society as a punishment for having crumbled society, and from his isolation he must learn the value of society. But it is his physical ailment which is the means to ensure that no person will have anything to do with him, as he is contagious both physically and spiritually.

Chasam Sofer's symbolic interpretation of *metzora* is very interesting. As we know, the works of *Chazal* contain numerous hints and allusions where actual events are related to the laws of the *metzora*. *Chasam Sofer* also linked events of his time to the *parashah*. He sees the *metzora* as the hypocrite, who acts as if he is *tahor* while poisoning his entire environment, as people do not recognize his true nature. It is not the evil people that are recognized as such by all that will harm others with their evil ways, because the members of society keep away from them. The worst people are those who appear to be righteous, but who are corrupt. Outwardly, they show the signs of *taharah*, as the Torah puts it (*Vayikra* 13:14), וּבְיוֹם הֵרָאוֹת בּוֹ בָּשָׂר חַי — and on the day that raw (living, חַי) flesh appears — giving an appearance of a straightforward person. But that is precisely when such a person is *tamei*. The signs of *tumah*, according to the Torah, are to be found in the person whose נֶגַע — blemish — is בּוֹ — "in him," i.e., in his internal character. His clothes are rent — ostensibly in mourning for Jerusalem. His head is unshaven — as if he had taken an oath to be a *nazir* forever. His lips are covered — so not to raise his voice, as if he is humble, and his head is covered in his *talis*. Yet he has the audacity to call others *tamei*, when he blames others for blemishes which are really his own. Such a man is a true *metzora*, from whom one must keep away and guard oneself. "All the days that his disease is within him, he is *tamei*" (ibid. v. 46) Their *tumah* makes others *tamei*, and one must exercise the utmost care to beware of them.

◈§ May a Metzora Remain in the Company of Other Metzora'im?

Toras Kohanim states in Chapter 12: בָּדָד יֵשֵׁב — אֵין לִי אֶלָּא זֶה בִּלְבָד. מְנַּיִן לְרַבּוֹת שְׁאָר הַמְנָגָּעִים? תּ"ל בָּדָד יֵשֵׁב '' 'He shall dwell alone' (ibid.). That applies to this person. How do I know that it includes others with *nega'im*? We deduce this from בָּדָד יֵשֵׁב."

Ra'avad explains that the reason for this is that the person is in חֵרֶם — "excommunication" — and one is forbidden to sit within four *amos* of such a person. That means that a *metzora* cannot sit within the same area as any other person with *nega'im*. On the other hand, *Tzofnas Pane'ach* brings *Chazal* on *Berachos* 54b, where we are told that Vahev and Sufah were two *metzora'im* who used to walk at the end of the camp — i.e., that both remained together. *Rashi* in *Menachos* 95 also says: "Those who are a *zav* or *metzora* are sent outside their boundaries, with the *metzora* outside the Camp of Yisrael, and they would walk along behind the Camp, as stated in *Berachos* 55, אֶת וָהֵב בְּסוּפָה." So too do we find in *Bava Basra* 20 that *Chazal* tell us that if a *metzora* is tied up, another *metzora* might come along and untie him. From all these we see that *metzora'im* may live together. The most striking proof of this is to be found in *Tanach* (II *Melachim* 7:3), where four *metzora'im* lived together outside the city. And indeed *HaTorah VeHaMitzvah* of *Malbim* proves from the meaning of the word בָּדָד, "alone" (ibid.), that the *metzora* may live with others like him. In his opinion, the word גַּלְמוּד is the more appropriate term for total isolation. The word בָּדָד, though, does not only refer to an individual, but also to a given group,

as we see in the verse (*Devarim* 32:12), "Hashem will lead him בָּדָד,"
where the reference is the whole Jewish people. And we also find
(*Bamidbar* 23:9), "the people shall dwell בָּדָד."

Michtav LeDavid, however, proves from *Chazal* that the *metzora*
cannot live with other *metzora'im*, for *Chazal* give as the reason for his
isolation the fact that he isolated people with his *lashon hara*, and he
should therefore be isolated from other people. That implies that he is to
be isolated from all people. He leaves unanswered the verses we have
quoted, as in *Melachim*, where four *metzora'im* lived together.

Ail Milu'im also proves from *Chazal* that *metzora'im* are forbidden
to stay in each other's company, because we are told in *Pesachim* 47 that
בָּדָד means that no other people who are *tamei* may sit near him. Nor
can one say that this refers to a *zav* or a person who is *tamei* by contact
with the dead, for the latter certainly do not sit together with the
metzora, since they are inside the camp; moreover, their contact with
the *metzora* would put them in danger of becoming *tamei* from him.
Finally, however, *Ail Milu'im* differentiates between various *metzora'im*, and says that those who became *metzora'im* as a result of
lashon hara are forbidden to sit together, because, as *Chazal* tell us, they
separated man from wife, etc. Other *metzora'im*, though, who became
such because of other sins, may live together.

This answers what *Chazal* tell us in *Sanhedrin* 107 on the verse (*II
Melachim* 7:3)," And there were four *metzora'im* at the entering in of
the gate." There the *gemara* asks: "Who were they? According to R'
Yochanan, these were Geichazi and his three sons." It can be asked,
what difference did it make who the four were? However, the question
of *Chazal* was how they were able to be together, for after all,
metzora'im are forbidden to stay together. The answer of *Chazal* is that
their sin was not that of *lashon hara*, and therefore they were permitted
to be together.

Rambam in *Hil. Tumas Tzara'as* 10:7 says: "He must live alone...
only in *Eretz Yisrael*." He does not explain whether "alone" includes
other *metzora'im* as well, but it is clear from *Rambam* that all must live
outside the city, as we are told in the Torah, "his habitation will be
outside the camp" (*Vayikra* 13:46). This refers to those cities which had
a wall around them, but it is not clear from *Rambam* whether the
intention is to all walled cities, or only those which had a wall around
them since the time of Yehoshua (see the first chapter of *Kelim* and the
explanations of *Rash* and *Bartenura* there). Yet the four *metzora'im*
were sitting outside the gate of Shomron, and we are told quite clearly
in *Tanach* that Shomron was built at the time of Omri king of Israel, as
we see in the verse (*I Melachim* 16:24), "and he bought the hill, and he

built up the hill, and he called the name of the city which he built, after the name of Shemer, owner of the hill, Shomron." *HaKesav VeHaKabalah* points out that the *Targum* translates this, "and he bought the city, and he built up the city..." meaning that Omri bought the city of Shomron and then built on it. In other words, Omri took a city which already existed from the time of Yehoshua, and rebuilt it. Afterwards, though, he concludes that *Rambam* holds that while such a city must be in *Eretz Yisrael*, there is no requirement that the wall should be from the time of Yehoshua. *Rambam's* ruling and source need to be clarified.

◀§ He Shall Call: Tamei! Tamei!

It is not enough for the *metzora* to be isolated. He must also keep proclaiming to all that he is *tamei*, so that all will hear him and keep away from him. That is the way that *Rashi* and Ibn Ezra explain it, and that is the way *Rambam* rules in *Hil. Tumas Tzara'as* 10, not only in reference to the *metzora*, but also referring to all those who can make others *tamei*.

According to *Chinuch*, "The crying out is (actually the) making of a sign on his body, so that they will recognize that he is *tamei*." It would thus appear that according to *Chinuch* the second half of the verse, that "He shall call: *Tamei! Tamei!*" is simply an explanation of the beginning of the verse, which notes that he must have a tear in his clothes as a sign of being a *metzora*. According to this view, it is the torn clothes which cry out, "*Tamei! Tamei!*"; the *metzora* himself does not have to say anything. *Sifre*, though, writes that he must announce: "Keep away."

Rambam in *Sefer HaMitzvos*, *Mitzvah* 112, writes: "We already have a tradition that the others who are *tamei* must also make themselves a distinguishing mark so that people will keep away from them ... as it states, 'He shall call: *Tamei! Tamei!*' Thus, every person who is *tamei* must announce that fact and must do something of a distinguishing nature to announce he is *tamei*." *Rambam's* language here seems ambiguous. One can understand that the distinguishing mark is the announcement, just as one can equally interpret it to mean that he must make the announcement in addition to a separate distinguishing mark. It is not clear why *Chinuch* explains that "calling out" means to implement some kind of distinguishing mark, when *Chazal* say that he must announce and give notice to all. But I looked into *Chazal* in *Moed Katan* 5, and found there the source of the two opinions. R' Abahu learns from the verse, "He shall call: *Tamei! Tamei!*" that graves are marked so that the *tumah* calls out and says, "Keep away!"

On the other hand, the *gemara* learns from that verse that "he must announce his distress in public, so that the community will pray for mercy on him." It is thus possible that the purpose of announcing that he is *tamei* is that he wishes others to pray for him, whereas if only a distinguishing mark were necessary, some type of sign on his clothes would be enough. I do not know why *Rashi* included both ideas here — that he must announce that he is *tamei* so that people will keep away from him. This deserves further study.

The Chassidic works explain that when a person calls someone else *tamei*, he himself is *tamei*. This interpretation is mentioned by the *Shaloh* and others, and before them by *Zohar* on *Parashas Vayishlach*. *Chazal* tell us in *Kiddushin* 70 in the name of Shmuel that כָּל הַפּוֹסֵל בְּמוּמוֹ פּוֹסֵל — "whoever wishes to disqualify another, disqualifies him with his own blemish."

Rambam even rules in *Hil. Isurei Bi'ah* 19:17 that: "One who disqualifies others constantly, such as claiming that families or individuals are *mamzerim*, is suspect that he may be a *mamzer*. And if he claims they are slaves, we suspect he may be a slave." It is not at all surprising that that principle appears in *Parashas Metzora*, which deals primarily with *lashon hara*. The punishment of one who denigrates others with his *lashon hara* is that he himself becomes *tamei* and is ostracized from society; and the telltale sign of his *tumah* is that he calls others *tamei*.

◆§ An External Sign

In addition to isolating him, the Torah commands also that the *metzora* must have some external distinguishing signs.

a) "His clothes shall be torn" (*Vayikra* 13:45). According to Ibn Ezra, *Chizkuni* and the other commentators, he must have a rip in his clothes as a sign of mourning, primarily to remind him to mourn his actions or because a *metzora* is considered as though he were dead.

HaKesav VeHaKabalah proves that when the Torah demands פְּרִימָה (tearing) of the *metzora*, it means many tears in his clothes, and he cannot simply have a single tear as does a mourner. We therefore find in the third chapter of Tractate *Makkos*: אִם נִקְרְעוּ נִקְרְעוּ וְאִם נִפְרְמוּ נִפְרְמוּ — "If they were torn, they were torn, and if there was פְּרִימָה, it was פְּרִימָה." From this, we see that קְרִיעָה, which is the kind of tearing done by a mourner, is not the same as פְּרִימָה, which is required of a *metzora*. It is logical to assume that פְּרִימָה is meant as a distinguishing mark. R' Sa'adiah Gaon did not include the commandment of "his clothes will be פְּרֻמִים (torn)" among the

613 commandments. This deserves further study.

b) "His head shall be פָרוּעַ" (ibid.). *Rashi* explains that he must let his hair grow, and that is the explanation of Abarbanel as well, for in this he is just like a mourner. *Rambam*, though, in *Hil. Tum'as Tzara'as* 10:6 rules like R' Akiva, that פָרוּעַ means that he must cover his hair. It is therefore surprising that in *Sefer HaMitzvos Mitzvos Lo Ta'aseh* 163, *Rambam* rules that this means to allow the hair to grow. That is also the way he explained the verse regarding the *Kohen Gadol* who loses one of his close relatives, at which time we are told in the Torah, "אֶת־רֹאשׁוֹ לֹא יִפְרָע", "he shall not cause his hair to be פָרוּעַ" (*Vayikra* 21:10). This agrees with his ruling in *Hil. Klei HaMikdash* 5. This too deserves further study.

c) "He shall wrap upon his mustache" (ibid.). According to *Rambam*, this means that his lips should be sealed and he should not inquire about the welfare of anyone else, just as with a mourner, but the other commentators, such as Abarbanel, *Chizkuni* and others, explain that his mouth must remain closed so that he will not infect others.

Kli Yakar explains all these distinguishing signs as a reminder to repent for his sins, which, according to *Chazal*, brought about the *tzara'as* in the first place. His head (i.e., hair) remains uncut to atone for his pride in attempting to be the head over others. His clothes are torn because of his envy, and his mouth is closed to atone for the sin of *lashon hara*.

It is interesting that *Targum Yehonasan* adds: וְעַל סַפְרַיָּא יְהֵא מְהַלֵּךְ, which some wish to explain to mean that he is to walk by the sea shore. That explanation, though, is not clear. Others have a different version — סַפְדַיָּא — namely that he must walk as a mourner, among "eulogizers" (סַפְדַיָּא). *Pardes Yosef* explains that סַפְרַיָּא refers to a border, namely that he can walk to the border of the camp, but cannot enter it. *Yehonasan's* intentions deserve further study, as does his apparent addition to that which the Torah itself says.

These distinguishing marks in his clothes and in other matters make the *metzora* conspicuous in the community, and this is meant to humble him and to hold him up as an example to warn others. *Shem MiShmuel* quotes his father, *Avnei Nezer*, as to why *Kohanim* have special garments. The reason is that each internal thing needs an external expression. The *Kohanim* have a certain inner *kedushah*, and therefore they must wear the special garments of the *kehunah*. In the case of the *metzora*, whose internal power of *kedushah* has left him to be replaced by an evil spirit, his garments must be torn.

IV.

And I Will Put a Plague in the House of Your Inheritance

Tzara'as, according to the commentators, is an outward manifestation of a spiritual and moral disease. At first, it appears in the home. Afterwards, it spreads to one's garments. If the person has still not taken heed of the warnings by Hashem, it appears in his body as well. As such, tzara'as is a supernatural phenomenon. At the time of our forefathers, it was part of the reality of life. There are some, however, who rely on what *Chazal* tell us in *Sanhedrin* 71, that "there never was a house with *nega'im*, nor will there be." If one examines that source, though, he will see that this is a quotation of R' Elazar, who does not deny the fact that *tzara'as* can appear in homes, but who simply states that the laws governing such a *tzara'as* are not to be implemented, because for a house to be declared afflicted by *nega'im* it requires the fulfillment of certain most unusual and uncommon conditions. He denies only the possibility of having a house with *nega'im* declared *tamei*, but does not deny the phenomenon itself.

This is what *Rambam* wrote in his commentary on the Mishnah, *Nega'im* Chapter 12, Mishnah 5:

> You can see that these are unnatural events, and under no circumstances are they diseases, for the houses are made of inert matter, which should not be affected by *tzara'as*. This is a miraculous event similar to the waters of the *sotah*, and is supernatural because houses and garments do not move on their own volition; and all that happens to them is not *tzara'as*, but the Torah only calls it that by way of comparison...

These words of *Rambam* parallel what he writes in *Mishneh Torah* and *Moreh Nevuchim*, that this is a miraculous phenomenon which cannot be explained through natural means. This phenomenon has since vanished. *S'forno's* opinion is that the earlier generations were worthy of having Hashem's mercy, and Hashem employed these means to caution them against sinning. But later generations have grown weaker spiritually, and are not worthy of such pity. That is why we have no *nega'im* in houses, these being meant to warn man before he receives his full punishment.

Alshech's explanation is a very interesting one. In former generations, men were full of kedushah and *taharah*, and if any *tumah* entered into them because of a sin they had committed, their bodies immediately rejected it in the form of *nega'im*. In later generations, though, our bodies are so steeped in *tumah* that we do not have the spiritual resistance necessary to expel the foreign intruder.

⋅≼ A Special Eretz Yisrael Merit

According to *Ramban*, *nega'im* as an outward expression of internal sin is a special quality linked to the holiness of *Eretz Yisrael*, and the Torah therefore stresses in our *parashah* that, "when you come to the Land of Canaan ... and I will put a *nega* ... in the land of your inheritance" (*Vayikra* 14:34), to teach us that *Eretz Yisrael* causes man's sins to be revealed. And these are his words:

> This is not at all a natural event nor was it ever. The same is with regard to the *nega'im* in houses. But when Israel were all perfect before Hashem, the spirit of Hashem was always upon them to preserve their bodies. Their clothes and homes all looked good. When it happened, though, that one sinned, it resulted in ugliness in his one's person, clothes or home, because the presence of Hashem departed from him. That is why the verse states, "and I will place a *nega tzara'as* in the house in the land of your inheritance." This is an affliction brought by Hashem upon the particular house, and is only in effect in the land which is Hashem's inheritance. This is not because it is a *mitzvah* related to the land, but because this event cannot occur except in the Chosen Land, which is always under the eyes of Hashem.

This view of *Ramban* characterizes his well-known approach to *Eretz Yisrael*. According to him, the kedushah of *Eretz Yisrael* is a tangible characteristic implanted in this wonderful land, and it is because the land is holy that *nega'im* befall the person who profanes it. Other commentators hold that the Torah links *nega'im* of houses to the arrival of the Jews in *Eretz Yisrael* because it was only there that the Jews began to live in proper homes. In the desert they lived in tents; there were no *nega'im* in houses there, because there were no houses. This view is brought by various *rishonim* in *Midrash Tadshei*. *Chizkuni* also explains the Torah this way.

Chida, though, in *Chomas Anach*, and the kabbalist R' Avraham Azulai, in his *Ba'alei Bris Avraham*, see the stress of the Torah, "when you come to the Land of Canaan" as having another meaning. *Chazal* in *Arachin* 16 say that the *nega'im* in houses come because of stinginess, and are meant to undermine man's feeling of security in his possessions, and his false belief that his possessions belong to him and that he has the right to withhold any enjoyment of them from others. The Torah therefore stresses that this land is "the Land of Canaan," and we are not its owners, as if we had taken possession of it with the sword. "I gave you this land," and you do not have the right to act to others as if you own it and to be stingy, for if you do so, I will take My possession back from you, and turn you out of your houses by means of *nega'im*.

A related interpretation is provided by *Netziv* in *Ha'amek Davar*. Canaan is the symbol of commercial life, as we see in the verse (*Yeshayahu* 23:8), "whose merchants (כְּנָעֶנֶיהָ) are honored ones of the land," where the word used for "merchant" is from the same linguistic root as כְּנַעַן, Canaan. The Canaanites lived on the Mediterranean Sea shores and alongside the Jordan River. Those who live by the sea are merchants. *Lashon hara* is deeply rooted in commercial life. According to *Chazal*, *nega'im* come only as a punishment for *lashon hara*. *Lashon hara* that did not harm anyone can be atoned for by the coat of the *Kohen Gadol* (*Arachin* 16a). The *lashon hara* which does cause injury to others is customary only among merchants, but not among farmers, who live off the earth. The Torah therefore stresses "when you come to the Land of Canaan," to show that *nega'im* in houses are more frequent among merchants, and those who are removed from agrarian and agricultural activities.

Perhaps the Torah wanted to teach us thereby to forsake the pursuit of luxuries by means of commerce, and to live the natural life of a nation on its land, in *kedushah* and *taharah*. *Tzara'as* comes to warn us of the moral and spiritual danger in dedicating ourselves to the exaggerated indulgence of our desires. The bricks of a person's house are silent witnesses to his greediness and evil behavior, which is why Hashem places the *nega tzara'as* "in the house of the land of your inheritance," so as to cleanse the Jewish people from the sickness of thievery, dishonesty and unjust behavior. With this basis, *Netziv* explains the words of the Midrash, "When you come to the Land of Canaan" — this is what is written (*Tehillim* 73:1), "[It] is but good to Israel." The word אַךְ (here translated as "but") refers to a life of suffering and of being content with little, as *Rashi* explains on the verse (*Bereishis* 7:23), "and only (אַךְ) Noach remained," that the word אַךְ connotes trouble and hard work. It is good for Israel to live a modest and upright life without any *lashon hara*, deception or theft, and thereby to save itself from *nega'im* and other hazards.

Indeed all the *rishonim* and the *acharonim* explain that *nega'im* were meant to implant in the Jewish people moral values and patterns of life, especially between man and his fellow. Among the eleven factors which *Chazal* give as causing *nega'im*, only two or three are *bein adam laMakom* — between man and Hashem; all the rest are social sins. It is logical to assume that the isolation of the *metzora*, as well as his clearly visible pollution, shows that the purpose of the punishment is to warn society and its individuals about those sins that remove the individual from the community, these, according to *Chazal*, being primarily *lashon hara*, pride, strife, stinginess, and so on. At first, *nega'im* appear in one's house and on one's garments, to warn him not to be too self-confident in his wealth and possessions and not to lord it over others, and to refrain from *lashon hara*, which injures others.

Chazal state clearly that *nega'im* in houses come about as a result of the person's stinginess. They do not explain the purpose of *nega'im* in garments. *Kli Yakar*, though, says that the punishment is due to pride, "because people normally pride themselves on fine clothes." Rot in clothes and homes removes the external covering which customarily hides man from the view of others, and displays his weakness. He stands naked as the day he was born, and he and others see him as a poor and weak creature in the world of Hashem; he is but dust of the earth. That is the purpose of what *Rambam* calls the "sign and portent" of *tzara'as*.

๙ Good News

Chazal tells us that *nega'im* imply good news:

> R' Shimon bar Yochai taught: "When the Canaanites heard that Israel were coming upon them, they arose and hid their money in their homes and fields. The Holy One, Blessed be He, said: 'I promised to their fathers that I would bring their children into a land filled with all good, as it states, "and houses filled with all good" ' (*Devarim* 6:11). What did the Holy One, Blessed be He, do? He brought about *nega'im* on their homes and they tore them down and found the treasures there" (*Chazal* in the Midrash and in *Horiyos* 11).

These words of *Chazal* are based, according to the commentators, on the language of the verse, וְנָתַתִּי נֶגַע צָרַעַת — "I will give a *nega* of *tzara'as*" (*Vayikra* 14:34) — which sounds like a promise. *Malbim* writes, on the basis of proofs from different verses, that the word נְתִינָה, meaning "to give," when used by itself refers only to good or to a good purpose. But it appears to me that the conclusion of *Chazal* is based on the positive expressions stressed in the Torah regarding inheriting the land: "which I am giving as a inheritance" (ibid.), and so too "in the house in the land of your inheritance" (ibid). Thus we see the Torah links *nega'im* to the promise of receiving the land, and it dulls the severity of the punishment by indicating the happiness in the promise by Hashem. The *nega'im* appear with the background of the "inheritance," and are meant to aid in finding hidden treasures in the land.

There are many commentators who nevertheless had difficulty with the meaning of *Chazal's* words, for we know that *nega'im* come for sin, and the appearance of a *nega* exposes a moral disease. How then can *Chazal* refer to *nega'im* as "good news"? There have been numerous interpretations of this.

Many *d'rush* works including *Anaf Yosef* on the Midrash hold that *nega'im* in the house are good news for the righteous and a warning for the wicked. Thus *nega'im* can be either a reward or a punishment. According to these commentaries, that is the reason that when the owner of a house comes to ask a *Kohen*, he says, "as a *nega*" and not simply "a *nega*." The owner is not in any position to know whether the *nega* is positive (for there may be a treasure buried), or negative. Only the *Kohen* can answer this after checking the signs. This *d'rush*, while rewarding in itself, does not answer the basic question, for a house in which a treasure might be found had to be *tamei*, since otherwise it was not torn down. How then can we reconcile the good news with the *tumah*?

Those who explain the Midrash tend to hold that R' Shimon bar Yochai's view is that *nega'im* in houses do not come as a punishment, and that he argues with those who hold that they are a punishment meant as a warning that precedes bodily *nega'im* (*Eitz Yosef* on the Midrash). But this is also a difficult explanation, for it not only rejects that *nega'im* are a punishment, but on the contrary — it seems to imply that the greater the *nega'im* in the house, the more the person stands to find the treasure underneath by having to tear down greater parts of his house. Thus the *nega'im* are a reward rather than a punishment. Can the different opinions be that far apart?

It may be possible to say, though, that R' Shimon bar Yochai intended to explain only why the Torah stresses the curse of the *nega'im* in houses as "good news." Thus he explains that when the Jews first came to *Eretz Yisrael*, the *nega'im* in houses were originally a blessing.

At that time, they were still not burdened with sin, and when there were nega'im in houses they served to reveal hidden treasures. It is for this reason that the Torah stresses the good news implicit in having nega'im in one's home. Afterwards, though, nega'im began to appear as signs of corruption of people's souls. I have found something similar in *Chinuch*, who writes:

> At first, when they conquered the land, Hashem brought nega'im upon a number of houses for their good, so that they would tear down the houses and discover the treasures hidden there by the Emorites. And even though it was possible to inform them of this by means of a prophet without nega'im, it is well known that God performs miracles to man in a secret manner.

It is also possible to say that the word בַּתְּחִילָה — "at first" — in *Chinuch's* words are in keeping with what *Ramban* brought, as quoted above, that nega'im appear because of the sanctity of *Eretz Yisrael*. When they first came into the land they had not yet impaired its *kedushah*, so that the nega'im then were יִסּוּרִין שֶׁל אַהֲבָה — "suffering of love," so that they would uncover the treasures. But with that very same house, once the Jews had profaned the *kedushah* of *Eretz Yisrael*, the blessing was turned into a curse.

Sefas Emes imparts a remarkable Chassidic significance into the words of *Chazal* on the good news of the treasures. Hashem gave the Jewish people a precious quality, enabling us to change חוֹל ("profane") to קֹדֶשׁ ("holy") and *tumah* to *taharah*. Nega'im in the houses are a sign of the *kedushah* of the Jewish people, who bring *kedushah* and *taharah* to the places where they live, to the extent that the *tumah* that might be present is ejected and leaves. And that is the good news — that the Jews have the power to impart spirituality to inert matter and plant life; that the Jewish people removed the Land of Canaan from its *tumah* and brought it to the highest level of *kedushah*. And that is indeed the true treasure — that in every material thing in the world there is a spark of *kedushah*.

V.
A Mitzvah Only in Eretz Yisrael

barbanel sees the *parashah* of *nega'im* in houses as an example of Hashem's extraordinary control of all phenomena, and as something which cannot be explained in natural terms. He disagrees with the commentators who explain *nega'im* in medical and natural terms. The Torah commanded that the *metzora* be healed and made *tahor* by sprinkling, and this shows conclusively that this is no medical or natural question. The entire phenomenon is extraordinary, and what is certainly remarkable is the last section on *nega'im*, that dealing with *nega'im* in houses. This *parashah* is next to the previous one to teach us that we should not be astonished at the nature of the supernatural process of *taharah*, for *Eretz Yisrael* is the land to which Hashem constantly directs His gaze, and there we will realize that the entire phenomenon of *nega'im* is miraculous. *Nega'im* strike a house by Divine Providence, whereby the very stones cry out a warning against our sins, and imply that allowing the spread of the *nega* of idolatry could result in the tearing down of the *Beis HaMikdash*. This particular instance of *nega'im* — in an inert object — is meant to teach us that all of *nega'im* are supernatural and that they expose a spiritual disease, one which must be cured.

Even those who explain the other *nega'im* as natural phenomena see the *nega'im* of houses as supernatural. *Ramban* notes that in regard to *nega'im* in the houses the Torah says, "If the *nega* returns and develops in the house." This is not like the *nega'im* in one's body, which return to their previous place. With houses, there is a new *nega*, in different stones and cement. If a *nega* returns to the body of a person there is a natural explanation for it, for on occasion the moisture is hidden beneath the skin and emerges only at a later point. With houses, though, the *nega* is caused only by an evil spiritual substance which has lodged in the house. Thus, even though the *nega* appears in another place, it is not considered as a new one but rather as stemming from the same source. The reason is that this evil substance does not depart from the house "but will always remain in one of the places to attack the owner." *Chazal* nevertheless see such *nega'im* as "good news," says *Sefas Emes*, because it shows that *tumah* is not absorbed by the Jewish people or their land, but is ejected to the outside, thereby forcing the person to rectify matters and to remove the evil from its lodging.

Chazal explained in a number of places what rectification is needed for *nega'im* in general and *nega'im* in the houses in particular. They give three reasons for *nega'im* in houses: a) *Nega'im* come as a punishment to a person who refuses to lend his belongings, claiming he doesn't have any. Now, when he must take all of his goods outside his house (see *Vayikra* 14:36), all see that he was lying. b)They come to expose items that a person stole and hid. c) They reveal treasures which the Canaanites concealed in their homes, and which could not be found unless the walls were torn down. Therefore, says *Likutei Basar Likutei*, the Torah mentions three ways to act in regard to *nega'im* in the house. If a person never sinned and the *nega'im* came to help him discover a treasure, the *nega* will spread and the stones with *nega'im* are to be removed until the treasure is exposed (see ibid. vs. 39-42). If a person sinned through stinginess in not lending out his things, it is enough just to expose to public view those things he wanted to keep out of sight, so that the *nega* does not need to recur and the house need not be destroyed. One, however, who was guilty of theft will be doubly punished. The *nega'im* will return until the house which he built dishonestly is destroyed (see ibid. vs. 43-45).

Rabbeinu Bachya says that there are ten types of *nega'im* in the two *parashiyos*, six relating to the human body, three to one's garments — wool, linen and leather — and one to the walls of the house. These ten parallel the *Aseres HaDibros* — the Ten Commandments. When the Jews kept the *Aseres HaDibros* in *Eretz Yisrael*, they were saved from *nega'im*. Further, Rabbeinu Bachya says that the reason that the Torah mentions the *nega'im* of the body before the *nega'im* of the house — even though according to *Chazal* the *nega'im* appear in the house first as a warning, then later they appear in the garments, and only at the end in the human body — is because the Torah did not wish to mention these items in order of increasing severity, and preferred to go from the most serious to the least serious.

◄§ To the Land of Canaan

According to all opinions, *nega'im* in houses occur only in *Eretz Yisrael*, as mentioned in the Torah. The reason, according to Ibn Ezra, is because of the sanctity of the land: "Because the *Beis Hamikdash* was within it, and the Glory (of Hashem) was within the *Beis HaMikdash*." *Riva* and other *rishonim*, though, say that the reason the Torah made *nega'im* of houses dependent on the land, unlike *nega'im* of garments and of the human body, is that in the desert they had only tents and no houses, and it was impossible to have *nega'im* of houses in the desert.

R' David Zvi Hoffmann too explains the word וְנָתַתִּי — "and I will place" (ibid. v. 34) — in regard to *nega'im* of houses as a warning of a new phenomenon, which will appear once the Jews own houses. In regard to *nega'im* of the body and of garments, the Torah uses the past tense, for these already appeared in the desert. With regard to *nega'im* of houses, though, these did not appear in the desert because of the absence of houses. R' David Zvi Hoffmann adds that the expression וְנָתַתִּי also implies a supernatural phenomenon in *Eretz Yisrael*. Other nations have *nega'im* of the body but not of their houses. This, then, is a supernatural phenomenon related to entering the land.

Kli Yakar sees the verses as a hint to the words of *Chazal* that this was a punishment for stinginess, for when the Torah says, "I will place a *nega tzara'as* in the house in the land of your possession," the stress is that if when you come to the land you treat it as your possession, as if it is yours because you took it by the sword, then the *nega'im* will appear to teach you that it was not your might and strength which achieved this for you, and you have no reason to be conceited and to think that you are the lords of the land.

Sifsei Kohen points out the use of the words אֶרֶץ כְּנַעַן — "the Land of Canaan" — used here. According to him, these words have a specific significance, for this refers to the land as one based on commerce. Commerce is a major cause of *nega'im*, which are brought about by miserliness and *lashon hara*. Up to this time, Hashem tells us, you lived in the desert and were engaged in learning Torah, so that there was no reason to warn you about *nega'im*. This era, though, is ending. From now on you will be living in a world of action, with all the spiritual *nega'im* involved in this. As a result, you are liable to have physical *nega'im* appear in your homes. *Ha'amek Davar* also explains this in a similar fashion. *Tzara'as* comes about primarily for the sin of *lashon hara*, where a person's words served to harm another person, as explained in *Arachin* 16. For *lashon hara* which does not harm another, the *me'il* — coat — of the *Kohen Gadol* atones. Such *lashon hara* applies primarily to merchants, where one is *masig g'vul* (encroaches) on the economic domain of another, so that the second comes to speak *lashon hara* about the first. Among those who work the land, though, such *lashon hara* is uncommon. It is for this reason that the Torah stresses *the Land of Canaan*, in its meaning of a land of merchants.

Rivash holds that all of the *nega'im*, even those that do not affect houses, do not appear outside of *Eretz Yisrael*. *Ramban* too says this, but not explicitly. One can rather infer this from his words. He writes in

Parashas Metzora on the verse (14:34), "When you come into the Land of Canaan, which I give to you for a possession, and I will put the plague of nega'im in a house of the land of your possession," that "It would have been fitting after 'And Hashem spoke to Moshe and Aharon' (ibid. v. 33) that He should say, 'Speak to the Children of Israel,' but the Torah abridges the meaning and implies that Hashem would speak to Moshe and Aharon, and not to all of Israel, thereby implying that the intention is to teach Moshe and Aharon all the laws of tzara'as so that they will teach them to the Kohanim. Moshe was not to warn Israel about it now. Only when they came to the land would he caution them to: 'Beware of the nega of tzara'as to guard against it diligently' (Devarim 24:8). This last verse refers to nega'im of the body, and nevertheless Ramban states that they were only commanded about it when they came to Eretz Yisrael.

Kli Chemdah also explains Ramban in this fashion, and he questions Ramban's view based on what Ra'avad said, that the Torah warning about nega'im was meant for the immediate time and for future generations. He also asks from the verse itself, which states, "He shall be brought to Aharon the Kohen," from which we see that this law applied in the desert as well. And again he asks from the fact that Chazal prove that poverty is like death from Dasan and Aviram of whom Hashem said, "all these men have died," only because they had lost their wealth and consequently their influence with Pharaoh. Ran there explains that Chazal were led to this interpretation because the other explanation, that having tzara'as is comparable to death, could not apply to Dasan and Aviram who were still in the midst of Israel. It appears from this, that to Ran it was obvious that already then the law of sending a metzora out of the camp was in effect. Kli Chemdah, though, says that that is no proof, because people nevertheless would stay away from those with skin diseases because of their bad breath and odor, and would not allow them to remain in the midst of Israel, without any connection to the laws of metzora. But he asks from the words of Chazal, who state in regard to Miriam that had there been a special place in the desert to put away metzora'im, if Miriam would have been put there. After a discussion, he reaches the conclusion that indeed Israel were warned about the laws of metzora in the desert, even according to Ramban, but the mitzvas asei and the lav (positive and negative commandments) of (Devarim 24:8), הִשָּׁמֶר בְּנֶגַע הַצָּרַעַת — "Beware of the nega of tzara'as" — went into effect only when they came into Eretz Yisrael. In Eretz Yisrael, their lives were conducted supernaturally, and they were forbidden to cut or peel off the tzara'as so as to bring about a natural cure. While they were in the desert, though, they were allowed to heal their nega in a natural way by cutting it off to heal it.

The other *acharonim*, however, hold that according to *Ramban*, it was not just the commandment, "Beware of the *nega* of *tzara'as*" that did not apply in the desert; none of the laws of *tzara'as* applied until Bnei Yisrael entered the land. *Nachalas Yaakov Yehoshua* brings proof to *Ramban's* view. *Chazal* in *Kerisus* 7 learn from the word וְהַצָּרוּעַ — "and the one afflicted by *tzara'as*" (*Vayikra* 13:45) — that women too are included in the laws of *nega'im*. This verse is apparently superfluous because we could learn the application to women from the fact that Miriam became a *metzora'as*. We are thus forced to say that we cannot learn anything from the *nega'im* that occurred in the desert, because then the laws of *nega'im* were not yet applicable.

◆§ Only Good for Israel

The Midrash at the beginning of our *parashah* brings the verse, אַךְ טוֹב לְיִשְׂרָאֵל אֱ-לֹהִים — (*Tehillim* 73:1 — "God [does] only good to Israel"). One might imagine that this applies to all. The verse therefore concludes: "to the purehearted," which *Chazal* interpret to mean — only to those whose heart is healthy because of their performance of *mitzvos*.

Yismach Moshe explains that the Midrash refers to the hidden treasures that the Emorites hid in their walls, and which the Jews found when they broke down their walls because of the *nega'im* in them, as stated by *Sifra*. Hashem promised those with a healthy heart that even אֱ-לֹהִים, which is Hashem's attribute of דִּין — strict judgment — would be good to them. Externally, it appears that the person has suffered a severe loss because his walls are torn down, while in reality it is to his benefit. *Chazal* deduced the good to be gained from *nega'im* from the word וְנָתַתִּי — "And I will give" (*Vayikra* 14:34) — used by the Torah in reference to *nega'im*, a verb in most cases used to refer to good news, as the Torah states: וְנָתַתִּי גִשְׁמֵיכֶם בְּעִתָּם — "And I will give your rains at their appointed time" (ibid. 26:4); וְנָתַתִּי שָׁלוֹם בָּאָרֶץ — "and I will make peace in the land" (ibid. v. 6); and so on. *Malbim* also writes that the verb נתן generally refers to something good. When it is used in reference to something bad, it refers to a continuous action, and one over a long period of time, such as וְנָתַתִּי אֶת־הָאָרֶץ שְׁמָמָה — "and I will render the land desolate" (*Yechezkel* 15:8). Here, in regard to *nega'im*, we do not refer to a continuous action, and therefore *Chazal* interpreted it to be a reference to the good, implying that *nega'im* are meant to be good news to Israel.

Ha'amek Davar explains this expression as Hashem's *Hashgachah P'ratis* — Divine Intervention — whether for the good or for the bad. He brings *Ramban's* view that this term is meant to indicate that

Hashem's hand has done this in a supernatural manner. *Ha'amek Davar* asks why the term וְנָתַתִּי is not used in regard to *nega'im* in clothes as well, for after all, that too is supernatural. He therefore explains that with regard to *nega'im* of houses, Hashem had a special positive aim, in accordance with the words of the *Zohar* that one who builds a house must be sure to build it on the foundations of Torah and *kedushah*. When the Canaanites built their homes, they built them from the outset on the basis of *tumah*. That is the reason that *nega'im* appeared in them, so that people would be forced to tear them down and rebuild them in *kedushah*. This is in itself good news, for it means that *tumah* is ejected by Jewish homes, and even though this may result in material damage to the person involved, the reward to him is much greater than any damage he suffered. This is the special *hashgachah* which is expressed in the word וְנָתַתִּי.

Tosefes Brachah wonders about the identity of the person who said that *nega'im* are considered good news for Israel. According to the way it is brought by *Chazal*, it was R' Shimon who said this. Whenever we are told "R' Shimon" said something, without any other clarification, it refers to R' Shimon bar Yochai. On the other hand, we find in *Sanhedrin* 4a that the son of R' Shimon, R' Elazar, was the author of the statement that "A house with *nega'im* never existed and will never exist." And this is the language of *Chazal*: "And according to whom is the view that we learned in a *beraisa* that a house with *nega'im* never existed and will never exist? According to R' Elazar ben R' Shimon, who said that a house is never declared *tamei* until one sees (the size of) two barley grains on two walls, in a corner, the length of two barley grains and the width of a barley grain." In other words, such a possibility is highly unlikely, and therefore the law of *nega'im* in houses was never put into effect.

Tosefes Brachah asks how it is possible that R' Elazar would disagree with his father, R' Shimon, as to whether *nega'im* ever existed in houses, for according to R' Shimon not only did *nega'im* exist, but they foretold good news for the occupants of the house, leading them to discover the treasures buried by the Emorites. How could his son say the exact opposite and deny the very existence of such a phenomenon? *Tosefes Brachah* gives a logical answer. R' Elazar is not arguing with his father as to the possibility of *nega'im* appearing in houses, but as to whether a house can be declared to be one with *nega'im*, due to the extremely rare conditions that must be met before the house can be declared to have *nega'im*. It is possible that R' Shimon will even agree to this, but that applies only to declaring a house *tamei*. As to finding treasures, if such were concealed they will be found when the walls are broken down.

Then they will see that the conditions for declaring a house *tamei* are not decisive, for meanwhile the treasures alluded to by R' Shimon will have been found.

It is also possible that the very unlikelihood of ever declaring a house *tamei* led R' Shimon to his statement that *nega'im* are good news, as they lead to tearing down the house and to finding the treasures of the Emorites, or, according to the *Zohar*, to rebuilding the house in *kedushah*, for otherwise why would the *nega'im* have appeared? After all, they would not fulfill the conditions necessary for declaring the house *tamei*.

It is interesting that the appearance of *nega'im* in houses does indeed depend on the Jews' coming into *Eretz Yisrael*, but it is not a phenomenon that depends on the land. Instead, it depends on the Jewish people living on its own land. The Emorites never saw any *nega'im* in their homes, even though were guilty of every type of depravity. This is proof, says R' Yehonasan, that the land belongs only to the Jews, and not to the other nations. The other nations, with their depravities, do not have the power to forbid something which does not belong to them. That is the reason for the stress here on "in a house in the land of your possession" (*Vayikra* 14:34) to teach us that this land is yours, and you have the power to make an impression on it, either positively or negatively. And again the Torah stresses, "and he who owns the house shall come" (ibid. v. 35), namely that the land is yours; and it is for that reason that the land is so sensitive to any *tumah* or injustice on your part. *Chida*, following the example of *Kli Yakar*, has a beautiful explanation of כִּי תָבֹאוּ אֶל־אֶרֶץ כְּנַעַן אֲשֶׁר אֲנִי נֹתֵן לָכֶם לַאֲחֻזָּה — "When you come to the land of Canaan which I am giving you as a possession" (ibid. v. 34). Your coming to the land must be marked by an awareness and recognition that *I*, and not your swords, am giving you this land. If, however, you attribute your conquest of the land to your endeavor and effort, וְנָתַתִּי נֶגַע צָרַעַת בְּבֵית אֶרֶץ אֲחֻזַּתְכֶם — "I will place the *nega* of *tzara'as* in the house in the land of your possession." The *nega* will appear when you consider this "the land of your possession," as if it is yours through your own power and might.

The *taharah* — purification — will come, says *Sha'arei Simchah*, when you confess and admit כְּנֶגַע נִרְאָה לִי בַּבָּיִת — "Something like a *nega* has appeared to me in the house" (ibid. v. 35) — where the sinner recognizes that it is not his house, but that of Hashem; it is only then that the cure can come.

Eretz Yisrael has the remarkable ability to reject any *tumah* in its midst and to implant in the hearts of those who live in it the lesson that miserliness brings about *tumah*. It also has the extraordinary ability to locate treasures, as a result of an event that seemed to be a curse. In this, *Eretz Yisrael* differs from any other country. In other countries, things that seem to be blessings turn out to be curses, while in *Eretz Yisrael* *nega'im* become blessings.

Chazal have discussed why the Torah mentions the *nega'im* of people before those of garments and houses, even though the last to be affected are people. *Or HaChaim* explains that in the desert there were only *nega'im* that afflicted people, for the other kinds of *nega'im* occurred only in *Eretz Yisrael*, as in the verse וְנָתַתִּי נֶגַע צָרַעַת בְּבֵית אֶרֶץ אֲחֻזַּתְכֶם — "I will place the *nega* of *tzara'as* in the house in the land of your possession." In *Eretz Yisrael*, the *nega'im* will first appear in your property, and only thereafter in your body, and that is good news for Israel.

Acharei Mos – אַחֲרֵי מוֹת

I.

The Significance of the Sa'ir La'Azazel

The *sa'ir la' Azazel* — the so-called "scapegoat" that was sent into the desert by the *Kohen Gadol* on *Yom Kippur*, is a central topic for the various commentators in all four areas of Torah interpretation — פַּרְדֵּס. *Rashi*, following the interpretations of *Chazal*, explains that *Azazel* means a high and craggy mountain, as if the Hebrew word עֲזָאזֵל was formed of two words: עַז (strong) and אֵל (mighty), namely sending forth the *sa'ir* — the goat — to a place where there are cliffs and mountains. Yehonasan ben Uzziel also explains it as "the desert of cliffs," and then adds the words בֵּית חָרוּרֵי. A number of commentators who have difficulty in determining the meaning of the latter two words suggest that Yehonasan is referring to a place filled with demons. However, the commentators on *Targum Yehonasan* say that the words are a scribal error, and should read בֵּית חָדוּדֵי, in accordance with the words of *Chazal* that "R' Yehudah said, 'They had a great sign, from Jerusalem to בֵּית חָדוּדֵי is three *mils*.'" According to this, the meaning of *Azazel* is simple and has nothing to do with Kabbalah. But the reason why the *sa'ir* was sent away remains unknown.

Chazal list the *sa'ir* that was sent away as one of those things that evoke responses by Satan, and they also refer here to the scoffers of each generation who claim that Jews do things which cannot be understood logically. Among those *halachos* listed by the *gemara* in this context are the prohibitions against eating pig and against wearing *sha'atnez*, the law of *chalitzah* when a man dies without having children, the *taharah* of a *metzora*, and the *sa'ir* that is sent away (*Chullin* 109). It is interesting that the *gemara* does not include *parah adumah* — the "red cow" — which too is a *chok* that defies human comprehension.

Maharsha in his *Chiddushei Aggados* on *Yoma* 67 says that the criticism of the heretics was based on the difference between what is permitted and what is forbidden in these matters, in accordance with what *Chazal* state in *Chullin*: "Whatever the Torah forbade to us, it permitted something resembling it . . . We are forbidden to eat pork, but were permitted the brain of the *shibuta* (a type of fish, whose brain tastes like pork)." In the purification of a *metzora*, there are two birds, one for the *taharah* and the second is sent away. And so with the *se'irim* of *Yom Kippur*, one for Hashem and the second for *Azazel*. Thus, the astonishment of the non-Jews was not at the *mitzvos* themselves, for which one might find a logical explanation, but on the internal differences and contradictions in the *mitzvos*, which cannot be explained logically. This idea is also found in *Maharitz Chayos*.

We find in *Chazal* that the Jewish heretics also scoffed at the *sa'ir* and would pull its hair, telling it, "hurry up and leave." According to *Rashi*, their scoffing was because they felt that the *sa'ir* was waiting for too long a time with their sins, and had not yet left. Rabbeinu Chananel, though, holds that they scoffed at the idea of having atonement come through a *sa'ir*. Would such a small *sa'ir* be able to carry on its neck such heavy sins? About such people, *Chazal* tell us in the Midrash and in *Yoma* that: "Lest you say that these are vain acts, it therefore states, 'I am Hashem.' I made these laws." Even so, the different commentators sought explanations for this *mitzvah*, and especially attempted to explain the difference between the two goats; why one was sacrificed and the other was sent to the desert, where it would die.

S'forno explains this simply. The *sa'ir* that carries all the sins of Israel is not fit to be sacrificed because of the great amount of *tumah* that it carries. In the eyes of other commentators, though, this is not so simple.

Or HaChaim states that "these matters are astonishing," and he seeks a conceptual and symbolic explanation for them. Punishment is the consequence of one's sins, as we see in (*Yirmiyahu* 2:19), "Your own wickedness will punish you." The purpose of a sacrifice is to have the impurities of the person transferred to the animal when he lays his hands on the animal's head and to release the person from the punishment that should result from the presence of these impurities. The *sa'ir* that is sacrificed in the *Beis HaMikdash* comes to atone only for deliberate sins related to the *Beis HaMikdash* and its *kodashim*, which is why Hashem accepts it as a sacrifice; but the *sa'ir la'Azazel* carries with it all the impurities of the Jewish people. It is the *goral* — the lot that is cast — indicating Hashem's choice, which decides which *sa'ir* is chosen to carry away all the impurities to a desolate place, where no man walks.

Ramban relies on the *goral* as being an indication of Hashem's will, even though both animals were chosen for Hashem. We bring both sacrifices to Hashem, but He decides through the *goral* that one of the goats will be sent away to a desolate place. We carry out this action in accordance with the commandment of Hashem, but it is not attributed to Him.

The Gaon of Lutzk, in his *Oznayim LeTorah*, provides a beautiful interpretation to the *parashah*. The *sa'irim* are two that are really one. Every *chatas* sacrifice requires *semichah* — the laying of the hands on the animal's head; *vidui* — confession; the sprinkling of the blood; and the burning of the *eimurim* — certain inner parts of the animal. On Yom Kippur, though, these duties are divided among the two *sa'irim*. The *sa'ir* that is for Hashem has no *vidui*, but its blood is sprinkled on the *paroches* and the golden altar, and its *eimurim* are burnt on the outer altar. On the other hand, the *sa'ir* that is sent away has no *shechitah*, neither is its blood sprinkled nor its *eimurim* burned. It does, though, have the *vidui* of the *Kohen Gadol* on its head. From this, we can see that both are in reality but a single sacrifice, and that because of all the sins that it carries, the *sa'ir la'Azazel* is not sacrificed.

⇜§ A Struggle Between Yaakov and Eisav

The kabbalistic works explain the idea of the *sa'ir la'Azazel*. It is similar to the bird that is sent away with the *taharah* of a *metzora*, as a gift to the forces of *tumah*, which are personified by the wicked Eisav and his שַׂר — his particular angel. All these commentators note the similarity in names between Mount Se'ir — the home of Eisav — and the *sa'ir* in this *parashah*. This explanation, even though far from *p'shat* — the plain meaning of the text — contains an idea that finds its expression in the *p'shat* literature, even though in a different garb.

Abarbanel develops this idea and says that the two *sa'irim* of Yom Kippur symbolize the eternal struggle between the two brothers, Yaakov and Eisav. They were born twins and were of the same height and appearance, yet separated later; one to eternal life and the other to infamy. By their nature, the two should have developed along the same lines, but because of Hashem's mercies and His Divine Intervention, it was the lot of the one of the two "*sa'irim*" to be part of Hashem's nation and to draw closer to Him, while the second "*sa'ir*" was moved away from Hashem's inheritance and was sent to an empty wasteland. The two *sa'irim* of Yom Kippur are a prayer to Hashem to have the eternal struggle between Yaakov and Eisav end that way. Just as the *sa'ir* la'Azazel is sent away, so too will the same occur to those forces which it represents. The *Kohen Gadol* confesses on the *sa'ir* which is sent away, indicating by this, that sins and immorality suit the personality of Eisav the *rasha*, while the children of Yaakov must be pure and clean of sin, for they are the Chosen People.

Akeidah also follows Abarbanel, but he says the *vidui* not only indicates that sin is suited to Eisav the *rasha*, but also serves to be *melamed zechus* — to indicate merit — for the Jews, who are tainted by sin only because of the pressures of Edom (i.e., Eisav), and only he is responsible for their spiritual and moral fall.

It is interesting that this approach is found repeatedly in the Chassidic works on our *parashah*, as well as in *Maharal* and in various *d'rush* works. All explain the verse, וְנָשָׂא הַשָּׂעִיר עָלָיו אֶת־כָּל־עֲוֹנֹתָם אֶל־אֶרֶץ — "and the *sa'ir* will carry upon himself all their sins to a land" (*Vayikra* 16:22) — that our exile and our suffering at the hands of the different nations have been the cause of our spiritual decline. R' Pinchas of Koretz explains the words of the *navi* (*Tehillim* 60:10), מוֹאָב סִיר רַחְצִי, עַל־אֱדוֹם אַשְׁלִיךְ נַעֲלִי — "Moab is my washpot; over Edom will I cast my lock" — along these lines.

Similarly, the Tzaddik, R' Elazar Shapira of Munkacz, would cry out on *Yom Kippur*: וְנָשָׂא אֶת־כָּל־עֲוֹנֹתָם אֶל־אֶרֶץ גְּזֵרָה — " 'It will carry all their sins to a wasteland (*eretz gezeirah*).' All the *gezeiros* (evil decrees) and pain brought upon us by our oppressors are the cause of our sins, and the source of all our cultural and spiritual problems." This has also been a theme of *tzaddikim* throughout the different generations to find merit for *Klal Yisrael* in their talks on *Yom Kippur*.

Chasam Sofer, too, in his *Toras Moshe* quotes *Chazal* in the Midrash, that Hashem loads all the sins of Israel on the shoulders of Eisav the *rasha*, who then screams out: "How can I bear all these sins?" *Chasam Sofer* explains that there are certain sins which one cannot attribute to the *galus*, and Eisav is not willing to take responsibility for these types of sins. There are, for example, sins of lust or passion, which should have disappeared because of the pain of exile. Hashem then places these sins on His own garments, because of the *tzedakah* and *chessed* which are such an integral part of Israel, as Chazal say: "And His garb is like a coat of mail." This refers to *tzedakah*. This *tzedakah* of Israel has the power to atone for those sins which cannot be blamed on Eisav.

Kli Yakar says that the two *sa'irim* are the two goats that Yaakov brought to his father, and by which he acquired the *brachos* — the blessings. Jewish history grew from that act. In the end, Eisav will be sent to the desert, into the arms of destruction and annihilation.

Rambam in *Moreh Nevuchim* 3:46 sees the idea of the *sa'ir* which is sent away as an action of arousing everyone to do *teshuvah*. According to him, "sins are not burdens that one can transfer from the back of one person to that of another, but all these actions [regarding the *sa'ir* on Yom Kippur] are all meant as lessons to bring about fear in one's soul, until one does *teshuvah*."

R' David Zvi Hoffmann in his work on *Vayikra* also follows this path. Whatever was said in regard to the *sa'ir* which is sent away is meant as a lesson to teach us that sins must be eradicated from within the borders of Israel. Hashem gives sinners an opportunity to improve their ways and demands that only sin be eliminated, not the sinners. This statement is very general, and does not relate to the specific laws involved or to the verses of the Torah.

HaKsav VeHaKabalah, though, attempts to show how this idea fits into the verses, symbolically and in educational and *hashkafah* terms. According to him, the purpose of the *sa'ir* which is sent away is to uproot various false beliefs from the heart, as in the verse, "they shall not sacrifice their sacrifices to the *sa'irim*" (*Vayikra* 17:7) The word עֲזָאזֵל is a composite of the words עַז and זָל, and implies a great and mighty denigration. The people see how the *sa'ir* is loaded up with all the sins and is then thrown over a cliff where it is torn apart, and as a result they are all greatly overwhelmed and impressed by an appreciation of how terrible it is to worship false gods, as symbolized by the sacrifices to the *sa'irim*. The results of this action are that וְנָשָׂא ... עָלָיו אֶת־כָּל־עֲוֹנֹתָם — "it shall carry upon itself all their sins." The contamination of idol worship leaves their souls and the people again cling to their Creator.

"Had I not been afraid of expressing so daring an idea," says *HaKesav VeHaKabalah*, "I would have explained that וְנָתַן אֹתָם עַל־רֹאשׁ הַשָּׂעִיר — 'and he shall put them [the sins] on the head of the *sa'ir*' (*Vayikra* 16:21) — means that the sinner will abandon his sins and will from now on forsake sin, for the word וְנָתַן may be defined in the sense of separation, as "my nard gave forth its scent." As to the verse וְנָשָׂא ... עֲוֹנֹתָם אֶל־אֶרֶץ גְּזֵרָה — "he will carry all their sins to a wasteland" — this refers to the one who carries the *sa'ir*. He will carry on his shoulders to a wasteland, עֲוֹנֹתָם — the *sa'ir* (עֲוֹנֹתָם has the same use here as חַטָּאת — which means literally "sin," but refers to the goat which is sanctified).

This idea is also found in *Ramban*, who explains that the intention of the Torah was to separate the people from idolatry, so that they should no longer offer their sacrifices to the *sa'irim*. One should note that the source of this idea of *HaKesav VeHaKabalah* is in *Akeidas Yitzchak*, who explains the sa'ir la'Azazel as an expression of scorn for idolatry and sa'irim, and as educating the people to serve Hashem.

Abarbanel and *Akeidah* have another explanation of the *parashah*. The two *sa'irim* are the two qualities of good and bad that were implanted in man so as to give him free will. The גּוֹרָל — the lot — is his lot, to choose between good and bad. The one is to Hashem, as in the verse, וּבָחַרְתָּ בַּחַיִּים — "choose life" (*Devarim* 30:19), while the other is to *Azazel*. This idea is elaborated upon by R' Samson Raphael Hirsch. (This can be found in *R' Samson Raphael Hirsch, His Teachings and Doctrine*, published by the Ezra study fund. This chapter in his teachings, covering many pages, should be on the table of everyone who studies our *parashah* in depth.)

The reader should also be aware of and know the views of the great Chassidic rabbis, that the letters of the word עֲזָאזֵל form the first letters (in different order) of the verse (*Koheles* 7:14), זֶה לְעֻמַּת־זֶה עָשָׂה הָאֱ־לֹהִים — "this as compared to this, Hashem created." This parallels a comment by *Chazal* that both goats must be identical in size and appearance. According to R' Leib of Sasov, this comparison shows that whatever exists in *kedushah* has a counterpart in *tumah*, and this is to provide the even balance of good and evil which makes free will possible as is explained at length by R' Samson Raphael Hirsch.

We should also note the words of *Tanna d'Bei R' Yishmael* (*Yoma* 67) that the sa'ir that is sent away is meant to atone for the sin of Uzza and Azazel, two angels who came down to earth at the time of Na'amah, sister of Tubal Cain, and who illicitly took mortal wives for themselves (see *Bereishis* 6:1-4). Some explain that we read all the laws of forbidden marriages at the afternoon service on *Yom Kippur* to remind us of that first corruption of forbidden marriages, for which the sa'ir that is sent away comes to atone. It may be that our atonement here is based on finding merit for ourselves, by showing that even angels sinned and fell into the trap of sin. What then can one say of the sins of man, who is but flesh and blood?

At the end of *Devarim Rabbah*, we find this same demand, in the name of the soul of Moshe *Rabbeinu*, which said: "Master of the Universe! From Your *Shechinah* on High, angels came and lusted for the women of the earth."

➻ Ibn Ezra's Comments

Ibn Ezra, in discussing the sa'ir that is sent away, makes the following remarkable comment: "And if you could understand the secret which is after the word עֲזָאזֵל you will know its secret and the secret of its name, for there are companions to this in the Torah, and I will reveal to you a little of the secret with a hint; when you are thirty-three-years old you will know it."

This secret mentioned by Ibn Ezra is concealed from us, and many commentators have struggled with what he means. *Ramban*, *Tosafos HaRosh* and other commentators explain that Ibn Ezra refers to thirty-three verses after this one, where the Torah states וְלֹא־יִזְבְּחוּ עוֹד אֶת־זִבְחֵיהֶם לַשְּׂעִירִם — "they shall no longer slaughter their sacrifices to the *s'irim*." *Ramban* adds that this *sa'ir* is Sammael, the angel of destruction, hostilities and war. Hashem ordered us to give His servant part of His sacrifice, as it were. Had it not been for the *goral*, the lots, we would not have been allowed to give anything to an angel, but the *goral* transforms this action so that the *sa'ir* is given, as it were, by Hashem.

This explanation of Ibn Ezra is not completely clear. If that is Ibn Ezra's meaning, what is the great "secret"? It is also difficult to understand why Ibn Ezra seems to be dealing with secrets. We can rely on *Ramban* in his interpretation of Ibn Ezra, though later commentators have also attempted to find the *p'shat* in his comment.

Avi Ezri offers a number of explanations. One of these is that this refers to Yaakov and his sons. When Yaakov met with Eisav (*Bereishis* ch. 30), the number of his sons and daughters was thirty-two, and when we include Yaakov there were thirty-three people. Yaakov then sent a gift to Eisav, and that is the source for the *sa'ir* which was sent away.

Chasam Sofer also discusses the words of Ibn Ezra, and especially the statement, "And if you could understand the secret which is after the word עֲזָאזֵל." The letters of the alphabet that follow each letter in the word עֲזָאזֵל are פחבהומ, which in *gematria* is equivalent to חָמֵץ — the leavening in the dough, which makes it ferment, and which is used by *Chazal* to indicate the *yetzer hara*. The letters following מִדְבָּר are נהגש, which in *gematria* is equivalent to נָחָשׁ, serpent, a reference to the serpent in Eden which *Chazal* identify as the *yetzer hara*.

II.

And the Land Will Not Vomit You Out

I n our *parashah*, the Torah warns us that the punishment that Israel suffers for עֲרָיוֹת — illicit sexual conduct — is *galus*, for that was the reason that the non-Jews who lived in *Eretz Yisrael* were evicted from the land. At the beginning of the *parashah*, the Torah warns us (*Vayikra* 18:3): כְּמַעֲשֵׂה אֶרֶץ־מִצְרַיִם אֲשֶׁר יְשַׁבְתֶּם־בָּהּ לֹא תַעֲשׂוּ וּכְמַעֲשֵׂה אֶרֶץ כְּנַעַן אֲשֶׁר אֲנִי מֵבִיא אֶתְכֶם שָׁמָּה לֹא תַעֲשׂוּ וּבְחֻקֹּתֵיהֶם לֹא תֵלֵכוּ — "You shall not do as the deeds of the land of Egypt where you dwelled, and you shall not do as the deeds of the Land of Canaan to which I am bringing you; and you shall not follow their statutes." The Torah does not specify what these deeds were.

Abarbanel explains that the deeds of the Land of Egypt were witchcraft, and those of the Land of Canaan were illicit sexual conduct. *Ramban*, though, following *Chazal*, says that the deeds of Egypt and Canaan were identical, and both refer to immoral sexual conduct, which preoccupied the Egyptians no less than the Canaanites. The Torah commands us not to follow in the pattern of such nations, whether we are already living in their midst or whether we are yet to live among them.

The behavior of nations, according to *Ha'amek Davar*, can be governed by one of two methods: either because it is the accepted mode of behavior in the place, or because it is a law enacted by the authorities. The first one is referred to as the "מַעֲשֶׂה" of the Land of Egypt, while as to the second, the Torah warns us, "וּבְחֻקֹּתֵיהֶם לֹא תֵלֵכוּ." This warning applies to Canaan, where immoral sexual conduct was the law of the land. At the end of the *parashah*, we are told of two punishments for these sins: first, the punishment of *galus*, וְלֹא־תָקִיא הָאָרֶץ אֶתְכֶם — "that the land should not vomit you out" (ibid. v. 28) and second, the punishment of *kares* (premature death) for individuals. According to *Ha'amek Davar*, the punishment of *galus* is imposed on a country whose immoral conduct becomes enshrined in law, while the punishment of *kares* comes for the acts themselves, whether these are by individuals or by an entire community, even though these acts are not the law of the land.

The other commentators of the Torah, and especially the Chassidic works, expand the concept of the מַעֲשִׂים — deeds — of the Land of Egypt and of the Land of Canaan to all aspects of life. The authors of *Shulchan Aruch* list innumerable matters that are forbidden because they resemble חֻקּוֹת הַגּוֹיִם — "the laws of the Gentiles."

Do not think, says the author of *Michtam LeDavid*, that as you have left Egypt already and you no longer have any ties with that nation, that you are permitted to imitate their customs and ways without needing to fear that you will be assimilated by them. This is not so. Do not do as the deeds of Egypt in which you lived, even though you once lived there. If you do not copy their customs, then you can be sure that "you shall not do as the deeds of the Land of Canaan to which I am bringing you." One who does not copy the nation in which he once lived will also not copy the nation in which he will live in the future. Do not copy therefore the customs of the country which you left, even though there is no fear of assimilation with that nation.

Ma'or VaShemesh has a different explanation. מַעֲשֵׂה אֶרֶץ מִצְרַיִם refers to the *chutzpah* of those who are insignificant, attacking those above them and telling them, as did Dasan and Aviram, "Who made you a leader?" (see *Shemos* 2:14). This is the מַעֲשֵׂה אֶרֶץ מִצְרַיִם, which we may not emulate under any circumstances. Instead, we must base our lives on לֹא תָסוּר מִן־הַדָּבָר אֲשֶׁר־יַגִּידוּ לְךָ — "Do not swerve from the things that they tell you" (*Devarim* 17:11) — that we must follow the path set for us by our *gedolim*, and may not emulate the actions of Dasan and Aviram in Egypt.

Kli Yakar offers an interpretation which is extremely practical for our days. The Torah is referring to *aliyah* — moving to *Eretz Yisrael*: "You shall not do as the deeds of the land of Egypt where you dwelled." Hashem commanded us to be no more than גֵּרִים — strangers or sojourners — in Egypt, but instead the Jews chose to settle there as citizens. Here Hashem commands us: In your future exiles, do not do the same thing. Similarly, "You shall not do as the deeds of the Land of Canaan to which I am bringing you"; do not repeat the sin of "rejecting the precious land" (*Tehillim* 106:24), where I was forced to bring you to the land against your will. Instead, come to *Eretz Yisrael* of your own free will, so that you may observe the *mitzvos* which apply only to it, and so that, as the verse quoted at the beginning of this section continues, אֶת מִשְׁפָּטַי תַּעֲשׂוּ וְאֶת־חֻקֹּתַי תִּשְׁמְרוּ לָלֶכֶת בָּהֶם — "You shall keep My commandments and observe My statutes to walk in them."

◆§ Immorality and the Sanctity of Eretz Yisrael

Ibn Ezra links the prohibition against illicit sexual conduct with living in *Eretz Yisrael*, noting that Yaakov married two sisters when he lived in Charan, and Amram married his aunt in Egypt. Abarbanel, though, doesn't agree with what Ibn Ezra said. Yaakov and Amram did not observe these laws as they lived before the Torah was given.

One who looks into what *Ramban* says here will see that he too says what Ibn Ezra said, but the style of his language is in accordance with his well-known view regarding *Eretz Yisrael*. The prohibition against *arayos* — illicit sexual conduct — says *Ramban*, is a prohibition which applies to the person and is not dependent on the land, but *Eretz Yisrael* does not tolerate idolaters or sexually immoral people, and it vomits them out, whereas the other countries which are under the rule of their own angels, and not of Hashem himself, do not have this quality.

Therefore,

Although everything belongs to Hashem, what is outside (of *Eretz Yisrael*) lacks complete *taharah* — spiritual purity — because of the heavenly hosts that rule there and the nations who stray after these ministers.

The Torah refers to Hashem as אֱ־לֹהֵי כָל הָאָרֶץ — 'God of *all* the land' — because He rules over all, and will in the end impose His will over all the hosts of heaven, in order to remove their rule and destroy the system of ministers.

Outside *Eretz Yisrael*, Hashem is "God of *all* the land," whereas in *Eretz Yisrael*, He is אֱ־לֹהֵי הָאָרֶץ — "God of the land" — the land which is נַחֲלַת הַשֵׁם — "the inheritance of Hashem," and that is the reason why *Eretz Yisrael* cannot tolerate the *tumah* of the other nations. It was because of this that when Sennacherib settled other nations in *Eretz Yisrael*, lions came and destroyed them.

Going on, *Ramban* tells us that the major purpose of the observance of *mitzvos* is to observe them in *Eretz Yisrael*. "Keeping *mitzvos* outside *Eretz Yisrael* is meant to ensure keeping them in *Eretz Yisrael*, for the main purpose of *mitzvos* is for those living in the land of Hashem." It is for this reason that Yechezkel told those that wished, after the destruction of the *Beis HaMikdash*, to abandon the observance of *mitzvos*, that (*Yechezkel* 20:32-33), "What has occurred to your spirit will never come to pass. . . As I live, says Hashem Elokim, surely with a mighty hand, and with an outstretched arm, and with fury poured out, will I rule over you."

As for Rachel, she died before she reached *Eretz Yisrael*, having become pregnant with Binyamin before she reached Shechem. She never reached *Eretz Yisrael*, so Yaakov never lived there with two wives. And one must be especially careful in *Eretz Yisrael* not to become *tameh* with the *tumah* of *avodah zarah* or *arayos*.

Ramban's view is almost identical to that of Ibn Ezra. It is not, God forbid, that there is no prohibition against illicit sexual behavior outside *Eretz Yisrael*, but the special quality of *Eretz Yisrael* is such that it vomits out sinners, something which does not happen elsewhere.

But *Ramban's* view that Yaakov never cohabited with Rachel in *Eretz Yisrael* is questioned by *Techeiles Mordechai*, based on *Chazal* in the first chapter of *Megillah*, where we are told that Yaakov lived in Sukkos for eleven months and after that another six months in Beit El, and that Rachel died while giving birth to Binyamin when they were travelling from Beit El. If that is so, she was living in *Eretz Yisrael* at the time she became pregnant, because Sukkos is in *Eretz Yisrael*. He answers that *Ramban* is consistent here with his view that the territory across the Jordan is not considered to be part of *Eretz Yisrael*, and Sukkos is across the Jordan, as we are told in *Bereishis* 33:17. *Ramban* therefore made a point of stating clearly that she became pregnant with Binyamin "before she came to Shechem," namely before she entered the western part of *Eretz Yisrael*.

The destruction of *Eretz Yisrael* resulted from its *kedushah*, because it cannot tolerate those who commit *aveiros*. *Sifsei Kohen*, though, explains the verse (*Vayikra* 18:25), וָאֶפְקֹד עֲוֹנָהּ עָלֶיהָ — "I visited its iniquity on it" — to mean that this refers to the sin *of the land itself*, in that it gives its fruit even to those not worthy of it, as *Chazal* tell us at the end of *Kesubos*: "R' Yehoshua ben Levi came to Gabla. He saw certain (extremely large) clusters of grapes . . . He said: 'Oh land! bring in (i.e., remove) your fruits! For whom are you producing these fruits? For the Arabs that have subjugated us because of our sins?' " That is the iniquity of the land, which will be visited upon it.

Sefas Emes quotes in regard to our topic an extraordinary section in *Toras Kohanim*, which blames living in *Eretz Yisrael* for Israel's sins. And this is the language of *Toras Kohanim*: "How do we know that the dwelling of *Bnei Yisrael* (in *Eretz Yisrael*) caused (punishments to befall) them? As it states (*Vayikra* 18:3), אֲשֶׁר אֲנִי מֵבִיא אֶתְכֶם שָׁמָּה — 'to which I am bringing you.' " In succinct fashion, *Sefas Emes* explains the other side of living in *Eretz Yisrael*. The Jews are suitable, by their souls, to live only in *Eretz Yisrael*, as we are told (*Chabbakuk* 3:6)), עָמַד וַיְמֹדֶד אֶרֶץ, "He stood and measured the earth" — that Hashem measured all the lands and found none more suitable for the Jewish people than *Eretz Yisrael*. But just as we know that the greater a person the greater his *yetzer hara*, the same applies to *Eretz Yisrael*. Because *Eretz Yisrael* suits the *kedushah* of *Bnei Yisrael*, it also offers greater temptations and pitfalls, more barriers that attempt to separate man from God. The latter cause people to sin, unless they are able to take heed. Thus the fact that the Jews live in *Eretz Yisrael* is an indirect cause of their sinning. It is this that is meant by the Torah when it states, וּכְמַעֲשֵׂה אֶרֶץ כְּנַעַן אֲשֶׁר אֲנִי מֵבִיא אֶתְכֶם שָׁמָּה לֹא תַעֲשׂוּ — "and you shall not do as the deeds of the Land of Canaan to which I am bringing you" (*Vayikra* 18:3). Your coming there will cause you to be exposed to the temptations and pitfalls of Canaan, and you must be especially careful not to allow yourselves to sin.

◆§ The Soul of the Person Craves These

As we mentioned, the Torah's primary warning is addressed to the prohibition of *gilui arayos*, sexual misconduct, which is the greatest contradiction to the inherent *kedushah* of *Eretz Yisrael*. Man craves *arayos*. In the desert, the Jews wept when they were told of the prohibitions against *arayos*. And in the days of Ezra, they suffered greatly when they had to evict their foreign wives from their homes. Therefore, says *Meshech Chochmah*, the Torah uses the language here of אֲנִי ה' אֱ-לֹהֵיכֶם, "I am Hashem your God" (*Vayikra* 18:2). Hashem says to Israel, "Do not be afraid of the craving for *arayos*. I am Hashem your God, and I know that I created you with a nature which is strong enough to resist these passions." We are told about the *mitzvos*, "that man should do them and live by them" (ibid. v. 5.). I give life to you, and not pain and apprehension. It is true that man craves *arayos* and finds it difficult to resist them, but not *you*. You are able to resist this impulse.

Or *HaChaim* also deals with this question at length. *Arayos* is one of those matters which is most tied to man's lusts and passions. But one can overcome these lusts by sanctifying his vision and his thought. Those who are not careful about their vision and thought are the ones who eventually sin. And one who has already tasted sin finds it even harder to resist it in the future, for the memory of the sin excites one's blood. That is the reason *Chazal* said that in the place where *ba'alei teshuvah* stand, even perfect *tzaddikim* cannot stand. *Ba'alei teshuvah*, who have already sinned, struggle much more strongly against sin.

The Torah warns us against doing כְּמַעֲשֵׂה אֶרֶץ מִצְרַיִם אֲשֶׁר יְשַׁבְתֶּם־בָּהּ לֹא תַעֲשׂוּ — "the deeds of the Land of Egypt where you dwelled" (ibid. v. 3). Do not act as you saw the Egyptians acting when they sinned, even though you became rooted in it. And even though it is difficult for you to separate yourselves from this sin, I command you to do so. And by the same token, וּכְמַעֲשֵׂה אֶרֶץ כְּנַעַן אֲשֶׁר אֲנִי מֵבִיא אֶתְכֶם שָׁמָּה לֹא תַעֲשׂוּ — "You shall not do as the deeds of the Land of Canaan to which I am bringing you" (ibid.). When you come to Canaan and become settled and established in the land, you will have free time for sinful thoughts, and it is against this that I am also warning you. Do not entertain sinful thoughts, so that you will not sin.

If you ask how this is possible, and how Hashem can command us to do something which is against human nature, Hashem assures us, אֲנִי ה' אֱ-לֹהֵיכֶם, "I am Hashem your God." I know your nature, and I know that you are capable of overcoming these material lusts. Your *neshamah* can overcome your passions, and thereby improve your heart, as in the verse (*Tehillim* 40:9), "I desire to do Your will, O my God: Your law is within my insides." Man's Torah and his striving for *kedushah* are embedded inside him. His soul was shaped in heaven, and it is with this nucleus that he can change for the better, until he wants to serve Hashem.

At the same time, though, Hashem warns man not to go to the other extreme and to withdraw completely from sexual contact, so that he will endanger the future of mankind by not having children and transgress the law of *piryah ve'rivyah* — "being fruitful and multiplying." The Torah commands, אֶת־מִשְׁפָּטַי תַּעֲשׂוּ — "You shall keep my laws" (ibid. v.4) — instructing us to distance ourselves from lewdness, but also tells us in the same verse, וְאֶת־חֻקֹּתַי תִּשְׁמְרוּ — "and observe My statutes" — indicating the requirement to maintain human existence.

The Torah tells us, אֲשֶׁר יַעֲשֶׂה אֹתָם הָאָדָם וָחַי בָּהֶם — "that man should do them and live by them." God does not ask us to destroy our bodies and our passions, but only to sanctify and purify these, so that we can live a life of *kedushah*. This is the way the Tzaddik of Kotzk explained the verse, וְאַנְשֵׁי קֹדֶשׁ תִּהְיוּן לִי (Sh'mos 22:30), which translated literally means: "You shall be holy people to me." The Kotzker, though, translated it as "You shall be holy in a *menshlich* fashion," a *kedushah* which takes into account the nature of man, and not a *kedushah* of asceticism which withdraws from all earthly pleasures.

And it is possible that the meaning of the verse, וְלֹא־תָקִיא הָאָרֶץ אֶתְכֶם בְּטַמַּאֲכֶם אֹתָהּ — "lest the land vomit you out when you make it *tamei*" (ibid. v. 28) — is also in accordance with the above. Hashem demands from us sanctified earthliness. And that is the purpose of our coming to *Eretz Yisrael* — to eat of its fruit, to be satisfied with its goodness, and to observe the *mitzvos*. The *tumah* of *arayos* profanes the earthliness and empties it of all *kedushah*. Therefore the land will vomit you out, for its basis is refined and sanctified earthliness. It has no right to exist without this *kedushah*. And that is the nature of your tie to *Eretz Yisrael*.

⋙ And the Land Vomited Out Its Inhabitants

The punishment for sinners is that *Eretz Yisrael* pushes them away from itself, said R' Zvi Hirsch Kalischer. Those who speak against *Eretz Yisrael* or who flee from it believe that they hate the land. In reality, though, the land hates them. As a result of the land's hatred of them, the people involved become nauseated by the land, and this is what the Torah speaks of when it refers to "vomiting," whereby the land vomits them up.

The simple meaning of the text is that the Torah decreed exile for those who sin, just as the nations that lived in it before Israel were exiled because of their abominations. The Torah includes both the past and the future in this, and refers both to the nations who lived in the country before the Jews, and who were evicted from it because of their sins, and those who will come later. But these various tenses cannot be explained as referring prophetically to the future, because the Torah states clearly, "for with all these, the nations which I send forth before you made themselves *tamei*" (ibid. v. 24).

Ramban says that this is written in the past tense because the decree had already been issued against these nations, and it is as if the land had already vomited them out. *HaKesav VeHaKabalah* and R' David Zvi Hoffmann both explain the verses in this spirit. According to *HaKesav VeHaKabalah*, the term כַּאֲשֶׁר קָאָה ("as it vomited out") is grammatically a form of the present, which refers to the future. He brings a number of examples, such as, הִנְּךָ שֹׁכֵב עִם־אֲבֹתֶיךָ, literally "behold you lie with your fathers" (*Devarim* 31:16), which really refers to an event in the near future. The word קָאָה is the same type of form, indicating that the land will in the near future vomit them out. And there are many other such examples.

Almost all the commentators contend with the meaning of וְלֹא תָקִיא הָאָרֶץ אֶתְכֶם בְּטַמַּאֲכֶם אֹתָהּ כַּאֲשֶׁר קָאָה אֶת־הַגּוֹי ... כִּי כָּל־אֲשֶׁר יַעֲשֶׂה מִכֹּל הַתּוֹעֵבֹת הָאֵלֶּה וְנִכְרְתוּ הַנְּפָשׁוֹת הָעֹשֹׂת מִקֶּרֶב עַמָּם — "That the land shall not vomit you out when you defile it as it vomited out the nation ... for all who practice these abominations, the souls which practice these shall be cut off from the midst of their nation" (*Vayikra* 18:28-29). The simple meaning of the text seems to imply that unlike the other nations, if Israel sins it will not be exiled, but will suffer *kares*. If one studies the verse, though, he will see that the punishment for these sins is exile, and that is the way *Chazal* explained it. Rabbeinu Bachya, *Chizkuni* and other commentators, both *rishonim* and *acharonim*, explain, "And the earth will not vomit you out" to mean that exile alone will not be enough to atone for your sins. Whereas the land vomited out the previous nations that sinned, if you sin not only will you be exiled from your land, but you will also incur the punishment of *kares*.

Chasam Sofer gives a beautiful explanation: If you say that the land will vomit up only those who are not deeply rooted in the land but not you who are so deeply rooted in it. Instead, all that do such abominations will suffer *kares*. Such people will be forcibly uprooted from their ties to the land, and as a consequence the land will vomit them out, as it did to the other nations.

Some of the later commentators explain the verse, "That the land shall not vomit you out when you defile it as it vomited out the nations" according to the simple meaning of the text. Unlike the other nations whom God banished permanently from the land, He will not do so to you. As the Maggid of Dubno puts it, if a stepchild turns bad, one banishes him from one's home forever, but in the case of one's own child, he is not permanently banished, but is punished until such time that he will return to the proper path.

Meleches Machsheves also explains this along similar lines. When the Canaanites and Perizites corrupted their ways, Hashem vented His anger upon the land and destroyed that entire nation, but if the Jewish people sin, only the sinners will be cut off, and the land will not vomit them out as it did the other nations. *Alshech* expands on this idea. If you ask what good is it that some individuals should observe the *mitzvos* when the majority defile them, as a result of which the land will vomit out the entire nation as it did to the other nations, the Torah assures us that that will not happen. If it is not the entire nation that sins, then "the land shall not vomit you out as it did the (other) nations." Those who sin will be judged as individuals, and they will be cut off from their people, but the rest of the people will remain in their land. This is unlike the other nations, which were evicted because some of their people did all the abominations.

Sifsei Kohen expresses this idea clearly. The land only vomited out the other nations, but not you, because it was conquered for you, as it states, "And the earth will be conquered before you" (*Bamidbar* 32:29). If you make the land *tamei*, then "the souls which practice these shall be cut off" (*Vayikra* 18:29); but no matter what the conditions and circumstances, the land will not be separated forever from Hashem's people.

III.

The Preservation of the Human Race: Taharah or Statute?

he laws of *arayos* — immoral sexual conduct — are defined by *Chazal* as being common-sense ordinances: "For had they not been written, it would have been appropriate to have them written" (*Yoma* 64). *Toras Kohanim* and *Sifra* on our *parashah*, though, state: "A person should not say, 'I do not want to have illegal sexual relations,' but rather (he should say), 'I do want, but what shall I do, as my Father in Heaven has made a statute — a *gezeirah* — forbidding me.' "

The commentators differentiate between those *arayos* which are detestable to man, and which, even if they had not been forbidden, would have been loathsome to him by his nature and common sense, and those *arayos* which man does covet. *Iyei HaYam* on *Sukkah* 52 says that *arayos* in regard to another man's wife is a common sense prohibition, as in the words of *Chazal* on *Eiruvin* 100: "Had the Torah not been given, we would have deduced (the prohibition of) theft from the ant and *arayos* from the dove." But the *arayos* of family relatives is a *gezeirah*, a decree above and beyond logic, as in the words of *Chazal* in *Parashas Beha'alosecha* 11: " 'Crying in their families' (*Bamidbar* 11:10) — crying because of (the prohibition of) *arayos* (related to) the family."

Ramban uses this general approach, and argues with the opinion of *Rambam* in *Moreh Nevuchim*, who gives the reason for the prohibition of *arayos* in families as being

> so as to minimize the amount of sexual intercourse and to make it loathsome, so that people will only wish to indulge a little ... for most of the time men are at home with women who are forbidden to them as *arayos*, and such women are close to the individual man and eager to do whatever he wishes and are familiar enough to be with him. And no magistrate can succeed in segregating anyone who is always in one's company. And with regard to a marriageable single woman, persons would succumb to sexual relations outside of wedlock. But once the Torah forbade sexual relations with these women [i.e., close relatives] under the death penalty by the *beis din* and by the penalty of *kares*, a man will not at all think of such women.

According to this, *Rambam's* opinion (3:49) is that even incest is something that one would be naturally inclined to, and it is for that reason that the Torah forbade it with a strong prohibition, so as to keep people far away from it.

Ramban does not disagree with the main thesis of *Rambam*, that the prohibition of *arayos* is one of a *gezeirah*. On the contrary, he adds that: "We have no traditional explanation [handed down from *Chazal*] about this," and the *arayos* are included within the *chukim* (laws which man cannot understand), which are decrees by the King. And (the definition of) a decree is that which a king wants, which he enacts in his wisdom, and He knows the need for and the value of this commandment which He commands us.

But *Ramban* argues with *Rambam* when the latter states that the reason for the prohibition is to prevent a person from becoming excessively habituated to marital relations. According to *Ramban*, "that is a very weak explanation," for a man is permitted to take many wives — even hundreds or thousands:

> And what harm will there be if a man takes just one daughter of his, this being permitted to *b'nei Noach* — the Noachides — i.e., anyone not a Jew, or if he marries two sisters, as did our father Jacob? And there is no more fitting marriage than having one's daughter marry her older brother, and this way they will inherit his inheritance. And they will be fruitful and multiply in his house, for the world was not created to remain void but to be populated.

Ramban therefore gives a different reason for the prohibition of *arayos*, which we will bring below.

Akeidah, however, is amazed at *Rambam*, who views marriages between relatives as something which would appear to be natural. He holds the exact opposite:

> *Arayos* of blood relatives, such as a father and daughter, or with a sister, more than the fact that the Torah forbids them, is such that man's natural healthy nature is to separate himself from them and to despise and abominate them utterly, to the extent that there is no nation where these are common, and the shame of Ammon and Moab proves this.

Akeidah adds that one cannot say that the Torah's prohibition against these *arayos* is what made them detestable and abominable, for the Torah also imposed a strenuous prohibition on taking another's wife, and yet there are sinners who violate this prohibition. *Akeidah* therefore concludes that the prohibition of *arayos* with relatives is a logical prohibition. It is not common among those with healthy minds, but only among those with diseased minds. The nations which lived in *Eretz Yisrael* had diseased minds and practiced all these abominations, "just as those who eat coal or raw meat or the flesh of their sons or daughters." But Hashem was merciful to us and implanted in our hearts a loathing for such prohibitions, for had that not been the case, there would be no future for the existence of the human race, for man would not recognize his brother or know who his children are. This is what the Torah means in the following *parashah* (*Vayikra* 20:17), "If a man takes his sister ... it is a *chessed*, and they shall be cut off." In other words, Hashem did us a *chessed* — kindness — in that He implanted within us a detestation of such action. Since the person involved here performed an action that is against the *chessed* of Hashem, that is the reason he suffers *kares*.

According to *Akeidah*, one who violates these prohibitions shows that he has diseased tendencies which developed in a diseased heart, and these tendencies are against human nature. The Torah mentioned them to make us realize that it was because of such actions that the former inhabitants of the land were vomited up by the land. But the prohibitions against such abominations are not a *gezeirah* by Hashem, but are meant to keep those people who have an animalistic nature away from such unnatural tendencies.

Many of the commentators exert themselves to explain this topic. It is interesting to mention *S'forno*, who holds that not only is marriage among relatives not an abomination, but that "since the two [marriage partners] are of a similar nature, the offspring, too, are likely to be more healthy and balanced, as occurred with Moshe, Aaron and Miriam, who were born of Amram and his aunt, Yocheved." But that happens only infrequently, when the person marries *l'shem shamayim* — for the sake of Heaven.

> In most cases, though, the intention is for pleasure ... and since relatives are readily accessible, and the lascivious thoughts and intimate pleasure shared between them is great, if the two believe that their union is not illicit they will indulge in it, whereas their intention is for pleasure alone, so that they will engage in extramarital sex without any intention of procreating, and the world will be filled with lechery.

It is for this reason that the Torah forbade this totally. This is *Rambam's* view. There are thus various opinions about the nature of man and his natural tendencies.

ᕮᔰ The Preservation of the Species

Ramban explains that the prohibition against *arayos* is due to the fact that:

> According to the Torah, sexual relations are held to be rejected and detestable except when they are for the preservation of the species, so that when no offspring can be born it is forbidden, as is also the case where the child that is born will not have a healthy existence or will not succeed in it, (all of which) the Torah forbids ... In all of these there is no marriage, for the issue will not succeed, and it is but lewdness, merely lust.

It appears that what *Ramban* means is that marriages of forbidden relatives do not succeed and do not produce a family, as doctors have shown that such marriages harm the existence of the family. Rabbeinu Bachya, in fact, says so specifically:

> There is no preservation of the species from close relatives. And the issue is not proper. And the Torah forbade such intercourse. And from this we learn that (the reason for) the prohibition of sexual relations is to preserve the species.

Both *Ramban* and Rabbeinu Bachya explain that the word, שְׁאֵר, used by the Torah to mean "close relative," is from the same root as נִשְׁאָר, "remain." Marriage with close relatives is forbidden because no descendants will remain from such a union.

HaKesav VeHaKabalah, in accordance with this logic, explains the word זִמָּה ("incest") to mean "closing off," and shows examples of the use of the word in such a sense in *Terumos* 9:3 and *Tehillim* 17. In such a marriage, the power of reproduction is closed off, proof of this being what *Chazal* say in *Yevamos* 78: "A *mamzer* does not live."

But *Ramban* finally concludes that the law is a *gezeirah* by Hashem, "Who is the Wise One in administering His kingdom, and it is He Who knows the need and the purpose of this which He commanded us, and He did not reveal this (reason) to the people, except to His wise advisers."

This is also the line adopted by the latest commentators, such as R' Samson Raphael Hirsch and R' Yitzchak Breuer. R' Samson Raphael Hirsch in his *Chorev* states,

> You cannot understand the laws of *arayos*, just as you cannot understand any purely logical basis for any *chok* of Hashem. And if you do have an idea of what you think might be the reason for that *chok*, you dare not value the *chok* just because of that reason and because of the principle which you think you have discovered in it ... "It is I who created man in the image of God for My reasons. I, only I alone, can tell you how to act according to My aims, and what the source is of justice and iniquity in your life" ... That is the call of Hashem's orderly arrangement of the universe. What Hashem gave us is a *chok* — a statute whose reason we cannot comprehend — to which all people and families of the earth must pay attention. He ordained and arranged the links between the sexes, in accordance with His wisdom, and it was He who determined how man is to act in His world. He arranged for us the sanctity of the couple, and sealed with His seal of truth the institution of marriage, to its ultimate root.

R' Yitzchak Breuer, in *Nachaliel*, states this in greater detail:

The Holy One, Blessed is He, did not cease to be an active participant in Creation after the initial step of "Let us create man" (*Bereishis* 1:26). Just as the gardener who wishes to grow exceptional plants will not permit them to grow arbitrarily and by chance but will take great care in the selection of the seed and seedlings and in the time for planting them, so too did the Gardener of mankind give us in His Torah the rules governing the birth of the Jew, whose nature only the Gardener, Blessed be He, knows and comprehends, making it our duty to accept these statutes as becoming the Jewish "species" — לְמִינֵהוּ.

"You shall do My commandments and observe My statutes, I am Hashem " (*Vayikra* 18:4). " No man shall approach his close relative to reveal the *ervah* (illicit union), I am Hashem" (ibid. v. 6). Do you not hear from the verses which preceded the prohibition against *arayos* the voice of the Gardener, "Who has sanctified us with His commandments and commanded us concerning the *arayos*, and forbade to us the *arusos* (a woman who has been "betrothed" — *kiddushin*) and permitted us the *nesu'os lanu* (a woman who has been married to us — *nisu'in*) by means of *chuppah* and *kiddushin*"? The Creator of the World decreed, and the King of the Universe commanded. "Let us create man" is the law governing family purity. Without this purity, the family is merely naturalistic and animalistic.

These latter-day commentators stressed this so much because of their understanding that there is no logic or reason for these statutes, and they are linked to our faith in the Creator of Man. He knows what is good and what is bad for man, just as the gardener knows the quality of his seedlings.

✥ Taharah and Kedushah

R' David Zvi Hoffmann sees the laws of *arayos* as stages in ascending in *kedushah*. Each person has his own character, even though it can be changed. The safeguards in *arayos* were meant to create a special type of person, who is sanctified and elevated by the laws of *tzniyus* — modesty — and the ways of *kedushah*. But one cannot explain all *arayos* in this fashion, because the prohibition against marrying a woman and her sister is obviously based on other factors.

There are certain reasons for some of the laws, but as a general rule they attempt to move man away from animalistic behavior and to make the Jewish people an *am kadosh* — a holy people — and a *mamleches kohanim* — a kingdom of priests. It is for this reason that the *parashah* begins with an emphasis on moving away from the *tumah* of the other nations, while the second section of *arayos* ends with the warning, "and you shall be holy because I am holy" (*Vayikra* 20:26). The purpose and aim is *kedushah*, and all the laws in their various forms are meant to achieve this purpose.

Kedushas Levi sees the commandments in our *parashah* as also implying the need to act with *kedushah* even with those matters which the Torah permitted. King Shlomo said: "Know Him in all your ways" (*Mishlei* 3:6). That means that even in those areas which are permissible one should act for the Sake of Heaven, and not in order to satisfy his bodily cravings. A man should marry a woman not because of his lust, but in order to fulfill the commandments of the Creator. This is what the Torah tells us here: אֶל־כָּל־שְׁאֵר בְּשָׂרוֹ לֹא תִקְרְבוּ לְגַלּוֹת עֶרְוָה — "You shall not approach any of your relatives to engage in *arayos*" (ibid. 18:6) — namely that even with his own wife — who, after all, is included in the term "*any*" of his relatives — he should not act lustfully, for "I am Hashem" (ibid.). You must act in all your deeds for the Sake of Heaven, so as to fulfill the commandment of פְּרוּ וּרְבוּ (*Bereishis* 1:28, 9:1) — to be fruitful and multiply.

Ibn Ezra goes even further in this regard, in that there is even an obligation to minimize relations with one's own wife. He says:

> And the reason it states "I am Hashem" is because Hashem loves the one who is separated, and who serves Him and obeys His words. And Mount Sinai is a witness. And also the first one. And that is the secret of man. And as man's lusts are as those of the animals, it could not be that all women should be forbidden. But (the Torah) did forbid those women who are with one constantly. And in *Parashas Ki Seitzei* I will reveal to you a sealed secret. And whoever acts contemptibly moves away from the Great Name. It therefore states, "I am Hashem."

Ibn Ezra's words seem difficult. *Ezrah Lehavin* explains that what he is saying is that Hashem loves those who are abstemious in marital relations if they do so in order to serve Him. "And Mount Sinai is a witness," because there the men were ordered to keep away from women for three days. "And also the first one" refers to Adam, the first man, who was created alone. "And that is the secret of man" — to know and recognize Hashem without any lusts. However, as man still has lusts, he was permitted certain women, while those that are constantly with him were prohibited. "And in *Parashas Ki Seitzei* I will reveal to you a sealed secret" — for there the Torah writes that when the people go out to fight, one who is a *ba'al keri* — who has had a seminal emission — must leave the camp, as the *Aron* — the Ark — was in their midst. By this, Ibn Ezra wishes to say that to minimize sexual relations is the appropriate practice for a person who wishes to draw closer to his Creator.

Or HaChaim, though, says that the reason why the verse before the *parashah* of *arayos* states "you shall observe My *mishpatim*" — My laws (*Vayikra* 18:5) — is to teach us that even though Hashem commanded us to keep apart from *arayos*, one should not go to the other extreme and separate himself totally from all women. Instead, "you shall observe My *mishpatim*," namely to fulfill the obligation of פְּרוּ וּרְבוּ — being fruitful and multiplying, by doing in accordance with the Torah and in holiness those acts which are otherwise prohibited if performed through *tumah* or in violation of Hashem's commandments.

❧ Not to Harm the Root

Another reason for the prohibition of *arayos* is brought by *Moreh Nevuchim* 3:49, in that an action which harms both the branch and root is outrageous. He says:

> The second reason is to warn of the attribute of shame, as the action between the root and the branch is extremely outrageous, namely to have intercourse with one's daughter or mother. And the root and branch are forbidden to have intercourse with each other. And it makes no difference if the root and branch are embodied in a third person [i.e., in a more distant relative such as an aunt or uncle].

Rambam explains that all the types of *arayos* indicate a lack of shame and *tzniyus*. He says that this is not only Torah morality, but is also accepted by philosophers.

A very exalted idea concerning the concept of root and branch is found in the Chassidic works of the *Besht*. All man's attributes and characteristics are derived from spiritual attributes above. Instead of utilizing them for lust, man must elevate these attributes to their roots. Man's attribute of love was created in order to bind him to the Infinite One, Who is the source of love. But his animalistic characteristics bring love down from on high to the depths of lust.

Chovos HaLevavos tells of a certain righteous man who, through his love, was able to achieve *teshuvah* and unification with the Source of Love, and to cling to the Infinite One. This is why the Torah mentioned "I am Hashem" in regard to *arayos*. Do not dirty yourself with physical lust, when lust is but a spark of the flame in the heart of man which must burn with the fire of Hashem. The Torah refers to *ahavah zarah* — false love — as *chessed* (see *Vayikra* 20:17), because the *aish zarah* — the foreign flame — of lust is but a perversion of the quality of *chessed* — kindness — from which love is derived. Rather than perverting this holy quality, man must cling to the source of *chessed*, "drag it into the *beis hamedrash*," for then you will understand that the Despicable One (i.e., the *yetzer hara*) is nothing but the perversion of true love, which is the love of Hashem and His Torah.

Kedoshim – קדשים

I.

You Shall be Holy Because I am Holy

The Sages of the Midrash on our *parashah* dwell on the equation between the *kedushah* of the Jewish people and the *kedushah* of Hashem. I would like to relate to the idea brought by one of the modern commentators, that the Torah wishes to tell us here that Hashem, although omnipotent and separate from the world, is nevertheless not divorced from it, and that He is to be found within the world. It is Israel's task to emulate Hashem in the same fashion: to be a holy nation, but not to divorce itself from the world. Rather it must exert its influence on the world in all areas of life. This idea is taken from Chassidic and other works.

Oheiv Yisrael states:

> One should not say, "How can we attain that level, since our lusts control our desires, etc.? And how is it possible, when one engages in physical pleasures, to add to these dimensions of *perishah* (separateness) and *kedushah?*" It is for this reason that (the Torah) states, "For I, Hashem, your God, am holy" (ibid.).

In other words, just as Hashem fills all the worlds and yet is separate from all of them, so too must Israel exist in the world, without becoming engulfed by it.

This idea is explained even more clearly by *Chiddushei HaRim*. He notes that we must be holy even within nature, for Hashem too is in nature, but is nevertheless separate from it and does not relinquish His being on its account.

This concept is expanded on by *Kesav Sofer*. There is the person who separates himself from other people, perfects his own soul, and does not deal with others, but that is not what Hashem desires. What Hashem wants is that one should always try to be of benefit to others and to guide them in how to serve Him. Hashem observes and supervises His creatures so as to increase their *zechuyos* — merits — and it was for that reason that He gave us Torah and *mitzvos*. This we see in the verse, קָדוֹשׁ קָדוֹשׁ קָדוֹשׁ ה׳ צְבָאוֹת — "Holy, holy holy is Hashem of hosts" (*Yeshayahu* 6:3): even though Hashem is the God of Hosts, nevertheless this verse concludes מְלֹא כָל־הָאָרֶץ כְּבוֹדוֹ — "the entire universe is His glory." Man must try to emulate his Creator in that he himself must be filled with *kedushah*, but must nevertheless be an active part of mankind, so as to bring others to perform meritorious deeds. This is what is meant by קְדֹשִׁים תִּהְיוּ — "you shall be holy" — but only in the way that קָדוֹשׁ אֲנִי ה׳ אֱ־לֹהֵיכֶם — "I, Hashem, your God, am holy:" even though I am holy and exalted, I am your God, in that I am directly involved in your life. You are to be holy — but nevertheless to remain part of the people.

Chasam Sofer follows this line in explaining the words of *Toras Kohanim* on this *Sidrah*: "This *parashah* was said in public assembly." Hashem does not love those who are removed from everyday life and those who separate themselves from mankind. Rather, he wants man to love his fellow-men and to bring them closer to Torah. This *parashah* of *kedushah* has no place in isolation, but must be in "*hakhel*," among the people, and with the people. That is the essence of Jewish *kedushah*.

It is along these lines that *Chasam Sofer* explains the words of the Midrash: " 'Because I am holy' — One might imagine just as I. It therefore states, 'Because I, Hashem, your God, am holy.'" There are two types of separation. The first of these is that of Chanoch ben Yered, who was holy "just as I," totally separate from this world; yet he was not really "just as I," for Hashem is aware of and plays a role in what happens in the world, while Chanoch totally ignored his generation, and by this was instrumental in enabling the generation of the Flood to develop. The other type of separation is that of Avraham, who was holy and exalted above the other people of his generation and yet was involved with them, preaching to people and bringing them close to Hashem. This *kedushah* is just like that of Hashem, who is known as our God, and who cares for us despite His immense separation from us. That is what *Chazal* meant when they wrote, "One might imagine just as I" referring to someone like Chanoch ben Yered. "It therefore states, 'because I, Hashem, your God, am holy,'" and I watch over you. You too, even though you are to be holy, must nevertheless look after the people of your generation.

Many commentators expand on the definition of the Jewish *kedushah*, which is markedly different from that of the other nations. *Chasam Sofer*, in *Toras Moshe*, says that there are non-Jews who separate themselves from the world far more than do our Sages, but that is due to their hatred of the world and a sense of despair. This is not true of the Jews who cling to Hashem, the Living God. They do not withdraw from life because of a sense of despair and of hatred. On the contrary, they find pleasure in the world and recite blessings of appreciation, as, for example, when they see trees in bloom. Jews sanctify themselves within life, in order to be sanctified by the *kedushah* of Hashem — "for I am holy."

Kesav Sofer, the son of *Chasam Sofer*, also explains the Midrash using this logic: "'You shall be holy' — this is as is written: 'And you who cling to Hashem your God are alive' (*Devarim* 4:4). In other words, the *kedushah* that is required is not that of asceticism, but rather that of the *kedushah* of life, by clinging to the living God.

R' Menachem Mendel of Kotzk used the same approach when he translated וְאַנְשֵׁי־קֹדֶשׁ תִּהְיוּן לִי — "you shall be holy people for Me" (*Sh'mos* 22:30) into Yiddish as "you shall be מענטשליך הייליג — holy in a *mentshlich* (human-like) fashion" — one that is not detached from life. The Rebbi of Kotzk also explained the words of *Chazal*, שְׁלֹמֹה תִּקֵּן עֵרוּבִין וּנְטִילַת יָדַיִם (literally, that King Shlomo was the one who instituted the different *eiruvin* and the requirement to wash the hands), to mean (homiletically, of course) that Shlomo instituted that men would be involved (מְעֹרָב) in what goes on in the world, and yet at the same time have their hands removed (נְטוּלוֹת) from the world, as quoted by R' Alexander Zusha Friedman in the name of the elder Chassidim: namely that the proper way to serve Hashem is to remain secluded while remaining part of society; to fast even as one is eating, and to sense the discomfort of rolling oneself in the snow even when in a warm bed.

The Jewish way of *kedushah* is to sanctify oneself within the midst of life, and not outside it. Thus *Techeiles Mordechai* explains the verse, לֹא תַעֲשֶׂה לְךָ פֶסֶל . . . אֲשֶׁר בַּשָּׁמַיִם מִמַּעַל וַאֲשֶׁר בָּאָרֶץ מִתָּחַת — "You shall not make for yourself a graven image. . . of that which is in the heavens above or of that which is in the earth below." A person is forbidden to resemble the angels above, but also to resemble the animals below. Both actions are wrong and are not the ways of the Jew. What path should the Jew then choose? That which brings honor to one's Creator and to one's fellow-men. In other words, this is the combined way of the *kedushah* of life, one that is worthy of honor above and below. That is the Jew's mission in the world. The Torah does not disparage the sex act, says *Or HaChaim*, but demands that it be carried out in *kedushah* and *taharah*.

Aperion, by R' Shlomo Ganzfried, follows this path in explaining why the command to respect one's mother and father (*Vayikra* 19:3) immediately follows the command to live a life of holiness. Those whose sexual relations are intended only to satisfy lust cause their children not to respect them, for why should such children respect parents whose only purpose in conceiving them was to satiate their lust? The Torah therefore commands us regarding the sanctity of life, for when that is present then there is respect for parents — the one depends on the other.

Michtam LeDavid also explains this *parashah* in terms of the *kedushah* of sexual relations. He quotes the Midrash: "'You shall be holy' — it is in accordance with this that it is written (*Tehillim* 20:3), 'He will send your help from *kodesh*, and strengthen you out of Zion.'" On this, he comments that one cannot have a one-sided *kedushah* in sexual relations. It requires both partners, as it is written, "I shall make him a help corresponding to him" (*Bereishis* 2:18). And that is the meaning of the Midrash: "He will send you help from *kodesh*." If you sanctify yourself, Hashem will give you a wife who will also sanctify herself. "And strengthen you out of Zion" — this refers to the holy children that will be born in *kedushah*, for these are one's true strength, the ones that support man. And such children are also referred to as צִיּוֹן — Zion — because they mark (מְצַיְּנִים) the essence of the person. This is how *Sefas Emes* interprets the Gemara's expression, "his interior matches his exterior" (תוֹכוֹ כְּבָרוֹ) — a man's children testify to his inner essence. Thus, *Chazal* said in *Yevamos* 12: "Children are equivalent to signs (of maturity)."

◄§ My Kedushah is Greater than Yours

The Magid of Mezerich explains the Midrash, "My *kedushah* is greater than (or alternately "above") yours," to mean that My *kedushah* stems from your *kedushah*. The more you sanctify yourselves below, the greater the *kedushah* on high. The two spheres aid one another. Thus we see in *Toras Kohanim*: "'You shall be holy' — You shall separate yourselves. 'Because I, Hashem, your God, am holy' — if you do not sanctify yourselves below, it is as if you did not sanctify Me."

The concluding section of *Toras Kohanim* seems puzzling. There it states, "Or maybe (this is not the meaning, but the meaning is as follows:) if you sanctify Me, I am sanctified, but if not, I am not sanctified. It therefore states (disproving the alternate meaning), 'for I am holy' — I remain in My sanctity, whether you sanctify Me or you do not sanctify Me. Abba Shaul says: 'the entourage of the king — how should it act? It should imitate the king.'"

It is difficult to understand the premise of the second attempted meaning of the Midrash: If the Jews do not sanctify Hashem, does that then mean that He is not sanctified? Does He need our acknowledgement? In reality, though, what the Midrash is teaching us is that our *kedushah* comes only for our own good, so that we may improve ourselves and resemble Hashem more closely. In doing so, man fulfills his mission on earth. He is not doing Hashem any favor by doing so, but only a favor to himself. Hashem created man to perfect himself and for no other reason.

Malbim has another interpretation of the Midrash. *Kedushah* means rising up above nature and matter, to spiritual and Godly concerns. There are degrees in *kedushah*. There are those who rise above specific material lusts, while others rise up above all material matters. The *kedushah* of Hashem rises up above the natural course of events to a miraculous course of events. Hashem created the world according to man's nature. If one behaves in accordance with nature, then Hashem acts naturally toward him. If, however, one raises himself above nature, then Hashem's dealings with him are also on a supernatural level. This is what the Midrash said when it stated, "If you sanctify yourselves, I will consider it as if you sanctified Me," namely that by your behavior you make Me enter the realm of dealing with you in *kedushah*: by means of the supernatural course of events. Of course, Hashem is holy and exalted of Himself, whether or not people sanctify Him. But the way one is treated depends on how one acts. This is what Abba Shaul said in regard to what the Torah tells us, "You shall be holy, because I, Hashem, your God, am holy." Man's behavior must reflect that of Hashem. Man was created in Hashem's image so that he can control his own little "chariot of divinity," namely his own body, by means of his free will in a manner of *kedushah*, just as Hashem controls the world. We must be the King's entourage, and must emulate the way He runs the world. That is what is meant by "You shall be holy, because I, Hashem, your God, am holy."

S'forno has a similar interpretation. In the previous *parashiyos*, the Torah commanded various separations: from the *tumah* of lust and human seed, as the *tumah* of *niddah* and the *nega'im* resulting therefrom, and from the *tumah* of *zivah* and the *tumah* of sin; and from the company of demons and the *tumah* of *arayos* — as it is written, "you shall be purified... from all your sins" (*Vayikra* 16:30). Now the Torah explains the reason for all these separations: "You shall be holy, because I, Hashem, your God, am holy." You must be a kingdom of *Kohanim* and a holy nation, so that you will resemble the Creator and will fulfill the requirements implied in "Let us make man in our image" (*Bereishis* 1:26). How does one attain this? By obeying all the commandments listed above and below, and — according to the Chassidic works — also by affiliating oneself with the entire Jewish people.

"This *parashah* was said at *hakhel*, in public assembly of the entire Jewish people," explains *Sefas Emes*, because by means of *hakhel* and one's joining with the Jewish people, he is granted the highest *kedushah*, as it is said, "Hashem, your God, walks in the midst of your camp" (*Devarim* 23:15). Where the camp is unified into a single unit, Hashem is present. *Sefas Emes* also explains that when one performs a *mitzvah* he should think he is doing it on behalf of the entire Jewish people, for then he clings to the eternal *kedushah*.

Or HaChaim has a different explanation as to why this *parashah* was said at *hakhel*. The Torah tells us that the attribute of *kedushah* was given to the entire Jewish people, and one should not say that this was granted only to specially worthy people, and only they can attain it. It was said to all. Each person can rise through ever higher levels of *kedushah* until he reaches the level of Moshe *Rabbeinu*.

R' Yosef Tzvi Dushinski, in his *Toras Mahariatz*, adds another element. Do not think that the *parashah* of *kedushah* is a personal matter, which is best observed discreetly. Rather, it obligates one even when in public. The commandment of "You shall be holy" applies at all times and to all places.

Neither is it a relative commandment, according to the Magid of Dubno. It is not enough to be holier than others, but one must be holy regardless of his environment. To what is this analogous? To a person who looked for and found the best scholar to be a groom for his daughter. Some time later, he found that the young man no longer studied diligently. When he commented on this to his son-in-law, the latter justified himself saying: "I still study more than anyone else in this city." The father-in-law told him: "When I took you as a son-in-law, I did not compare you to the people of this city, but to those in the *yeshivah* where you were studying." Similarly, says the Magid of Dubno, that is the meaning of the Midrash when it says: "The Holy One, Blessed be He, said to Israel, "As I sanctified you even before I created the world, therefore you are to be holy." This *kedushah* stems purely from the *kedushah* on High, that of "for I, Hashem, your God, am holy." It is only measurable against that yardstick, and therefore there is no limit to it.

☙ Sanctify Yourself with what Is Permitted You

The commandment of "You shall be holy" is said as a positive commandment, a *mitzvas asei*. *Or HaChaim* holds that the purpose of the *mitzvah* is also to make the laws of *arayos* subject to a *mitzvas asei*, and not only a negative commandment — a *lav*. R' Sa'adiah Gaon and *Rashbatz* preceded him, in that they included the *mitzvah* among the 613 and explained that there is a special *mitzvah* to sanctify oneself even with what is permitted.

This is also the opinion of *Ramban* in our *parashah*, even though he does not list this as a separate *mitzvah* in his comments on *Rambam's Sefer HaMitzvos*. He explains this differently from *Rashi*, who interprets the term *kedoshim* to mean refraining from the prohibitions of *arayos* and other sins, for wherever one keeps away from *arayos* there is *kedushah*. In this, *Rashi* follows the Midrash. *Ramban*, though, adds that the Torah commandment also includes sanctifying oneself with that which is permitted. Previously, the Torah had given the various prohibitions regarding food and sexual relations. The Torah, though, was afraid that there might be people who are so lustful that they act in an improper manner, even though they are within the bounds of what is permitted, so that they will be *nevalim* — despicable — within the bounds of Torah law. The Torah therefore gave a general commandment, commanding one to refrain even from what is permitted: that a man should not overindulge in sexual relations with his wife; that one should not drink too much wine and should remember the evil that befell Noach and Lot as a result of their drinking; that one should keep away from *tumah*; one should guard one's mouth against gluttony and improper language; and remain sanctified and careful in one's actions even where the Torah did not prohibit them as such.

Kli Yakar also explains the words of *Chazal*: "Where you find a fence against *ervah* (*arayos*), there you find *kedushah*," to mean "sanctify yourself with what is permitted to you." A fence in this sense refers to refraining from doing what would otherwise be permitted. This we see in regard to the sanctity of the *nazir*, who keeps away from what the Torah permitted. And the same was true at the giving of the Torah on Sinai, where the men were told, "Do not approach a woman" (*Sh'mos* 19:15), meaning their own wives. It is in this context that *Am Yisrael* is called a "holy people" (ibid. v. 6). Similarly, we are told, "Do not draw close to reveal *ervah*" (*Vayikra* 18:6); that we are to refrain from any contact with the opposite sex that might lead to an illicit sexual relationship. By the same token, we see that *Kohanim*, who are more sanctified than the rest of Israel, are forbidden to marry a *zonah* or *challalah* (see *Vayikra* 21:7), women whose *kedushah* has been tainted by their own behavior or that of their parents, although such women are permitted in marriage to other Jews.

Akeidah explains at length the concept of *kedushah*, seeing it as an intermediate step in Judaism. There are certain matters of which there is no concept of intermediate, such as day and night. There is no time that is neither day nor night. In regard to cold and hot, though, there is an intermediate step, that of lukewarm. And the same is true between black and white. *Kedushah*, too, is an intermediate stage, between what is permitted and what is forbidden, being neither one nor the other but rather, "sanctify yourself with that which is permitted to you."

HaKesav VeHaKabalah brings the question of *Korban Aharon*, that one who forbids something which is permitted to him is regarded as only a *chassid* and not a *kadosh*. *HaKesav VeHaKabalah* therefore explains that the concept of *kedushah* means being holy even when engaged in physical activities. This means not seeking pleasure in one's actions, but rather involving one's intellect and realizing that he is observing the *mitzvah* of his Creator. This way, the person himself will be purely intellectual and devoid of all materialism.

R' Yitzchak Breuer in *Nachaliel* defines in a decisive manner the concepts of *kedushah* and *tumah*. Whatever aids a person in wrong beliefs, as if man is no more than an advanced animal and as if there is nothing after death, is *tumah*. On the other hand, whatever is far from death and which serves to elevate man above the animals, is *taharah*. But *taharah* is not the final stage; it is but an intermediate stage on the way to *kedushah*. "Because I, Hashem, your God, am holy" (*kadosh*) — Hashem has the true *kedushah*, and man was given the continuous desire to strive for that *kedushah*. The Torah teaches us how to free ourselves of the bondage of our lusts and to ascend in *kedushah*. But do not think that this goal can ever be totally achieved in one's lifetime. "For I, Hashem, your God, am holy," and My *kedushah* is infinite (*Melo HaOmer*).

Abarbanel says that in this *parashah*, the Torah repeats *mitzvos* that were already mentioned earlier, so as to stress that they are to be performed with an awareness of *kedushah*, and not only with our natural feelings. While by our nature we would understand the observance of the *Aseres HaDibros* or certain of the moral laws and laws of modesty, for the Jew what counts is the concept of *kedushah* and nothing else. This *parashah* was therefore said at *hakhel*, so as to obligate all of Israel together, with a covenant to fulfill the laws of morality out of a desire to attain *kedushah* and exaltation. This is the guarantee that the laws will continue to be observed in all generations.

According to *Rambam* in *Moreh Nevuchim* (3:47), the meaning of the verse, "You shall be holy," is that we must become sanctified through the observance of the *mitzvos*, which impart *kedushah* to Israel. R' Tzadok HaKohen of Lublin also develops this idea in his own way. We say in our blessings, "...Who has sanctified us with His *mitzvos*," so as to inform all that the *mitzvos* are the source of *kedushah*. And if you should claim that it is difficult to observe the *mitzvos* as decreed by Hashem, know that "I, Hashem, your God, am holy," and *I* will help you. *I* am the source of *kedushah*, and this source imparts *kedushah* to all those who come to cling to His attributes, as in the saying of *Chazal*: "Whoever sanctifies himself below, they sanctify him above." "Be holy because I, Hashem, your God, am holy." You do not need to create *kedushah*, for it already exists, and whoever acts in accordance with the ways of the Torah has *kedushah* cling to him, even without realizing it.

II.

What Is Included in Loving and Hating One's Neighbor?

The commandment, "Do not hate your brother in your heart," in Chapter 19, verse 17, is the introduction to a series of moral commandments dealing with man's relations with his fellow-man. The next verse ends with, "You shall love your neighbor as yourself." We begin with a *lav* — a negative commandment — that one may not hate one's neighbor, and continue with a *mitzvas asei* — a positive commandment — to love one's neighbor. It is therefore logical to assume that those matters mentioned between the two sections: "you shall surely admonish your neighbor and you shall not bear a sin because of him"; and "you shall not bear vengeance nor take a grudge against those of your nation"; are related to the hatred and love mentioned above. Indeed *Rashbam* explains the verses as a single unit: "If he did you a wrong, do not act as if you are his friend while plotting against him. Instead, you should admonish him for what he did, and this way there will be peace. You shall not bear a sin because of him in your heart." The Torah continues: "Do not wreak vengeance by paying him back evil for evil, nor bear a grudge even in your heart. Instead be forgiving."

All the *mitzvos* here are various forms of removing enmity from one's heart. Even admonishment is meant for that same purpose. *Ramban*, though, wants to explain admonishment as being separate from the rest, in that a person must admonish his fellow-man if he sees him doing something wrong, so that he does not become responsible for the other person's sin. *Ramban* relies here on *Targum Onkelos*, who explains this as, "So that you should not become liable to punishment because of his sin." Later, though, *Ramban* ties all the commandments here together, and explains the purpose of admonishment in terms of "and Avraham admonished Avimelech" (*Bereishis* 21:25), namely that one must speak openly to his fellow-man rather than bearing his sin in one's heart. This way, the other person will apologize and admit his error.

The Torah warns us also that not only may one not hate one's neighbor, but one is even forbidden to remember the evil action that the person did against him. Thus one must totally remove any memory of the sin from his heart. Not only that, but one must love the person, "as yourself."

Ramban ponders what the Torah means when it says that one must love one's neighbor as oneself, for R' Akiva stated that one's own life takes precedence over that of another. *Ramban* therefore explains that what the Torah means is that one must not harbor any jealousy toward his neighbor, but should desire only good for him, just as one would wish for his own self. Proof that this is what the Torah meant is that the Torah did not say, "You shall love אֶת־רֵעֲךָ", but לְרֵעֲךָ, literally "to your neighbor," namely that you should be happy with whatever belongs to your neighbor (לְרֵעֲךָ) and not envy whatever he has, just as you are not envious of what you yourself have. This type of emotion is feasible. We find an example of this in the love of Yehonasan for David. Yehonasan removed all envy from his heart, to the extent that he said to David, "you shall rule over Israel" (*I Shmuel* 23:17). It is for this reason that we are told that אֲהֵבוֹ נַפְשׁוֹ אֲהֵבוֹ (ibid. 20:17) — that he loved him as his soul. It is this love that the Torah commands all of Israel.

Rivash, *Paane'ach Raza* and *Abarbanel* all follow this approach. They expand the concept of endearment to include even the Jew who has sinned. One is forbidden to hate him in one's heart. Instead one has to admonish him. One is to hate the deeds, says *Abarbanel*, but not the person. One should thus admonish him so that he will not commit the same sin again.

◆§The Actual Performance of the Mitzvah of Love

R' David Zvi Hoffmann sees the five *mitzvos* contained in verses 17-18 — "do not hate . . . you shall surely admonish . . . do not wreak vengeance . . . do not bear a grudge . . . you shall love your neighbor . . ." — as paralleling the last of the Ten Commandments, לֹא־תַחְמֹד — "you shall not covet" (*Shemos* 20:14). The actual violation of this *mitzvah* is when one performs covetous actions against the owner because one coveted the owner's property in his heart. Similarly, the five *mitzvos* mentioned in our *parashah* all involve actual deeds, but originate in the heart.

The commandment of "you shall love" refers to acts of kindness and generosity which stem from love, for a person cannot love someone who is not pleasing to him. Thus, with regard to Hashem, the Torah uses the grammatical form of the "direct object" — "you shall love אֶת ה׳" (*Devarim* 6:5). But with regard to loving one's fellow-man, it uses the form of the "indirect object" — "you shall love לְרֵעֲךָ," literally, "you shall love to your neighbor." Love of one's fellow-man is not an abstract feeling, but is expressed through the things one does "to your neighbor." Hillel expressed this in a negative form: "What is hateful to you, do not do to your fellow," for he wished to stress that the commandment is not to be expressed in quantity but rather in quality. In terms of quantity, a person certainly aids himself more than he aids his neighbor, but in terms of quality he must treat his fellow-man as he treats himself. The example of this is in refraining from doing to one's neighbor what one hates being done to oneself. Of course, the more one aids his neighbor in quantity the better, and the person fulfills with that the *mitzvah* of the Torah in full.

Rambam in *Hil. Eivel* 14 gives this *mitzvah* a positive interpretation:

> It is a *mitzvas asei* — a positive commandment — of *Chazal* to visit the sick, to comfort the mourners, to bury the dead, to facilitate the marriage of a bride, to escort guests, to deal with all aspects of burial etc. All these are *gemilas chasadim* — deeds of loving kindness — performed by personal action, for which there is no set measure. Even though all these *mitzvos* are from *Chazal*, they are included in the general commandment, "you shall love your neighbor as yourself." All those things which you want others to do for you, you do them for your fellow-man in Torah and *mitzvos*.

In *Sefer HaMitzvos*, *Asei* 66, on the other hand, *Rambam* explains love for one's fellow in an abstract form, and says: "He commanded us to love others as we love ourselves, and that one's love and pity for his fellow should be as one's love and pity for himself."

Ramban, though, holds that it is not natural to expect a person to love another as he loves himself. Following him, other commentators on the Torah explain the *mitzvah* in concrete terms. Of course the concrete expression of love cannot be defined specifically, for it includes numerous types and variations of kindness. It is for this reason that Hillel phrased the *mitzvah* negatively, giving us a dimension that we can understand, namely not to do something to someone if one would consider that action bad for oneself.

Hillel's interpretation is beautifully explained by *Chiddushei HaRim*. There is no doubt that one must treat others kindly and show them love in a positive fashion. Hillel though, who taught ethics to a non-Jew who was interested in converting, knew that the mind of the non-Jew could not comprehend the idea of love for one's fellow in positive terms and he therefore translated this entire concept into a negative fashion, namely that one should not do bad to others. This the non-Jew could understand, but the idea of doing good to others requires a Jewish heart.

◄§ You Shall Love Your Fellow as Yourself

HaKesav VeHaKabalah explains that one's love for the other person must be "as yourself" — with the same devotion that one expects another person to show oneself. One does not have to give him everything one owns, for one does not expect that of him. The love that the Torah demands is that which a person expects to be shown to himself. *HaKesav VeHaKabalah* lists such loves: a) being frank and not hypocritical; b) treating the other with respect; c) inquiring about his welfare; d) participating in his grief; e) being cordial to him; f) giving him the benefit of the doubt; g) going out of the way at least to some extent on his behalf; h) lending him items. This is the sort of behavior towards our fellow-man required by the Torah in the fulfillment of the positive *mitzvah*.

Indeed the Torah made sure that this command would be one that one can accept logically. It is based on man's self-perception. Whatever I demand of others for myself, I must do for others. According to Hillel, this is a basic ethical principle of the Torah, and all the rest is to be deduced by study. R' Akiva too stresses that, " this is a major principle in the Torah" (*Yerushalmi Nedarim* 4:9). What our Sages wished to tell us is the value of each person, for all were created in the image of Hashem, and that all men are "as yourself," the works of the Creator.

R' David Zvi Hoffmann explains that this is the meaning of the Torah when it adds after this *mitzvah*, אֲנִי ה' — "I am Hashem" (*Vayikra* 19:17). In other words, I am Hashem, who created you all, and it is I that demand the unity of the human species, by means of human ethics, for that is the source for this unity.

Avnei Ezel explains beautifully the words of R' Akiva that "This is a major principle in the Torah." This unity depends solely on the Torah of Hashem and on its *mitzvos*, and on faith in the Creator of man. The unity that men create by means of their own humanitarian or social ideologies cannot endure, for they have no true basis. In fact, we can all see what has befallen man as a result of democratic universalism or material socialism. Where there is no "I am Hashem" as the basis for the love of one's fellow, love has no enduring practical basis.

In *Sifra*, there is an argument among *tannaim* as to the meaning of "You shall love your fellow-man as yourself." R' Akiva says that this is a major principle in the Torah, while Ben Azzai quotes the verse, "This is the book of the generations of man" (*Bereishis* 5:1). Many commentators have given explanations as to what the difference is between the two.

Malbim in *HaTorah VeHaMitzvah* analyzes the two views. There is a general principle among philosophers who deal with ethics that one should examine in universal terms whatever one wishes to do to others, namely that the same rules should apply to oneself as well. The personal benefit that one wants to achieve from the law has to apply to others as well. In this way, ethics are equal for all, even though the underlying principle is the good one gains personally. According to *Malbim*, that is the view of R' Akiva when he says "this is a major principle of the Torah." The word כָּמוֹךְ — "as yourself" — is the "major principle" upon which human ethics is built. Do to others what you wish them to do to you.

Moralists, though, do not content themselves with an assumption based on egotism. According to them, this is not a completely ethical position, but is merely a utilitarian ethical position — one that serves a purpose. A completely ethical position is one based on ideological and spiritual grounds, and is derived from the unity of all mankind, all of whom were created by God, and it is that fact which requires one to help his fellow-man. It is this view that Ben Azzai expounded when he said, "This is the book of the generations of man." The fact that all men come from a single source is the basis for our ethical system. Mankind is one, and it is only natural that we should help others, just as we help ourselves. It is difficult to understand, though, what forces *Malbim* to explain that R' Akiva's view is that human ethics is egotistical.

It is possible to say that the two views here are clear. R' Akiva holds that loving one's fellow-man is a major principle of the Torah, without which the Torah and the *mitzvos* are impossible, while Ben Azzai holds that without that rule all of humanity is impossible. Not only is it a major principle, but it is the entire book of the generations of man — the principle which enables mankind to exist. Indeed, *Chinuch* in *Mitzvah* 243 explains the words of R' Akiva as follows:

> "This is a major principle in the Torah" means that many *mitzvos* of the Torah depend on it, for one who loves his neighbor as himself will not steal from him, will not commit adultery with his wife, will not cheat him out of money, and will not harm him in any way. There are numerous other *mitzvos* in the Torah that depend on this, as anyone with intelligence will realize. The logic behind the *mitzvah* is well known, for just as he does to his fellow-man man so will his fellow-man will do to him, and this way there will be peace among mankind.

Hashem's seal appears upon all these *mitzvos*, as we see in the concluding words, "I am Hashem." Sadly, there are very few that heed this seal, and there are very few who love their fellow-man כָּמוֹךְ — as yourself. Yet we must realize that the same way we treat others, we are treated.

It was along these lines that *Besht* explained the words of the verse, 'ה צִלְּךָ — "Hashem is your shadow" (i.e., your protector; *Tehillim* 121:5) — to mean that just as a person's shadow does whatever he himself does, so too does Hashem treat the person the way he treats others. *Besht* also interprets "I am Hashem" at the end of these verses along the same lines. Hashem will act toward you as you act. If you are kind and merciful, He will act to you accordingly. God's actions toward you will be as your actions to others.

◆§ The Mitzvah of Admonishment

The *mitzvah* to admonish others is clearly stated in the *halachah*. One of its rules, for example, is that one should not do it in such a way as to have the face of the person involved change color due to embarrassment (*Arachin* 16). There are innumerable other laws. *Avnei Ezel* says that admonishment is effective only when it comes from a loving heart. If a father rebukes his son, his words are accepted, because the son knows that the words come from the father's heart. "Do not hate your fellow-man in your heart" (*Vayikra* 19:17), and then you will be able to fulfill the *mitzvah* which concludes this same verse: "you shall admonish your neighbor."

In *Yoma*, *Chazal* tell us that the Second *Beis HaMikdash* was destroyed because of *sin'as chinam* — groundless hatred, and in *Shabbos* 119 we are told that the Destruction happened because they did not admonish one another. There is no contradiction between the two. One implies the other. If they hated one another, of course their rebukes would have no effect.

The Chassidic works discuss at length the *mitzvah* of admonishing one's fellow-man, and the ideas implicit in the Torah text here. Rebuke yourself and examine your own behavior first, and only if you find yourself to be pure should you admonish your neighbor. If you behave so, then the concluding words וְלֹא־תִשָּׂא עָלָיו חֵטְא — "and do not bear a sin for him" — will apply to you in the sense that you will not have transferred the sin within you to him.

The Chassidic works also explain that one should admonish in a way that does not arouse heavenly accusation against the other person — "and do not put a sin upon him."

In *Arachin* 16, *Chazal* tell us in the name of R' Elazar ben Azaryah: "I wonder if there is anyone in this generation who has the ability to offer *tochachah*." On the basis of this latter statement *Chazon Ish* rules in his commentary on *Rambam's Hilchos De'os*, that:

> Jewish sinners are in the category of רֵעֶךָ — your neighbor, for *Chazal* said in *Sanhedrin* 52 that even regarding a person deserving the death penalty, "choose for him the easier death, because of וְאָהַבְתָּ לְרֵעֲךָ כָּמוֹךָ." (Thus we see that even a person who committed a capital crime is considered to be רֵעֶךָ — your neighbor — and you are required to love him.) As to the fact that *Chazal* said that it is a *mitzvah* to hate a רָשָׁע — a wicked person — that is only after the person was given proper *tochachah*, admonishment, and did not accept it (*Rambam Hilchos De'os*) As we nowadays do not know how to admonish, as indicated by R' Elazar ben Azaryah, every person is considered as if he had not yet been given *tochachah*, so that his wicked actions are regarded as being involuntary, and it therefore remains a *mitzvah* to love him.

This is the ruling of the *gaon* of our generation, the *Chazon Ish*.

It is clear that the *mitzvah* of *tochachah* is limited by the *mitzvah* of "You shall not hate your fellow-man in your heart." Admonishment is a part of the *mitzvah* to love one's neighbor and to guide him to the proper way, so that he should be כָּמוֹךָ — "as yourself" — both in heavenly and in earthly matters.

III.

The Prohibition of Orlah in Eretz Yisrael and Outside It

Rambam in *Moreh Nevuchim* 3 gives as the reason for *orlah* — the prohibition of the fruit of a newly planted tree for the first three years (*Vayikra* 19:23-25) — a means to move the Jewish people away from idolatry. The sorcerers of the time would do all types of things to speed up, as it were, the production of fruit on the tree. After the trees gave fruit, the fruit would be offered to their gods.

According to *Rambam*, this explains the statement by R' Yoshiyahu regarding the Torah's prohibition against *Kilayim* — sowing a field with more than one kind of seed — that "it is not forbidden until he sows wheat, barley and grapes with one throw." This type of planting was part of the idolatry of the time, and that is why it was forbidden, and the same is true for *orlah*. *Ramban* quotes this statement of *Rambam* without comment.

Many of the *rishonim* differed with *Rambam's* explanations in *Moreh Nevuchim*, for they felt that these explanations tended to undermine the principle that the *mitzvos* must be observed in *all* generations, including those in which idolatry is not a common temptation. *Rambam* himself stated that his work was only for those who were perplexed, so that the explanations that he gave for the *mitzvos* in that work were meant only for such individuals. In his *Yad HaChazakah*, which is meant to be for the entire Jewish nation as a whole, *Rambam* adopted an entirely different approach.

Ramban, however, gives an entirely natural explanation for the prohibition of *orlah* and, unlike his normal practice, ignores the kabbalistic interpretations he so often quotes. He merges his reasons with those of his predecessors, that the *mitzvah* of *orlah* is meant to have us set aside our first fruits for Hashem, as we do with *bikkurim* — the first fruits of the crop each year. According to *Ramban*, the setting aside of fruit for Hashem begins only after the third year, because during the first three years the excessive moisture in the fruit is harmful, "and most (fruit) rots or (the trees) do not produce fruit at all until the fourth year." Ibn Ezra also states simply that "the fruit that grows the first three years is of no benefit, and is harmful."

These explanations, though, are very difficult, because the *halachah* is that if there is doubt whether a certain fruit is *orlah* or not, if it grew in *Eretz Yisrael*, one is forbidden to eat it, whereas if it grew elsewhere, one is permitted to do so. If the reason for the prohibition is because of danger to one's health, what difference should there be between the two? If the reason for the prohibition is simply because the Torah forbids the use of such fruit, we can understand the distinction between *Eretz Yisrael* and other countries, but not if the reason is because of danger to one's health, which halachically is considered more weighty than a simple prohibition.

One could, of course, say that the nature of *Eretz Yisrael* is different from that of other countries, in a way that is known only to Hashem, and that is the difference in the *halachah* between the two. But using the explanation that *orlah* is prohibited for health reasons fails to answer other aspects of the laws of *orlah*. Thus, for example, we are told explicitly by the Mishnah in the first chapter of *Orlah* that when our forefathers entered *Eretz Yisrael* with Yehoshua, if they found trees that had just been planted, these would be exempt from the laws of *orlah*. *Chazal* deduced this from the verse, וּנְטַעְתֶּם כָּל־עֵץ — "and [when] you plant any tree" (*Vayikra* 19:23) — thereby excluding any tree planted before by non-Jews. If the reason for the prohibition of *orlah* is that it is injurious to one's health, what difference should there be in who did the planting?

Similarly, we are told in *Toras Kohanim*: "I might think that this (the law of *orlah*) applied when they reached Transjordan; it therefore states אֶל הָאָרֶץ — "to the land" (ibid.) — the special land." What difference should there be in the danger in *Eretz Yisrael* and that on the other side of the Jordan? Also, in *Yerushalmi Orlah* 1:2, we are told: "A tree planted within a house is subject to *orlah*," and this is deduced from a verse. Why should we need a separate verse to teach us this, if the reason for the prohibition is because of danger?

A very strong question on the view that the prohibition is due to danger is asked by one of the *acharonim*, who quotes the Midrash Rabbah on *Bereishis*:

> R' Yehudah ben Pazzi taught: "Who will roll away the dust from your eyes, Adam? You were not able to observe your *mitzvah* even for a single hour, while your children wait three years (because of the laws of *orlah*)."

If the prohibition of *orlah* is due to danger, what comparison is there between the two? Israel waits for three years so that they will not be harmed, while Adam was specifically told by Hashem, "The tree is good for food" (*Bereishis* 2:9).

The kabbalists see the prohibition of *orlah* as being a separation between good and bad, which became mingled together after Adam's sin. *Sefas Emes* discusses this at length, seeing the *mitzvah* as serving also to purify the land and to take it out of its curse, through the סוּר מֵרָע (*Tehillim* 34:15) — turning away from bad — for three years, before reaching the עֲשֵׂה־טוֹב (ibid.) — doing good — in treating the fourth year's crop as holy.

Some of the recent commentators are not far in their explanations from the view of the kabbalists. R' David Zvi Hoffmann and R' Samson Raphael Hirsch do not offer a natural explanation for this *mitzvah*. According to them, the *mitzvah* serves an educational function in teaching us that Hashem is the Master of all of creation, and in uprooting from within us the idea that whatever we have comes from our own efforts. Refraining from using the fruits of trees for the first three years because of Hashem's command forces man to consider what it means to "own" anything, and what the relation is between a creature and his Creator. But this reason also needs to be explained. Why do we need specifically three years to consider these matters? There are those who explain that this was the time that it took our forefather to recognize the existence of God, as in the words of *Chazal*, "At the age of three, Avraham recognized his Creator." But the reason for specifically a three-year wait is still unclear.

Kli Yakar sees this *mitzvah* as "a remembrance of the act of creation." While trees were created on the third day of creation, their fruit had not yet ripened. Only on the fourth day, when the sun and moon were created, did the fruit become ripe. That is the reason we may not eat the fruit of the first three years. The fourth year parallels the fourth day of Creation when the fruits ripened, and the fruit of the fourth year is holy and may be eaten only in Jerusalem. On the fifth day of Creation, many of the creatures who would enjoy the various plants were created, and therefore we may eat the fruit wherever we wish in the fifth year. This is an interesting explanation, but is much closer to homiletics (*d'rush*) than to the plain meaning (*p'shat*). It is clear that this *mitzvah*, as many other *mitzvos*, shows us that the human intellect cannot fathom Hashem's commands, and that the reason is beyond our comprehension.

☙ Orlah Within and Outside Eretz Yisrael

In *Kiddushin* 37, *Chazal* tell us that the prohibition of *orlah* is "from the Torah" in *Eretz Yisrael* and is הֲלָכָה לְמֹשֶׁה מִסִּינַי — an oral law handed down by Hashem to Moshe on Sinai — in all other countries. This makes a difference in *halachah*. Thus, if we are unsure if a certain fruit is *orlah* or not, in *Eretz Yisrael* it is forbidden to be eaten, while if such a doubt arises concerning fruit which grew in any other country the fruit is permitted.

At first, *Chazal* wanted to say that only in *Eretz Yisrael* is the *halachah* "from the Torah" because it states, "When you come to the land and plant ..." (*Vayikra* 19:23). Afterwards they rejected this because of a question: "After all, regarding *tefillin* and the firstborn domestic animal (*petter rechem*), both verses (also) refer to coming (to *Eretz Yisrael*) and yet they are in effect both in *Eretz Yisrael* and outside it." *Chazal* therefore give the reason for this law applying to *Eretz Yisrael* as being that this is one of those laws which is חוֹבַת הַקַּרְקַע — literally "an obligation of the land" — namely that it is an agricultural law. Such laws are given specifically for the land of *Eretz Yisrael*.

Rambam, though, in *Hilchos Ma'achalos Asuros* 10:10, when mentioning that the laws of *orlah* are Torah law only in *Eretz Yisrael*, links it to the verse, "When you come to the land." The commentators on *Rambam* have sought to explain why *Rambam* ignores the question posed by the *gemara*, and which caused it to find another explanation.

One may be able to answer that *Rambam*, even though he knew that it was not "the coming into the land" which determined the law of *orlah*, nevertheless used the verse as an *asmachta* (support), because in reality on the Scriptural level ("from the Torah") the laws of *orlah* only apply in *Eretz Yisrael*. Thus he was able to explain the verse in its plain sense as referring to *Eretz Yisrael*, even though in other lands there is an obligation of *orlah* which does not depend upon "coming into the land." *Orlah* is, after all, an agricultural law dependent upon the land. Therefore, on the Scriptural level, the verse can be interpreted literally. Outside *Eretz Yisrael*, the *mitzvah* of *orlah* is not a Scriptural obligation, but derives from a הֲלָכָה לְמֹשֶׁה מִסִּינַי, an oral law handed down to Moshe at Sinai. It is somewhat surprising that none of the commentators of the Torah attempted to explain why the Torah mentions "when you come to the land" in connection with this *mitzvah*. The only one who did was *Or HaChaim*, who saw here the merging of three different *mitzvos*: a) the duty of *aliyah* to *Eretz Yisrael*; b) the duty to plant trees in *Eretz Yisrael*; and c) the duty to keep the *mitzvah* of *orlah*. It was not for nothing that *Chazal* in the Midrash on our *parashah* greatly praised those who plant trees in *Eretz Yisrael*, to the extent of comparing them to Hashem, Who also began by planting trees, He created man. The mention of coming to *Eretz*

Yisrael in our *parashah*, even though the *mitzvah* of *orlah* applies outside *Eretz Yisrael* as well, tells us, as it were, that there is a link between this *mitzvah* and the land, which is not the case outside *Eretz Yisrael*. In *Eretz Yisrael* we have a duty to plant trees, while outside *Eretz Yisrael* we have no such duty, and all we are commanded to do is to observe the prohibitions of *orlah*.

Sifsei Kohen, among the disciples of *Ari Hakadosh*, sees in this *parashah* a special meaning: that we are not to come to terms with plantings by the Canaanites, but that instead we should have new planting in *kedushah* and *taharah*.

The *Magid* of *Dubno* uses a similar approach in his *Ohel Yaakov*. There he adds that there is an obligation to plant and build in *Eretz Yisrael*, in order to fulfill the verse, "a land flowing with milk and honey, where nothing is lacking."

Chazal in *Kiddushin* 39, based on the difference in the laws of *orlah* in *Eretz Yisrael* and elsewhere (that the first is "from the Torah," while the second is הֲלָכָה לְמשֶׁה מִסִּינַי, as mentioned above), state that a difference in *halachah* results where there is a doubt if a fruit is *orlah* or not: It is forbidden if it grew in *Eretz Yisrael*, but permitted if it grew elsewhere. *Beis Yosef* expresses surprise at this difference in *halachah*, because throughout *shas* we accept that הֲלָכָה לְמשֶׁה מִסִּינַי is considered just as any law which is דְּאוֹרַיְתָא — from the Torah. Similarly, what is the difference between the fact that *orlah* in *Eretz Yisrael* is "from the Torah," while outside *Eretz Yisrael* it is הֲלָכָה לְמשֶׁה מִסִּינַי? Why should there be such a distinction in the case of *orlah*?

Taz in *Yoreh De'ah* 294 combines these two questions and answers them jointly. He says that all that *Chazal* knew was that the law in *Eretz Yisrael* is "from the Torah" and that outside *Eretz Yisrael* it was הֲלָכָה לְמשֶׁה מִסִּינַי, without any further details. This set them wondering: Why should such a difference exist? It was on the basis of that question that *Chazal* reached the conclusion that there must be a difference between the two in *halachah*. What difference is there? that in a case of doubt in *Eretz Yisrael*, the fruit is forbidden, while in the same situation elsewhere, the fruit is permitted. This difference stems from the fact that there is a difference in the reason given for the prohibition in each case.

Based on the comment by *Taz*, the Rav of Lutzk, in *Oznayim LeTorah*, answers a famous question on *Rambam*, who rules that whenever there is a question of doubt on a law which is דְּאוֹרַיְתָא, "from the Torah" [according to the Torah], one always adopts the lenient view, *l'kula*. According to this view, why do we have to be told that since the law of *orlah* outside *Eretz Yisrael* is הֲלָכָה לְמשֶׁה מִסִּינַי we therefore are lenient in a case of doubt? According to *Rambam's* view, even if it a regular case of דְּאוֹרַיְתָא one should adopt the lenient view! According to *Taz*, though, we can answer this question. All that we were told is that the law of *orlah* outside *Eretz Yisrael* is הֲלָכָה לְמֹשֶׁה מִסִּינַי, as opposed to *Eretz Yisrael* itself, where it is "from the Torah." We thus conclude that there must be a difference in *halachah* between the two in this instance, unlike everywhere else, where there is no difference between them.

We can thus answer the question on *Rambam*. It is true that in every instance of doubt on a דְּאוֹרַיְתָא law, we are lenient. In the case of *orlah*, though, since the Torah made a distinction between *Eretz Yisrael* and elsewhere, this must mean that the Torah came to be stringent — to go *l'chumra* — in a doubt regarding *orlah* on the דְּאוֹרַיְתָא level, unlike all other *mitzvos*, in which we are lenient. Thus there is a difference regarding *orlah* between a דְּאוֹרַיְתָא law and הֲלָכָה לְמֹשֶׁה מִסִּינַי, a difference that does not exist regarding any other *mitzvah*. *Ran* at the end of the first chapter of *Kiddushin* answers the question asked on *Rambam*, who holds that all doubts in דְּאוֹרַיְתָא are to be treated leniently. Based on that view, what difference is there between a doubt concerning *orlah* outside *Eretz Yisrael* and doubts which are דְּאוֹרַיְתָא? According to him, the *kula* — the leniency — of a doubt of *orlah* is different than other doubts. In a case of a doubt of *orlah* outside *Eretz Yisrael*, there is no prohibition whatsoever, and a person may even give that fruit to another to eat without the other person knowing its nature, without violating the prohibition of *lifnei iveir* — of being instrumental in causing another person to sin. But this is not true for other forbidden foods of the Torah. In the case of doubt regarding other forbidden foods, one may not give another person that item to eat if the person who will eat it does not know its nature. *Ran's* source is the words of *Chazal* in *Kiddushin* 39: "Rav Iva and Rava ben Rav Chanan would give each other to eat" (foods whose nature the receiver did not know, but the giver did know). From this we see that there is no prohibition of *lifnei iveir* in feeding someone something of which there is a doubt of *orlah* outside *Eretz Yisrael*.

Shev Shematsa, in his first chapter, asks a basic question on *Ran*. True, the person who feeds the other is not guilty of *lifnei iveir*, but it should nevertheless be forbidden for him to do so because he (the giver) is receiving benefit from that *orlah*, in accordance with *Tosafos* on *Pesachim* 22b, that if one gives another an object or supplies the other with a service of some kind, he is considered to have received *hana'ah* — pleasure — because the other person is now indebted to him. Thus, if a person knows that something is *orlah* and he gives it to another without telling him what it is, the giver is deriving benefit from the *orlah*. How then is he permitted to give it to the other person? Many *acharonim* have attempted to answer this question. The commentators on *Rambam* have also dealt with it.

Kesef Mishneh holds that only Shmuel, who holds that *orlah* outside *Eretz Yisrael* is not forbidden at all by הֲלָכָה לְמשֶׁה מִסִּינַי but merely by a stringency (*chumra*) adopted by the people there, would permit someone to feed another person something of which there is a doubt of *orlah*. Indeed, *Rambam* did not include the law of feeding another in his *Yad HaChazakah*, because according to him, *orlah* is forbidden as הֲלָכָה לְמשֶׁה מִסִּינַי, and one is therefore definitely forbidden to derive any benefit from it.

Rambam did not even include the *halachah* brought by *Chinuch*: "One who has a tree of *orlah* in his garden, and if his neighbor came and ate of it, is not required at all to tell him that it is *orlah*." From the way *Chinuch* phrases it, he only permits a person to allow someone else who does not know about the *orlah* to eat it undisturbed, but does not permit one person to actually feed another. This position of *Chinuch* to some extent avoids the problem raised by *Shev Shematsa* (above), about deriving benefit from *orlah* by feeding it to someone else.

It appears that *Rambam*, who did not bring this law either, holds that even this act of passive permission would require the eater to be grateful to the owner of the tree, and therefore is also forbidden. He permits a person only to buy grapes outside *Eretz Yisrael*, even when he sees that the seller brought them from an *orlah* vineyard, provided that he did not see the grapes being cut. In *Eretz Yisrael*, even such a doubt would be forbidden.

IV.

Who is Duty Bound by Kiddush Hashem?

The source of the *mitzvah* of *kiddush Hashem* — of sanctifying Hashem's name, even if necessary dying for Him — is found in the verse, וְנִקְדַּשְׁתִּי בְּתוֹךְ בְּנֵי יִשְׂרָאֵל — "and I will be sanctified in the midst of *Bnei Yisrael*" (*Vayikra* 22:32). *Chazal* in *Toras Kohanim* 9:4 tell us:

As it says וְלֹא תְחַלְּלוּ — "and you shall not desecrate" (ibid.) — I hear that you must sanctify. When it says וְנִקְדַּשְׁתִּי — "and I will be sanctified" — it means give yourself up (to death) and sanctify My name. I might imagine that this is true even when one is by himself; it therefore states, בְּתוֹךְ בְּנֵי יִשְׂרָאֵל — "in the midst of *Bnei Yisrael*" — when there are many (people).

The details of the laws of *kiddush Hashem* are brought by *Chazal* in *Sanhedrin* 74 and in other places. *Rambam* in *Hil. Yesodei HaTorah* 5:1, says:

All the house of Israel are commanded concerning the sanctification of this Great Name, as it states, וְנִקְדַּשְׁתִּי בְּתוֹךְ בְּנֵי יִשְׂרָאֵל, "and I will be sanctified in the midst of *Bnei Yisrael*." How is this? If a gentile arises and forces a Jew to transgress any one of the *mitzvos* written in the Torah, or else he will kill him, he is to transgress it and not be killed . . . and if he died (i.e., chose death) and did not transgress it, he is guilty of taking his own life.

In the following sections, *Rambam* rules that the *mitzvah* of *kiddush Hashem* applies when force is applied to have a Jew transgress a law of the Torah "in public," namely before ten Jews, provided that the motivation of the gentile is to have the Jew transgress a law of the Torah. If, however, this is "in private" (i.e., with less than ten Jews present) or if the motivation of the person applying the force is simply because he wants to gain some benefit for himself (e.g., by forcing a Jew to drive him on *Shabbos*, where the person applying the force wishes transportation to a certain destination), there is no requirement of *kiddush Hashem*, except in the case of three prohibitions: *avodah zarah* (idolatry), *gilui arayos* (sexual immorality), and *shefichas damim* (murder). For these three, *Chazal* deduced that regardless of the circumstances one must allow himself to be killed rather than to commit the sin. (Later on, we will clarify *Rambam's* position.)

The commentators are surprised at *Rambam's* use of the phrase, "all the house of Israel" (בֵּית יִשְׂרָאֵל), "the whole House of Israel." After all, does not every *mitzvah* apply to the whole Jewish people? *Avnei Shoham* has a beautiful explanation. According to him, *Rambam* wishes to stress that even if all the Jews are gathered together in a single place, where, God forbid, they are offered the option of either committing idolatry or having the entire nation annihilated, they should not reason that if the nation is annihilated that will be a tremendous *chilul Hashem*, since His promises to His children will go unfulfilled. In spite of that, all of Israel are required to die for *kiddush Hashem*, as we see from *Chazal* (*Berachos* 6a), where we are told: "What business of yours are the hidden things of Hashem? What you were commanded to do you must do, and whatever He wishes to, the Holy One, Blessed be He, will do." *Avnei Shoham* also adds that in regard to a question of *kiddush Hashem* concerning the entire Jewish people, there is a difference between committing *gilui arayos* (forbidden relations) and *avodah zarah* (idolatry). We also find in *Meiri* on *Sanhedrin* (p. 227) that Yael was right to comply with Sisera "for the sake of saving the community." Thus, *Maharik* writes in *Shoresh* 165: "Esther went to Achashverosh voluntarily in order to save all of Israel." *Rambam* accordingly tells us here that this leniency regarding *kiddush Hashem* is only in regard to *gilui arayos*, but in regard to *avodah zarah* "all" of Israel must sanctify Hashem's name, by being willing to die for it, even if by committing the sin they could save the entire Jewish people.

The wording in which *Rambam* arranges the laws here offers the commentators the opportunity to conclude that *Rambam's* view is that in regard to the three severe prohibitions listed above there is a *mitzvah* of *kiddush Hashem* even "in private," while with the other *mitzvos* there is only such an obligation "in public." This is not the opinion of *Lechem Mishneh*. He holds that the law of *kiddush Hashem* does not apply in private, even with the three *halachos* listed above. His view is based on *Chazal* in *Sanhedrin* and other places, who learn from the phrase, בְּתוֹךְ בְּנֵי יִשְׂרָאֵל — "in the midst of *Bnei Yisrael*" — that the *mitzvah* of *kiddush Hashem* requires the presence of ten Jews. *Rambam*, though, states clearly, "in those places where it is stated that one should be killed rather than transgress, should he be killed and not transgress, he has sanctified the Name, and if there were ten of Israel present, he sanctified the Name publicly." According to this, in regard to these three sins there are two types of *kiddush Hashem*: in private we have the obligation of *kiddush Hashem*, while in public we have the obligation of *kiddush Hashem b'rabim* — sanctifying the Name in public. *Lechem Mishneh* thus asks how it is that *Rambam* says something which is the opposite of what *Chazal* said.

If we look in *Rambam's Sefer HaMitzvos*, *mitzvah* 9, we will see the strong foundation for *Lechem Mishneh's* opinion that according to *Rambam*, *kiddush Hashem* applies only in the presence of ten Jews. In *Sefer HaMitzvos*, *Rambam* writes clearly:

> This *mitzvah* was not commanded except in such a great gathering as that which terrified the entire world (that of Chananyah, Mishael and Azaryah). For the purpose of publicizing in this way Hashem's Oneness, He saw to it through Yeshayahu that Israel would not be completely disgraced on that occasion, and that young men would step forth at that difficult time, and they would not be afraid of death, and that they would be prepared to

die, thereby proclaiming the faith, and sanctifying Hashem's Name publicly.

This, in keeping with the verse: "Not now will Yaakov be shamed, and not now will his face pale, for when seeing his children, the work of his hands in his midst, they will sanctify My Name."

It appears from the above that *Rambam's* opinion is that the purpose of the *mitzvah* of *kiddush* Hashem is to cause a revolution in the hearts of those who are apathetic, to rouse them up not to accept spiritual subjugation, and to demonstrate Israel's adhering to its faith. This *mitzvah* of וְנִקְדַּשְׁתִּי — "and I will be sanctified" — is different from that which is required in regard to the violation of the three prohibitions, where the terrible nature of the sin requires one to choose death. וְנִקְדַּשְׁתִּי supposes public demonstration.

It would therefore appear, that *Rambam's* ruling, that one must be willing to forfeit his life rather than violate any of the three prohibitions even in private, does not stem from the *mitzvah* of *kiddush Hashem*, which is primarily in public and is meant to arouse the community. One might venture to say that, according to *Rambam*, there are two types of *kiddush Hashem*: The first is *kiddush Hashem* before non-Jews, so that they will not say that the Jews make a mockery of their religion and faith. This is the counterpart of the sin of *chilul Hashem*, as expressed by the verse,"you shall not desecrate My holy name," and is meant to impart respect for Judaism in the hearts of the non-Jews, as they realize how Jews are willing to sacrifice their lives for their faith.

The *kiddush Hashem* that *Rambam* discusses in *Sefer HaMitzvos*, though, is meant to strengthen the faith of the Jews themselves and to strengthen their spiritual resistance against those who wish to force them to violate their faith. This *kiddush Hashem* applies only in the presence of ten Jews or more, in accordance with its aim of strengthening the resolve among young Jewish men and of encouraging them to observe the Torah without fear of death or of evil decrees.

From this point of view, *Lechem Mishneh* appears to be correct when he says that the law of *kiddush Hashem* applies even before less than ten (Jews). When there are ten Jews present, though, there are two elements: וְנִקְדַּשְׁתִּי — "and I shall be sanctified" — and וְלֹא תְחַלְּלוּ — "you shall not desecrate." The purpose of the latter negative commandment is to have the non-Jews respect Judaism and its adherents. Any Jew who gives in to the pressures and violates one of the three severe prohibitions has desecrated the holiness of Israel among the other nations. If he allows himself to be killed rather than to transgress, the non-Jews must stand in amazement at the strength of the faith of the

Jewish people, and that is a *kiddush Hashem*. If the person is killed in public, his act of sacrifice serves as an example to his brothers, and he fulfills the positive commandment of וְנִקְדַּשְׁתִּי בְּתוֹךְ בְּנֵי יִשְׂרָאֵל — "and I shall be sanctified in the midst of *Bnei Yisrael*" — as explained by *Rambam* in his *Sefer HaMitzvos*.

Indeed later, in his *Yad HaChazakah*, *Rambam* says that whoever transgressed rather than allowing himself to be killed "before ten of Israel" has not fulfilled a *mitzvas asei* — a positive commandment — that of *kiddush Hashem*, and has transgressed a *lav* — a negative commandment — of *chilul Hashem*. Here *Rambam* uses the phrase, "the positive commandment of *kiddush Hashem*," in order to teach us that there is another type of *kiddush Hashem*, one that does not stem from the positive commandment, "I will be sanctified," but which stems solely from the prohibition of *chilul Hashem*. And that is the same *kiddush Hashem* that applies to allowing oneself to be killed rather than to transgress in private.

Rambam's words are in keeping with *Toras Kohanim* that we brought above: "as it states, 'you shall not desecrate,' that implies 'sanctify.' " In other words, there is a *kiddush Hashem* that stems from the prohibition of וְלֹא תְחַלְּלוּ — "you shall not desecrate." "Then when it says וְנִקְדַּשְׁתִּי — 'and I will be sanctified' — give yourself over (to being killed) and sanctify My name." This latter *mitzvah* applies only in public, as it states, בְּתוֹךְ בְּנֵי יִשְׂרָאֵל — in the midst of *Bnei Yisrael*.

◆§ "And I Will be Sanctified" — as Seen Through the Eyes of the Commentators

Most of the commentators on the Torah, and even those who do not normally adopt a purely textual explanation, hold that the commandment of וְנִקְדַּשְׁתִּי refers to the laws of sacrifices addressed to the *Kohanim* in the immediately preceding verses. The Torah comes here to warn the *Kohanim* that there may be an element of *chilul Hashem* if they transgress the *mitzvos* they were commanded, namely if they sacrifice an animal with a blemish or a mother and its young on the same day. This is the way *Abarbanel*, *S'forno*, *Akeidah* and Ibn Ezra explain it. Ibn Ezra even proves that this verse refers to *Kohanim*, for only afterwards does the Torah state: "Speak to *Bnei Yisrael*" (*Vayikra* 23:2).

R' David Zvi Hoffmann also follows the lines of the *rishonim*, for in interpreting the Torah we use the principle, אֵין מִקְרָא יוֹצֵא מִידֵי פְשׁוּטוֹ — that regardless of what other interpretations may be given to a verse, the plain meaning of the text nevertheless remains valid.

Meshech Chochmah notes that the Torah mentions *yetzias Mitzrayim* — the Exodus from Egypt — here, as the warnings above concern matters of which only the person himself can know whether he is guilty. For example, if a person brings a sacrifice with the intention to eat it after the appointed time, only he himself knows that fact, and by having the animal sacrificed he can cause others to sin. Similarly, only he may know that an animal and its young are to be sacrificed on the same day. By the same token, a person can claim that a *todah* offering whose time for eating has elapsed is really a *shelamim*, for which an additional period of time is available. Thus the Torah mentions *yetzias Mitzrayim* here to tell us:

> I am Hashem, Who distinguished in Egypt between the drop which made a *bechor* — firstborn — and that which did not make a *bechor*. I am also He Who can distinguish between a sacrifice that is proper and one that is not, and I will punish those who attempt to cheat.

Rashi and *Ramban* explain the verse of וְנִקְדַּשְׁתִּי in accordance with *Chazal*, that here we are commanded a *mitzvas asei* of *kiddush Hashem*; to allow ourselves to be killed for the *mitzvos* of the Torah.

Rashi quotes *Sifra*: "When a person gives himself over, he should give himself over in order to die, for one who gives himself over expecting a miracle does not have a miracle done for him." Many are surprised at this addition, for it is only good advice directed to a person prepared to sacrifice his life for the sake of Heaven, but is certainly not specified in the Torah.

In general, the commentators are surprised at the significance attached by *Sifra* (as quoted by *Rashi*) to the intentions of the person who is ready to die on *kiddush Hashem*. After all, the Torah commands us about the deed, and what is the importance of the person's intention here? *Sefas Emes* says that *Rashi* wishes to warn us that a person should not expect that God will cause a miracle — calculating to himself that a miracle which occurs in public is also a *kiddush Hashem*. Expecting a miracle makes the miracle less likely, and thus it diminishes the *mitzvah* of *kiddush Hashem*.

Maharal, in his *Gur Aryeh*, explains *Rashi's* words along *hashkafah* lines. A person who is willing to accept death for *kiddush Hashem* removes himself from the natural framework, and as a result he merits his salvation from a world which is beyond nature. If however his will to survive is so great that he expects a miracle, that means that he is still within the world of nature and cannot draw to him salvation by supernatural means.

The Tzaddik of Sochachow gives a profound explanation of this. When a person is willing to give his life for *kiddush Hashem*, it is an act of annulling his very essence. Man is permitted to slaughter animals for food, because their existence is subservient to that of the human. By the same token, man's existence is infinitely more subservient to that of God in regard to dying for *kiddush Hashem*. It follows that man's body and soul — even his share of the World to Come — are meaningless where there is *kiddush Hashem*. It is for this reason that the *mitzvah* of *kiddush Hashem* is such that man should not even consider the reward he may obtain for his act, but must be willing to totally annul his existence and offer up his life purely out of love for Hashem.

Sefas Emes expands and develops this idea. He says that each Jew has, at least potentially, a spark of *kedushah* which enables him to free himself from the rules of nature and to offer up his life for Hashem's glory. *Yetzias Mitzrayim* — the Exodus from Egypt — is mentioned here "because during the departure from Egypt Hashem made miracles for us which took us out of the realm of nature, and as a result we were able to overcome all the limitations of nature."

The same approach is adopted by R' Simchah Zissel of Kelm, who notes that the Torah here uses the נִפְעַל — the passive form — of the verb, וְנִקְדַּשְׁתִּי — "and you shall be sanctified" — rather than the צִוּוּי — the imperative. In this, the Torah hints to us that each Jew must develop within himself this wondrous trait that enables him to give his life for *kiddush Hashem*, if it ever becomes necessary. There is no direct command, because *kiddush Hashem* is not required in all circumstances. Under normal conditions, the rule is וְחַי בָּהֶם וְלֹא שֶׁיָּמוּת בָּהֶם — "You shall live by them (the *mitzvos*) and not die by them." At the same time, we must always be ready to carry out this trait in practice when it becomes necessary. This *mitzvah* was written right next to the laws governing the *todah* — thanksgiving-offering — because this trait derives from man's appreciation of all the good Hashem has bestowed upon him, which obligates him to give up his life for the One who gave him life.

◆§ The Essence of Life and the Sanctity of Life

In Judaism, life is the supreme value. The *mitzvah* of *kiddush Hashem* is given in the passive grammatical form, because the active form is to live. The Torah gives us a basic rule in the observing of the *mitzvos* — וְחַי בָּהֶם וְלֹא שֶׁיָּמוּת בָּהֶם — "you shall live by them (the *mitzvos*), and not die by them." *Pikuach nefesh* — danger to human life — supersedes all the *mitzvos* in the Torah. But there are three *aveiros* —

sins — to which the rule of *pikuach nefesh* does not apply, because these sins undermine the Jew's very existence and the superiority of his soul, and transgressing these sins would leave his life with no value. These *aveiros* reduce man to the level of an animal. They destroy the entire fabric of life in the world, because when we have *arayos* — sexual immorality — *shefichas damim* — the shedding of human blood — and *avodah zarah* — idolatry — there is no value to life, and thus no right to defend such life.

As to all the other *mitzvos* and *aveiros*, the value of life is decisive. The only exception to this is when an attempt is made to force a Jew to commit an *aveirah* other than the three, where the entire motivation is to have the Jew violate the *halachah*. In such a case, it is the personal example which lends sanctity to life, and which encourages the rest of our nation to remain firm in the sanctity of its life and not to give in to our oppressors. In the latter case, the person must be willing to give his life, so as to encourage the remaining Jews to sanctify their lives. Thus, we find that R' Samson Raphael Hirsch writes in *Chorev*:

> In dying a saintly death, you leave a faithful personal example of the greatness of your faith in Hashem and His holy religion, as a sign and beacon for your generation and the following generations, that by your death you teach even your grandchildren how to purify their lives, and to elevate themselves to such a sanctified life.

As this *mitzvah* is an educational one for future generations, and its aim is to serve as an example of spiritual bravery, there are innumerable limitations to it, and it applies only when the person attempting to force the Jew to commit the sin is doing it clearly so as to have the Jew violate his religion, and provided it is in the presence of ten other Jews. *Rambam's* view is that a person may not undertake to give up his life in circumstances where the Torah exempted him from such action. There are *rishonim* who disagree, and bring proof from *Chazal* of many great Sages who gave their lives where they were not required to do so by *halachah*. On that basis, they attempt to differentiate between a prominent Torah Sage and other people. But this is not a clear *halachic* ruling.

The laws of *kiddush Hashem* have been accepted throughout Jewish history, based on the individual's personal decision, given the fact that in most such cases there has not been time to ask a question as to the *halachah*. As is known, a special blessing was composed during the period of the Crusades for those dying for *kiddush Hashem*.

The *poskim* argue as to whether one has the right to sacrifice others for *kiddush Hashem*. Some bring proof from Shaul, who told his arms bearer to kill him. *Beis Yosef* in *Yoreh De'ah* 157 quotes those who forbid this, and who hold that what Shaul did was against the *halachah*. *Yefei To'ar* on the Midrash holds that Shaul knew that he would die because Shmuel had told him that Hashem said to him, "Tomorrow you and your sons will be with Me" (*I Shmuel* 28:19), but in general one is not permitted to give up hope of the possibility of Hashem saving him at the last moment. There are various opinions on this among the *rishonim* and *acharonim*. What is clear is that we do not have the right, living in comfort and peace, to judge those who came before us and who were subjected to forces which we cannot begin to fathom. The fact is, that while we Jews are not *nevi'im*, prophets, we are nevertheless *b'nei nevi'im*, descended from prophets — we have a sense of what is proper and what is required of us — and we have known how to sanctify Hashem's name and to glorify it, and to exemplify the sanctity of our lives in accordance with Hashem's command of וְנִקְדַּשְׁתִּי, "I shall be sanctified."

The fact that our people have so often laid down their lives for *kiddush Hashem* requires us to follow in the pattern of their lives. *Chazal* say that after Chananyah, Mishael and Azaryah were saved from the furnace, "they drowned in spit." *Rashi* to *Sanhedrin* 93a explains that they drowned in the spit of the non-Jews, who said to the Jews: "You have such a great God, and yet you do not serve Him." *Chasam Sofer* explains that it is about this that the Torah warns us וְלֹא תְחַלְּלוּ אֶת־שֵׁם קָדְשִׁי וְנִקְדַּשְׁתִּי בְּתוֹךְ בְּנֵי יִשְׂרָאֵל — "You shall not desecrate My name and I will be sanctified in the midst of *Bnei Yisrael*." Do not bring about a situation, God forbid, where your behavior after a *kiddush Hashem* results in *chilul Hashem* when the nations see that you continue as before without change or improvement. Instead, you must continue to sanctify your lives, because only that way can you indicate the *kiddush Hashem* of your fathers, on the basis of וְנִקְדַּשְׁתִּי.

Emor – אמר

I.

The Reason for the Counting of the Omer

ccording to many commentators, the reason for the counting of the *omer* is related to a basic fact established by *Chazal* and disputed by the apostates known as *Tzeddukim* (Sadducees). As we shall see below, the *Tzeddukim* interpreted the Torah as commanding that the count should always start from the day after *Shabbos*. But *Chazal* interpreted that the count always begins the day after the first day of *Pesach*. Thus, according to *Chazal*, the *omer* is the time from the Exodus until the giving of the Torah. The counting comes to link these two events, or — to be more precise — to supply a reason for the freedom that the Jews were granted through signs and miracles.

The giving of the Torah was the purpose for which the Jews were redeemed from Egypt, and therefore, says *Chinuch*,

> We were commanded to count from the day after the day of the
> Yom Tov of Pesach until the day of the giving of the Torah, to
> show by our actions how beloved the great and longed-for day is
> to our hearts. Just as a slave who seeks refuge and always counts the
> time until the longed-for day that he will go free, for by counting,
> the person shows that his total desire is to attain that day.

This reason is also brought in *Eileh HaMitzvos* by R' Moshe Hagiz, who notes that this purpose was already told to Moshe when he was chosen to lead Israel, as we see in the verse (*Sh'mos* 3:12), "and this will be the sign for you ... when you take the nation out of Egypt you will serve God on this mountain."

Chinuch explains why we do not begin counting the *omer* on the first day of *Pesach*, as that was the day the Jews left Egypt and that day was set aside to remember that extraordinary miracle, one which showed how Hashem created and leads the world. Thus we do not allow any other signs on that day nor mix any other joy with that joy.

The other commentators also see the counting along *hashkafah* lines, stressing the freedom we were granted when we left Egypt as a means, and the giving of the Torah as the final purpose. R' Samson Raphael Hirsch comments that just as the days of the week are counted in relation to and culminate with *Shabbos*, the counting of the days of the *omer*, a count that begins at the time of our liberation, is meant to culminate in our ultimate purpose — the receiving of the Torah at Sinai.

The Lubavitcher Rebbi states that it is due to the links between the counting of the *omer* and the giving of the Torah that require each individual to count for himself. This is unlike the *shemittah*- and *yovel*-year countings, which were only done by the *beis din*. As the counting of the *omer* is meant to symbolize our link to the Torah, the duty to count applies to each person individually, just as we find that the beginning of the *Aseres HaDibros* is addressed to the individual: אָנֹכִי ה' אֱ‑לֹהֶיךָ — "I am Hashem, your God," where the word "your" is in the singular.

Some of the commentators, though, and not only the kabbalists among them, see this as a type of counting off of days of *taharah* — of purity — as a *niddah* does before she goes to the *mikveh*. This *taharah* is meant to purify us of the impurity of Egypt, in anticipation of receiving the Torah, and is a *mitzvah* in itself just as in the case of *niddah*. A *niddah*, though, counts seven days of *taharah*, while here the count is seven times seven days. This reason is given in the *Zohar* and other kabbalistic works, and both *rishonim* and *acharonim* discuss it. *Or HaChaim* uses this reason to explain why we start counting only after the first day of *Pesach*. The Jews were still in Egypt for part of the first day, so that the days of *taharah* could only begin on the following day.

It is interesting that R' Baruch Epstein in his *Tosefes Brachah* uses this reason to explain why marriages are forbidden during this time period. These days are days of *taharah* from the impurity of *niddah*, and thus sexual relations are forbidden, just as, according to *Or HaChaim*, the counting is meant to prepare for the union between Hashem and the Assembly of Israel. (Author's note: If that is the case, then all men should have to keep apart from their wives during the entire period!)

Meshech Chochmah uses this reason to explain why the counting of the *omer* must be said aloud. The counting here is one of *taharah*, just as that of a *zav* or *zavah*, but there is a difference here. For the *zav* and *zavah*, the count indicates the number of days that no discharge was seen; it is related to a clear physical phenomenon. With the *omer*, though, there is no such physical phenomenon, so in order to differentiate between what came before and the condition now, it is necessary to count aloud.

Ridvaz gives a beautiful explanation of the reason the counting must be aloud. If a *niddah* begins to menstruate while counting her "seven clean days," it is evident retroactively that there had been no need to count. Moreover, if a *niddah* does not wish to have relations with her husband, she is not required to make a count. Thus we see that the count of the *niddah* is not always mandatory. The *omer*, though, is not optional, and therefore the count must be made aloud.

✥ Linking Nature to God

Maharal holds that the reason for counting the *omer* is to link it to the Torah, and to implant in us the realization that אִם אֵין קֶמַח, אֵין תּוֹרָה — "without flour (the *omer* was a meal-offering of barley) there is no Torah."

A similar idea is expressed in Abarbanel. The *omer* relates to the labor of reaping the harvest. At that time, most Jews are engaged in working in their fields, and they are liable to forget that they are obliged to go up to Jerusalem for *Shavuos*. The counting thus reminds every Jew that the festival is drawing near.

Ramban has a similar explanation. The counting commences at the beginning of the harvest season of barley, and then the Jews bring an *omer* of barley. The counting of the *omer* ends at the beginning of the wheat harvest, and at the time they bring an offering of fine wheat flour. That is why, says *Ramban*, our present *parashah* mentions only these two offerings, and not the *musaf* sacrifices.

This is brought out more clearly by *S'forno*. These actions are meant as a prayer and as a way of expressing our thanks to Hashem. In the spring festival, *Pesach*, we have the prayer of spring, and our thanksgiving for our redemption. The success of the harvest depends on the weather between springtime and the harvest. The *omer* is a thanksgiving for the springtime, just as one brings his first fruits, and the sacrifice that is brought with it is a prayer for the future. The counting is a daily remembrance of that prayer. The festival of the harvest (*Shavuos*) is thanksgiving for the quality of the harvest, while the festival of ingathering (*Sukkos*) is thanksgiving for the quality of the produce which was gathered in. A similar idea is found in *Mateh Moshe* in the name of R' Yehudah the Chassid.

This link between the counting and the seasons of nature is in essence the source for the argument between the *Perushim* (Pharisees) and the *Tzeddukim* (Saducees). While we, the spiritual descendants of the

Perushim, count the *omer* from the second day of *Pesach*, the *Tzeddukim* counted it from the Sunday after the first day of *Pesach* (as do the Samaritans today). The *Tzeddukim* evidently based themselves on the fact that the Torah says מִמָּחֳרַת הַשַּׁבָּת — "from the day after *Shabbos*" (*Vayikra* 23:15) — which they take to mean the first Sunday, but the verse is used only to lend support to their *hashkafah* that seeks to sever the links between nature and man's spiritual life. Such a link exists only if the counting of the *omer* is linked to the Exodus and the harvest is linked to the giving of the Torah, namely that the counting of the *omer* begins with *Pesach* and ends with *Shavuos*. According to the *Tzeddukim*, though, there is no necessary link between these matters, for the counting of the *omer* can sometimes start as much as a week after the first day of *Pesach* and ends after the seventh *Shabbos*. Thus these festivals are secular events whose essence is strictly the celebration of nature itself. There is no doubt that this difference is a major — if not the decisive — reason for the disagreement between the two sides.

⊷§ On the Day after Shabbos

The argument between the *Tzeddukim* and *Chazal* about the interpretation of the words מִמָּחֳרַת הַשַּׁבָּת — "from the day after the *Shabbos*," continued for a long time and played a decisive role in the details of the *mitzvos* relative to the bringing of the *omer* and the celebration of *Shavuos*. We have in our possession details of those disputes in the works of *Chazal*, and *lehavdil*, in the works of the *Tzeddukim*. The *Tzeddukim* argued that the words must be taken literally, and they also argued with the fact that we interpret "שַׁבָּת" (*Shabbos*) here to refer to *Pesach*, so that when the Torah says we have to count "seven *Shabbosos*" we interpret it to mean seven weeks. It would incorrectly seem, at first glance, that there is room for people to indeed interpret the Torah according to the view of the *Tzeddukim*, but *Chazal* have convincing proof that any doubts as to our interpretation can be dispelled purely by logic. Below we will give some of these proofs, which go to the very root of the fundamentals of the written Torah and the *Torah She'be'al Peh*.

In *Menachos* 65-66, the *gemara* lists the arguments of *Chazal*, quoting different *tanna'im*. a) The Torah says we must count fifty days. According to the *Tzeddukim*, if *Pesach* falls on a Sunday, there will be fifty-six days between the two festivals. b) The *omer* on *Pesach* resembles the *Two Loaves* on *Shavuos*. Just as the Two Loaves were brought at the beginning of the festival, the *omer* too had to be brought at the beginning of the festival. c) The Torah said that the months are to be proclaimed at a fixed time relative to the moon cycle. The same must apply to *Shavuos*, which must occur on a fixed date of the month, and that is only possible if there is a fixed date on which one begins to count the *omer*. d) The Torah states in one place "fifty days" while in another it states "seven weeks." How can both be correct? The answer is that they apply to two sets of circumstances: If *Pesach* falls on *Shabbos*, then we have seven full weeks, whereas if it falls in the middle of the week, we count the days. e) The Torah says תִּסְפָּר לָךְ, [i.e., וּסְפַרְתֶּם לָכֶם; ibid.], "and you shall count for yourselves," namely that the counting depends on the *beis din*, which sets the festivals. Now, when the *beis din* sets *Pesach*, *Shavuos* follows based on the day set by the *beis din*. If, however, the counting is based on *Shabbos*, it has nothing to do with the *beis din*, because everyone knows when *Shabbos* is. f) The Torah says מִמָּחֳרַת הַשַּׁבָּת — "on the day after *Shabbos*," but it does not say מִמָּחֳרַת שַׁבָּת שֶׁל הַפֶּסַח — "on the day after *Shabbos* of *Pesach*." The entire year is full of *Shabbosos*, and had it not been for the tradition handed down by *Chazal*, how would we know which *Shabbos* is referred to? g) One verse says שֵׁשֶׁת יָמִים תֹּאכַל מַצּוֹת — "six days you shall eat *matzos*" (*Devarim* 16:8), while another says שִׁבְעַת יָמִים מַצּוֹת תֹּאכֵלוּ — "seven days you shall eat *matzos*" (*Sh'mos* 12:15). How do we reconcile the two? It means you may eat *matzos* of the old crop for seven days, but you may eat *matzos* from the new crop for six days.

These interpretations are brought by *Chazal* in *Menachos* 65-66 and in *Sifra*. The fact that there is such a major discussion and so many proofs, of which there are very few counterparts in *shas*, shows that this was a major debate at the time. Proofs are brought to support both views, but of course the main thing here is the *kabbalah* — the tradition that was handed down from one generation to the next.

According to *Rambam* in *Hilchos Temidin U'Musafin* 7, the error on the proper interpretation of this verse was created intentionally during the Second *Beis HaMikdash* period by "those who left *Klal Yisrael*." *Rambam* enumerates the various laws related to the *omer* which are meant to make public the correct date for the cutting of the *omer*, and to disprove those who claim that מִמָּחֳרַת הַשַּׁבָּת — the "day after *Shabbos*," refers to the first Sunday after *Pesach*. Thus the prophets and the *Sanhedrin* throughout the generations always waved the *omer* on the 16th of *Nissan*, whether it was a weekday or *Shabbos*.

In regard to the day of the *omer* offering, we are told in the Torah that (*Vayikra* 23:14), "You shall eat neither bread, nor parched corn, nor green ears [from the current year's crop], until that very day," and we are further told that when the Jews entered *Eretz Yisrael* (*Yehoshua* 5:11), "They ate of the produce of the land [i.e., from the current year's crop] on the day after *Pesach*; *matzos* and parched corn." Thus we see that one is permitted to eat of the current year's crop from the second day of *Pesach*. If, however, one wishes to claim that that is no proof, because the year the Jews entered *Eretz Yisrael*, *Pesach* just happened to occur on *Shabbos* (in which case the *Tzeddukim* would bring the *omer* on the same day as *Chazal*), that is an illogical assumption, because why would the verse in *Yehoshua* connect the eating of the new grain with *Pesach*, if that day was not the main reason for the permission to eat, but merely happened to occur on *Shabbos*? Thus, when the verse in *Yehoshua* states "on the day after *Pesach*" that must mean that *Pesach* was the cause of the permission, regardless which day of the week it happened to fall on.

Rambam tells us here a new fact: that the view of the *Tzeddukim* was not an ancient one, but traced back to the time of the Second *Beis HaMikdash*. Of course we must search for a historical basis for that novel claim. One might be able to say that this is what we indicated earlier on the basis of the major debate on the subject that was conducted in the Talmud during that period. Thus, *Rambam* in his commentary on the Mishnah *Avos* 1:2, says clearly that the *Beitusim* (Boethusians) — what we would call the Reform movement in our time —

> wanted to remove from themselves the various obligations and rabbinic decrees and regulations. As they were unable to reject outright all of the accepted traditions and the Torah, they sought the right to explain (the Torah) as they wished, for if interpretation is open to each individual, he is able to be lenient wherever he wishes.

It was *Rambam* who pointed out, regarding the verse, "And they ate of the produce of the land" in *Yehoshua*, that there we are told "on the day after *Pesach*," and not "on the day after *Shabbos*." This proof is discussed at length by *Ralbag* in his commentary on *Yehoshua*.

⇜§ A Dispute Which Left Its Mark

As we mentioned above, this dispute left permanent traces in the form of many specific *halachos* concerning the cutting of the *omer*, as mentioned by *Rambam* in *Hilchos Temidin U'Musafin* 7:11, but there is no doubt that there are other areas which we find difficult to understand which trace back to this dispute. For example, R' Zvi Hirsch Chajes says that the reason that we say "today is one day in the *omer*" rather than "the first day," is to stress that this does not necessarily have to be the first day of the week (i.e., Sunday).

Bnei Yisas'char explains that the reason the *Shabbos* before *Pesach* is known as *Shabbos HaGadol* is to stress that the words of the Torah מִמָּחֳרַת הַשַּׁבָּת — "from the day after the *Shabbos*," refer to the day after *Pesach* and not to Sunday. There are literally hundreds of such comments among the *rishonim* and *acharonim* along these lines.

Chasam Sofer explains that the *Tzeddukim* went off the proper path because of their opposition to the *Torah She'be'al Peh*. He mentions, along the lines of *d'rush*, that it seems puzzling that *Yom Tov* in the Torah is based on *yetzias Mitzrayim*, the Exodus, and not on *matan Torah* — the giving of the Torah. He answers that since the Torah was given to us under coercion and not of our own free will (as *Chazal* tell us, Hashem placed Mount Sinai over the Jewish people and told them that unless they accepted the Torah, this would be their grave), that occasion is not the basis of the *simchah*.

Tosafos hold that Hashem forced the Jewish people only to accept the *Torah She'be'al Peh*, but as to the written Torah, all proclaimed: נַעֲשֶׂה וְנִשְׁמָע — "we will do and we will hear" (*Sh'mos* 24:7). According to the *Tzeddukim*, who reject the *Torah She'be'al Peh*, the coercion must thus have been on the written Torah. They therefore felt no reason whatsoever to link the giving of the Torah to any *Yom Tov*. While this explanation is indeed *d'rush*, in essence it goes along with what we mentioned earlier; namely that the *Tzeddukim* wanted to uproot *Shavuos* from its origins, and to make it entirely secular, even though based on a religious ceremonial.

There are also more recent proofs of the correctness of *Chazal* in determining the date of the *omer*. There are those who attach importance to the word בְּשָׁבֻעֹתֵיכֶם — "in your weeks" — in *Parashas Pinchas* (*Bamidbar* 28:26), regarding the new *minchah*. If מִמָּחֳרַת הַשַּׁבָּת — "the day after the *Shabbos*," refers to the day after *Pesach*, then the counting depends on our weeks, because it is the *beis din* which decides when the month of *Nissan* will begin. That in turn determines when *Pesach* will fall, the *omer* will be brought, and the counting of the *omer* begun. Thus, בְּשָׁבֻעֹתֵיכֶם refers to our weeks, as determined by the *beis din*. However, if הַשַּׁבָּת refers to the Sunday after *Pesach*, then those are not our weeks at all.

Most commentators also explain why the Torah preferred to refer to the first day of *Pesach* as "*Shabbos*." *HaKesav VeHaKabalah* has an interesting comment on this. It means "*Shabbos*" in terms of "a rest," in that it is a rest from eating the new grain, which is forbidden until the next day. He also points out that even though the *omer* has been brought, one is still forbidden to use the new year's crop in the *Beis HaMikdash* until שְׁתֵּי הַלֶּחֶם — the Two Loaves — are brought on *Shavuos*. Thus the Torah speaks here, in our *parashah*, of "seven *Shabbosos*" — שֶׁבַע

שַׁבָּתוֹת — seven weeks of "rest." In *Parashas Re'eh*, on the other hand, the Torah (*Devarim* 16:9) speaks of "seven weeks," (שִׁבְעָה שָׁבֻעֹת) because there the time is not linked to מָחֳרַת הַשַּׁבָּת — the time when the *omer* is brought.

There is also an explanation that the Torah did not want to write מִמָּחֳרַת הַפֶּסַח — "from the day after the *Pesach*," because that might imply the day after the *Pesach* sacrifice is brought, or the 15th of *Nissan*. Nor did it want to write מִמָּחֳרַת הַחַג — "from the day after the festival," because that might be taken to mean the day after the last day of the festival. It therefore wrote מִמָּחֳרַת הַשַּׁבָּת — "from the day after the *Shabbos*.

Iturei Torah quotes an explanation of R' M.Y.L. Sachs. The first day of *Pesach* is referred to as *Shabbos*, because of the day's similarity to *Shabbos*. Just as on *Shabbos* it is forbidden to carry things out of one's house (unless there is an *eiruv* to make carrying possible), so too it is forbidden to take the meat of the *Pesach* sacrifice out of the house; and just as on *Shabbos*, one violates the prohibition only after he has put the meat down outside the home.

◈§ A Festival to Celebrate Victory over the Tzeddukim

Chazal tell us in *Menachos* 65 that they established a festival when they were able to defeat the *Beitusim*. The *gemara* does not explain what this victory was, and what the dispute was about. What we do find in *Chazal*, though, are debates about the meanings of various verses, and different proofs to justify the interpretations of *Chazal*. This is evidence that the opinions of the *Beitusim* were deeply rooted and there was need to fight these by logic and conclusive proofs.

Chazal in the Mishnah in *Menachos* 65 specify the great amount of publicity that was given to the cutting of the *omer* on the evening after the first day of *Pesach*, all of this to counteract the view of the *Tzeddukim*, who said that מִמָּחֳרַת הַשַּׁבָּת referred to the first Sunday after the first day of *Pesach*. The *Tzeddukim* based their view on the claim that nowhere do we see that the Torah refers to a festival by the word *Shabbos*. Another claim was that the view of *Chazal* was impossible, because according to *Chazal* there are exactly forty-nine days between *Pesach* and *Shavuos*, even though the Torah stated "fifty days" (*Vayikra* 23:16). According to the *Tzeddukim*, though, there might be as many as fifty-six days between the two festivals. Thus, according to them, there were years when there would be exactly fifty days, but this was simply impossible according to *Chazal's* interpretation.

Rabbeinu Asher ben Yechiel, the *Rosh*, at the end of *Pesachim* explains the reference to "fifty days" in keeping with the Torah's preference to round numbers off to the nearest ten, as in when it calls for "forty" lashes (*Devarim* 25:3) while the *halachah* is that one receives thirty- nine. Similarly, we are told that "seventy" souls (*Bereishis* 46:27; *Sh'mos* 1:5) came down to Egypt with Yaakov, even though in reality there were only sixty-nine.

In any event, the dispute between the two groups was a bitter and serious one that had a very clear *hashkafah* element. *Chazal* held that the counting of the *omer* was meant to join *Pesach* to *Shavuos*, and to make the redemption from Egypt a prologue to receiving the Torah at Mount Sinai. By this, the natural festivals of the Harvest (*Succos*) and of the First Fruits (*Shavuos*) were also connected, and all three Pilgrimage Festivals became one unified sequence. The *Tzeddukim*, though, wanted to divide the spiritual and national elements; they wanted to keep Torah and nature apart, and made the harvest of the *omer* separate from *Pesach*. Thus, according to them, the counting of the *omer* linked only the harvest and the firstfruits, both of which deal with natural events, and sometimes there were as many as fifty-six days between *Pesach* and *Shavuos*.

On the question as to why the *Pesach* festival was referred to as *Shabbos*, and why the seven subsequent weeks are called "seven *Shabbasos*," *Ramban* and Ibn Ezra note that we also find in *II Melachim* 7:9 and *II Divrei HaYamim* 23:4,8 that the word *Shabbos* is used to mean a full week, and not just *Shabbos*. On the other hand, the Torah in Chapter 23 of *Vayikra*, verses 24, 32 and 39 refers to *Rosh Hashanah*, *Yom Kippur, and Sukkos*, respectively, as *Shabboson* or *Shabbos Shabboson*. Thus *Pesach* too can be referred to as *Shabbos*, as in מִמָּחֳרַת הַשַׁבָּת, "from the day after the *Shabbos*." Of course, none of this is sufficient to prove that when the Torah refers to *Shabbos*, it refers to a festival and not to *Shabbos*. This is based more on our traditions than on proof.

It appears that *Kuzari* too did not see the proofs alone as a firm basis for *Chazal's* view, and in 3:41 he writes surprisingly:

> Even if we say that the verse is as they claim, nevertheless *Chazal* realized that the meaning is not the beginning of the week, but that the count must be forty-nine days, no matter which day of the week this begins. The Torah only gave us a sign in stating the beginning of the week, namely if "the sickle begins among the standing wheat" (*Devarim* 16:9) on Sunday, then the number will begin on Sunday. And if it is on Monday, then "the sickle among the standing wheat" will be on Monday. This interpretation is from

the Torah and is obligatory in the Torah, for it is not contradictory to the Torah, or to what was said by the Creator through the prophets.

Kuzari thus accepts as given that when the Torah said מִמָּחֳרַת הַשַּׁבָּת — "from the day after the *Shabbos*," it referred to Sunday, but this day of the week is meant only as an example, and what counts is that there should be forty-nine days between *Pesach* and *Shavuos*, regardless of when the harvest begins. He says that this was told prophetically to the Sages of the generations.

Ibn Ezra also accepts the meaning of "the day after the *Shabbos*" to be Sunday, and says that it is possible that the very first *Pesach* outside Egypt, in the year the Torah was given, occurred on *Shabbos*. Therefore, when the Torah speaks of "the day after the *Shabbos*," it refers back to that first *Pesach*, even though that year they did not yet bring the *omer*. The Torah, though, simply uses this date as an example. Ibn Ezra then proves that the first *Pesach* after the giving of the Torah occurred on *Shabbos*. According to *Sh'mos* 40:23, the Showbread was set up on the day that the *Mishkan* was erected (the first of *Nissan* in the first full year after leaving Egypt), and according to *Vayikra* 24:8, that had to take place on *Shabbos*. If the first of *Nissan* falls on *Shabbos*, so does *Pesach*, the 15th of *Nissan*. Therefore that year indeed the beginning of the *omer* count was on "the day after the *Shabbos*," and when the Torah used that phrase, it meant it only as an example.

HaKesav VeHaKabalah also attempts to use this approach, but if one looks into *Chazal* in *Menachos* and *Sifra* and in the earliest commentators, he will find clear proof that "from the day after the *Shabbos*" always means the day after the festival, and there is no reason to go far afield and to explain the words as actually referring to *Shabbos*.

⧉ R' Yochanan Mocks the Beitusim

As we mentioned, *Chazal* in *shas* and *Sifra* bring various proofs to justify their view. The names of the *tanna'im* involved change from one source to the other, but the proofs are identical. R' Yochanan mocked the *Tzeddukim*. He referred to them as "fools," and asked them how they deduced what they did. (In other words, did they have any proof that מִמָּחֳרַת הַשַּׁבָּת — "from the day after the *Shabbos* — referred to the weekly *Shabbos*?) They had only a single old man, who mumbled something about "Moshe loved Israel, and we know that *Shavuos* is a single day. He therefore instituted it after *Shabbos*, so that Israel should rest two days." R' Yochanan answered him mockingly, and said to him:

"It is an eleven-day trip from Chorev to Mount Se'ir, and if Moshe loved Israel, why did he keep them in the desert for forty years?" The *Beitusi* said to him: "Is that the way you wish to get rid of me?" R' Yochanan said to him: "Should our perfect Torah simply be as nothing more than your small talk?" (According to *Maharsha*, R' Yochanan was angry that this old man rejected Torah from Sinai, and preferred to believe that the date of the festival was decided independently by Moshe. For this reason he answered him mockingly.)

R' David Zvi Hoffmann, in his commentary, discusses the views of the *Tzeddukim* and other heretical sects. He brings all the views quoted above, but adds a number of proofs. a) According to the *Tzeddukim*, there is no fixed date for the festival of *Shavuos*, and it varies from year to year, based on the date when the *Shabbos* following *Pesach* occurs. It is not logical to assume that *Shavuos* does not have a fixed date. b) All of our festivals are based on the number seven. Between *Pesach* and *Shavuos* there are seven weeks. From one *shemittah* to the next are seven years. From one *yovel* to the next are seven *shemittah* cycles. *Sukkos* occurs in the seventh month after *Pesach*. If we count the days from *Pesach* until *Shavuos* differently, we do not preserve the number that determines the timing of the Jewish festivals. c) The Torah, when it states, "from the beginning of the sickle in the standing wheat" (*Devarim* 16:9), certainly does not intend to make this date an open one. There is a special day for this, and as *Pesach* is celebrated by everyone making the pilgrimage to Jerusalem, after which we are told, "and in the morning you shall go to your tent" (*Devarim* 16:7), it must be because that is the time of the harvest for all.

Hirsch too takes the example from *shemittah* and *yovel*, which are also based on periods of seven years, and which always begin on a specific day and date.

◆§ Why the Double Count?

R' Benzion Firer proves the erroneous ways of the *Tzeddukim* in an incisive manner:

Abaye says in *Chagigah* 18, "It is a *mitzvah* to count the days, and a *mitzvah* to count the weeks." Why should we need this double count? Why count both days and weeks?

A famous question of the *Ba'al HaMa'or* is why we do not count two different numbers each day, since there is a doubt as to when *Pesach* really began (which is the reason that outside *Eretz Yisrael* we must keep two days of *Yom Tov*). He answers that this is not done so that people will not have any doubts that the first day of *Shavuos* is such by

Torah law. The second day of *Yom Tov* is kept only because it is a custom handed down from our fathers (*Beitzah* 4). The first day of *Shavuos* is undoubtedly so by Torah law, but people might question this certainty if we counted two different days of the *omer* each day.

The *acharonim* explain that counting can only be carried out when one is certain; when there is a doubt, there can be no counting.

But the question remains: In those places which were far from Jerusalem, and where they could not find out in time when the first day of *Pesach* occurred, what did they do about the counting, for a doubtful count is not considered to be a count? It is possibly because of this that the Torah commanded that the weeks must be counted as well. The view of the *acharonim* (see *Tur, Orach Chaim* 489) is well known that the counting of the weeks needs to be done only once a week, at the end of the week. Now, even if there is a doubt about days, there is no doubt about weeks, and that is why the counting is considered definite.

That was the error of the *Tzeddukim*. According to them, the doubt can result in being off by an entire week, as where there is doubt whether *Rosh Chodesh Nissan* should begin on *Shabbos* or Sunday. In the first case, according to the *Tzeddukim*, the counting begins on Sunday, and in the second case *Pesach* is on Sunday and the counting of the *omer* is postponed for a week. If that is so, there is a doubt not only about the days, but about the weeks as well, and then we come back to our original question: Why the double count?

II.

The Day of the Giving of the Torah

The early commentators wonder at the fact that nowhere in our *parashah* or in any other place in the Torah is there a mention of *Shavuos* being the day on which the Torah was given. We have received this fact by tradition from our fathers and it appears in our prayers.

Akeidah gives two answers for this absence: a) *Bahag* did not include in his list of the 613 *mitzvos* the existence of Hashem, because according to him that is the fundamental premise for all the *mitzvos*; had there been no one to command the *mitzvos*, there would be no need to observe them. *Akeidah* holds that the same applies to the receiving of the Torah. The value and nature of the Torah are based on the fact that it was given by Hashem. The receiving of the Torah is the first fundamental of Judaism, without which we could not have Torah or *mitzvos*. It is therefore unnecessary to mention it. b) The receiving of the Torah does not depend on time, unlike the other *mitzvos* which are tied to times. The Torah is received at all times, as it states (*Yehoshua* 1:8), "This book of the Torah shall not depart from your mouth; and you shall meditate in it day and night." The Torah's words must always appear to us fresh and precious, as if we had just received them, as in (*Devarim* 26:16), "This day Hashem your God is commanding you." The Torah therefore did not set aside a special time for the receiving of the Torah, and only mentioned *bikkurim* — the first fruits — in regard to *Shavuos*. The Torah relied on its description of the giving of the Torah, which begins with the words (*Sh'mos* 19:1) "In the third month" (i.e., *Sivan*) as indicating the time of the giving of the Torah.

Abarbanel holds that the link between *Shavuos* and the giving of the Torah is coincidental. *Shavuos* is a festival of thanksgiving to the Creator Who gives food to all, and that is why it takes place at the time of the harvest. So too do we read in *Mishpatim* (*Sh'mos* 23:16), "And the feast of harvest, the first fruits of your labors, which you have sown in the field: and the feast of ingathering ... when you have gathered in your labors out of the field." Further we read in *Ki Sisa* (*Sh'mos* 34:22), "And you shall observe the feast of weeks, of the firstfruits of wheat harvest, and the feast of ingathering." And again in *Re'eh* (*Devarim* 16:9), "Seven weeks shall you number unto you: Begin to number the seven weeks from such time as you begin to put the sickle to the wheat." We therefore read in our *parashah* (*Vayikra* 23:21), "And you shall proclaim on the same day, that it may be a holy convocation unto you." It is the fact that it is the day of the first fruits of wheat harvest which imparts the holiness to the festival. It is true that the Torah was given to Israel on this day, but that is not the reason for the festival, for there is no need to make a special day to remember that exalted event. Torah and prophecy are the testimony and the remembrance of the event.

At the same time, Abarbanel sees a number of symbolic matters in the observance of *Shavuos*, which is meant to make us mindful of our excellence as a people following our receipt of the Torah. On *Pesach*, we bring an *omer* of barley, a grain normally used for animal fodder, as when we left Egypt we still lacked Torah and culture and were more like animals. On *Shavuos* we received the Torah and acquired intelligence and understanding, and it was then that we were commanded to bring a *minchah chadashah* — a meal offering of the new crop — to symbolize the new spirit that Hashem put into us. This *minchah* consisted of two loaves of bread, the food of civilized and cultured people. The counting between *Pesach* and *Shavuos* is also symbolic, indicating our longing to receive the Torah and to achieve the rank of a holy nation and a kingdom of *Kohanim*.

R' David Zvi Hoffmann also deals at length with the explanation of the reason there is no mention made on *Shavuos* of the receiving of the Torah. He explains that the vision of Sinai cannot be made into a concrete symbol. The Jews must place on their hearts that they did not see any picture on the day that Hashem spoke on Chorev out of the fire, so that they should not fall into the trap of making graven images. The Jews must simply remember the great events, and as a result they will celebrate the festival of the harvest on the day the Torah was given. Then by bringing their first fruits to the *Beis HaMikdash*, they will thank Hashem for blessing the land. By doing so, they will acknowledge that Hashem is the ruler of all and it is He that we must serve and His *mitzvos* that we must obey. By this means, we can relive the events of the receiving of the Torah, when we proclaimed, "we will do and we will hear" (*Sh'mos* 24:7). The reason there is not even the slightest hint of a link between the giving of the Torah and *Shavuos* is simply that the Torah did not want to have any symbols of those events in which the Divine Presence revealed Itself.

In reality, we were not given historical reasons for any of the festivals, except for *Pesach*. We learn of the content of each festival from the name of the festival or from its date, from the *mitzvos* that the Torah commands us to do, or from hints that indicate its nature indirectly. Thus, for example, we find the aim of a festival from its name in the case of *Yom HaKippurim* (the Day of Atonement), *Chag HaKatzir* (the Festival of Harvest), *Chag Ha'Asif* (the Festival of the Ingathering). We see also from the fact that the Torah stresses that *Pesach* must be in the spring that this festival also reminds us of the beginning of the harvest. So too do we see in *Vayikra* 23:43 that there is a historical basis for sitting in the *Sukkah*. Only in regard to *Pesach* does the Torah give us a precise explanation (*Sh'mos* 12:14), "And this day shall be unto you for a memorial; and you shall keep it a feast to Hashem." This is because of the special significance that the Torah attaches to the Exodus, which was the prelude to receiving the *mitzvos*.

Later, R' David Zvi Hoffmann proves the link between *Shavuos* and the giving of the Torah. The great commentators all agree that *Shavuos* is to be seen as the conclusion of *Pesach* (see Rabbenu Bachya, who states that the reason that there was no special commandment about *Shavuos* is because this festival follows on the *mitzvah* of the *omer*, and the 49 days between the two are like a type of *chol ha'moed*, intermediate days of a festival, between *Pesach* and *Shavuos*). The giving of the Torah was the completion of the freedom the Jews acquired on *Pesach*. When Moshe was first told of his mission, he was told, "When you take the nation out of Egypt, you will serve God on this mountain" (*Sh'mos* 3:12). Moshe always spoke to Pharaoh in the name of Hashem: "Send forth My nation and they will celebrate to Me in the desert" (ibid. 5:1), and there Moshe referred to it as "a festival to Hashem" (ibid. 10:9). Moshe and Israel expected that the service of Hashem would mean the bringing of sacrifices, as Moshe said to Pharaoh: "And you too will give in our hands, sacrifices and burnt offerings" (ibid. v. 25). When the time came, though, the nation was not ordered to bring any sacrifices, but only to listen to the voice of Hashem and to observe His covenant. That is the meaning of *Yirmiyahu* 7:22-23, "For I did not speak to your fathers, nor did I command them in the day that I brought them out of the land of Egypt, concerning burnt offerings or sacrifices: But this thing I commanded them, saying, Obey My voice, and I will be your God, and you shall be My people." What this means is that at Sinai they were told the *Aseres HaDibros* — the Ten Commandments — and not all the laws of the sacrifices. Thus *yetzias Mitzrayim* and serving Hashem on Sinai were one event.

Pesach is the beginning of the harvest and *Shavuos* is its end, just as *Pesach* is the beginning of the process of the liberation of the Jewish people and *Shavuos* is its end. This opinion is reinforced when we take note of the fact that *Shavuos* is on the fiftieth day after *Pesach*, which is a perfect parallel to the *yovel* year which was the fiftieth year, after seven *shemittah* cycles. Just as at the time of the receiving of the Torah the Jews all gained their spiritual freedom, at the *yovel* all Jewish slaves were given their freedom. On *Shavuos* the Jews were given the name "the servants of Hashem," and they were forbidden to enslave themselves to anyone else.

⋙§ Shavuos and the Giving of the Torah

Rivash in Section 96 states that the Torah did not link *Shavuos* to the giving of the Torah but to the fiftieth day of the *omer*. Nowadays, though, when we have a set calendar, the fiftieth day falls on the 6th of *Sivan*, which is the day, according to *Chazal*, that the Torah was given. In earlier times there was no fixed date for commemorating the giving of the Torah, for *Chazal* stated clearly in *Rosh HaShanah* 6 that *Shavuos* can come out on the 5th of *Sivan*, on the 6th, or, on the 7th. Indeed, all the early works display only hints in the Torah to link *Shavuos* to the giving of the Torah. *Rokeach* in *Hilchos Atzeres* 295

sees such a hint in the word לָכֶם in the verse, וּקְרָאתֶם בְּעֶצֶם הַיּוֹם הַזֶּה מִקְרָא
קֹדֶשׁ יִהְיֶה לָכֶם — "And you shall call on this very day, a holy convocation
it shall be to you." The word לָכֶם — "to you" — is superfluous, and is
a hint at the giving of the Torah, of which we read in *Parashas
Va'eschanan*, prior to the Ten Commandments, וַיִּקְרָא מֹשֶׁה אֶל כָּל יִשְׂרָאֵל
— "And Moshe called to all of Israel." Similarly, in *Parashas Yisro*, at the
first account of the Ten Commandments, we find, וַיָּבֹא מֹשֶׁה וַיִּקְרָא לְזִקְנֵי
הָעָם — "And [Moshe] came and called to the elders of the nation." Thus,
Shavuos is called a holy convocation "to you" (לָכֶם) because Moshe
called "to you," i.e., to "all of Israel" and "to the elders" prior to the giving
of the Torah.

The *halachic* source for linking *Shavuos* to the giving of the Torah is
found in *Tosefta Megillah* and is also brought in the *gemara Megillah*,
regarding the Torah reading on *Shavuos*, where we are told that some
say the reading is the passage describing the giving of the Torah,
beginning (*Sh'mos* 19:1), בַּחֹדֶשׁ הַשְּׁלִישִׁי — "In the third month" —
because *Shavuos* is the day the Torah was given to Israel. We find also
in *Pesachim* 68 that R' Elazar said regarding *Shavuos* that all agree that
we also need לָכֶם — "to you" (i.e. that the day is not to be devoted solely
to Hashem's matters, but must have an element of feasting). What is the
reason? Because it is the day the Torah was given to Israel.

The source, though, lies in the words that *Chazal* instituted for the
prayers of the day, when we say זְמַן מַתַּן תּוֹרָתֵנוּ — "the time of the giving
of our Torah," as mentioned above by *Rivash*. This refers to when we
have a fixed calendar and where we have a fixed date of *Shavuos*, the
6th of *Sivan*. Indeed, *Ran* at the end of *Pesachim* quotes a Midrash
which links the counting of the *omer* and the giving of the Torah. These
are his words:

> We are told that when Moshe said to Israel, "You will serve God on
> this mountain," Israel said to him: "Moshe, our teacher, when will
> this be?" He said to them: "At the conclusion of fifty days," and
> each counted for himself. It was because of this that the Sages set
> the counting of the *omer*. That is to say: In our days, where there
> is no bringing of the *omer* to count from, we count fifty days until
> the receiving of the Torah, just as Israel counted at that time. [The
> Torah relates the count to the *omer* offering, but the Sages related
> it to the giving of the Torah.]

Chizkuni also links the counting of the *omer* to the giving of the
Torah, and this is what he writes:

> The reason that the Torah did not specify which month and what
> date of that month, as it did with the other festivals, is because if

it had told us the date, we would not have counted seven weeks, but would simply have celebrated the festival on its date. Yet the counting is a very important matter. Now that we count seven weeks from the time of the cutting of the *omer*, the fiftieth day will automatically fall on the 6th of *Sivan*, which is the day on which the Ten Commandments were given.

Chizkuni's explanation is puzzling: If the Torah had mentioned the month and the date, would that mean that the counting of the *omer* would not apply? What he apparently means is that had the Torah specified the date of *Shavuos*, we would have thought that the counting of the *omer* and the festival are two separate things, with no connection between the two. *Chizkuni* also wishes to stress what we said above, that this festival extends from *Pesach* until *Shavuos*, which is the end of the process of liberation, and it was for that reason that the Torah made the festival dependent on the counting and stated that the fiftieth day of the *omer* would be *Shavuos*. Thus we learn from this that the two are linked.

S'forno, though, explains that the reason for *Shavuos*, as with the other festivals, is an agricultural one, in which we celebrate the bounty of nature and no more. He says:

> The references to *Shavuos* begin with the *omer*, for that is when the harvest of the *omer* begins as does the counting of the weeks, this being related to the festival, which is known as the Festival of the Harvest. The Festival of *Shavuos* is the time at which thanks is given to Hashem, may He be Blessed, on the harvest which He reserves for us, for indeed one of the aims of the festivals is prayer and thanksgiving, as in the season of the month of spring we pray for the spring and are thankful for our redemption. As the success of the harvest depends on the weather from the beginning of the spring until the harvest, as it states (*Yirmiyahu* 5:24), "He reserves unto us the appointed weeks of the harvest," the *omer* is thanksgiving for the spring, as one who brings the first fruits of his field. The sacrifice brought with it was a prayer for the future, and the counting was a daily reminder of that prayer. The Festival of the Harvest was thanksgiving for the quality of the harvest, while the Festival of the Ingathering for the quality of the ingathering.

⊷§ The Counting of the Omer as a Link

According to all the views above, the counting of the *omer* links *Pesach* to *Shavuos*, either in terms of the beginning and the end of the harvest, or in terms of the beginning and the end of the redemption process, that being the giving of the Torah. *Akeidah* finds three things that link the *mitzvah* of counting the *omer* to the Torah and Hashem's rule over the world.

a) The *mitzvah* of the *omer* ties working the land and other passing concerns to the study of the Torah. It therefore states (*Vayikra* 23:10),

> When you come to the land that I give you and you harvest its harvest, you shall bring an *omer* of the beginning of your harvest to the *Kohen*, and he shall wave the *omer* before Hashem for your benefit, on the day after *Shabbos* the *Kohen* shall wave it.

And we find in another place (*Devarim* 8:7-10):

> For Hashem your God is bringing you to a good land ... a land of wheat and barley ... and you shall eat and be satisfied and shall bless ... Take heed for yourself, lest you forget.

To stress this principle, when the time for the barley harvest comes, we are not permitted to derive any benefit from the new crop until we bring its first fruits to Hashem, for this is the first grain that ripens. The *Kohen* waves the *omer* before Hashem so that all will realize that everything comes from Him, and does not come by itself, as the simple folk believe. The Torah set the date as the second day of *Pesach*, the festival that symbolizes Hashem's supernatural control of the world, and not the day after *Shabbos*, which symbolizes the natural course of the world.

b) The counting represents our anticipation of what is yet to come, just as we find in the counting of days of purification in other cases. The purpose of the Exodus from Egypt was: "When you take the nation out of Egypt, you shall serve Hashem on this mountain" (*Sh'mos* 3:12). The counting reminds all future generations that our fathers rose to a higher level when they forsook their foreign gods and counted seven weeks, this number symbolizing the count of the impure who are sent away from their marital satisfactions [during the *niddah* count of seven days]. Because of the pain involved in this yearning and the waiting for the longed-for day, we do not recite the blessing of *shehecheyanu* ("...Who kept us alive and preserved us and caused us to reach this day") for the beginning of the *omer*-count.

c) In terms of the quality of the *minchah* — the meal offering — that was brought, we see the central idea of elevation from the lowest rungs of *gashmiyus* — materialism — to the highest rung of *ruchniyus* — spiritual life. On the day after the first day of *Pesach*, they brought barley to show that even though Israel had left the ranks of the other nations — who are all like straw or thorns — and had reached the level of grain, they were still on the lowest level of grain, that of barley, which is eaten by both man and beast, and had not yet reached their true perfection as symbolized by food for man. Only at the very end of the process did they bring a sacrifice of wheat, because, with Hashem's help, they attained the level of receiving the Torah, which is the bread which Hashem gave to His chosen people to eat.

This idea is also expanded upon by R' Yitzchak Breuer in *Nachaliel*. He says:

> What is freedom for Israel without Torah? And what is *Eretz Yisrael* to the nation of Israel without Torah? ... What the other nations see as an end is only the beginning for Israel. All its longing is for another goal, a loftier aim, and that is why the counting comes.

According to this interpretation, the counting is meant to direct us to the goal for which our nation was redeemed from Egypt. It comes to transfer man from the slavery of the other nations to eternal freedom, and to raise up his sacrifice from barley to wheat, from food for the beast to food for man, and to a superior culture.

HaKesav VeHaKabalah holds that the entire intention of the *omer* is to subjugate nature to Hashem, so that people should not come to rebel against Hashem by deceiving themselves into believing that it was their efforts that accomplished for them the bountiful good that they have enjoyed.

The waving of the *omer* in all four directions symbolizes our recognition of the control by Hashem of His world. The reason the sacrifice is called an *omer*, which is a measure of volume, and not *minchas bikkurim* — "the meal offering of the first fruits" — is because the word *omer* hints at our subjugation of ourselves to the will of Hashem, as in the verse (*Devarim* 24:7), "and he will make merchandise (וְהִתְעַמֶּר) of him, and sell him." In other words, these are days that we subjugate ourselves to Hashem, and we count the days from when we began this process. The counting reaches its peak with the giving of the Torah. Just as the *omer* symbolizes control of the sheaves, it symbolizes the spiritual control of subjugating all the lusts of our hearts so that we can serve Hashem properly. Thus, when the days of counting are over, we refer to the festival as *Shavuos*, which also includes an element of spiritual control, since the word "*Shavuos*" (שָׁבוּעוֹת) is related to the word "captivity" (שְׁבִי). This is also the reason the festival is known as עֲצֶרֶת — *Atzeres* — which has a connotation of holding back. *HaKesav VeHaKabalah* adds that this interpretation is not far from the truth.

III.

And the Son of an Israelite Woman Went out

This *parashah* is interpreted by our commentators in terms of *d'rush*, following *Toras Kohanim* and the Midrash quoted by *Rashi*. The verse reads, וַיֵּצֵא בֶּן־אִשָּׁה יִשְׂרְאֵלִית — "And the son of an Israelite woman went out." Where did he go out of? ask *Chazal*. R' Levi said: "He went out of his world" (עוֹלָמוֹ). (The previous *parashah* ended with the words חָק־עוֹלָם, — "an eternal law," so that the *d'rush* here is that he left his spiritual world and cursed Hashem.)

R' Berachiah said, "He went out of the earlier *parashah*, which states (in regard to the *Lechem HaPanim* — the Showbread) that "on each *Shabbos* day he shall arrange it." It is customary for a king to eat fresh bread daily. Will Hashem eat stale bread nine days old? (In other words, the son of the Israelite woman mocked the Torah. As a result he quarreled with his neighbor, and eventually came to curse Hashem.)

In a *beraisa* we learn that he "went out" from the *beis din* of Moshe. He asked to pitch his tent with the tribe of Dan, but they refused to permit him to do so and told him: "It states (*Bamidbar* 2:2), 'each man according to his flag, according to their fathers' houses,'" and as he was the son of an Egyptian father, he had no share in the place in the camp. He then went to the *beis din* of Moshe [where he lost the case and] he began cursing.

In this vein, *Chazal* explain the verses in the Torah (*Vayikra* 24:10), וַיִּנָּצוּ בַּמַּחֲנֶה — "and they quarreled in the camp" — that they quarreled concerning matters of the camp. The son of the Jewish woman wanted to pitch his tent within the tribe of Dan but was opposed by a Jew, who offended him by taunting him and reminding him that he was the son of the Egyptian killed by Moshe using the *Shem HaMeforash* — Hashem's Name.

According to Rabbenu Bachya, this was the reason for the anger and cursing by the son of the Jewish woman. Because his opponent reminded him of the shame in his family, in that his father had been killed by Moshe by the use of the *Shem HaMeforash*, he began to curse Hashem — the Name of Hashem with which his father had been killed.

Toras Kohanim adds that the son of the Jewish woman had been converted, but he nevertheless still had the law of a *mamzer* — a child of a forbidden sexual relationship.

The *rishonim* follow *Chazal* in explaining the verses. This is evidently due to the fact that the Torah stressed that "the son of an Israelite woman, and he was the son of an Egyptian man, went out among *Bnei Yisrael*, and they quarreled in the camp, the son of the Israelite woman and the Israelite man." From the way the Torah repeatedly mentions the parentage of the persons involved, we see that a blemish in the man's ancestry caused him to act as he did.

Ramban says that the emphasis teaches us that the child of a non-Jew and Jewish woman is not Jewish. Even though the *Gemara* rules that such a child is "kosher," whether the woman was single or married at the time, the fact is that a daughter of such a union cannot marry a *Kohen*, nor can such a child enjoy such rights as being under the tribal flag of his mother or inheriting the land, for it says in the Torah, "according to their fathers' houses."

Ramban is surprised at the fact that *Toras Kohanim* states that the man converted. If his mother was Jewish, why did he need to convert? He therefore explains that at the time of the giving of the Torah, the son of the Jewish woman and an Egyptian father entered the covenant, like all the rest of the Jewish people, by *tevilah* in a *mikveh* and by a *bris milah*, and by the blood of the Covenant which Moshe *Rabbeinu* sprinkled on them (see *Sh'mos* 24:8) and became part of the Jewish people. Yet in spite of this, when it came to inheritance in the land, he was still considered the son of a non-Jewish father, and his conversion did nothing to change that. This is still surprising, for why, according to *Toras Kohanim*, was he considered as a *mamzer*, since the *Gemara* rules that such an offspring is a kosher Jew?

Ramban asserts that *Toras Kohanim's* view is that of one individual, and is not the *halachah*. *Ramban* cites the explanation of the Sages of France that the man was born before the Torah was given, at which time the Israelites were still considered as non-Jews, and in the case of non-Jews the child is attributed to his father's nationality. That was the reason why he did not have a *bris milah*. Consequently, he converted and was circumcised when he grew up. *Ramban*, though, refutes this explanation. From the time that Avraham made his covenant with Hashem, his children were considered as Jews and not as non-Jews. If this man was born of a Jewish mother, he did not need to be converted or to have a *bris milah*. And it would be all the more true after the Torah was given that the son of a Jewish mother and a non-Jewish father would be considered a Jew.

Malbim says that whenever *Sifra* states anything without attributing it to any person, it is R' Yehudah (סְתָם סִפְרָא ר׳ יְהוּדָה), and he is the one who holds that the child of a union between a non-Jew and a Jewish woman is a *mamzer*. As such, considering the fact that the event in the *parashah* occurred before the giving of the Torah, if *Bnei Yisrael* were already considered to be Jews, then the son of the Jewish woman would have had the status of a *mamzer*, but would not need to convert. If, though, before the giving of the Torah the Jews had the status of non-Jews, then the son would follow his father, and would need to convert. The son of the Israelite woman assumed that he was a Jew but also a *mamzer*, and that was why he wished to pitch his tent with Dan. They rejected him, claiming he was an Egyptian like his father. He went to the *beis din* where he thought that they would rule that he was Jewish. He reasoned as follows: If the Jews before Sinai were considered to be Jews, then Moshe could be justified to kill his father the Egyptian, because a non-Jew who strikes a Jew deserves death. If, however, the Jews were still considered as non-Jews at that time, what right did Moshe have to kill his father? He therefore cursed Hashem.

Of course all of this is *d'rush*. The other commentators, though, follow a similar path here. *Divrei Shaul* also derives from this clear proof to the view of *Tosafos* in *Kiddushin* 75b and in *Maharsha* there, that the offspring of a non-Jew and a Jewish woman must be converted, and until doing so is considered to be a non-Jew. Therefore *Toras Kohanim* explains the words בְּתוֹךְ בְּנֵי יִשְׂרָאֵל — "among *Bnei Yisrael*" — to mean that the son of the Jewish woman had converted, but that it did not help him gain an inheritance in the land, for it states "according to their fathers' houses."

◆§ Is He Considered a Jew or a Non-Jew?

Abarbanel also deals with the question of whether such a person is considered a Jew or a non-Jew. He says that the man was placed under guard in order to establish the answer to that question. After all, if he was a Jew, he deserved the death penalty for having cursed Hashem, while if he was considered to follow his father and was hence an Egyptian, he was not obliged to keep the *mitzvos*. Moshe himself was unsure of the answer. He ordered that the man's mother be brought to determine who his father was, Jewish or Egyptian. She admitted that the father was an Egyptian, and then a new doubt arose, as to whether he followed his father's or his mother lineage. Hashem ordered that he be put to death regardless, because even a non-Jew who curses Hashem is put to death. This is the reason that this *parashah* is right next to those dealing with a person who hits an animal or a human, where we are told clearly that it is irrelevant if it is a Jew or a convert. If the convert is equal in rights, he is also equal in obligations, and therefore the man deserved to die as any Jew.

Abarbanel explains the emphasis given the quarrel between "the son of an Israelite woman and the Israelite." In mentioning both in this way, the Torah was stressing that both were to blame, because they fought within the camp. If they had wanted to argue, they should have gone out to the field, and there whoever prevailed would be the winner (כָּל דְּאָלִים גָּבַר). Because both were dishonorable, they fought within the camp. The Jewish man won, at which point the son of the Jewish woman cursed Hashem.

Rabbenu Bachya also holds that the Torah stresses the man's moral inferiority, but this did not originate with himself. It was because of his ancestry. One who comes from holy seed cannot ever commit such a terrible sin. An evil man who curses Hashem must have faulty ancestry on both his mother's and his father's sides. The Torah mentions the mother's name here, because she was the most to blame. If one finds a person who shows signs of such terrible behavior, one should first investigate his mother. Rabbenu Bachya brings a number of proofs to this from *Tanach*. By the same token, when a person is worthy of praise, it traces back to his mother as well.

R' Samson Raphael Hirsch uses the same approach. The Torah revealed the name of the mother to stress that she was the only one in Israel who had relations with an Egyptian — and see what happened as a result.

Kli Yokar sees a defect not only in the son of the Jewish woman, but also in his opponent, the Jewish man. The Torah deliberately does not mention either name, to tell us that both suffered from a defect of ancestry. Whoever embarks on a quarrel is defective and is not a person worthy of praise. The reason the Torah says וַיִּנָּצוּ בַּמַּחֲנֶה — "and they quarreled in the camp" — is because they were people who were constantly involved in strife. Whoever is involved in quarrels is not worthy of praise, and the most one can mention of them is their ancestry. The reason why the *parashah* is next to that of striking a beast or man is to indicate that all these actions are the outcome of fighting and quarreling.

Or HaChaim also comments on the fact that the Jewish man's name was *not* mentioned. The reason is that it was through him that Hashem's name came to be cursed. Thus he too was to blame, for "guilt comes about through the guilty." But Hashem did not wish to mention his name and to have him condemned forever. Some of the *rishonim*, though, do reveal who this man was. He was the stepbrother of the other man. The Israelite woman had another son, this one from her Jewish husband. The two brothers were arguing, because the son of the Egyptian father wanted equal rights of inheritance. As a result, Hashem's name was cursed.

◂§ To Resolve It for Them According to Hashem

Rashi explains the differences between the מְקוֹשֵׁשׁ — the man who gathered wood on *Shabbos* — where we are told that he was put under guard כִּי לֹא פֹרַשׁ מַה־יֵּעָשֶׂה לוֹ — "for it had not been explained what was to be done with him" (*Bamidbar* 15:34) — and the present case, where we are told, "לִפְרשׁ לָהֶם עַל־פִּי ה' — "to resolve it for them according to Hashem" (*Vayikra* 24:12). In the case of the man who gathered wood they knew that he deserved death, but they did not know which death penalty to give him, whereas with the מקלל — the one who cursed Hashem — they did not know if he even deserved the death penalty. Thus they imprisoned him to find out from Hashem what the law was.

We explained above what the doubts were with the מְקַלֵּל. *Rivash* further explains their doubts. After all, they should have been able to deduce the death penalty from the fact that even a person who curses his parents gets the death penalty, except that there is a rule that we never deduce punishments simply on the basis of *a fortiori* logic (אֵין עוֹנְשִׁין מָן הַדִּין). As a result, Moshe had to ask Hashem.

Taz in his *Divrei David* says that they were in doubt as to what to do, because they had not warned the man in advance of the penalty (הַתְרָאָה). According to the *Gemara* in *Sanhedrin* 8, a person is not executed if he is not warned before his actions that what he is about to do is prohibited by the Torah. Here though, Hashem gave special instructions for this time alone, and therefore a special law was needed.

Nachal Kedumim, by *Chida*, holds that the doubt stemmed from the seriousness of the offense. When a person is put to death, this punishment constitutes a כַּפָּרָה — an atonement for his sins. The *halachah* though, in the case of one who passes his children through fire to Moloch, is that he is not put to death, and this is to his disadvantage, because this way he does not atone for his sins. Moshe was thus uncertain whether the מְקַלֵּל, who had cursed God, was fit to receive a punishment that involved atonement.

Divrei Shaul holds that Moshe's doubt was whether all of Israel needed atonement, after they had heard the man cursing Hashem. To this, Hashem replied (*Vayikra* 24:14), "Take the one who cursed outside the camp and let all those who heard him place their hands on his head." By that action, it would be an atonement for all of Israel. *Kanfei Nesharim*, though, says that the witnesses placing their hands on the sinner's head was meant to place the sin of the witnesses on the man's head as well. Their sin was that in testifying they had to repeat all the curses the man had said against Hashem.

Using this foundation, *Machazeh Avraham* explains the end of the *parashah*, "and they took the מְקַלֵּל outside the camp and they stoned him with stones." Here it does not say anything about laying their hands on his head. The law of *semichah* — of the witnesses laying their hands on the condemned man's head — only applied in the future, should another such case occur. If such a case occurs where the witnesses have to repeat the terrible things a man has said, the Torah tells us that the witnesses are to lay their hands on him, and that sin too will fall on his head. Here, however, they had no need to lay their hands on him, because they killed him by the command of Hashem, and not under the normal procedures of hearing witnesses.

Melo HaOmer has a beautiful interpretation of the verse, לִפְרשׁ לָהֶם עַל־פִּי ה׳ — "to resolve it for them according to Hashem." The witnesses would have to repeat the curses they had heard, but they were afraid to do so. They demanded that it be ascertained with Hashem whether they had to do so or were even permitted to do so. That is the reason that the *parashah* ends (ibid.), "and *Bnei Yisrael* did as Hashem commanded Moshe." After they heard from Moshe that Hashem had ruled that they were permitted to repeat the words, they did so.

Rivash explains this in a similar fashion. He adds that when they laid their hands on the one who cursed, that was meant to be an atonement for them, just as one lays one's hands on a sacrifice before it is offered. In this case, though, there was an additional aim of the laying of the hands, in that by doing so the witnesses avenged the honor of Hashem and were physically involved in pushing the man off the roof of *beis haskilah*, the house of execution. After that, the man was stoned by everyone (see ibid. v. 16), for once they saw that the witnesses had pushed him over, they knew for sure that he had cursed Hashem. Had it not been true, they would not have taken an action such as this, which, if unjustified, would be punishable by death. That is also why the Torah demands (*Devarim* 17:7), "and the hands of the witnesses shall be upon him first to kill him."

Ha'amek Davar also explains the reason for the *semichah*, because the one who cursed had forced the witnesses to hear Hashem's name cursed, and should they be in any way guilty for this, the man's death would atone for them all. Listening is counted as a sin, as we see in *Tosefta Shevuos*: R' Elazar b. Matia would say: "A person is not forced to listen unless he was liable for a sin (i.e., previously), as it states (*Vayikra* 5:1), 'If a soul sins and hears the sound of a curse.'" So too would he say: "One who sees others committing a sin was condemned to see it. One who sees others performing a *mitzvah* had the merit to see it."

Now we understand why it was so difficult for the witnesses and the *beis din* to hear and repeat the cursing of Hashem. In fact the *halachah* is that one who hears this must tear his garments, as we see in *Sanhedrin*. And that was the reason the witnesses laid their hands on him.

At the end of the *parashah*, we are told (ibid. 24:23) וַיִּרְגְּמוּ אֹתוֹ אָבֶן — "and they stoned him with a stone;" while with the person who gathered wood it states וַיִּרְגְּמוּ אֹתוֹ בָּאֲבָנִים — "and they stoned him with stones" (*Bamidbar* 15:36). R' Yeshaya Prager, and some say this in the name of R' Heschel, said that in regard to the one who gathered wood, there is a dispute among *Chazal* whether he was really a sinner. There are some who hold that he did it *l'shem shamayim* — for the sake of Heaven, so that people would learn the severity of *chilul Shabbos*. Those who stoned him were also divided among themselves. There were some who thought that he was wicked and stoned him wholeheartedly, while others held he was a *tzaddik* and stoned him only because that was Hashem's command. Thus in that case, the Torah says "with stones," because there were different opinions. In the case of the one who cursed all were united in their view. They stoned him, as it were, "with one stone and with one mind."

☙ As Hashem Commanded Moshe

The *rishonim* and *acharonim* ask what the above phrase teaches us. Ibn Ezra explains that from that day on, the Jewish people executed the appropriate sentence in all similar circumstances. *Ramban*, though, disagrees. The language of the verse refers to the present and not to the future. *Ramban* therefore has a new, ethical explanation. The Torah testifies that the Jews were freed of all hatred against the son of the Egyptian father, and they put him to death, not because he had quarreled with a member of the Jewish nation, but because this was what Hashem had commanded; that in these circumstances it was necessary to destroy this blemished person.

S'forno also explains that "they did not stone him because of enmity that he was a convert and had fought with a natural-born Israelite, but they did this so as not to depart from the *mitzvah*."

Meshech Chochmah states that the verse comes to tell us that even though the one who cursed laughed at the לֶחֶם הַפָּנִים — the Showbread — his mockery did not accomplish what it was meant to. Israel continued to light the menorah and to bring the לֶחֶם הַפָּנִים, as Hashem had commanded Moshe, without paying any attention to the claims of the apostate.

Alsheich has an interesting explanation: Hashem commanded Moshe to personally take the man out to be stoned, as it states, "take out the one who cursed" (ibid. v. 14). Afterwards, though, the Torah tells us, "And Moshe spoke to *Bnei Yisrael* and they took out the one who cursed" (ibid. v. 23). This change came about because the *Bnei Yisrael* wanted to prevent people from the slander of saying that first Moshe had killed this one's father, and now he had killed his son as well. Therefore they decided to take Moshe's place, and it was they who carried out the verdict. Hashem knew that what *Bnei Yisrael* did was *l'shem shamayim*, for the sake of Heaven, and therefore He considered it as if they had done "as Hashem commanded Moshe."

R' Yosef Tzvi Dushinsky has a beautiful interpretation along the lines of *d'rush*. When there is an evil man in the camp of Israel, that is a stumbling block for serving Hashem and hinders others in serving Him. Now that they had killed the wicked man, Israel could observe the Torah and *mitzvos* without disturbance. Indeed from then on Israel did as Hashem commanded Moshe.

Behar – בהר

I.

The Uniqueness of Shemittah

ven though our obedience to Hashem's *mitzvos* does not depend on knowing the reasons behind them, almost all commentators seek an explanation for the *mitzvah* of *shemittah*, the *mitzvah* of giving the land a rest from agricultural work once every seven years. *Ramban* and Abarbanel see it as commemorating the renewal of the world. The days of the week commemorate the creation of the world, while the years suggest what will be in the future. The seventh year symbolizes the seventh millennium (from the year 6001 on). Abarbanel says that after 6000 years there will be a partial destruction of the world, but the heavens and earth will remain, while in the *yovel* (jubilee) year, which is seven times seven, the world will return to its roots, as in "Return, each man to his own possession" (*Vayikra* 25:13).

Chinuch too brings as one of the reasons of *shemittah* the commemoration of the renewal of the world as symbolized by the number seven, but he also sees this *mitzvah* as an educational tool in instructing man to trust in Hashem, on the one hand, and in teaching him generosity on the other. *Shemittah* is also a proclamation by Hashem of His ownership of the universe. It is He who makes the world function, and it is He who can make it cease to function when He desires, and man must know and recognize this.

Rambam in *Moreh Nevuchim* 3:39 also sees this *mitzvah* as a means to implant mercy and pity in man. There, he writes that "the *mitzvos* of *shemittah* and *yovel* include pity for others and being generous to all men, as it states (*Sh'mos* 23:11), 'and the poor of your nation shall eat,' and that the earth should increase its produce ..." These *mitzvos* also include release for slaves and impoverished [debtors], and means for constant regulation of the economy [through the return of the land to its original owners]."

Akeidas Yitzchak, however, disputes the comment by *Rambam* that *shemittah* serves to increase the produce of the land. He asks: "If that is indeed the reason, why do the Torah and the prophets stress how great the punishment is for violating *shemittah*?" *Akeidas Yitzchak* therefore says that *shemittah* and *yovel* are "windows to open blind eyes, which are immersed in the sights of the (immediate) time." They are meant to make man aware that the world was created by and functions through the desires of Hashem. *Shemittah* is also intended to take man out of his rote style of living, where he is totally involved in his work and subjected to drudgery. He must know that the perfection of man, and not work, is his mission in life. The Torah therefore sets a time to declare all the land a person possesses as ownerless, so that he should not become enslaved to his own labor. Instead, he should be content with earning just enough to sustain himself.

Rabbenu Bachya also views *shemittah* as an educational tool, but he sees a different message in it. Whereas, according to *Akeidah*, *shemittah* is meant to teach us that a person should not be a slave to his work, according to Rabbenu Bachya it is meant to teach us that man should not convince himself that he is the master of his work:

> The general rule is that one is not permitted to act in his field or vineyard in any way as the owner, but all his produce should be ownerless (and available) to all; that even the simplest Jew may take it. The Torah therefore commanded this *mitzvah*, that all types of governing or ownership in this lower world should be annulled in regard to working the land, so that man should consider that neither governing nor ownership mean anything, since everything belongs to the Master of All.

R' Yitzchak Breuer elaborates on this in a number of chapters in *Nachaliel*. We will summarize his views here. In *shemittah*, all natural processes are a recognition of the sovereignty of Hashem and testify to His *kedushah*, as in (*Sh'mos* 3:5): "take off your shoes from your feet, for the place upon which you are standing is holy ground." That is the virtue of *Eretz Yisrael*. All the other countries of the world are a turmoil of blood and tears, where all fight one another over rivalry for bread, while *Eretz Yisrael* rests in the arms of its Creator. *Shemittah* comes to teach us that not only does the Jew have *Shabbos*, but the land too has its own *Shabbos*. The land is only lent to man, and it passes back to Hashem's sovereignty. In addition, *shemittah* ensures that man does not enslave himself to civilization nor become a victim of automation. *Shemittah* is a halt in the sovereignty of man's domination over nature and creation.

R' Breuer also notes the concept of equality in the *mitzvah* of *shemit-*

tah. He says that *shemittah* comes to abolish the different classes of people and of property ownership for a year. It is true that this is only temporary, but it proves that man's property is not truly his own and he must still justify his ownership of it.

R' Breuer adds another interesting point: that during *shemittah* there is equality between man and beast. Both have the right to eat freely in any field. The educational lesson of the *mitzvah* of *shemittah* lies in its answer to the question, "What shall we eat?" The *mitzvah* proclaims that it is not the laws of economics that control the world, but Hashem's will.

R' Yitzchak Breuer's words here contain a variety of reasons and explanations, almost all of which are hinted at among the *rishonim*.

R' David Zvi Hoffmann, though, sees *shemittah* as having an educational value to teach us the *kedushah* (sanctity) of *Eretz Yisrael*, as the land that is under the supervision of the Master of All. *Chazal* said in *Sanhedrin* 39: "The Holy One, Blessed be He, said to Israel, 'Sow for six years and rest the seventh, so that you should know that the land is Mine.'" The purpose of *shemittah*, according to R' Hoffmann, is not the same as that of *yovel* (the Jubilee Year). The latter comes to teach us that we should not become conceited over our wealth, while the former comes to instill in us "the *kedushah* of *Eretz Yisrael*." It follows that the punishment for not keeping *shemittah* is *galus* — exile — because when one violates the laws of *shemittah*, he is desecrating *Eretz Yisrael*.

Abarbanel also brings this idea and notes, among other reasons, that this is meant to inform us that *Eretz Yisrael* is the chosen land, just as man is chosen among all created things, and that it has it own *Shabbos*, just as the Jew has his *Shabbos*.

Kuzari, too, in 2:18 states: "The scholar said: 'You can see how the land received *Shabbosos*, as it states (*Vayikra* 25:2) וְשָׁבְתָה הָאָרֶץ שַׁבָּת לַה׳ — 'the land shall observe a *Shabbos* for Hashem.'" *Otzar Nechmad*, in his commentary on *Kuzari*, adds:

> The land too is subject to the rules of the Torah, for even the *Shabbos* that we are commanded has its parallel in the land, as it states, שַׁבָּת הָאָרֶץ — "the *Shabbos* of the land" (ibid. v. 6). The commandment does not refer to us — that we should be sure not to harvest or plow in the seventh year, but it states "the *Shabbos* of the land" to teach us that this rule is meant for the land.

According to this, the land appears as a living and active body, and it must follow Hashem's commandments just as man must.

It is worth mentioning here the interesting explanation of *Matteh Moshe* 473, and in a similar vein, *Tiferes Yehonasan* of R' Yehonasan Eybeschutz. *Shemittah* is meant to have the land rest for all the

Shabbosos of the year that it violated *Shabbos* as it were, by growing produce. There are 52 *Shabbosos* in the year, and in seven years that adds up to 364 *Shabbosos*. Against this, the land rests for 364 days during the *shemittah* year. But as there are still wild plants that grow during the *shemittah* year, the *yovel* was decreed against all the *shemittah* years.

Meshech Chochmah has an interesting and original explanation of *shemittah*. The six years of the *shemittah* cycle when one may grow crops parallel the six days of Creation as we mentioned above. The third and sixth days of Creation were the days "שֶׁהֻכְפַּל בּוֹ כִּי טוֹב" — that the expression כִּי טוֹב — "that it was good" — was repeated. That is why in the third and sixth years of the *shemittah* cycle we must give *ma'aser ani* — a "tithe to the poor" — to help others. *Meshech Chochmah* adds that the seventh year is referred to as שַׁבָּת לַה' — a "Shabbos to Hashem" (ibid. v. 2) — just as the regular *Shabbos* (*Sh'mos* 20:10). That phrase is not used in regard to *yovel*, and that has *halachic* significance. *Shemittah* resembles *Shabbos* in that it is fixed in time. It does not require the *beis din* to proclaim it. *Yovel*, though, is like the festivals of the year, and is unlike *Shabbos*. The day on which the festival occurs depends on when the *beis din* (Torah Court) proclaims *Rosh Chodesh* and the leap years, and with *yovel* too the Torah tells us (*Vayikra* 25:10), וְקִדַּשְׁתֶּם — "you shall sanctify" — that for *yovel* to occur requires the proclamation of *beis din*. *Shemittah*, by contrast, is independent of *beis din*. Like *Shabbos*, it is "the King's own cessation."

৵§ What Link Is There Between Shemittah and Mount Sinai?

Rashi, quoting *Toras Kohanim*, answers the question, מָה עִנְיָן שְׁמִטָּה אֵצֶל הַר סִינַי? — What is the connection between Mount Sinai and *shemittah* that the Torah saw fit to link the two in our *parashah*? He says that the words בְּהַר סִינַי teach us that "just as in the case of *shemittah* its general principles and its details were said from Sinai, so too is this true for all the *mitzvos*." The commentators on *Rashi* expand on these words of *Toras Kohanim*. If one looks into Mizrachi, *Gur Aryeh*, *Turei Zahav* and the other commentators on *Rashi*, one will find all types of questions and queries, but no simple and complete explanation. Two fundamental approaches to explaining *Toras Kohanim* emerge here:

Rashi's view is that the way we can establish that *shemittah* with all its detail was stated at Sinai is from the fact that this *mitzvah* was not repeated in the Plains of Moab (i.e., in the Book of *Devarim*), whereas other *mitzvos* were repeated there. It was not repeated because all of its laws had already been specified in detail at Sinai. From this we learn a

בִּנְיַן אָב — a standard rule — to the other *mitzvos*.

Ramban's view is that the general rules governing *shemittah* are mentioned above in *Parashas Mishpatim*: וְהַשְּׁבִיעִת תִּשְׁמְטֶנָּה וּנְטַשְׁתָּה — "and the seventh year, you shall let it rest and leave off from it" (*Sh'mos* 23:11), while all the details of *shemittah* are to be found in our *parashah*. Here we read (*Vayikra* 25:1) בְּהַר סִינַי — "on Mount Sinai" — while in the last verse of *Vayikra* we are told, "These are the *mitzvos* that Hashem commanded to *Bnei Yisrael* on Mount Sinai". From this, *Chazal* learned a הֶקֵּשׁ — an analogy — that just as the general principles and details of *shemittah* were said at Sinai, the same is true for the other *mitzvos*.

We are still left with a fundamental question that *Ramban* asks on *Rashi*: After all, there were other *mitzvos* besides *shemittah* which were not mentioned in the Plains of Moab, so why should it be specifically *shemittah* that serves as the בִּנְיַן אָב, the model for the other *mitzvos*?

Many attempt to reconcile *Rashi's* words, but it would appear that *Rashi's* view is based on the special moral and philosophical importance of the *mitzvah* of *shemittah*, in accordance with the explanations given above. *Shemittah* serves as a model for the other *mitzvos*, because it has in it principles of the renewal of the world, of the rectification of the world, of social justice, and of faith and trust in Hashem. No other *mitzvah*, among those *mitzvos* which were not repeated in the Plains of Moab, has similar values to those of *shemittah*.

We can thus understand *Rashi's* view that differs from that of *Ramban*. The latter's view is that *shemittah* was mentioned in general in *Parashas Mishpatim*, with its details brought here. *Rashi*, though, would be able to point out that all the festivals were also mentioned in *Parashas Mishpatim* and were repeated in *Parashas Emor* and *Parashas Pinchas*, in even greater detail than *shemittah*. Why, then, should not the festivals serve as the model for deducing the other *mitzvos*, and why does the Torah not write "on Mount Sinai" about them? It is for this reason that *Rashi* learned that *Chazal* in *Toras Kohanim* deduced the rule from the fact that *shemittah* was not repeated in the plains of Moab. It is true that there are other *mitzvos* that were not repeated in the plains of Moab, and the Torah could have written "on Mount Sinai" about them as well, but because the *mitzvah* of *shemittah* is so precious, as a fundamental *mitzvah* with such great value, the Torah wrote "on Mount Sinai" about it, so that it can serve as a model for the other *mitzvos*.

Chizkuni explains this in a different fashion. Two topics are covered in this *parashah*: the laws of the עֶבֶד עִבְרִי — the Jewish slave — and the laws of *shemittah*. The laws regarding the Jewish slave were repeated in the plains of Moab, while those of *shemittah* were not. Thus the words "on Mount Sinai" come to teach us that even those laws that were repeated in the plains of Moab were already given, in general and in detail, at Sinai, just as those that were not repeated there.

According to a number of commentators, the Torah adds the words "on Mount Sinai" here to stress the ties between the Torah and *Eretz Yisrael*. *Or HaChaim* says that just as the Torah mentions here the giving of the land: "When you come to the land which I am giving you", it also mentions "on Mount Sinai" to let us know that we will only receive the land conditionally, provided we observe the Torah in it.

R' Shlomo Ganzfried uses this to explain why the punishment of not keeping *shemittah* is exile from *Eretz Yisrael*. There is a famous question: Why should the Jews be exiled for not keeping the Torah, when they were forced to accept the Torah in the first place? In fact *Chazal* stated: "This provides a major excuse for [those who violate] the Torah" מוֹדָעָה רַבָּא לְאוֹרַיְתָא. *Rashba* answers this question by stating that the giving of the land to the Jews was made conditional upon accepting the Torah. As it is said in *Tehillim* 105:44-45 בַּעֲבוּר . . . וַיִּתֵּן לָהֶם אַרְצוֹת גּוֹיִם יִשְׁמְרוּ חֻקָּיו וְתוֹרֹתָיו יִנְצֹרוּ — "And He gave them the lands of nations . . . in return for heeding His statutes and keeping His Torah." After the Jews accepted the land, they were no longer able to claim that they had been forced to receive the Torah. As a result, when Hashem commanded us about the מִצְוֹת הַתְּלוּיוֹת בָּאָרֶץ — the *mitzvos*, such as *Shemittah* that are dependent on the land — the Torah stresses אֲשֶׁר אֲנִי נֹתֵן לָכֶם — "that I am giving you" — to let us know that this gift requires us to observe all the laws said "on Mount Sinai."

Sefas Emes expands on this idea. The Jews cannot fulfill their role to raise up nature to a higher spiritual level unless they are living in their own land. As long as the Jews live elsewhere, they are enslaved and are unable to fulfill their function in the world. When the Jews come to *Eretz Yisrael*, it enables them to sanctify the earthliness, and to raise nature to a degree of *kedushah*, sanctity. On the basis of your coming to *Eretz Yisrael*, I command you, וְשָׁבְתָה הָאָרֶץ שַׁבָּת לַה׳ — "the land shall observe a *Shabbos* for Hashem" — you must make nature too serve Hashem, just as you serve Him, to prove with this that you are free of any other considerations, and serve only Hashem and Him alone.

Kli Yokar also finds a direct link between the *mitzvah* of *shemittah* and Sinai. Moshe went up to the mountain seven weeks after they left Egypt, namely after forty-nine days. The *mitzvah* of *shemittah* is in the seventh year, while the *yovel* is after seven times seven years. These numbers parallel the number of days and weeks between the Exodus and the giving of the Torah. The phrase "on Mount Sinai" hints at this hidden link between the receiving of the Torah and the *mitzvah* of *shemittah*.

Chasam Sofer gives an interesting explanation of the phrase "on Mount Sinai". *Shemittah* was certainly said to Moshe at Sinai, for how could anyone but Hashem himself promise (*Vayikra* 25:21): "I will command My blessing ... for three years"? Therefore all the *mitzvos* were compared to *shemittah*. Just as it was definitely said at Sinai, so too were all the other *mitzvos*.

This approach is also followed by *Kli Chemdah*. The Torah was given to those who were eating manna. When the Jews entered *Eretz Yisrael*, the manna ended. The *mitzvah* of *shemittah*, though, perpetuates the manna in a different form. The Jews still eat "the bread of heaven" in terms of the promise of Hashem: "I will command My blessing ... for three years."

The term שַׁבָּת לַה' — a "*Shabbos* to Hashem" (ibid. v.2) — also reminds us what we are told about the manna and the double portion that was provided on the sixth day in preparation for the *Shabbos*. The sixth year is a preparation for the following years. The crops of the sixth year were twice and three times as great as normal.

Avnei Shoham discusses a specific difference between *shemittah* and *Shabbos*. In regard to *shemittah*, the Jews were commanded to rest after having worked, as it states (ibid. v. 3-4), "six years you shall sow your field and six years you shall prune your vineyard, and you shall gather its produce, and in the seventh year the land shall have a שַׁבַּת שַׁבָּתוֹן — a complete rest. In regard to *Shabbos*, though, the order is reversed: "Remember the *Shabbos* day to sanctify it. Six days you shall work ... and the seventh day is *Shabbos* to Hashem your God" (*Sh'mos* 20:8-10). Here, the Torah mentions rest *before* work. There is significance in this difference. The sanctity of *Shabbos* is a result of the renewal of the world, but it is holy in itself. The *shemittah* year, though, depends on the work of the years preceding it, as *Chazal* tell us in *Arachin* 12 and *Kiddushin* 40, that after the fourteen years the Jews spent conquering and dividing up *Eretz Yisrael* at the time of Yehoshua, they began to count off six years of work, followed by *shemittah*. This justifies what *Rambam* writes: that the purpose of *shemittah* is so that the land should rest after long years of work, and thereby to improve its productivity, or else we must seek another reason for this. The term שַׁבָּת לַה' thus does not entail a complete parallel between *Shabbos* and *shemittah*.

According to the *Yerushalmi Orlah* 7:7, this term, "a *Shabbos* to Hashem," teaches us a *halachah* that even if a person plants a vineyard for *hekdesh* (for the benefit of the *Beis HaMikdash*), the laws of *shemittah* apply, because "even anything which is לַה׳ — 'to Hashem' — has *shemittah* apply to it. *Minchas Chinuch* thus sees a contradiction between this *gemara* and *Tosafos* in *Menachos* 4a, where one is permitted to preserve סְפִיחִין — wild shoots of grain — that grew in *shemittah*, for the *omer*, "because the Torah said קְצִירְךָ — 'your harvest' (*Vayikra* 25:5) — and not that of *hekdesh*." He does not give an answer.

Meshech Chochmah uses an analogy to explain the reason of the *Yerushalmi*. If a person declares his property *hefker* (ownerless) and then makes a vow about it, the vow is invalid, since the property had already become ownerless. Similarly, Hashem gave the land to the Jewish people provided that *shemittah* is observed in it. Thus *shemittah* applies to *hekdesh* too, since its status of being subject to *shemittah* preceded its status as *hekdesh*. Using this logic, one may be able to differentiate between a *kinyan* — acquisition — of the land itself, and a *kinyan* of the produce that grew during *shemittah*. When produce was once privately possessed, it can be transferred to the possession of *hekdesh*. *Tosafos* therefore holds that the wild shoots may be harvested for *hekdesh* — for the *Beis HaMikdash omer* use — and that is not a contradiction to the *Yerushalmi*.

I also think that the *halachah* that *hekdesh* — land donated to the *Beis Hamikdash* — is subject to the laws of *shemittah*, stems from the *hashkafah* aspect of the *mitzvah* of *shemittah*. The sanctity of *shemittah* is such that, by Hashem's royal decree, all rights to ownership are terminated. That is the basis under which the land was given to us. Without that, there can be no concept of possessing the land. The people live in *Eretz Yisrael* because of the sanctity of *shemittah*, which justifies their ownership of it during the other six years. Without this justification, there can be no holiness and no Holy Temple, because Israel would be without any land. That is the reason the *kinyan* of *hekdesh* cannot apply during *shemittah*.

II.

For Bnei Yisrael Are Slaves unto Me

The social basis of Judaism is contained in the words of the Torah (*Vayikra* 25:55), "for *Bnei Yisrael* are slaves unto Me," as interpreted by *Chazal*, "and not slaves unto slaves" (*Kiddushin* 22), with all the laws related to this. Of course we cannot define this in the terms customarily used in the modern world. The Torah given by Hashem cannot be classified as "socialist" or "capitalist." In the Torah, for example, we find the complete negation of private property, side by side with the acceptance of slavery. If, however, we delve deeply into the Torah — its views, its visions, its *hashkafah* (philosophical basis) — as these are reflected in countless *halachos*, from *shemittah* and *yovel*, to the laws of social justice to the basic rule that "*Bnei Yisrael* are slaves unto Me," we find a clear direction in this area.

The *rishonim* and *acharonim*, each in his own way and according to his own approach, describe the views of the Torah on the subject. Two great Torah-true ideologists of recent times, R' Avraham Yitzchak HaKohen Kook and R' Yitzchak Breuer, did so in an all-encompassing manner. Both of them, in their greatness, holy fearlessness, and depth of understanding, described the Torah's viewpoint in a most remarkable manner.

R' Kook, in his introduction to his *Shabbos HaAretz*, writes as follows:

> Individuals of the nation may lower themselves from the level of a life filled with the light of *kedushah* and freedom and become slaves, forgetting their noble status, [as the Sages said], "and the ear which heard on Mount Sinai, 'for *Bnei Yisrael* are slaves unto Me' — they are My slaves and not slaves unto slaves, and yet this one went and acquired a master for himself." But then along comes the restoration of each one's personal respect and freedom [in the *yovel*], from the life force of the Supreme Holiness, which is suffused from the Highest Source and from which the nation nurtures the source of its soul. Freedom is proclaimed to all the land's inhabitants, replacing the inequality of land ownership, which arises from weakness of hands and spirit because of all of man's sins, which so detract from his strength, until he loses the inheritance of his fathers. Along comes the *Shabbos [Yovel]* which restores, in accordance with the nation's value at its outset, this fundamental property, to those upon whom the conflict of life has become too great, and upsets their balance.

This explanation of *shemittah* and *yovel* does not deal with the economic regime involved. It only adds a spiritual dimension to the life of society, which automatically causes a balance in social life. Later on, R' Kook clarifies the ultimate goal behind the commandment of *shemittah* with the following words: "A year of peace and tranquility, without oppressor or tyrant, "he shall not demand (repayment) from his fellow and his brother, because a *shemittah* has been proclaimed for Hashem" (*Devarim* 15:2).

There is no private property, no zealous pursuit of property rights, and Divine peace dwells upon all those who have breath in their nostrils. There is no desecration of the sacred by zealous attention to private property in the crop of this year, and the lust for wealth which is whetted by trade is forgotten.

R' Yitzchak Breuer is even more drastic in discussing this subject in *Nachaliel*. In his chapter on the social aspirations of the Torah, he expresses his opinion that the Torah advocates the abolition of ownership of property and money, in order to set up in the world what he calls 'The Social Sabbath." According to him, the Exodus was also meant to implant into the heart of man the Torah perception that a person who was rescued from slavery does not have the right to enslave others.

> Every Jew who exploits his workers, and who deals with them ruthlessly, shows that he has already forgotten that he himself was once a slave in Egypt, and in my eyes he is as one who is desecrating the Social Sabbath.

In talking about the prohibition against taking interest, R' Yitzchak Breuer explains this as being due to the fact that when a person takes interest, his money has "multiplied" in a non- productive fashion. In his *Moriah*, he says things that not even the most radical reformer would dare to say in criticism of society:

> And we? Where is our state, the state of the Torah, which is the only one that can regulate our national economy according to the laws of the Torah, according to the rules of uprooting money, to the extent that there will be no reason to use any but these laws, which show all the glory and beauty of the Torah? The *shtar iska* (a halachic arrangement which permits the investor to receive interest on his investment)? Woe to us that we sinned, and that we have neither a Torah state nor a Torah economy, and may Hashem have mercy on us.

In speaking of slavery, R' Breuer writes:

> If, through animalistic desires one man is made the slave of another, it is nothing less than a tremendous desecration of the honor and glory of mankind, for all have but one Father. There is no greater injustice than 'human justice' which recognizes slavery. If the Creator, may He be blessed, decrees that one of His sons is to be the master of this slave, then the Creator, Blessed be He, has placed upon both an enormous duty: You (the master) are to treat him in a brotherly fashion and he is to act in a servile manner. Study the laws of slavery and you will find this.

According to R' Breuer, *shemittah* has two aims: "the *Shabbos* of the land against national sovereignty," and "the *Shabbos* of money against sovereignty of property." He adds:

> The *shemittah* of money depends, by Torah law, on the *shemittah* of the land. "The earth is Mine! And money is Mine!" And what does the capitalist say? He says: "The money is not the Lord's, nor is the money mine, but I belong to money."

This is but a small portion of what R' Breuer writes in his book, but it is enough to raise the curtain and to illuminate the viewpoint of the Torah and its intentions in the *mitzvos* in our *parashah*.

⊰§ Hashem's Sovereignty over Property

R' Yitzchak Breuer stresses a number of times that the Torah does not negate private property, but only imposes spiritual limitations on it, so that the amount involved automatically contracts to a quantity that expresses Hashem's sovereignty over creation, in accordance with His declaration (*Vayikra* 25:23), "The earth is Mine."

Akeidah explains this problem in a less radical fashion. The number seven in regard to days (of the week); years (of the *shemittah* cycle); *shemittah* cycles (of the *yovel*) is always meant to revolve about a central point, that being Hashem and His desire in the world. The Torah tells us that we were not sent into this world to be slaves that are sold to the land, but we have a different and much loftier task to perform, and that we should labor solely to buy our food and other necessities. Our entry to *Eretz Yisrael* was not so as to become enslaved to it or to working it, or to amass wealth, as is the purpose of other nations with their lands. Instead, our purpose is to gain control of ourselves and strive to perfect ourselves in order to follow the desire of Hashem, and in the course of that, Hashem will supply us with our needs. Thus the concept of the land resting in *shemittah* is so that we should know that nothing is permitted to us from what we produce except what is necessary for all of us, including the poor, and that the owners should take only what is necessary. The basic principle is that the more wealth is produced, the more people should benefit from it, and the owners have no right to it except what is essential to them, and this they will never lack.

Thus *Akeidah's* view is that the owner is entitled only to what he needs. The Torah demonstrates this countless times. The most prominent of these are *shemittah* and *yovel*.

R' Yaakov Emden made a very interesting comment in *Pirkei Avos* on the two approaches to private property, which are expressed in the argument: "One who says 'what is mine is mine and what is yours is yours' — that is an average quality; while others say that is the quality of S'dom." *Chazal* tell us in *Sifra* regarding one who owns a slave:

> He must be with you in food, with you in drink, with you in clean clothing — that you should not eat fine bread while he eats inferior bread, or that you drink old wine while he drinks new wine; or that you sleep on upholstery and he sleeps on straw.

That illustrates to us best of all man's limitations in doing whatever he wants with his property. It is true that *Sifra* is dealing with how one must treat his Jewish slave, where *Chazal* tell us that "Whoever buys a slave for himself, buys a master for himself," but the way other nations regarded their slaves in those days was no different than the views of those who advocate private property without any limitations. It is not the object that is involved here, but the principle, and there is no doubt that the Torah principle is the subjugation of all possessions and property to the control of Hashem, and to deal with it in an ethically and socially responsible manner.

✑§ The Hashkafah and Halachah Aspects

There are literally hundreds of *halachos* and sayings of *Chazal* which illuminate to us the holy Torah's approach to social questions, an approach to which no modern ideology can compare. This is not the place to expand on this, for it is a matter which requires many volumes. This is certainly not the place to discuss the relationship between employer and employee, which also has a direct bearing on the topic. If, by Torah law, a person sold as a slave in order to repay his thefts must be treated like a master, how much more must one give respectful treatment to a person who works for his living, and regard him as an equal.

The principle which tells us to remember how we were exploited as slaves in Egypt, is of significance in all our endeavors. There are numerous laws in this regard, even though the *hashkafah* side as revealed in our *parashah* is not always explicitly stated. The laws of *shemittah* are the most far reaching, in terms of social responsibility and ethical considerations. But there are countless other examples where an employee or a laborer is given precedence, even though this infringes on the private property of the employer.

I would like to mention a few of the examples, of the many that might be given. The law is that a hired laborer may choose to cease working in the middle of the day and must be paid for his work until that time, but a person who hired another to work for him cannot terminate his work in the middle.

The law, in general, is that a person is responsible for any damages that he causes, but an employee must sometimes be given special exemption, because we are told, לְמַעַן תֵּלֵךְ בְּדֶרֶךְ טוֹבִים — "so that you shall follow the ways of the good" (*Mishlei* 2:20).

The law is that where one person sues another, in the absence of decisive evidence, the person being sued must take an oath that he does not owe the amount in dispute, and then he is cleared of the claim against him. In the case of an employee, though, the law changes to his benefit, and where he claims that he was not paid his wage, he is the one to take the oath, and on the basis of that oath, the employer must pay him any outstanding wages.

Similarly, special halachic considerations are given to artisans; for example, the law is that one cannot seize an artisan's tools as security for a debt.

These are but a sprinkling of the vast compendium of laws involved. Some contemporary rabbis in Israel have indeed compiled such sets of laws, and it is imperative that a nation which has such laws should legislate their implementation in our daily lives.

◆§ This is the Book of the Generations of Man

Meshech Chochmah in *Parashas Kedoshim* explains the words of Ben Azzai in *Toras Kohanim*. Ben Azzai interpreted the verse, "You shall love your fellow-man as yourself" (*Vayikra* 19:18), by quoting another verse: "This is the book of the generations of man" (*Bereishis* 5:1). The holy Torah is not only a book of laws, but is also the exact opposite of all those systems not based on the *kedushah*, sanctity, of man. Whatever is found in ideologies today already existed in earlier times. Tyranny ruled at the time of the Flood, when the land was filled with violence. Communism was the order of the world at the time of the Tower of Babel, when society was organized on the basis of complete sharing of all property. There is nothing new under the sun. The Torah though, in our *parashah*, stresses that "they are My slaves" (*Vayikra* 25:55), which *Sifra* explains to mean, "My deed of ownership takes precedence," namely that whatever position a person wishes to adopt, it must be in keeping with Hashem's prior claim on us. The spiritual foundations of "in the image of God He created [man]" (*Bereishis* 1:27), and our redemption from the slavery of Egypt, must leave their imprint on our ethical behavior and our laws, and these foundations represent a promissory note that has not been paid to this day. This vision is not dependent on man's desires: Even if he agrees to give up his freedom, he does not have the ability to do so. Thus, *S'forno* explains the verse, "they are My slaves" as follows: "Even though a person went and acquired a master for himself, which means that it is proper that he should work for him, nevertheless, as he is My slave, he has no right to sell himself."

Ketzos HaChoshen raises a question: The *halachah* is that an artisan who makes something acquires that object by the added value that he has contributed by his labor. Now, in general, the added value is worth more than the labor invested in the object, and as the artisan gets paid only for his labor, is the person who hired him not cheating him? As is known, the entire doctrine of Karl Marx ימ״ש is that the added value should belong to the laborer. Thus even in this, we see that he adds no new insight that is not to be found in our sources. R' Yitzchak Breuer, in *Moriah*, in the chapter on "Society," shows the differences, though, between the false doctrines of Marx against the truth of our Torah on the question of society:

> According to our Torah, Man was created in the image of God. Marxism vehemently denies the chosenness of man. Our Torah proclaims the independent value of justice. According to Marxism, justice is only a temporary "reflex" of the economics of that era. Our Torah teaches that there is an eternally valid law, and that it is God's law, which He revealed to the Jewish society. According to the Marxist doctrine, only economics establishes justice from time to time. According to this doctrine, justice is not Divine, but is a product of economics. Marxism bows down and supplicates itself before economics, and that is indeed the idolatry of our era.

According to R' Breuer, slavery is idolatry, "because *Bnei Yisrael* are My slaves, and not slaves to slaves." His opposition to an anti-Torah social system stems from his opposition to idolatry.

III.

The Nature of the Mitzvah of Yovel

he *mitzvah* of *yovel*, the Jubilee Year, is a religious and social *mitzvah*, and much more than that, as we will cite below based on the views and interpretations of the Torah commentators on this great and remarkable *mitzvah*. This *mitzvah* includes (*Rosh*

Hashanah 9) a number of *chukim* and three *mitzvos*, these being blowing the *shofar*, freeing the slaves, and the return of the land to its original owners. When these three *mitzvos* are observed, then all the others as well — not to harvest, not to sow, etc. — also apply. Yet, it seems strange why it is that when these three are not being observed that the others also need not be observed. Should the guilty be rewarded?

A question to be considered is whether this rule of everything being dependent on these three *mitzvos* refers to the nation as a whole — i.e., that when these three *mitzvos* are not kept, there simply is no *yovel* — or whether it applies at the individual level as well. *Tosafos* in *Eiruvin* 32 says that the rule whereby all the laws of *yovel* are abrogated applies even in the case of individual sinners, and not necessarily only in a situation where *yovel* is not in effect. If that is the case, we certainly need an explanation as to why the Torah allowed the sinner to benefit from his transgression of the *mitzvos*.

In *yovel*, there is also a commandment of וְקִדַּשְׁתֶּם — "and you shall sanctify the fiftieth year" (*Vayikra* 25:10). *Chinuch* holds that the sanctity here is not an additional *mitzvah*, but is identical with the essential nature of this year, whereby the land's produce is ownerless, and the slaves go free. Nevertheless, he adds that "it would appear that the Sanhedrin are to gather and to consecrate the year, and to recite a blessing 'לְקַדֵּשׁ הַשָּׁנָה' — 'to sanctify the year.'" Sadly, in the years of our exile, these laws were forgotten. Now that we have returned to our land, we should delve into them and clarify them.

According to the Torah, *galus*, exile, comes for the sin of not observing the *mitzvos* of *yovel* and of *shemittah*. The Torah states this quite clearly a number of times in *Parashas Bechukosai*. So too do we read in *II Divrei HaYamim* (36:21), "To fulfill the word of Hashem by the mouth of Yirmiyahu, until the land had compensated her *Sabbaths*." According to *halachah*, *galus* exempts us from keeping these *mitzvos*, and, in fact,

> from the time that the Tribes of Reuven and Gad and half the Tribe of Menasheh were exiled, the *yovel* was abolished, because it states, "and you shall proclaim liberty throughout the land to all its inhabitants" (ibid.) — namely as long as all live in it (*Rambam Hilchos Yovel*).

Meshech Chochmah deduces and explains this law from a verse, "and the land shall not be sold in perpetuity, because the entire land is Mine, for you are strangers and sojourners with Me." When the land is yours, it is also Mine, but when Israel does not live on its land, the *Shechinah* is also in exile with them — "for you are strangers and sojourners with

Me — you, together with Me, are strangers when Israel is not on its land." Hashem links His redemption, as it were, to our redemption, with the keeping of the *mitzvah* of *yovel* in *Eretz Yisrael*. On the greatness and importance of this *mitzvah* and the underlying motifs in it, we will bring various commentators below.

◄§ One Generation Follows Another

Ramban chooses, among the various explanations, one "along the way of the *emes*" (i.e., the truth, which is the way he refers to kabbalah). The word דְּרוֹר — "freedom" — is, according to him, a contraction of the phrase, דּוֹר הוֹלֵךְ וְדוֹר בָּא — "One generation goes and another generation comes." According to him, the word *yovel* is related to הוֹבָלָה (*hovalah*) — moving or transportation. Everything returns to its original root through this *mitzvah*, that root, of course, being Hashem.

Rabbenu Bachya uses a similar approach. The word *yovel* is as seen in the verse (*Yirmiyahu* 17:8) וְעַל-יוּבַל יְשַׁלַּח שָׁרָשָׁיו — "that spreads out his roots by the river (*Yuval*)." All the generations trace back to the Prime Cause — Hashem. The *yovel* is also referred to as *dror*, because through it all the generations (*doros*) are attached to their First Root.

Chinuch also states that, "one of the reasons for this *mitzvah* according to the plain meaning (*p'shat*) is that Hashem wanted to tell His people that all is His, and that in the end everything will return to whomever He originally wanted to give it, for 'Mine is the land.' He adds that this will also bring about the mending of society. People will "keep far away from stealing the land of their fellows and will not covet it in their hearts, knowing that everything will return to whomever Hashem wished to give it." *Chinuch* says that *yovel* resembles what happens in earthly kingdoms, where kings take away fortified cities from the nobility, just to remind them to fear their lord. In the case of mortal kings, that is done only to instill fear so that the noblemen do not rebel, whereas Hashem commanded His people for their benefit. According to *Chinuch*, whoever violates the *halachah* of freeing slaves not only violates a negative commandment, *mitzvas lo ta'aseh*, but, much more basic, denies the Creation and renewal of the world, as described above in the reason for *yovel*, where all returns to its First Root.

The commentators give other explanations of *yovel*. Abarbanel states that the *mitzvos* of *shemittah* and *yovel* come to remind us of two great kindnesses of Hashem, these being: the first *Shabbos* after the world was created, and the giving of the Torah fifty days after the Jews left Egypt. The fifty years of *yovel* symbolize those fifty days. Thus the required blowing of the *shofar* (הַיּוֹבֵל) at the beginning of *yovel* reminds us of, "when the *shofar* sounds, they may ascend the mountain" (*Sh'mos* 19:13). Hashem commanded us to be free in *yovel*, just as we were when we left Egypt. Similarly, we should not sow in order to remind us that we wandered through land that was not sown.

Eitz HaDa'as by R' Chaim Vital also explains, evidently following in Abarbanel's footsteps, that just as the Jews who left Egypt counted seven weeks and then received the Torah, we are commanded to count seven *shemittah* cycles, each of seven years. The number seven is meant to remind us of Hashem's creation of the world, in that He created it during six days and rested on the seventh.

This idea of the number seven being a reminder of the Creation is brought also by *Chinuch*. The Torah commanded that we are to rest on the seventh day. *Shemittah* is at the end of seven years. *Pesach* is seven days. *Shavu'os* comes after seven weeks. *Sukkos* is seven days, and then we have *Shemini Atzeres*. Thus the number seven is repeated over and over in the Torah and by the Prophets.

Akeidah also expands on this. We are always commanded to make a circuit of seven and then to return to our starting point. The last circuit is that of *yovel*, which is meant to symbolize the ultimate and final return to our roots: "Each man to his estate and each man to his family" (*Vayikra* 25:10). The kabbalistic and Chassidic literature deal with this at length. While the different commentators have various opinions, the common element in all is that the *mitzvah* of *yovel* is meant to return us to our sources, and to remind us of a basic concept about mankind in general and the Jewish people in particular.

⊷§ Putting the World Right

Rambam in his *Moreh Nevuchim* explains the *mitzvah* of *yovel* differently. According to him, Hashem's plan with *yovel*, as well as with *shemittah*, was to improve the social and economic conditions of the nation and of society. In 3:39, he states:

> With all the *mitzvos* that we enumerated in regard to the laws of *shemittah* and *yovel*, some of them are out of pity for people, and to ease matters for all, as it states, "and the poor of your nation shall eat" (*Sh'mos* 23:11) and that the earth will increase its produce, and will be strengthened by its resting during *shemittah*. Others are meant to grant reprieve to slaves and the poor, these being the freeing of slaves and the canceling of debts. Others are meant to ensure one's income and sustenance in perpetuity, and that is because the land is reserved for its owners and cannot be sold

permanently, so that a person's property is preserved for him and his descendants.

Rambam thus stresses the benefits to the community and to the individual in the *mitzvos* of *shemittah* and *yovel*: the preservation of family ownership over its property; support for the poor; and the improvement of economic conditions of the nation by increased productivity of the land.

Ramban, too, explains the word *yovel* (יוֹבֵל) to mean that the *mitzvah* leads — הַמּוֹבִיל — man back to his previous status before he was forced to sell all his property.

Oznayim LaTorah also explains the *kedushah*, sanctity, of the *yovel* along these lines:

> The *kedushah* is the total freedom that exists in creation; a year in which there are no masters or slaves; there is no ownership of the land and of the produce of the land; and there is no indebtedness.

S'forno says that the reason for the blowing of the *shofar* is "because of the joy of the freedom of the slaves and the returning of fields to their owners."

Actually, *Rambam* had already said this in *Sefer HaMitzvos*, where he wrote that:

> The blowing (of the *shofar*) on the *yovel* is to publicize freedom and is part of that announcement. This is as stated, "proclaim liberty" (*Vayikra* 25:10). This is not like the blowing on *Rosh Hashanah*, which is as a reminder before Hashem, but it is for the freeing of slaves.

Chinuch too follows that direction, and gives the blowing of the *shofar* a psychological meaning: The sound of the *shofar* comes to strengthen the hands of the master, as a measure of צָרַת רַבִּים חֲצִי נֶחָמָה — the suffering of the multitude is half a consolation ("misery loves company") — when all masters see that all of them were commanded to free their slaves, that is in itself somewhat of a consolation. The slave too is aroused by this to go out free. This is not only an announcement of freedom, but serves to impress its meaning on both the master and the slave.

It is interesting that *Zohar* explains the word תְּרוּעָה of the blowing of the *shofar* as "breaking," as in the verse, "break them (תְּרֹעֵם) with an iron rod" (*Tehillim* 2:9), in that the *shofar* "breaks the chains — rule over all slaves is broken."

HaKesav VeHaKabalah explains this in a very similar fashion. He takes תְּרוּעָה to be close to רֵעוּת — friendship, as in the verse "the friendship of (וּתְרוּעַת) the King is in him" (*Bamidbar* 23:21) — the *yovel* being "a year of joy for the poor and the rich, for those who own property and for the slaves. There is no work of the fields, and all rejoice."

This meaning of *yovel*, as coming to rectify society and to free the Jew of all types of entanglements, is the basis for the social *hashkafah* of the Torah of many commentators. R' Yitzchak Breuer describes the event:

> The sound of the *shofar* on *Yom Kippur* of *yovel*, went forth from the *Beis HaMikdash*! From the home of eternal *kedushah*! The Sanhedrin gave the sign. With lightning speed, the sound spread throughout the land, from mountain to hill and from hill to mountain. From place to place, and from house to house. The sound of this *shofar* brings the old and antiquated economy crashing down — as the wall of Jericho, and there echoes forth the piercing and revolutionary cry: Freedom! It breaks the chains of the economic past, and all the downtrodden are sent free, each man to his own estate and each man to his own family (*Nachaliel* 447-448).

Earlier too, when talking about *yovel* and *shemittah*, R' Breuer reaches the conclusion that "the uprooting of money is one of the basic principles of the law of the Torah. And another is the uprooting of (private) land (ownership), so that it should not be an item of profiteering" (p. 430).

◆§ Courtyards and Walled Cities

In regard to *yovel*, the Torah establishes a different law for fields than for houses inside walled cities. Whereas fields are returned in *yovel*, sales of such houses become permanent if the houses are not redeemed within a year. Houses in open areas have the same rules as fields. Many reasons have been given for these differences. *Ramban* finds the laws governing houses in walled cities as having elements of both *kula* and *chumra* (leniency and stringency). It is a heavy blow to a person if he has to sell his house, and therefore the Torah allows him a year to redeem it. If he has not redeemed it within a year, it is evident that he has resigned himself to its loss. Since his livelihood is not dependent on that house, he has no doubt found other accommodations and has settled down. That is not true for a person's fields, which are the basis for his sustenance. Therefore, though he sold his land when he was in difficult financial straits, it returns to him in *yovel*. Houses in the open are also considered like fields, because they serve to guard the fields and to be the living quarters of those who work the ground. The Torah therefore requires them to be returned in *yovel*.

Rivash and *Chizkuni* give a similar explanation. If the city is surrounded by a wall, then the land upon which the house stands is not intended for sowing. Hashem required only land that man uses to earn his living, such as a crop field or a vineyard, to be returned. When the land produces crops, Hashem does not want the person's source of sustenance to end, and He therefore decreed that the land cannot be sold in perpetuity. With a residential dwelling, the law is different; yet Hashem allowed the person a year to redeem it. Similarly, with houses in open land, where such land may be used at a later time for raising crops, the land cannot be sold permanently.

Meshech Chochmah gives a remarkable explanation as to why the laws of returning the land do not apply to houses in walled cities. Walled cities must be able to withstand the onslaught of enemies from without, and that requires a stable population. If a considerable part of the population was replaced each *yovel*, it would result in many people living in the city who did not know all its hidden alleys and streets, so that the city defense would be weakened.

There is a controversy among *poskim* whether one who sells his land with the intent that it be permanent has transgressed a commandment of the Torah. *Rambam*, in *Sefer HaMitzvos*, *Mitzvas Lo Ta'aseh* 227 takes the prohibition as such, among the 613 *mitzvos*. *Ramban*, though, disagrees: "What difference does it make to us if a person sells his land and does not state that the sale is only to *yovel*? In any event, when *yovel* comes, Hashem removes the ownership (from the buyer)." Indeed, *Bahag* does not list this as one of the 613 *mitzvos*. According to *Ramban*, the Torah meant that one is not permitted to sell the land permanently to a non-Jew, because then it does not return in *yovel*, and since "the land is Mine" (*Vayikra* 25:23) we are forbidden to settle any others but Jews on it.

Chinuch sees another purpose in the prohibition against the perpetual sale of land. It is to inform us that there is a difference between the canceling of debts during *shemittah* and the sale of land. In the case of the canceling of debts during *shemittah*, the responsibility is entirely that of the lender, who may not ask for repayment. It does not apply to the borrower, who has the right, if he so wishes, to repay his debt to the lender. In the case of the sale of land, though, the prohibition against selling the land permanently falls on both seller and buyer, and the seller cannot, during *yovel*, tell the buyer that he may still own the land.

Michtam LeDavid explains the Torah verse in a *d'rush* fashion, as a promise — that the land will never be taken over in perpetuity by other nations, and a time will come when it will be redeemed and restored to its legitimate owners, the people of Israel.

IV.

You Shall Not Oppress One Another

he *parashah* of אוֹנָאָה (cheating, oppressing) appears in the middle of the laws of *yovel*, the Jubilee Year, and as *Meleches Machsheves* points out, there is a link between the two: "When one realizes that his ownership of the land will eventually be terminated he will refrain from stealing and cheating." That applies only to the buyer. As to the seller, there is a simpler explanation. Since his sale of the land is only temporary, he will not feel as great an urge to cheat his fellow.

Taz in *Divrei David* says that the warning against cheating appears here because it is possible that a first buyer may attempt to cheat a second buyer by overcharging him for the land as if it were being sold permanently, since as far as the first buyer is concerned, the land will not return to him in *yovel*. The fact that the second buyer will eventually have to return the land in *yovel* to the original owner is not the first buyer's concern, he might claim, just as when a person sells an animal to another to be used as a sacrifice, the parts of the animal that must be given to the *Kohanim* obviously are taken from the buyer. The Torah, therefore, wished to call the attention of the first buyer to the fact that when he sells the land he must realize that it is being sold only for a limited time, namely until *yovel*, and he should adjust the price accordingly.

R' Dushinsky explains the tie between the two *mitzvos* in accordance with *Chazal*, who hold that a person who violates the laws of *shemittah* becomes poor and is forced to sell, first his land, and eventually all his goods. The Torah thus feared that a person buying the land might rationalize to himself and say: "The fact that this fellow must sell his land proves that he is wicked, and I may therefore cheat him." That is why the Torah warned us here against cheating others.

Chazal in *Bava Metzia* 58b explain that the Torah uses the phrase לֹא תוֹנוּ twice (*Vayikra* 25:14,17) here to apply to cheating financially as well as to oppressing with one's speech, as we will explain below.

Binah L'Itim explains this according to *d'rush*. The first mention in the Torah forbids cheating אָחִיו בְּמִצְוֹת — "one's brother in *mitzvos*" — as it states אַל־תּוֹנוּ אִישׁ אֶת־אָחִיו — "do not cheat your brother." The second mention, though, prohibits cheating even a swindler like oneself, who is "his fellow" in swindling, as it states וְלֹא תוֹנוּ אִישׁ אֶת־עֲמִיתוֹ — "do not cheat your fellow." No one has the right to sin in order to treat people according to their behavior. Instead, we are commanded in this same verse to "fear your God" — וְיָרֵאתָ מֵאֱ־לֹהֶיךָ. It is for Hashem to repay people, and not you.

Chinuch explains the reason for this *mitzvah* as a moral rule which is the basis for all of humanity:

> It is not proper to take people's money by lies or cheating, but rather each person must merit his earnings by laboring with what Hashem has granted him rightfully in the world. This benefits everyone, because just as a person will not cheat others, others will not cheat him. Even if the person is more capable of cheating others than they him, his sons may not be like that and others will cheat them. Thus these laws are worthy of being observed by all, and are essential for the functioning of the world. This law is a general social need, whose value is clear to all.

Ma'ayanah Shel Torah quotes *Me'or Einayim* that when a person deals fairly and is careful not to cheat, and has correct weights, not only does he aid in the functioning of the world, but he also serves Hashem's work by acting thus. He adds that the *Besht* said if one observes the Torah laws governing "one who trades a cow for a donkey" merely by learning these laws, how much more does one observe the Torah when one actually carries out the laws. This is a typical view of how Chassidism pictures the world.

◆§ "Do Not Cheat" in Land

According to the plain meaning of these verses, the prohibition of אַל תּוֹנוּ — "do not cheat," refers to the sale of land, as it states, "in accordance with the number of years after the *yovel* shall you buy from your fellow ..." (*Vayikra* 25:15). Indeed, following this *p'shat*, *Rashi* explains that the verse is a warning that when a person sells or buys land, he must take into account how many years remain to *yovel*, and it is on the basis of the number of crops that will remain until then, that the price is to be set. On this, the Torah states אַל תּוֹנוּ, referring to both the seller and the buyer.

Ramban is surprised at *Rashi's* view. After all, *Chazal* learn from a verse that the law of *ona'ah*, overcharging, does not apply to land, as deduced from the verse אוֹ קָנֹה מִיַּד עֲמִיתֶךָ — "or that you buy from the hand of your fellow" (ibid. v. 14) — that this refers to movable goods which are bought from hand to hand. This is found in *Toras Kohanim*. There, however, we are told both: a) that the verse applies to land; and b) that there is no *ona'ah* in land. This is the language of *Toras Kohanim*:

> I only know that the verse refers to land. How do I know that includes everything even movable goods? This we deduce from the word מִמְכָּר, — "merchandise" (ibid.), to include something which is movable. How do I know that there is no *ona'ah* in land? For it states אוֹ קָנֹה מִיַּד עֲמִיתֶךָ אַל־תּוֹנוּ, — "or that you buy from the hand of your fellow do not cheat" — there is *ona'ah* in movable goods, but there is no *ona'ah* in land.

This quotation seems to be contradicting itself: Is there or is there not *ona'ah* with land?

Ramban first attempts to reconcile the verses in accordance with the *halachah* that there is no *ona'ah* in land, and that the admonition to sell land only by the number of years remaining until *yovel* is not related to *ona'ah*, but is part of the law of *yovel*. The purpose is to remind each seller and buyer that a field cannot be sold permanently, but only for the number of years until *yovel*. Afterwards, though, *Ramban* reconciles the verses in a way that has implications on the *halachah*. The *poskim* have dealt with this extensively.

According to one view of *Ramban*, the prohibition of *ona'ah* applies to both land and movable goods. However, when *Chazal* deduced from the verses that there is no *ona'ah* in land, they were referring to a different aspect of *ona'ah*. In general, if one sells anything for one sixth above the market price, the overcharge must be returned. If he overcharges more than a sixth the sale is null and void. That law, though, applies only to movable goods and not to land. There are two possible explanations why land should not be included in this rule: a) *Chazal* assumed that even if the price exceeds the market price by more than a sixth, the buyer is willing to buy the land, or b) because *Chazal* had a tradition that only in the case of movable goods does the halachah require that the sale be canceled. According to the latter view, the rule governing being overcharged by one-sixth depends on what the average man feels, and with regard to land, this varies from place to place. Whereas a person would wish to cancel a purchase of movable goods where the price was more than a sixth above market value, he might not wish to do so when he buys land. This, says *Ramban*, is analogous to the halachah regarding a sale of movable goods by a private homeowner, in contrast to a store. Since it is generally accepted that a private homeowner charges high prices, the rule of one-sixth does not apply.

Ramban also reconciles these verses in another manner: There is no cancellation of the sale of land if the *ona'ah* consisted of too high a price, but when the *ona'ah* is related to how large the tract is or to any other measure of quantity, where the seller misrepresented such figures, the sale is canceled. In our *parashah*, since the *ona'ah* revolves about the number of years involved, the sale is void.

The *acharonim* explain this interpretation of *Ramban*. If the error was one of price, a person will normally be willing to accept the deal in spite of that fact, but when the error is one in the quantity involved, a person will not accept the deal. These two explanations of *Ramban* also answer the question regarding the passage from *Toras Kohanim* quoted above; for sometimes there is *ona'ah* with land, and other times there is not.

Some of the early commentators, such as *Chinuch* and *Paane'ach Raza*, hold as the first view of *Ramban*, that the law of *ona'ah* applies to land as well as to movable goods, and this question has been discussed at length by both *rishonim* and *acharonim*. *S'forno* and others, though, hold as the second view of *Ramban*, that in the case of land there is *ona'ah* only in quantity or measure, but not in price.

Chasam Sofer answers *Ramban's* question on *Rashi* by means of *d'rush*. As we noted earlier, *Ramban* asks how *Rashi* can explain this verse to refer to land, when the law of *ona'ah* does not apply to land. As an introduction to *Chasam Sofer's* explanation, we must note that there is a law that grapes that are ready to be harvested are considered as if already harvested. The *gemara* (*Gittin* 48) tells us also that if a person sells his fields during a period of history when the laws of *yovel* apply, all that he sells is the produce, and not the field itself. Hence, whoever sells his field has, as it were, sold only the produce that the land is expected to grow. Since such produce is considered to be as if harvested, it has the classification of movable objects, which are subject to *ona'ah*.

Along these lines, *Rashbam* explains the verse, "for he sells you a number of crops" (*Vayikra* 25:16), to mean that all that one sells is the yields until *yovel*, but not the fields themselves.

HaKesav VeHaKabalah, however, states that such a sale of "years of crops" would be even inferior to a person's sale of the crops of his field to another person, and in the latter case the buyer is not permitted to use the field at all, and cannot even enter it except to take out the produce, while the owner of the field can do whatever he wants to with it. Such a sale of "years of crops" would be no sale at all. He therefore explains the words "for he sells you a number of crops" to mean that the person "sells you the fields for their crops." In such a case, the seller cannot enter the field without the buyer's permission, whereas the buyer can do whatever he wants: building, demolishing, or taking any other action that an owner of a field can take, as given by *Rambam* in *Hilchos Mechirah* 5-7, while at the end returning the field to the original owner. It therefore follows that if one sells a field for its fruit, it is a sale of the land and not of movable objects, and *Ramban's* question returns.

Or HaChaim answers the question simply. The Torah warns the seller not to deceive a person who is ignorant of Torah law by selling him a field as if in perpetuity, and then go back to the buyer later with the excuse that it is Torah law that the land must be returned, as we mentioned above. Such *ona'ah* is similar to the case of a person who sells property to which he claims he has full title, and later it is discovered that there are indeed claims against the title, in which case the sale is annulled as *ona'ah*. Our case is similar, for there is no bigger claim to the title of land than someone who has the Torah law backing him. And this type of deception is indeed considered *ona'ah* on land.

Or HaChaim also states, as does *Ramban*, that even if there is no *ona'ah* on land in general and a sale cannot be annulled on the base of overcharging, there is still a *lav* — a negative prohibition — involved in overcharging on land, in terms of וְלֹא תוֹנוּ אִישׁ אֶת־עֲמִיתוֹ — "do not cheat your fellow." While it is true that *Chazal* interpreted this to refer to אוֹנָאַת דְּבָרִים — oppressing someone with words — nevertheless the plain meaning of the text is that even though there is no *ona'ah* with land, in that the sale is not canceled, there is nevertheless a sin against God involved in such deception, and it is for this reason that we are told in the same verse, וְיָרֵאתָ מֵאֱ-לֹהֶיךָ — "You shall fear your God."

The reason there is no *ona'ah* in regard to land, is that the *beis din* cannot fathom the intentions of the seller. To the latter, indeed, the price that he set — which to an outsider now appears so high — might be eminently reasonable, if that is what the property is worth to him. It is just because the question of *ona'ah* depends on the seller's intentions that the seller is told, "You shall fear God." Hashem knows whether the seller was sincere or whether he was bent on fraud, and that is why this law is left to Heaven to determine.

Or HaChaim adds that all kinds of trickery are included in the prohibition of *ona'as devarim*, oppressing with words, so that in the present case, i.e., that of land, even though there might not be *ona'ah* in terms of money, where such *ona'ah* can annul a purchase, there is still *ona'as devarim*, oppressing with words, that being a prohibition of the Torah as well. This is unlike *Ramban's* view, which considers this to be *ona'as mammon* — financial cheating, and not simply oppressing with words.

Ha'amek Davar proves *Ramban's* second theory, namely that *ona'ah* in quantity or measure applies to land as well, from the implications of the verses themselves. The Torah details the form of *ona'ah* in land: "according to the years after the *yovel*," which indicates that the error was in the number of years. Only such an *ona'ah* applies to land, and not an error in the price. On the other hand, with movable objects, where the *ona'ah* cannot refer to the number of years, all types of *ona'ah* are possible, including errors in price. Thus we see that the interpretation of *Chazal* fits exactly into the words of the Torah.

Kli Yakar also offers a logical reason for the law that there is no *ona'ah* in land: "There is never a constant price or value for real estate. It is possible that a piece of land that is worthless now may become extremely valuable later. Thus there can only be *ona'ah* with movable objects, where the price remains stable over their life, for they are consumed over a period of time. As to land, it lasts forever; hence even if a person was overcharged now, he will be compensated later when the price increases. That is why there is no *ona'ah* with land."

This explanation, while seeming to be suitable for land, does not explain why there is also no *ona'ah* with slaves. *Tosafos* in *Bava Basra* 61b use this argument to contradict the view that there is no *ona'ah* in land because land is worth more, for why then should there also not be *ona'ah* with *hekdesh*, sacred property of the *Beis Hamikdash*, and with slaves? Evidently, though, it is a decree of the Torah, a *chok*, statute whose reasons we cannot fathom.

◄§ According to the Number of Years after Yovel

Rashi explains, as we mentioned above, that the above verse comes to warn the seller and the buyer to calculate the sale according to the number of years left until the *yovel*, so that if there are few years to *yovel* and the seller sells the land for a high price, the buyer is cheated and if there are many years to *yovel* and the buyer pays a low price, the seller is cheated. Thus the price should be in accordance with the time until *yovel*. This is what the Torah means when it writes, "according to the number of years of crops he will sell it to you" (*Vayikra* 25:15), namely the number of crops that the buyer will enjoy.

Even though *Rashi* says this is the plain meaning (*p'shat*), there are commentators who ask why the Torah states, "according to the number of years after *yovel*" (ibid.), and not, "according to the number of years before *yovel*." After all, the sale is based on the number of crops the buyer will enjoy until *yovel*!

Mizrachi finds it difficult to explain *Rashi*, but *HaKesav VeHaKabalah* gives a simple interpretation. The word אַחַר (which was translated here as "after" sometimes means "within," as in (Sh'mos 3:1) אַחַר הַמִּדְבָּר, which Onkeles renders, "into the desert." And in fact the yovel year is the beginning of a new fifty-year count. Moreover, the end of a thing is called its "after part" (אָחוֹר), as in (Yeshayahu 42:23): "Who will listen and hear until the end (לְאָחוֹר)." Thus, the term, אַחַר הַיּוֹבֵל, should not be translated "after the yovel," but "into the yovel, with regard to the end." And there is a reason why the Torah chose precisely this word, whose more usual meaning is "after." As far as yovel is concerned, the Torah wants to point out that if a person sells his land during the yovel, the sale has no validity, because the seller does not own the land that he has attempted to sell. And indeed in Arachin 29 Shmuel learns that if a person sells his field during yovel, the action is meaningless. It is true that Shmuel deduces this by reasoning a fortiori (kal va'chomer), but this is apparent from the meaning of the verse itself.

According to Ramban in his commentary on our parashah, both the seller and the buyer must specify the number of years until the yovel. The commentators wonder: Doesn't Ramban himself in his commentary on Sefer HaMitzvos, Lo Ta'aseh 227, state that,

> A person need not mention when he sells land, that "I am selling it to you until yovel," for all sales are made by stating, without any further qualification, "I have sold you my field," or "My house has been acquired by you," and during the yovel the sold property returns to its owner, whether they were sold without specifying or were explicitly sold "forever," as Chazal state, "Yovel is a cancellation by the King."

Many struggle to answer this difficult question. R' Chavel answers it simply. We are dealing with two separate topics. It is true that in regard to ona'ah, the prohibition against overcharging, when discussing the terms one must mention the number of years until yovel, but when the sale is concluded, in regard to making it a binding sale governed by the laws of yovel, there is no need to mention that it is until yovel. This is just what Ramban said: "A person is not required to mention when he sells (to the other), 'I am selling this to you until yovel,' because this is so whether he said so or not."

S'forno explains the verse (Vayikra 25:16), "According to the multitude of years you shall increase its price, and according to the fewness of years you shall diminish its price": this means that one must calculate not only the number of years, but also according to the best estimate possible, what the field can produce during these years. When a person buys for many years, he uses the land for building pens for his animals as well, and not only for grain. That is not so when one buys for a few years. The maximum value which he can obtain in this sale must also be reflected in the sale, and if it is not reflected it is *ona'ah*, because "according to the number of years he is selling it to you." Thus, if a person sells land for a few years, he cannot use the land except for grain, as *Chazal* state in *Bava Metzia*, Chapter *HaMekabel*, "One who receives a field from his fellow for a small number of years should not plant flax," as it weakens the field. The limitation on the use of the field must lower the price, in addition to the number of years, and in this too we are warned, לֹא־תוֹנוּ, "do not cheat.".

Chazal learned from the words בְּמִסְפַּר שְׁנֵי־תְבוּאֹת — "according to the number of years of crops" (*Vayikra* 25:15) — that a person who sells his field when *yovel* is in effect in the land cannot redeem it until at least two years have passed. If there was a year of blight, it is not included in this calculation. R' Eliezer says that if a person sold his fellow a field from *Rosh Hashanah* and it was full of ripe produce, the buyer can enjoy three crops (i.e., in the two years). Not only the seller must wait two years, but the buyer as well, and this is a *mitzvas asei* (*Arachin* 29).

Here we have four *halachos*: a) The law that the field is not to be redeemed for the first two years applies to the buyer as well as to the seller; b) if there are three crops in the two years, they all belong to the buyer; c) if there was no produce because of blight, the year is not included; d) and another rule — which we did not mention above — that if the buyer managed only to obtain a single year's produce before *yovel*, he is given the year after *yovel* to complete his two years.

Or HaChaim finds all four laws in the plain meaning of the verses according to "the number of years after the *yovel*" (ibid.) — namely that if the buyer did not have two years of crops before *yovel*, he is given the land after *yovel*. At different times the Torah used the word תִּקְנֶה — "you will buy" (ibid.) — and at other times it used יִמְכָּר — "he sells" (ibid.) — to teach that the law applies equally to the seller and the buyer. The Torah also refers to שְׁנֵי תְבוּאֹת — "years of crops" [in the plural] — to teach us that the buyer is entitled to buy land for a period of time that will ensure at least two crops. Finally, the Torah states מִסְפַּר תְּבוּאֹת — "the number ... of crops" — rather than מִסְפַּר תְּבוּאָה, "the number of the crop," to teach us that the buyer is entitled to more than one crop, and if there is a year of blight it is not included in the two years.

Bechukosai – בחקתי

I.

The National Promises and Their Significance

The blessings at the beginning of this *parashah* are directed at the nation as a whole, if it observes the Torah. As to the individual, promises to him are made in countless places in the Torah. Here, though, the promises are made to the entire community.

Ikarim uses this differentiation to explain why, among all the promises, there is not a single spiritual one here, one that relates to *Olam Haba*, the World to Come. The blessings here are directed at the whole nation, that it will be firmly entrenched in its land, and that its citizens will be happy. *Akeidah* sees a most exalted spiritual promise here, that being "I will place My dwelling place in their midst" (*Vayikra* 26:11).

The *rishonim* all deal with the question of why the Torah does not mention *Olam Haba* here. *Kli Yakar* lists some of the views on this. *Rambam* devotes considerable space to this in a number of places, and primarily in his commentary on *Pirkei Avos*. The promises mentioned in the Torah, says *Rambam*, are promises to man, whereby if he performs the *mitzvos* as they should be performed, Hashem will eliminate all impediments and obstacles, thereby enabling all to live in tranquility, so that we can realize our aspirations on earth, and receive a reward such as no eye has seen, i.e., in the World to Come. As such, the rewards mentioned in the Torah are but a means to fulfilling the Torah completely, and not a payment for fulfilling it.

Abarbanel and *Akeidah* classify the blessings in our *parashah* into groups. This idea of categories is especially stressed by R' David Zvi Hoffmann in his work on *Vayikra*. According to R' Hoffmann, there are five kinds of blessings here:

a) the blessing of the fruitfulness of the earth, that being, "I will give your rains in their season" (ibid. v. 3) which, according to *Ramban*, is an extremely fundamental blessing; one that guarantees not only that we will have abundant food, but also that we will have clear air and fresh water, which are primary to man's health. There is also an assurance (v.5) that threshing the grain (דַּיִשׁ) will continue until it is time to harvest the grapes (בָּצִיר), and that the harvesting of the grapes will last until the time to sow the next crop of grain (זָרַע). This abundance will enable a person to support himself.

b) The second blessing is the blessing of peace. Peace will reign throughout the land. People will feel deeply rooted in the land: וִישַׁבְתֶּם לָבֶטַח בְּאַרְצְכֶם — "and you will dwell in your land in security" (ibid.). There will be no need to wander from place to place in search of work. Everything will be fine, and it will follow automatically that there will be no crime. "You will lie down and there will be none to make you fear" (v. 6). Even the animals will not disturb your tranquility, because the land will be settled throughout: "I will rid evil beasts out of the land" (ibid.). If all this is true, then it is all the more obvious that no one from elsewhere will disturb you: "neither shall the sword go through your land" (ibid.).

c) The third blessing is victory over your enemies should they dare to disturb your tranquility: "You shall chase your enemies" (v. 7). You will defeat your enemies easily, and you will not only defeat them but destroy them: "They shall fall before you by the sword" (ibid.).

d) The fourth blessing is multiplying in numbers, a flourishing economy, and Hashem's *hashgachah pratis*, special Providence, over the nation. "I will turn to you" (v. 9) with special *hashgachah*; "and make you fruitful, and multiply you" (ibid.) — a growing population and a minimal death rate. "You shall eat well-aged produce" (v. 10) — there will be economic growth. Your crops will not rot or mildew, and will be of good quality.

e) The fifth blessing is that of Hashem's *Shechinah*, Divine Presence, remaining with Israel: "I will set My dwelling (*Mishkan*) among you," (v. 11) with Hashem's open and public *hashgachah*. "My soul will not abhor you" (ibid.) — there will be no reason to remove the *Shechinah*, because one who comes to purify himself is aided in his quest. I will help you to be worthy of it. As a result, "I will walk among you, and will be your God" (v. 12).

All the above are promised to our nation if the kingdom of the Torah is established and the nation as a whole observes the Torah. The Lubavitcher Rebbi remarked beautifully in his *Sichos* that the word בְּחֻקֹּתַי — "in My statutes" (ibid. v. 3) — means legislation and the imposition of the burden of laws. The Torah does not content itself with a person merely identifying himself with it ideologically, but what the Torah demands is practical legislation, for the individual and for the community, through which the blessings we were promised regarding a life of stability in *Eretz Yisrael* will be fulfilled.

We will follow the division of R' David Zvi Hoffmann of the blessings into five categories, and will see how the commentators deal with the matter.

◆§ The Blessing of the Fruitfulness of the Land

We have mentioned *Ramban's* view that this is the most fundamental of all blessings, and that is why the Torah mentions it first. Rains at the correct time purify the air and springs of water, and this in turn produces better crops and larger and healthier animals and people, as a result of which the latter live longer.

Abarbanel, though, holds that this blessing is linked to the *mitzvos* of the land in the previous *parashah*. If you observe *shemittah* and *yovel*, you have no cause to fear that you will suffer economically by your actions. The reverse will be true: by keeping these *mitzvos*, the land will become even more abundant.

According to Abarbanel, when the Torah uses גִּשְׁמֵיכֶם — "your rains" (v. 4), it means the rains of the land. If you keep these *mitzvos*, the rains of the land will be yours.

Toras Kohanim, however, explains the personal aspect of this blessing of rain, to indicate that only in your case will there be an abundant crop, so that all the other nations will come to you to buy grain. *Or HaChaim* comments that rains which come as a result of your actions are "your rains," and it is as if you had brought them.

The blessing of the fruitfulness of the land also is connected with the assurance of וִישַׁבְתֶּם לָבֶטַח בְּאַרְצְכֶם — "you shall live in security in your land" (v. 5). Ibn Ezra and other commentators note that famine causes a person to wander into exile, and the *halachah* permits a person to leave *Eretz Yisrael* when there is a famine in the land.

Sifre writes regarding the verse "and you shall live in security in your land": "On your land, you live in security, and you do not live in security outside the land." On this, R' Sorotzkin's *Oznayim LaTorah* comments that when the Jews live in security in *Eretz Yisrael*, it is because of this blessing of Hashem, whereas when Jews outside *Eretz Yisrael* live in security, it is not because of the blessing of the Torah.

Ha'amek Davar has an interesting comment regarding the blessing that the threshing period will continue until the time of the harvest of the grapes, etc. He relates this to the productive life of *Eretz Yisrael*. The purpose of this blessing is that we will always be busy working, and as a result, וַאֲכַלְתֶּם לַחְמְכֶם לָשֹׂבַע — "you will eat your bread to the full" (ibid.). This will also lead to the blessing of וִישַׁבְתֶּם לָבֶטַח בְּאַרְצְכֶם — "you shall live in security in your land" (ibid.) — because those who are idle, leave the land. If, however, you will be busy with your work, you will surely remain in the land.

Meshech Chochmah expands on the blessing of the fruitfulness of the land to discuss the topic of the natural and the miraculous, and of the harmony between the laws of nature and the Torah and *mitzvos*. The greatest miracle of all is the miracle of nature. Man, though, is so used to nature that he fails to see in it the marvels of Hashem. The miracle, therefore, comes to arouse man and to take him out of his everyday existence. The miracle is a one-time event, while nature supports all of the world continuously.

Our keeping of the Torah leads to nature being blessed, and that is the greatest revelation of Hashem in the world. It is the blessings of nature working within the laws of heaven and earth which come from our observance of the Torah which are the purpose of the world, and not the miracle.

✥ The Blessing of Peace

The *rishonim* discuss the seeming repetition in וִישַׁבְתֶּם לָבֶטַח בְּאַרְצְכֶם — "and you shall live in security in your land"(v. 5) — and וְנָתַתִּי שָׁלוֹם בָּאָרֶץ — "and I will give peace in the land" (v. 6). After all, if the people live in security, doesn't that imply that there is peace in the land? One of the *rishonim* explains that what the Torah wishes to tell us is that it will be a real peace and not one that just appears to be that way by people who ignore the evil around them. This is the interpretation of *Rivash*, who evidently was well aware of the optimism of people, who often perceive of the situation in a way that simply ignores reality.

Or HaChaim and other commentators state that peace here refers to a state of calm between various groups in the country itself. If the country has an abundance of food and satisfaction, the internal peace will be more stable. *Or HaChaim* also explains that the word אֶרֶץ — "land" — in this verse refers to the entire world. If there is no peace in the entire world, then there will not be any security in *Eretz Yisrael* either. Where there is no such peace, rumors fly and affect people's lives; people live in fear, even though there is no war in the country itself. The Torah promises us that in order to ensure our security, there will be peace throughout the world. *Meleches Machsheves* limits the area involved. There will be peace among the nations living around *Eretz Yisrael*.

They will not even fight among themselves, and as a result there will be no tension or fear in *Eretz Yisrael*. The peace of *Eretz Yisrael* will affect its neighbors.

Chasam Sofer explains, "and I will give peace in the land," in terms of contentment. Even though Hashem promised Israel all of the best, that does not mean that they will be satisfied with this, because one who has a hundred dollars wants two hundred.

Hafla'ah explains וּמַשְׂבִּיעַ לְכָל־חַי רָצוֹן — "You satisfy the desire of every living thing" (*Tehillim* 145:16) — that the main thing is the person's desire and his contentment. This is a special gift of Hashem. The Torah promises Israel that not only will there be an abundance in the land, but contentment. People will be content with what they have, and that is true spiritual serenity.

Likutei Basar Likutei has an interesting interpretation of his own: In stating "and I will give peace in the land," the Torah wished to guarantee harmony also among the natural elements of which the earth is composed. There will be no earthquakes, and the earth itself will also be secure.

This peace is also the one we long for, in which "the wolf will live with the lamb" (*Yeshayahu* 11:6). According to R' Shimon, animals too are part of this peace. R' Yehudah holds that the words of the verse are to be taken literally, in that if cities are populated, there is no room for wild animals to roam. R' Shimon, though, holds "[the animals] will be prevented from doing harm." *Ramban's* opinion is that this is what the Torah meant when it said, "I will rid evil beasts out of the land." Before the sin of Adam, says *Ramban*, there was no such a thing as prey, even among animals. If the Jews live in *Eretz Yisrael* according to the Torah, the earth will revert to that state, and the lion will eat straw like the cow. Peace will envelop *Eretz Yisrael* and the surrounding countries, the entire world, and even all animals. The kingdom of the spirit will reign in the world, as it did before the sin.

◆§ The Blessing of Victory over the Enemy

This blessing, first of all, promises that we will pursue our enemies: "And you will chase your enemies, and they will fall before you by the sword" (*Vayikra* 26:7). After that, we are promised the deliverance of the many into the hands of the few: "And five of you will chase a hundred, and a hundred of you will chase ten thousand" (ibid. v.8). And an additional blessing: "and your enemies will fall before you by the sword" (ibid.).

The *rishonim* discuss the fact that the Torah repeats the phrase about our enemies who will fall by the sword. They also ask about the equation involved with five pursuing a hundred (twenty times as many) and a hundred pursuing ten thousand (a hundred times as many). The latter question is answered by *HaKesav VeHaKabalah*, who says that the word five refers to both parts of the verse, so that the second part is as if to say, "and five hundred of you will put ten thousand to flight," so that the ratio remains twenty times as many.

The reason why "falling by the sword" is repeated, says *Ramban*, is that after the Torah had promised that five will pursue a hundred, one might imagine that such a small ratio, even with all the expertise and energy of the Jewish fighters, could only put the enemy to flight, but could not kill them. The Torah therefore repeats that the enemy will die by the sword, to tell us that even with this ratio, the enemy will be killed. Ibn Ezra holds that there is a promise here that our enemies will fall repeatedly, until they will not be able to arise again.

Rashi's comment on the verse, "and your enemies will fall before you by the sword," is that they will fall "in an abnormal way," while on the verse, "and they will fall before you by the sword," he says that they will kill one another. *Ma'asei Hashem* asks what the source is for *Rashi's* interpretation. He says that *Rashi* drew his first conclusion from the apparently superfluous term, "your enemies," as a result of which *Rashi* says that this refers to your enemies who will die in an abnormal way, whereas *Rashi* deduces the second one from the fact that the Torah could have stopped with the words, "and you will chase." Why then the extra words, "and they will fall before you by the sword"? The meaning must be that you will find them killed next to one another. This innovative explanation is surprising, for *Rashi's* interpretation is based on *Toras Kohanim*, and there we are told clearly where the interpretations are taken from. The first is derived from the fact that the Torah repeats the verse, while the second is deduced from the fact that the Torah writes וְנָפְלוּ — "and they will fall" — rather than וְהִפַּלְתֶּם אוֹתָם — "and you will make them fall," which implies that they have already fallen.

The fourth blessing, of a flourishing economy and multiplying in numbers, has very little commentary on it. Its meaning is clear. According to *Ramban*, וְהִפְרֵיתִי — "and I will make you fruitful" (ibid. v. 9) — means that no man or woman will be barren, whereas וְהִרְבֵּיתִי — "and I will multiply you" (ibid.) — means that you will have many children. Others explain the first to refer to many children, and the second to a decrease in the mortality rate. *Or HaChaim* explains the former to refer to quantity and the latter to quality. The increases in your numbers will not affect your quality.

It is interesting that S'forno refers וְיָשָׁן מִפְּנֵי חָדָשׁ תּוֹצִיאוּ — "you will bring forth the old because of the new" (ibid. v. 10) — to exports. The *halachah* is that anything that is vital to life may not be exported from *Eretz Yisrael*, as we see from *Chazal* in *Kesubos*, *Perek Shnei Dayanei Gezeros*, that they did not export from *Eretz Yisrael* wine, oil, and fine flour. Here, though, the Torah promises that the economy will flourish so much that you will be able to export the old grain in your barns, because you will need the space for the new grain.

◄§ The Blessing that the Shechinah Will Dwell in Israel

According to the Midrash, the verse, וְנָתַתִּי מִשְׁכָּנִי בְּתוֹכְכֶם — "And I will set My dwelling (*Mishkan*) among you" (*Vayikra* 26:11) — refers to the *Beis HaMikdash*. The *rishonim* extend the concept to include the public and open revelation of the *Shechinah*, Divine Presence, and the Kingdom of Hashem as happened during the existence of the *Beis HaMikdash*. *Zohar*, though, states that the Torah is even referring to a state of exile (as if it were written, "and I will set My *mashkon* — My pawned object — among you"). Even when the *Shechinah* is, as it were, "pawned" (מִשְׁכָּן) when Israel is in exile, nevertheless "My soul shall not reject you" (ibid.).

Me'iri, too, follows this direction, and sees this as a promise of the return to Zion and the ingathering of the exiles. In his opinion, "And I will set My *Mishkan* among you" is a reference to the communities of exile which are like pawns and collateral in the hands of the nations. The verse assures us that these communities shall again be "among you," as it is written: "The redeemed of Hashem shall return" (*Yeshayahu* 35:10; 55:11).

The addition to this blessing of the phrase, "My soul will not reject you," arouses surprise. This is noted especially by *Ramban*. After the promise that the *Shechinah* will dwell in Israel, is there any need for such a statement? After all, we are told that even after Israel broke the covenant with Hashem, He did not reject them, and this should be all the more true when they keep the *mitzvos*.

The other *rishonim* also discuss the verse. *Ramban* explains this in his way. *Ralbag*, though, tells us that this is a new promise, that Hashem will not remove his *Shechinah* from Israel even when they sin and Hashem should, by right, reject them. *Ha'amek Davar* also explains it along these lines, but he does not interpret the sins here to be those of the nation as a whole, but rather the sins of individuals. Hashem will not remove His *Shechinah* because of the sins of individuals.

Abarbanel sees here a special stress against those who hold that there is no *hashgachah pratis* — direct Divine intervention. Hashem does not dwell only in the Heavens, disdaining the lower realms. He is also directly involved with the creatures on earth.

Akeidah, though, explains the words at their face value. In spite of the distance between Me and you, you can still rise up in knowledge to such an extent that you deserve to be drawn close and not rejected. Among mortals, if a prince marries a commoner, there has to be some distance between the two. However there will be perfect harmony between Me and you.

As opposed to this, *HaKesav VeHaKabalah* explains the verse as a condition, that if you ensure that "My soul does not reject you," then I will dwell among you.

Oznayim LaTorah, by R' Sorotzkin, says that this is a promise to Israel that there will not be a third destruction. When the promise of "I will set my *Mishkan* among you" is fulfilled, there will never again be a case that I will reject you. "And I will walk among you" (*Vayikra* 26:12), namely that Hashem will walk among us throughout the land, and He will not limit His *Shechinah* to one city or another. Instead, His kingdom will spread throughout the land and into every corner.

According to *Ramban*, these blessings have not yet been fulfilled, and they will only be fulfilled when Israel attains the heights of perfection.

II.

The Curses of the Rebuke and the Blessings of Consolation

The *parashah* of the *tochachah* — "the rebuke" — is a very difficult and painful one, foretelling much grief to the Jewish people, but at the same time it carries a message of hope. He who carried out the punishments listed in the *tochachah* will also carry out the vision of redemption and will fulfill His promises of good to Israel. From this point of view, the *tochachah* is but an episode in the ultimate redemption. Thus we see that after the destruction of the second *Beis HaMikdash*, when R' Akiva saw foxes running out of what had been the *Kodesh Kedashim* — the Holy of Holies — he rejoiced and said: "He who kept His word about the punishments will also keep His word regarding His promise of retribution and reward" (*Makkos* 24b).

The commentators on the Torah deal with explaining the *tochachah* and with relating it to their own generation or the generations before them. From that point of view, we, the generation of the Holocaust, can testify that in our time, because of our sins, the *tochachah* has been fulfilled in every last detail. But the consolation of the *tochachah* is to be found in the Torah itself, in the verse, "And even when they are in the land of their enemies, I shall not abhor them or reject them to destroy them" (*Vayikra* 26:44). As the commentators on the Torah explain it, even when we are affected by the greatest of troubles, the troubles will never bring us to the stage of destroying us. Rather, there will always be a nucleus that will remain alive, and from which will again grow the live tree of our nation.

One cannot understand this phenomenon with our limited mortal understanding. How we can be driven to the very brink of destruction and nevertheless emerge to live again? The very fact that this is so encourages us, as *Chazal* tell us: "That is His greatness; these are His mighty deeds." The fact that a single little lamb can exist among seventy wolves is no less remarkable than the destruction of all the wolves and only the lamb remaining alive. The fact that the lamb exists under all circumstances is a proof that Hashem's word exists forever, and that after the *tochachah* will come the full consolation, just as the *tochachah* came to pass in every detail.

Galus, exile, is a stage in the redemption which will follow. In fact, *galus* itself testifies to the eternity of our nation, which has existed under more bitter conditions than any other nation.

Ikarim 42 deals at length with the awesome phenomenon of the continued existence of the Jewish people under conditions approaching total destruction. He proves that there is a purpose for our existence, and that our nation is safeguarded for the remarkable day that awaits us in the future. There are nations — says *Ikarim* — whose race remains stable, but whose name is destroyed or changed, such as Philistia, Ammon, Moab, etc. And there are those whose name remains, but the race disappears, such as Egypt. The Jewish people is the only one in history that has maintained both its name and its race, thus fulfilling the remarkable prophecy (*Yeshayahu* 66:22), "'For as the new heavens and the new earth, which I will make, shall remain before Me,' says Hashem, 'so shall your seed and your name remain.'"

Chazal defined the miracle of the continued existence of the Jew with the words, based on *Vayikra* 26:44:

"I did not abhor them" — at the time of the Chaldeans; "and I did not reject them" — at the time of the Greeks; "to annul My covenant with them" — at the time of the Romans. "I am Hashem their God" — in the future, that no nation or folk can rule over them.

The *tochachah* is a preface to the redemption. If something remains alive under all conditions and circumstances, it is proof that there is a reason and a purpose for its existence. All those who tried have failed to annihilate the Jewish people, because "I am Hashem your God."

Maharal in his *Netzach Yisrael* deals at length with these proofs. The most convincing proof of the prophecy of redemption is the fact that we see the *tochachah* so clearly. If we are able to talk about the *galus* and its significance, there is no better proof of our eternity.

All the commentators on the Torah attempt to determine the nature of our eternity when they write about the *tochachah*. The *tochachah* and the consolation are two sides of the same coin. The Holocaust, too, is also remarkable in terms of our faith, no less than our revival. It of course presents us with questions: Why was this fate decreed upon us? The fact that it is so totally out of the range of the ordinary indicates clearly that it is a sign of the eternity of our nation, which passes through fire but is not consumed, and this must necessarily be for a purpose: to achieve our calling as determined by Hashem.

◆§ Exile and Its Purpose

The commentators on the Torah all explain, each in his own way, the purpose of our *galus*, exile, and the suffering that we have undergone as a result of it. It is clear that מִפְּנֵי חֲטָאֵינוּ גָּלִינוּ מֵאַרְצֵנוּ — "because of our sins we were exiled from our land" — but one who observes the results of *galus* finds many aspects to it.

Rabbeinu Bachya in his *Kad HaKemach*, under the topic of גְּאֻלָּה — "redemption" — sees the purpose of *galus* as the means for spreading knowledge and awareness of Hashem among the nations and to teach them about Him and His Torah. This is the awareness (תעודה) theory that many think originated with the school of R' Samson Raphael Hirsch.

According to *Chazal*, our dispersion among the nations has been a blessing in the midst of a curse, because through it the nations were unable to destroy us totally. A nucleus always remained somewhere from which the Jewish tree grew again. The fact that we had to wander from one place to another is also explained by the commentators as being good and with a positive aim, so that we would not be assimilated among the nations, as a result of becoming too deeply rooted in a single place.

In the same vein, *Chasam Sofer* (*Parashas Ki Savo*) notes the extraordinary phenomenon that "the more Israel draws closer to the other nations, the more [the nations'] hatred increases. And this (theory) is tried and tested." He explains the verse (*Devarim* 28:63), "Hashem will rejoice over you to destroy you, and to bring you to naught; and you shall be plucked from off the land where you go to possess it," that the other nations will attempt to destroy us physically, but this too will have a good side to it, in that it will preserve the existence of the Jew and Jewish eternity.

Meshech Chochmah also discusses this at length. He analyzes Jewish history in the light of one astounding fact: From the time of Yaakov, the Jews have been a foreign and separate element among the other nations, and they have always made a point of erecting various barriers to keep themselves separate from the other nations. It is only when the Jews come to terms with the fact that they are living among others and attempt to become part of them, that they become as thorns in the sides of the other nations. An outside storm then uproots them from their place, one that seemed to them so secure, and again throws them among strangers whose language they cannot speak. And again they find it impossible to assimilate.

According to the Gaon of Dvinsk, this forced move from one place to another has a certain "national" value to us, in that it prevents assimilation. This forced move from one place to another prevents the "progress" which occurs when all is calm, and when the people again begin to assimilate. The forced move thus creates a "freezing" in the spiritual realm, and we again return to our original sources and independence.

The purpose of our wandering is to undermine our imaginary security and to instill in us the recognition that it is our duty to fortify ourselves with our spiritual treasures, and not to seek new ways, which our fathers did not know. It is a fact that after every such storm we begin to build anew from the beginning, using new paths, rather than simply "progressing," in the way of other nations as happens at times of peace and security.

Akeidah, too, explains the phenomenon of *galus* along these lines, and in accordance with the conditions he saw in his days. He explains the verse (*Devarim* 28:65), "And among these nations you shall find no ease," as a promise and a warning. Your attempts at assimilation among the other nations will not help you. Hashem will take you out of those nations among whom you were assimilated, and even there He will decree annihilation upon you. There is no fleeing your destiny as a Jew. According to *Akeidah*, the curse of "You shall be sold there to your enemies as slaves and maidservants, and none will buy" (ibid. v. 68) is also a blessing. Almost never, in all our exiles, were we sold as slaves, as were the blacks. Instead, we were subject to the good graces of various kings, and their desires, which were subject to Hashem. The same is true for the other curses in the *tochachah*. These are all mixed curses and blessings, and what might in one era be considered a curse is shown in another era to have been a blessing.

◄§ The Days of the Second Beis HaMikdash — Redemption or Remembrance?

In commenting on the *tochachah*, the different commentators disagree whether the era of the Second *Beis HaMikdash* is considered as part of the *tochachah* or as a *redemption*. *Ramban* holds that the *tochachah* in our *parashah* refers only to the First *Beis HaMikdash*. The punishments listed here are what occurred at that time. אָז תִּרְצֶה הָאָרֶץ אֶת־שַׁבְּתֹתֶיהָ — "then the land shall make up for its *Sabbaths*" (*Vayikra* 26:34) — namely, that the seventy years of *galus* in Babylonia paralleled the number of *shemittah* years that were not kept in the days of the First *Beis HaMikdash*. In the *tochachah* in our *parashah*, there is no mention of the ingathering of the exiles, because not all the Jews moved back to *Eretz Yisrael* from Babylonia. The *tochachah* also does not mention that Israel will do *teshuvah* (repent). It only says that they "will confess," which is what happened at the time of Ezra and Nechemiah, as explained in *Tanach*.

On the other hand, the *tochachah* in *Devarim* deals with the Second *Beis HaMikdash*. In that *tochachah*, there is no time limit mentioned for the *galus*, because the end depends on *teshuvah* and nothing else. Nor is there any mention in it of *avodah zarah* — idolatry — because by that time, *avodah zarah* had been uprooted from Israel. Nor, again, is there any mention of the *Beis HaMikdash* and the fragrance of the sacrifices, because the fire that had devoured the sacrifices during the First *Beis HaMikdash* had been hidden away, and no longer came down to consume the sacrifices.

In the *tochachah* in *Devarim* 28:49 we read, "Hashem shall bring a nation against you from far ... a nation whose tongue you will not understand," and that refers to Rome, whose language, unlike that of the surrounding nations such as the Chaldeans, the Jews did not know at all. There (v. 64) it states, "And Hashem will scatter you among all the peoples," because Titus took the captives of Israel and spread them in many countries, taking the younger ones captive and leaving their elders to weep, as it states in the second *tochachah* (v. 32): "Your sons and your daughters will be given unto another people." Similarly, when it states there (v. 36), "Hashem shall bring you, and your king which you will set over you," this refers to when Agrippas was taken to Rome, which led to the destruction of the Second *Beis HaMikdash*. This explains also why the verse says "your king which you will set over you" rather than "your king who will rule over you," because Agrippas was a foreigner and a non-Jew, and his fathers had seized the throne for themselves.

Ramban's interpretation on the following verse is especially interesting: "And I will bring them to the land of their enemies" (*Vayikra* 26:41), which comes immediately after the verse, "and they will confess." All the commentators are astonished at why they should be punished after they have already confessed their sins. *Ramban*, though, says that this is not a punishment but a means to have them subjugate their stubborn hearts.

"The land of their enemies" is not *galus*, but *Eretz Yisrael* under the rule *of our enemies*, as it was at the time of Ezra. According to *Ramban's* interpretation, there were two exiles. The first followed the destruction of the First *Beis HaMikdash*, and the other followed the destruction of the Second *Beis HaMikdash*, and each *tochachah* (that in *Vayikra* and that in *Devarim*) referred to one of them. Between these two destructions, the Jews lived for a time free of any foreign yoke, sovereign in its own land.

Abarbanel has a different view. According to him, there were not two destructions with a redemption between the two, but a single destruction: that of the First *Beis HaMikdash*, which has continued and will continue until *Mashiach* arrives, quickly in our day, Amen.

Abarbanel states that at the time of the Second *Beis HaMikdash* there was no גְּאֻלָּה — "redemption" — but there was only פְּקִידָה — "remembrance." When Ezra came back to *Eretz Yisrael*, that did not change the destruction, and that was not yet the fulfillment of the words of the *nevi'im* — the prophets. These were merely days of remembrance, where Israel was given the opportunity to rectify its sins and thereby to be worthy of the redemption. As Israel did not utilize this opportunity and did not rectify its wrongs, the *galus* continued without a break.

Abarbanel has a number of proofs that the days of the Second *Beis HaMikdash* were not a time of redemption. Firstly, only 42,000 people came back; only those who had been exiled to close areas returned, while those who had been exiled to distant areas did not return at all. Most of the time of the Second *Beis HaMikdash*, the Jews lived under foreign occupation, and there was almost never a period of tranquility. The kings of the Second *Beis HaMikdash* period were not of the House of David. The Second *Beis HaMikdash* was missing a number of key elements, such as the *aron* (ark) in which the Tablets of the Law (*luchos habris*) had been kept, the *keruvim* (cherubs), the *Ruach HaKodesh* (Divine Inspiration), and the Anointing Oil.

As to the legal basis for the Jews' stay in *Eretz Yisrael* during the Second *Beis HaMikdash* period, it was based on "permission" by Koresh to move to *Eretz Yisrael*, to build the *Beis HaMikdash*, and to set up a spiritual and culture center for the Jews. That and no more. According to Abarbanel, that center was no more important than the spiritual center which the Jews had in Alexandria. Abarbanel therefore holds that the *tochachah* in our *parashah* is a curse which has extended since the destruction of the First *Beis HaMikdash*. It includes *both Batei Mikdash*, for it states clearly, "your Temples" (*Vayikra* 26:31) in the plural. After the seventy years in Babylon came the "Day of Remembrance," which had the potential of developing into the full redemption, but the opportunity was lost. It is true that there was no longer idolatry, but in its place came the heretics, the *apikorsim*. As a result, "I will bring them to the land of their enemies," meaning literally that, and those who had come up with Ezra were again exiled, as part of the first *tochachah*.

Abarbanel explains many historical incidents and reveals his opinion on many events. According to him, the Jews came to Spain after the destruction of the First *Beis HaMikdash*, and did not even have a partial redemption at the time of Ezra. He explains the events in his days according to the verses of the *tochachah*. He finds three typical characteristics of the time in which he was living: a) A great deal of fear. The mighty warriors of Israel of the Second *Beis Hamikdash* era had become cowards, fearing even the sound of a blowing leaf; even the wealthy were not sure of their wealth, because a catastrophe might come which might wipe out all. b) Even though there were times that the Jews enjoyed peace and tranquility in the *golah*, they were never granted the blessing of "land." It is not for nothing that *Chazal* see a sign of the redemption in (*Yechezkel* 36:8), "But you, O mountains of Israel, you shall give forth your branches, and yield your fruit to My people, Israel." The blessing of the land is a clear sign of the redemption; before the redemption the Jews will not enjoy this blessing. c) The fact that Jews are spread throughout the world is a clear indication of *galus*. There is no stability in any place. One lives in a certain place for some time, and is then forced to wander elsewhere. "Among these nations you shall find no ease" (*Devarim* 28:65). There is no rest as long as we are in exile. Fear pursues those who are in exile, and causes them to flee to every country in the world. In any event, according to Abarbanel, the period of the Second *Beis HaMikdash* was only an intermediate stop, which cannot be considered a redemption.

This is also the view of R' Samson Raphael Hirsch, who states that the period of the Second *Beis HaMikdash* was nothing but an inoculation shot for Israel, so that they would be inoculated with the *Torah She'Be'al Peh*, the Oral Torah, and would be able to live afterwards in the long *galus* with the power of the *Torah She'Be'al Peh*.

The days of the Second *Beis HaMikdash* remain a mystery for many of the commentators of the Torah. They are unsure whether to consider it part of the destruction or of the redemption. The contrasting views of *Ramban* and Abarbanel on this are still evident in our times, for we too have seen a certain measure of deliverance, but have not yet experienced the גְּאֻלָה — the redemption, and many seek to find an answer to the question as to what this event means in our history. If we look in the *rishonim*, we will find that they too sought to find the answer to a similar question — the historical meaning of the Second *Beis HaMikdash*.

Chasam Sofer in his *Teshuvos*, *Yoreh De'ah* 333, states that Titus destroyed the Second *Beis HaMikdash* of his own free will and not by the orders of any prophet. This was unlike the redemption at the beginning of the Second *Beis HaMikdash* era, which came about at the command of a prophet. That is the reason the second *kedushah* which *Eretz Yisrael* acquired in the days of Ezra and Nechemiah continues, unlike the *kedushah* of the first occupation in the time of Yehoshua, which was annulled by the destruction of the First *Beis HaMikdash*.

◈§ The End of the Tochachah and the Confession

At the end of the *parashah* of the *tochachah*, after the Torah concludes all the curses and terrible punishment that will befall those who violate the laws of the Torah in *Eretz Yisrael*, the Torah promises that a time will also come of regret: וְהִתְוַדּוּ אֶת־עֲוֹנָם וְאֶת עֲוֹן אֲבֹתָם בְּמַעֲלָם אֲשֶׁר מָעֲלוּ־בִי וְאַף אֲשֶׁר הָלְכוּ עִמִּי בְּקֶרִי — "they will confess their sins and the sin of their fathers, with their trespass which they trespassed against Me, and that also they have walked contrary to Me" (*Vayikra* 26:40).

Immediately after this regret, a new punishment is listed: אַף־אֲנִי אֵלֵךְ

עִמָּם בְּקֶרִי וְהֵבֵאתִי אֹתָם בְּאֶרֶץ אֹיְבֵיהֶם אוֹ־אָז יִכָּנַע לְבָבָם הֶעָרֵל וְאָז יִרְצוּ אֶת־ עֲוֹנָם — "I also will walk contrary unto them, and will bring them into the land of their enemies; then their uncircumcised heart will be humbled, and they will then pay for their iniquity."

As we mentioned earlier, many of the commentators on the Torah wonder why the people's confession (vidui) is not accepted. After this, in the next verse, again the Torah returns with words of comfort: וְזָכַרְתִּי אֶת־בְּרִיתִי יַעֲקוֹב ... וְהָאָרֶץ אֶזְכֹּר — "Then will I remember my covenant with Yaakov ... and I will remember the land."

Immediately thereafter the following words of punishment reverberate: וְהָאָרֶץ תֵּעָזֵב מֵהֶם וְתִרֶץ אֶת שַׁבְּתֹתֶיהָ בָּהְשַׁמָּה מֵהֶם וְהֵם יִרְצוּ אֶת־עֲוֹנָם — "The land will be bereft of them, and will make up for her Sabbaths, while she lies desolate without them: and they will pay for their iniquity."

This back-and-forth movement between punishment and forgiveness has aroused discussion among the commentators.

Akeidah holds that this *vidui* is not one of people who have acknowledged their sin, but is similar to טוֹבֵל וְשֶׁרֶץ בְּיָדוֹ — a person who enters the waters of the *mikveh* to purify himself while holding on to the very creature that caused him to be *tamei*, impure. What the Torah is telling us is that the people have indeed confessed their sins, but have done so while still sinning, "with their trespass which they trespassed against Me," and did not forsake their sins. For this reason Hashem will send them to a far-off land, until they are cleansed of all their sins, not only through *vidui*, verbal confessions, but also through *teshuvah*, inner repentance.

Kli Yakar also explains the verse in a similar fashion. Had the people confessed and forsaken their sins, the Torah would have said, "they will confess their sins and their trespasses," but as the Torah states, "with their trespass which they trespassed against Me," it means to tell us that even after their *vidui* they continue trespassing. *Kli Yakar* adds that this is the custom of our times. People know that certain specific sins have caused all the suffering of the exile, yet they don't repent.

Some late commentators also explain this along these lines. *Meleches Machsheves* says that the *vidui* here is only lip service, and that is why Hashem continues to punish the people, as the Torah states, "if then their uncircumcised hearts are humbled." There is no place for *teshuvah* unless one confesses and forsakes the sin. One cannot simply confess and continue with his wicked ways.

Chafetz Chaim, too, says this *vidui* lacks the element of accepting not to sin in the future, and without that the *teshuvah* has no value. Consequently, Hashem has no alternative but to continue punishing the people to purify and refine them until they do proper *teshuvah*.

Binah L'Itim sees the defect in the *vidui* in that "they confessed their sins and the sin of their fathers." The people do not admit that it was they who reached the lowest levels by their actions, but instead blame their fathers. The truth, though, is that it is the sons themselves who committed the sins and who deserve the punishment. By blaming their parents for their sins, the sons free themselves of even feeling guilty. Their claim is that they were educated that way, and are unable to change their habits.

R' Yosef Tzvi Dushinky also explains this in a similar fashion. He adds that this is what Hashem means when he states, "I will bring them into the land of their enemies." Hashem cannot accept that "their habits" brought the people to abandon the Torah. He will thus create a situation in which the most assimilated of them will realize that they are in the land of their enemies. Hashem will allow the hostility of their enemies to appear, and He will uproot the Jews from their comfortable lives among the other nations. Afterwards the Torah (*Vayikra* 26:44) promises that, "And even when they are in the land of their enemies," if they recognize that they are living among other nations and not in their own home, "I will not abhor them, or reject them, to destroy them," and then there will be hope for their future and they will return from the land of their enemies.

Malbim, too, explains the Torah this way: "I will bring them to a situation where they will find it impossible to be friends with the nations and to assimilate with them, and then, 'their uncircumcised hearts will be humbled.' "

⋖§ At the End, All Is Vidui

R' David Zvi Hoffmann has a novel explanation of the verse after the *vidui*, confession, which reads אַף־אֲנִי אֵלֵךְ עִמָּם בְּקֶרִי —"I too walked (literally, "will walk") contrary unto them" (*Vayikra* 26:41). That verse, too, is part of the confession. Those who confess finally realize that Hashem was contrary with us: "I brought them into the land of their enemies" (ibid.), but they come to the realization that He exiled them so that "their uncircumcised heart will be humbled" (ibid.). After they realize this, the Torah tells us in the next verse that, "I will remember My covenant with Yaakov, and also My covenant with Yitzchak, and also My covenant with Avraham will I remember; and I will remember the land."

It is interesting that R' David Zvi Hoffmann was preceded in this interpretation by *Or HaChaim*, who says that the verse, "I too walked contrary unto them, and I brought them into the land of their enemies" is said by the Jews as part of their *vidui*.

HaKesav VeHaKabalah also follows this approach. According to him, not only this verse, but the five verses after it are all part of the *vidui*. None of the verses is a promise. The people confess that in spite of their sins Hashem did not remove His *hashgachah*, Providence, from the Jewish people, He remembered His covenant, and even when they were in the lands of their enemies He did not reject them to destroy them. After this long and detailed *vidui*, which includes Hashem's mercies and kindnesses in spite of all, the Torah ends the *tochachah* with words of *appeasement* (ibid. v. 45): וְזָכַרְתִּי לָהֶם בְּרִית רִאשֹׁנִים אֲשֶׁר הוֹצֵאתִי־אֹתָם מֵאֶרֶץ מִצְרַיִם — "I will for their sake remember the covenant of their ancestors, whom I brought forth out of the land of Egypt." This interpretation explains the seeming changes in mood in these verses and the shift from *tochachah* to appeasement and back again, the entire text of which is recited by those who confess. When they finally realize their sins and justify the punishments which they suffered, they also note the kindnesses in Hashem's treatment of them.

According to the various commentators, the concluding verse, וְזָכַרְתִּי לָהֶם בְּרִית רִאשֹׁנִים — "I will for their sake remember the covenant of their ancestors," is said by Hashem. He accepts their *teshuvah* (repentance) and their *vidui*.

According to *Sifsei Kohen*, Hashem says, "I remember that they were the first (רִאשֹׁנִים — translated in the verse above as "ancestors") in the world to enter into a covenant with God, and they were the first to accept the Yoke of Heaven."

Kedushas Levi also explains this delightfully:

> I remember how they appeared when I took them out of Egypt. Then too they were no better than now, and yet they elevated themselves and received the Torah. I cannot therefore despair of their present condition. They will still awaken and ascend to the spiritual heights. This is analogous to a man who married the daughter of someone who he thought was wealthy, and then he found out the man was poor. In such a case, the man has the right to be upset. If, however, at the time he was married he knew his prospective father-in-law was poor, he certainly cannot complain about that fact later. So, too, with Hashem: He did not choose us at a time when we were spiritually wealthy, because when He took us out of Egypt we had sunk to all but the lowest rung of *tumah*, spiritual defilement. What, then, is the tumult

when he sees us spiritually poor now? Are we worse now than we were then?

The Torah states (ibid.), לְעֵינֵי הַגּוֹיִם לִהְיוֹת לָהֶם לֵא-לֹהִים — "Before the eyes of the nations, to be to them a God." Now He must help us so that there is no desecration of Hashem's name among the other nations, says *Ramban*. We may not deserve His help, because we have not done *teshuvah* and have not atoned for our sins, but Hashem will remember the covenant with our ancestors in order to preserve His great name, "whether in *Eretz Yisrael* or outside it, in the *galus* (exile) alluded to here, and in all other generations."

⊰§ I Will Remember the Land

Eretz Yisrael appears as an independent unit, which is not dependent on those living in it. Hashem will remember it for the good, just as He does with people. If you sinned, says *Kli Yakar*, why is the land to blame? R' Shimon ben Lakish said that this is analogous to a king who had three daughters and a maidservant who raised them. Whenever the king inquired about the welfare of his daughters, he also asked how the maidservant was.

Ramban, though, explains the verse according to the plain meaning of the words, "I will remember the land," after it has completed the punishment for its sins. Following that, the Torah states (ibid. v. 43), "The land will be bereft of them." This hints at the fact that even after the land is remembered, the Jews will not yet return to it. This, says *Ramban*, refers to the Second *Beis HaMikdash* period. Even after King Koresh announced that the Jews could return, and the land had lain waste enough time to atone for all the *shemittah* years that had not been kept, there were still another nineteen years until the *Beis HaMikdash* was erected and the city was once more consecrated. It was only then that the *kedushah* (sanctity) of the land was restored, and the Jews pledged to keep *shemittah* and the *mitzvos*, as we read in the book of *Ezra* and *Nechemiah*. According to *Ramban*, all of these events are hinted at in our *parashah*.

Tosefes Brachah, though, explains the verses according to *d'rush*. *Chazal* in *Midrash Eichah* 4 referred to the verse in *Tehillim* 79, "A Song of Asaph. Hashem, the non-Jews have come into Your inheritance." They said to Asaph: "Hashem destroyed the *Heichal* and the *Mikdash*, and you are singing?" He said to them, "I am singing that He poured out His wrath on wood and stone, and not on Israel." The consolation here is that wood and stone can be replaced, but if the Jewish people were wiped out, there would be no replacement. According to this, the fact that "the land will be bereft of them" is also a blessing. Hashem takes out His rage, as it were, on wood and stone, because of the covenant He made with our forefathers.

The simple meaning of our text, though, is that Hashem will redeem not only the Jewish people, but also His land. Just as He did not exchange us for another nation, He will not exchange His land for another. Hashem's remembering the land is coupled here with His remembering our forefathers. "The land will make up for her *Sabbaths*," and because of this, its remembrance will come before Hashem. The land was not created to remain desolate, and there is no choice but to return Israel to its ancient home.

III.

The Value of Man . . . and the Daughter of Yiftach

I f a person says עֶרְכִּי עָלַי — "my value upon myself" — in other words, if he vows to donate to the *Beis HaMikdash* a sum of money equal to his own value — he has to pay the amount set by the Torah. The amount involved depends on the person's age and sex. Between the ages of 20 and 60, a male pays 50 *sela'im* while a female pays 30. From 5 to 20 years old, a male pays 20 *sela'im* and a female 10. From one month to five years, a male pays 5 *sela'im* and a female 3. Finally, over 60 years old, a male pays 15 *sela'im* and a woman 10. We will explain the differences due to age and sex below, based on the different commentators, but these explanations are all forced.

It is surprising that *Rambam* in *Moreh Nevuchim* 3:40, when discussing the *erech* — value — of a slave, which is 30 *sela'im*, states that, "the value of the slave is calculated at half that of a free man, for we find that the highest *erech* for a free man is sixty *sela'im*." The different commentators of the *Moreh Nevuchim* find this astonishing, because the highest *erech* for a free man is only fifty *sela'im*. Some wish to change the text from sixty to fifty, but then *Rambam's* whole point of half the value is lost. Crescas explains *Rambam* to mean that the value of a free man is sixty *sela'im*, regardless of his physical condition, but the fact is that the Torah value is fifty *sela'im*. This question requires further study.

The *Chozeh* of Lublin states that the reason the *parashah* of *arachin* ("values") follows the *tochachah*, is that the Torah was afraid that when people would hear the curses there they might become depressed. The Torah therefore gave us the *parashah* of *arachin*, to stress the value of the individual Jew and to demonstrate his greatness to him.

Abarbanel notes that these values should, theoretically, have been in accordance with the person's wisdom or abilities. The Torah, though, did not want to differentiate between one Jew and another, and to have some considered no more than beasts of burden. It is also an insult to a person, made in the image of Hashem, to be valued in accordance with his strength and ability to work. Valuing people in such a manner will also cause envy between different people. In order to remove these stumbling blocks, the Torah set a standard value for everyone, whether rich or poor, whether wise or foolish.

Chinuch holds that the basis and the reason for the *mitzvah* of *arachin*, "values," is the holiness of man's speech. Man's soul is linked to his power of speech, as Onkelos translated נֶפֶשׁ חַיָּה ("living soul," *Bereishis* 2:7) as רוּחַ מְמַלְלָא ("speaking spirit"). A person must fulfill whatever he says, both in regard to sacred and non-sacred matters. There is no clear *mitzvah* in the Torah to this effect, but *Chazal* uttered a curse (מִי שֶׁפָּרַע) against one who does not keep his word. The *parashah* of *arachin* came to stress the great value that the Torah attaches to a person's talk. *Akeidah* too states that only speech is what distinguishes creatures of intellect, and this is what makes us different from any other species. This is seen in the *mitzvah* of *arachin*.

⊷§ The Differences in Values

Chazal in *Arachin* 19 explain why the value of a woman of sixty is a third of one who is twenty, while the value at age sixty of a man is less than a third of the value of a man of twenty. According to *Chazal*, women age better than men: "People say that an old man in the house is a breach in the house, while an old woman in the house is a treasure in the house." This interpretation explains the difference in values by age, but there are still many other differences that have not been explained. Ibn Ezra notes that, "According to many, the laws of *arachin* are decrees of the King, because one cannot explain the differences in any other way." There are nevertheless many commentators who grapple with the question.

HaDrash VeHaIyun uses *d'rush* to explain why a man at the peak of his strength is worth fifty *sela'im*. The Midrash says that a *revi'is* (roughly a third of a cup) of blood and a *k'zayis* (size of an olive) of flesh of a dead person make one *tamei*, ritually impure, because that amount of blood and flesh is the beginning of the formation of the person. In *Sotah* 5, the *gemara* explains that the weight of a *revi'is* of blood is 25 *sela'im*, and according to *Shabbos* 77 a *k'zayis* of flesh is equivalent to a *revi'is* of blood. Together their weight totals fifty *sela'im*. Thus the value of a man at the peak of his strength is fifty *sela'im*. Before the age of twenty and after the age of sixty, though, he is worth less, because at both extremes he is not at his full strength. Even this *d'rush*, though, does not explain why the values before age twenty and after age sixty are what they are, or the differences between the value of a male and of a female.

Abarbanel attempts to find an explanation for these differences. From the ages of twenty to sixty a woman is weaker than a man, because, according to *Chazal*, a male is formed in forty days and a female in eighty days. It would, therefore, be appropriate for the value of the female to be half that of the male, but the Torah added five *sela'im* to her value as she can give birth to children. The value of the male from age five to age twenty is still not complete, but he is still worth more then than after the age of sixty, for by then he is declining. Until the age of twenty, a woman has not reached full maturity with regard to her ability to conceive and give birth, and therefore her value is half that of the male of that age. After the age of sixty, though, the value of the female is relatively higher, in accordance with *Chazal* that we quoted above. From the ages of one month to five years, the Torah valued the male at five *sela'im*, while the female should be worth half that, or two-and-a-half *sela'im*. As the Torah did not want to divide the *sela* into two, the value of the female was set at three *sela'im*.

In accordance with the view of Abarbanel that the Torah did not want to divide up *sela'im*, *Tiferes Yisrael* explains in the last chapter of *Beitzah* all the types of *arachin*. The value of a female is half that of a male, because she is considered half of his body [since woman was created from man's "side" — *Bereishis* 2:21]. The Torah did not wish to divide *sela'im* into two, nor to divide ten *sela'im* into two parts. As a result, where half the value of the male should have been two-and-a-half *sela'im*, the Torah assigned a value of three *sela'im*. Where the value of the female should have been twenty-five *sela'im*, which are two groups of ten *sela'im* and half a group of ten *sela'im*, the Torah rounded it off to thirty *sela'im*. Where, after the age of sixty, it should have been seven-and-a-half *sela'im*, the Torah rounded it off to ten *sela'im*.

Akeidah explains the differences as follows: From the ages of one month to five years there is no special value for boys, but their value is based on the future. The difference between the male and the female is a relative one. The same relative difference exists between the ages of twenty and sixty. Above the age of sixty, the value of females is proportionally higher, as mentioned above. The only question we must ask is the difference between the value of males and females from the ages of five to twenty. It is possible that the value of the female is less proportionally because at that time her father enjoys legal rights to whatever she earns. [That is only until twelve-and-a-half — Ed. note.]

R' David Zvi Hoffmann also attempts to find an explanation for these differences. According to him, since a woman is not commanded to observe all the 613 *mitzvos*, a woman of twenty has the same value as a non-Jewish slave, who is obligated to keep the same *mitzvos* as a woman. When a slave is killed, his master must be paid thirty *shekalim* (*Sh'mos* 21:32), and that is the value of a female of twenty and up. The value of a female under twenty is relatively less than that of a male of that age, and the reason may be that a woman's life is more endangered in those years, as we see from *Chazal* in *Sanhedrin* 100b, "Happy is he whose children are males; woe to him whose children are females." From one month until five years, the value of a male is five *sela'im*, just as for the redemption of the firstborn, *pidyon haben* (*Bamidbar* 18:16). The value of a female of that age is three *sela'im*, which is more than half, because at that age, females are not yet exposed to the dangers they will face at a later time. The value of a female up to the age of five is a tenth of her value after the age of twenty. After the age of sixty, her value is relatively higher, as discussed above.

In spite of all of these explanations, there is no clear reason and logic for the various differences. It is best to return to the opinion of Ibn Ezra, that the reasons are the decrees of the King, and only known to Him Who gave us the Torah.

◆§ If a Human Being Is Donated to Hashem

"If a human being is declared חֵרֶם — donated to Hashem — he cannot be redeemed and must be put to death" (*Vayikra* 27:29). This is one of the most astonishing verses in the Torah. How can a person be made חֵרֶם? Is he to be put to death if he is חֵרֶם? *Chazal* in *Arachin* 6 explain the verse in two ways:

a) If a person is sentenced to death and on the way declares עֶרְכִּי עָלַי — "my value upon me" (see the preceding section) — his statement has no meaning, because he now has no value. Such a חֵרֶם by a person is not redeemed, and the Torah explains that the reason for this is because "he must be put to death" and is therefore of no value.

b) There are cases where a person deserves מִיתָה בִּידֵי שָׁמַיִם — to be put to death by Hashem — but he pays a ransom for his life and achieves atonement for his sin. An example is where a person's bull killed another person, where the Torah writes that he must be put to death. After he pays the amount specified, he atones for his sin (see Sh'mos 21:29-32). One might then imagine that a person who is to be put to death by man can also pay a life-saving ransom. The Torah therefore stresses that he must be put to death. Only his execution by the beis din will serve as his atonement, and he cannot redeem himself with money.

Ramban, however, explains this passage literally. The Torah refers to a person who declares his enemies חֵרֶם to Hashem, meaning that rather than taking them as slaves and their property as spoils of war, all will be destroyed, as we see in Bamidbar 21:2, "If you give this nation in my hands, I will make their cities חֵרֶם." Such a חֵרֶם is valid, and one cannot redeem whatever was declared חֵרֶם. Rather, whoever was declared חֵרֶם must be put to death.

R' David Zvi Hoffmann adds that it is impossible for any person to have the right to declare whomever he wants to be חֵרֶם. The verse therefore must be referring to a body with legal authority, such as an authorized beis din or the nation as a whole, or their authorized representatives, as we can see from the word יָחֳרָם — "shall be declared חֵרֶם" (Vayikra 27:29). We find this type of חֵרֶם in many places in Tanach, and such a declaration is more severe than declaring something הֶקְדֵּשׁ — "sanctified" for the use of the Beis HaMikdash — for here there is no redemption for the objects.

Ramban brings examples of such חֲרָמוֹת (plural of חֵרֶם). The people of Yavesh Gilead (Shoftim 21:10) violated the oath of the congregation and did not come to Mitzpah, and we are told there:

> The congregation sent there twelve thousand men of the army, and commanded them, saying, "Go and smite the inhabitants of Yavesh Gilead with the edge of the sword, including the women and the children."

So too do we find that Yehonasan, son of King Shaul, transgressed a חֵרֶם, and his father declared (I Shmuel 14:44), "Yehonasan shall surely die."

Why did all these instances justify the death penalty? The answer is, says Ramban, that the beis din or the congregation has the right to punish by death anyone who violates a חֵרֶם. The source of this law is the verse above. The question we can ask is why the people of Yavesh Gilead did not ask הַתָּרָה — a release — of the חֵרֶם and the oath of the other tribes, who had sworn to kill anyone not coming to Mitzpah.

Abarbanel answers that they held that the oath could not be annulled, because "there was no king in Israel" (*Shoftim* 21:25) at the time. Had there been a king or judge, he would have annulled the oath on behalf of all. As there was no judge, the people of Yavesh Gilead thought that they needed to annul the oath in the presence of everyone, and that was by then impossible, because many had died in war.

Again, Abarbanel notes that this was an extraordinary event. At the time of their distress they had vowed that the entire nation would gather together and they would not be smitten by their enemies. Thus the decree they made was extremely severe, and they did not want to annul it.

In the case of Yehonasan, Shaul had ordered all of Israel to fast until evening, and anyone who failed to do so was to be put to death. Yehonasan, not having heard of this, found a honey-like substance on the ground and tasted it. Later, when Shaul consulted the *Urim* and *Tummim*, the prophetic breastplate of the High Priest, regarding the conduct of the war, he received no answer. This indicated that someone had sinned, and when lots were cast to determine the guilty party, Yehonasan was singled out. In regard to Yehonasan, we are told, "And the people redeemed Yehonasan" (*I Shmuel* 14:45). How can there be any redemption, when the Torah states clearly that in such cases of חֵרֶם, there is no redemption? *Ramban* answers that this was not that he was redeemed with money, but that the people justified his behavior, claiming that he had erred in doing what he did (and this is stated clearly in *Pirkei d'Rebbi Eliezer* 38: "The nation said to Shaul, 'Our lord the king! it was an error' "). The word used here is indeed וַיִּפְדּוּ, which means "they redeemed," but it has a different meaning here.

If Yehonasan did not sin, why did Hashem not answer Shaul through the *Urim* and *Tummim*? R' Saadiah Gaon answers that Hashem did not answer him so that people should not say that He showed favoritism to the king's son, but indeed Yehonasan's sin was unintentional. Abarbanel and *Radak* also explain that the fact that the people succeeded in saving him was known as פְּדִיָּה, as in the verse פָּדָה בְשָׁלוֹם נַפְשִׁי, — "He rescued (redeemed) my soul in peace."

Radak brings a controversy in *Chazal* on this: R' Elazar says: "They gave his weight in gold and redeemed him" — namely that they redeemed him for money; while R' Yochanan said, "Did he eat bread? Indeed, he merely tasted honey." R' Avahu said, "A taste is not considered eating or drinking and does not interrupt a fast, and does not require a blessing. Thus they redeemed Yehonasan." In other words, the redemption was by persuasion.

Akeidah has an original approach in explaining this verse. The Torah commands that if we place people in חֵרֶם, we must ask for a Torah Sage to annul the חֵרֶם, as the people did with Yehonasan, so that he did not die. When the Torah writes about a חֵרֶם not being redeemed, it refers to a case where a person declared a חֵרֶם on another, and instead of going to a Torah Sage to have the חֵרֶם redeemed, went ahead and killed the person. Such an action is considered to be murder, and therefore "he (the one who put the other to death) must be put to death."

✥§ The Daughter of Yiftach

Ramban says that it was Yiftach's misunderstanding of this verse that led him to offer his daughter as a sacrifice (see *Shoftim* ch. 11). He thought that just as a leader has the right in war to declare people חֵרֶם and to have them killed, the same, God forbid, would apply if a person pledged another person as an *olah*. *Ramban* disagrees with Ibn Ezra, who holds that Yiftach's pledge, that whatever would come out of his house, וְהַעֲלִיתִיהוּ עוֹלָה — "I will offer him as an *olah*," did not refer to a sacrifice, but simply meant that he would offer that person to serve Hashem. Yiftach, says Ibn Ezra, kept his promise, and made a house for his daughter outside the city, where she lived alone. He supported her all her life, and she was imprisoned there forever.

Ramban says that this explanation of Ibn Ezra is דִּבְרֵי רוּחַ — without substance. There is nothing in our traditions regarding that type of separation and monastism, except for the type of vow taken by Channah, who gave her son Shmuel to serve and be educated in the House of Hashem. According to the Torah, a person cannot take a vow concerning members of his household, forcing them to remain apart from everyone else, just as he cannot make a vow to offer them as a sacrifice. Had this been possible, what is the meaning of the verses where we are told that the daughter of Yiftach went to cry over her youth, with her friends? God forbid that there should be a custom to visit the site of the event four days a year for the daughter of Yiftach (see *Shoftim* 11:40) just because she did not marry and instead served Hashem in *taharah*. What the verses really mean there is exactly what they say: that Yiftach offered up his daughter as a human sacrifice, because of his ignorance in understanding the Torah.

Ralbag and *Radak*, though, both explain the section in accordance with Ibn Ezra, that Yiftach took a vow that his daughter would be a hermitess her whole life. Abarbanel too follows this path, and adds something remarkable, that it was from Yiftach that the Christians learned of making their daughters nuns and of entering them into nunneries, where they remain the rest of their lives. After Yiftach's vow, his daughter remained isolated from people, and never again saw another man or woman. It became a custom to go to the place where she stayed once a year, to talk to her and to comfort her.

The basis for this controversy among the commentators on *Shmuel* is the verse "If a human being is declared חֵרֶם he cannot be redeemed; he must be put to death" (*Vayikra* 27:29), which, according to *Ramban*, led to Yiftach's making a mistake, as if he was permitted to offer his daughter as a burnt-offering (*olah*).